# Sree Narayana Guru

## A Critical Study

## By the same Author

### Research Works

*The Autobiograhic Literature — A Study.*

*The Works of Vaikom Muhammed Basheer — A Study.*

*The Love Lives of World Literateurs.*

*The Progress of Science in India.*

*Humerous Literature Through the Ages.*

### Biographies

*Sri Sathya Sai Baba.*

*Sree Shirdi Sai Baba.*

### Novels

*Kunti — Delight in Distress*

*Lakshmana Vishadam*

# Sree Narayana Guru
## A Critical Study

*By*
Vijayalayam Jayakumar

*Translated into English by*
K. Sadanandan

PRINTWORLD
Publishers of Indian Traditions

**Cataloging in Publication Data — DK**
[Courtesy: D.K. Agencies (P) Ltd. <docinfo@dkagencies.com>]

Jayakumar, Vijayalayam, 1924 -
Sree Narayana Guru.
Includes bibliographical references. (p. ).

1. Narayana Guru, 1856-1928 — Criticism and interpretation. I. Title

**ISBN 9788124601204 (Hb)**
**ISBN 9788124608784 (Pb)**

*First published in India in 1999*
*Reprinted in 2017*


*Printed and published by:*
D.K. Printworld (P) Ltd.
*Regd. Office* : *Vedaśrī*, F-395, Sudarshan Park
(Metro Station: Ramesh Nagar)
New Delhi - 110 015
*Phones* : (011) 2545 3975; 2546 6019
*e-mail* : indology@dkprintworld.com
*Web* : www.dkprintworld.com

# Prologue

THOSE enlightened on the mysteries of life are honoured everywhere and are considered great. Their awakening arouses those who happen to be around, triggering off at times social transformations across the country that may even gradually penetrate the world. Subtle is the way such great souls influence history.

Indiscreet man who happen to be in seats of high political authority also can create upheavals in history. Their wrong decisions taken at weak moments of disturbed emotions could end up in world wars, toppling over history headlong. Such decision-makers too find their place in history, but only to be remembered with all antipathy.

The tumbling down of normal human life across the world owing to war-mongers sometimes is abrupt. The influence of the intuitive vision of the great, on the other hand, is mostly gradual and time-consuming, often taking generations or even centuries. Its way is that of seeping slowly into the fabric of human life. The contemporaries of visionaries may mostly treat them as aberrations, unmindful even of crucifying them, charging them with the crime of corrupting the innocent youth or challenging the crown. That prophets are not honoured at home has thus become an accepted dictum. Rare indeed is the phenomenon of a visionary or prophet being honoured, with people throwing around to take his lead to bring about deliberate changes in history. Sri Narayana Guru was one. At least two million people of a country treated him as God-incarnate and as their deliverer. Yet he always remained a contemplative catalyst, absorbed always in his natural quietitude. His sublime calmness and inner clarity aroused but an adoring attitude in anyone who happend to come across him. The spontaneous expression of feelings of the poet Rabindranath Tagore, after his visiting Guru at his *āśrama*, for example, was thus:

> I have been touring different parts of the world. During these travels, I have had the good fortune to come in contact with several Saints and Maharishis. But I am frankly to admit that I can never come across one who is spiritually greater than Swamy Sree Narayana Guru of Malayalam, nay a person who is on par with him in spiritual attainment.
>
> I shall never forget his radiant face illuminated by the self-effulgent light of divine glory and his yogic eyes; whose gaze fixed at a far remote point in the distant horizon.

What made Guru so unique and mysterious was his inner clarity, his life as a materialisation of that vision, and his intense, kindly wish to see the lives of people attain the same clarity and normality. Summarised in his own words, that vision in essence is:

> What is understood as 'that person' or 'this person',
> In the world, thought of properly,
> Is but one primeval Self in essence.

All the worlds and the beings in them are none other than various manifest forms of the one radiant Sun that shines in the transcendental space. One of this awareness, Guru loved every being as he did himself. Born of one Self-Reality, all were brothers for him.

### The Struggle Against Casteism

Yet what he saw around him was all in discord with this vision. Children of one nature, though, one set of people suffered serfdom under another. Mankind biologically belongs to one species, yet human beings are seen to be treated as belonging to various caste layers that have no *raison d'être*. He saw how much this senselessness had rendered human life miserable, he himself belonging to one such supposedly lower stratum. Those in the lower strata should not touch those in the upper one; some still lower should not even go near. Sweating blood, those of the lower strata produced food for all, which readily is acceptable to those of the upper layers who hoard it in their storehouses and enjoy, whereas its producers are untouchables!

People were made to believe that this caste discrimination had the sanction of religious scriptures; its sole basis being interpretations given to scriptures by the upper caste people. All such books, being in Sanskrit, were unreachable to ordinary man, not to mention that he had no chance of reading and understanding them first hand. The miseries one had to suffer in this life was the fallout of one's *karma*s in past lives, and the only way to make amends for them was doing meritorious deeds in the present life, doing service to Brahmins being the best of all such deeds. Such was the lesson they were taught. Reference to *cāturvarṇya* (four-fold classification of mental colouration) found in scriptures was often quoted in support of such claims, not knowing or deliberately concealing the fact that those references do relate only to psychological types, not to any social stratification. The poor believed what they were taught; the others too believed or tried to believe in what they were teaching. To expose this ignorance and enlighten people and to set things straight was taken by Guru as his life's assignment. The real essence of Indian wisdom itself was with him for a formidable support.

Absence of knowledge, ignorance is a negative phenomenon. Eradicating it also has to be in a negative way. Any other type of means to get rid of it will help only to make it more deep-rooted. The way, therefore, to wipe out caste system, Guru suggested, is not to ask, not to speak and not to think of caste. Debarring it from mind, words and deeds will end up in the gradual disappearance of caste notion from human affairs, enabling people to live as everywhere else in the world. As a positive back up for this negative way, Guru thought also of having a broad-based organisation of human beings in which discrimination on any count would be absent. Many were the young enthusiasts around him at that time, fully willing to act on it, most of them those who were denied any job that the education they managed to get deserved, their only disqualification being born in a low caste. Nevertheless, the organisation they gave final shape to, contrary to all the expectations of Guru, was in effect of the community to which they belonged, and was meant for the spiritual and worldly uplift of that community. Guru naturally was very unhappy about it. This ended up later in his publicly declaring that he would give up that organisation his mind, words and deeds.

It was the first ever communal organisation not only of Kerala, but of India as a whole, its fall-out being all the communities, irrespective of caste status, getting organised one by one, each staking its own claims. Guru's honest wish for having a casteless organisation of human beings thus ended up having as many organisations as there are caste-communities.

Though caste-mindedness thus got more strengthened, caste-discrimination and social evils such as untouchability, unapproachability and denial of opportunites in life ameliorated much; as far as Kerala is concerned they almost disappeared. Practice of untouchability became unlawful all over India. Encouraging inter-caste marriage and inter-caste communal feeding were the sole purpose for which certain organisations shooted up. Kerala eventually became the Indian state with the least caste-discrimination in the social front, all being the net result of Narayana Guru's quiet way of creating history.

## Religious Front

That caste-discrimination had a sort of approval of religion, we know, was a common notion. Religiousness and its culture had since long been seeping into the populace with temples as epicentres. In temples people felt the presence of the almighty God, the Creator, Sustainer and Dissolver of the world. Equally the children of God, all did not enjoy the equal privilege of going near God's presence in temples. The low-castes were not to go near God and worship Him, as though God too practised untouchability with His own children. Still the offerings made by such untouchables were not untouchable to God, for they eventually reached the hands of the upper caste. Even God thus became a tool at the hands of orthodoxy to promote its own selfish interests. If others wanted to go near God's presence and pray, they had to make their own temples — often make-shift ones — where they were to install only certain crude forms of deities to be worshipped in equally crude and often vulgar ways. To practise purer ways of worship was taboo to them, no one knowing or thinking of who tabooed it and why. To make amends for this social evil, the way Guru chose was not a forced entry into the orthodox temples. Instead, he took the initiative to make new temples open for all with the purest and most beautiful forms of worshipping. The deities installed were also equally beautiful and meaningful, even educative. His installing the image of Śiva at the newly conceived temple at Aruvippuram near Trivandrum marked the beginning of this new revolutionary religious movement.

Guru's new venture did not only make available a place of worship free of all caste discriminations, put it also was a silent challenge to the longstanding convention that Brahmin priests alone had the right to install a temple-deity. It was a silent proclamation that caste discrimination was not God-made but man-made, that too owing to man's ignorance. This set in motion a new religious reawakening among the downtrodden right across the whole of Kerala with demand for more new temples from different corners, and Guru too was willing to meet the new demands by consecrating more temples and installing deities like Śiva, Subrāhmaṇya and Devī. Many old temples with crude forms of worship were renovated with new deities installed and new forms of worship introduced. It indeed was a turning point in the temple-culture of Kerala. Priests well-trained in their craft emerged in legions from among the low-caste. Side by side with this was gaining momentum the demand for admittance to all in the old orthodox temples; and its climax was the Vaikam Satyagraha conducted at the instance of Mahatma Gandhi, which had all the moral support of Guru. He even let the *satyāgraha* volunteers use his own premises at that place as their camp. This movement, gradually gaining more momentum, ended up in the Crown making the famous Temple Entry Proclamation of 1936 which let open the doors of all temples to all. Neither mere political pressure nor the Crown's open-mindedness and generosity is to be considered the sole factor that prompted the authorities to make such a proclamation. The low-caste, though had no admittance to temples, were the main source of income for almost all the orthodox temples, for they formed majority of the population. A major portion of that income was being diverted to the newly-formed temples bringing the sustenance of the orthodox temples to the brink of a crisis, or the authorities were scared of such an eventuality. This too should have been one of the background aspects that led to the Proclamation.

## Educational Front

Social evils like caste-discrimination are the ill-effects of ignorance, their eradication possible only through education. Guru, therefore, insisted on the importance of universalising education, himself taking the initiative in starting an English School at Varkala and a Sanskrit School at Alwaye. He knew how English had become a world language and how indispensable the modern English education was. Equally well he knew that the Indian culture was rooted in the Sanskrit language. Hence, his starting both the schools on his own. Later he even discouraged having more temples and asked people to make more schools instead. Those were the days when none thought of having schools of their own, mainly, because people couldn't believe that education was accessible to them too. Things have so changed since that such initiatives are to be curbed by government regulations. Even temples, Guru conceived, are to be served as educational and cultural centres. Their clean ambience should encourage people to gather there in evenings and discuss matters of spiritual and cultural import, to be given a push to by organising occasional formal discussions in which invited distinguished scholars would be participating. Attached good libraries should enliven the quest for knowledge. Guru in order to transform even temple-deities into educational means, composed poetically sublime hymns either in the Malayalam, Sanskrit or Tamil language, on the occasion of installing a new temple deity, revealing how symbolically rich it was in meaning. But the followers of Guru, who got attracted by the new trend, need not be taken as having fully imbibed the high ideas and ideals Guru conceived.

For this reason, most of such new temples turned out to be a mere replica of the already existing orthodox temples but run by those of the lower strata. Instead of becoming places of worship for all, they in effect, became temples of the community concerned, yet always open for all. All the same, the new enlivening of temple culture and religious awakening among the downtrodden and the new open-mindedness and reasonableness the orthodox were brought down to in Kerala were tremendous.

## Social Front

Each community then had certain of its own customs and social events observed almost with a religious fervour as symbols of their self-esteem and pride, though most of them were meaningless, unreasonable, unscientific, not befitting the modern age, and, above all, pushing families down to utter poverty. Celebrating the first menstruation of a girl as a mark of recognising her as a grown-up girl, eight-year-old girls having to undergo a sort of formal marriage which in their later life will have no marital value, some ceremonies and social gathering at the first pregnancy of a girl, were some among them. Guru discouraged all such practices. He once even dared to walk into the scene of a group-child-marriage and stop it. He blessed the little girls giving them some sweets, and the public gathered there took the oath to discontinue the practice. Such customs and practices, various in kind and details in different communities, eventually vanished altogether. Even on occasions like marriage and funeral, spending much money on feasts and showy things were discouraged by Guru. He showed how marriages could be simplified and made less expensive with only ten participating. The spirit with which Guru showed these new lines of social life, though acceptable in principle, were not fully adaptable to all in practice, especially when social pride and showiness of the well-to-do prevailed over principles and ideals. Separate social movements bringing forth people to practise what they preach did therefore shoot up, the most notable among them the *Sahodara Prasthānam* (Fraternity Movement) initiated by K. Ayyappan.

The new awakening the downtrodden were thus brought to was reflected in the political front as well. Kerala in due course became unparalleled in political awareness and labour movements among the Indian States.

## Religious Tolerance

Christian missionaries, mostly from the West, by that time had begun to open new schools here and there. Their aim rather was using such schools as tools for converting more people to Christianity than uplifting them educationally and culturally. Those who got converted only were admitted to such schools in those days. Such forced conversion was much resented by Hindus, though caste-discrimination prevailing in Hinduism was another factor that the missionaries took advantage of. Guru's support for this anti-convertionism was also sought for, taking advantage of Mahatma Gandhi's visit to him. But Guru's attitude in this matter remained perfectly neutral. One leaves one's religion as he loses belief in it, and his leaving it gives that religion the benefit of getting rid of one non-believer, whereas the other religion gets the benefit of gaining one more believer. Such was Guru's neutrality. Born though as a Hindu, in religious matters his identity was not of *Hindutva*. He always remained the embodiment of the spiritual enlightenment that formed the glowing core of all religions, yet the birthright of no particular religion. He could not love one religion and hate another. Of course, the temples he initiated and consecrated were of the Hindu heritage. Why did not he make or consecrate places of worship of other religions? He himself cleared this doubt: none of those religions demanded such of him; had anyone demanded he would gladly have complied. The real followers of one religion should necessarily have the knowledge of what other religions teach. He felt also the need of having some institution where all religions are taught with an open-mindedness. Creating such new trends in religions was what he aimed at when he organised a Parliament of Religions at his own ashram in Alwaye in 1924. It was the first ever inter-religious meet in India and the second in world history, the first being the one held in 1893 in Chicago. "Not to argue and win, but to know and make know" was the motto written large at the entrance to the venue. Such new moves initiated by Guru made Kerala the Indian State of most religious tolerance and least religious turbulence.

The last decades of Guru's life was when the National Movement in India was warming up, led by the Indian National Congress. That gaining political freedom would be meaningless unless social freedom is ensured to the oppressed classes of India did not strike the minds of the political leadership until Mahatma Gandhi visited Guru. Gandhiji, though against untouchability, was then an advocate of the *cāturvarṇya* caste system, his ideal being *Rāmarājya*, a Vaiṣṇavite social order in which each caste group sticks to its hereditary vocation. The topic happened to be highlighted in the discussion during his visit too. "Look at the leaves of that mango tree", Gandhiji said, "each leaf has its own peculiarity; so too is there difference between human beings." "Chew the different leaves of a mango tree; they will taste the same", was Guru's reply. Gandhiji eventually became a spokesman of the downtrodden and he even re-christened his beloved newspaper 'Navajeevan' as 'Harijan'. This influence of Narayana Guru on the Indian National Movement is an aspect not much evaluated by historians.

## In the History of Indian Thought

Epochal is the place of Narayana Guru in the history of Indian Philosophy, in that he represented the ancient Upaniṣadic non-dual vision in the age of modern science. It was in order to codify the Upaniṣadic speculations into a well-structured system of thought that Bādarāyaṇa in the ancient days wrote the *Brahma-Sūtras*, also known as the *Vedānta-Sūtras*. Yet, normal to its *sūtra* style, it was a text so condensed that, without a proper commentary it was not understandable at all. Such commentaries that arose later were many and varied, each portraying Bādarāyaṇa's vision as a different one. Twenty-one such commentaries appeared. It even became a convention in India that a person, to be recognised as an adept in Vedānta, should write a new commentary of his own on the *Brahma-Sūtras* of Bādarāyana. The dominant schools of Vedānta which thus sprang up were those of Śaṅkara, Rāmānuja, Madhva, Vallabha, Nimbārka, Caitanya-Mahāprabhu and the like. A modern student in search of the original philosophy of Bādarāyaṇa, will find himself confused and lost among the conflicting commentaries and commentaries on commentaries, of the many schools. Guru did find a final solution: in his *Ātmopadeśa-Śatakam* he resuscitated the original non-dual vision of the Upaniṣadic seers, presenting it in a tone familiar to the ears of the age of science.

Writing more and move commentaries, as we have just noted, was what the later Vedāntins were interested in, each making the essential teaching vaguer and remoter. Many were those who wrote introductory and elucidatory works on Vedānta in all its schools, but none wrote a new *sūtra* text of Vedānta to clarify all the obscurities. Narayana Guru did do it. His *Vedānta-Sūtras* was the result of it. He thus, though a continuator of the philosophy of Śaṅkara, as he acknowledged once himself, was not simply repeating what Śaṅkara said, had Śaṅkara's philosophy is elucidated mainly in his comments on the *Brahma-Sūtras* of Bādarāyaṇa, the Upaniṣads and the *Bhagavad Gītā*. Guru, on the other hand, wrote no commentary on any of the already existing basic texts. Instead, he wrote the new *Vedānta-Sūtras*, *Ātmopadeśa-Śatakam* as original as the *Gītā*, and *Darśanamālā*, a work of the genre of the Upaniṣads but more concise and precise, natural to the modern times. Guru differed from Śaṅkara thuswise. He brought in many revisions and revaluations of the nuances of Vedānta. Also Guru did not have to, and did not, compromise with the teachings of Vedānta in practical life, while Śaṅkara had to, for historical reasons, at least in the matter of observing caste system as he himself confessed in the *Manīṣā Pañcakam*.

A hitherto unfamiliar way of presenting the philosophy of non-dualism was adopted by Guru in his *Darśanamālā*. Many were the profound works on Vedānta that have emerged in the Sanskrit language between Śaṅkara's time and his. Viewing the non-dual Reality from various philosophical perspectives, one following the other in a logical sequence, and leaving the seeker to intuitively perceive the Reality on his own, is the new method adopted by Guru in this work, its name itself, 'A Garland of Visions of the Absolute' (*Darśanamālā*) indicating it. Unparalleled though this style is in India, semblance to it could be seen in the philosophy of Henri Bergson, especially in his *Introduction to Metaphysics*. Nevertheless, Bergson, with his Western bend of mind, when facing the transparency of the non-dual vision, turns out to be a face-saver. No such conditioning contains Guru's spontaneous expositions of the clarity of vision. Preciseness of thinking and a clarity of mystical intuitive vision are like two sides of a coin in the philosophy of Guru.

### In the World Thought

Unique are the contributions of Guru to world thought also, especially in the field of Ethics, one of the serious topics in all philosophy. It, as a normative science, teaches what kind of activities are morally justifiable and not; it, as a descriptive science, examines human behaviour from moral point of view. Determining what is justifiable and not must needs have a criterion universally valid. Such a criterion had been lacking in all systems of thought in spite of all the ethical theorisations, the net result, all such evaluations remaining relative. Narayana Guru filled up this lacuna — his original contribution to world thought.

One Reality — the Self or the Absolute — alone exists. All multiple appearances are but Its ever-changing manifestations. The essential content in one being and another thus is one and the same, whatever the form it appears in. One who knows this basic reality sees himself in everyone else. Self-love thus gets transformed as the love for all, where loving others becomes spontaneous. Doing something beneficial to oneself and harmful to another thus becomes incongruent to the oneness of Reality. Oneness of the all-abiding Reality thus serves as the universal basis for all Ethics. An ethically sound human behaviour ensures the happiness of oneself and others. Such actions which are beneficial to one and harmful to another are unsound. Harming oneself for the sake of helping others also thus is unethical. Guru deals with this problem in Verses 21 to 25 of the *Ātmopadeśa-Śatakam*.

## The World Government

Getting inspired by Guru's teachings, Garry Davis, a Second World War American bomber pilot, who happened to bomb a German hospital, brought forth the ideal. "One Human family, One World, One-World Government." He realised that accepting this principle alone will bring about world peace. He therefore declared, with the philosophical and moral backing of Nataraja Guru, the disciple-successor of Narayana Guru, that the world is already one; admitting it alone is needed. He even initiated the 'World Government of World Citizens', a movement that fully honours the famous U.N. Charter of Human Rights, a document signed by all member-nations of that world body, but none honouring it in practice. The world passport issued by the World

Government at times had been a legal and moral headache to many nations including India and America. Peace lovers right across the world extended their moral support to this movement. Through the books *The World is My Country* and *Passport to Freedom*, Garry Davis let the world know all his ideas and ideals, all an application of the teachings of Narayana Guru in the world political scenario. The World Government, based in America, published the newspaper 'World Citizens News' also. Garry Davis has been travelling around the world disseminating the idea of the World Government, always on the strength of the passport he himself issued. During his first visit to India he met the then Prime Minister, Mr. Nehru and presented him with a world passport.

The world, with all the wonders achieved by modern science and technology and all the communication and transportation facilities made available, is gradually shrinking into a global village. Yet religious fundamentalism, economic interests, political ideologies and many such factors, along with their unholy alliances, together go on disintegrating the world into more and more fragmented political units. The number of member-nations of the U.N. at its inception was 51 only. Gradually increasing, the number has reached 184, the world yet remaining the same. It is mutual mistrust and fear that bring about such disintegration which in turn furthers the mistrust and fear. The only way out of this vicious predicament is nurturing the attitude of oneness, the only meaningful application of intelligence human race is gifted with. It alone will ensure even the existence of this planet of life.

The United Nations whose charter recognises all human beings as equal and which the entire human race puts all its hopes on, has proved itself a failure. Despite all its high sounding ideals it has no right to function without admitting the sovereignty of the member-nations. It can take no decision not complying with the interests of the top five members either. No organisation of sovereign states will ensure world-peace, a fact already proved in practice. Admitting the world as a political unit, which it already is geographically, is the only way to a world without wars, which in effect will be a world without armies. All the world leaders are aware of this naked truth, but none knows how to work it out. Garry Davis, with the sound support of the non-dual vision of Narayana Guru and the guidance of Nataraja Guru, was shedding a new light on this ever vexing world problem. Presently Guru Nitya Chaitanya Yati is giving all the spiritual guidance he needs. The one-world dreamed by these Gurus has inevitably to become a political reality. The only question is 'When'?

*Gurukulam, Varkala* **Guru Muni Narayana Prasad**
*23-12-1998*

# Foreword

VIEWED from whatever perspective or criterion, because of their relevance to modernity, Guru's life and vision have adorned themselves with an aura of illustriousness. In them the magnificance of fullness vibrates in all its glory. In the pinacle of thought which ends on a non-existence of analytical conjunction of ideas, lustrous spirituality issues forth in purebred ripeness. When the spontaneous flux of that spirituality is automatically articulated visions come to light.

The attribute of withdrawing from an infructuous endeavour to contain within oneself one's mind and thought in a harmonious blend is gorgeousness of the *ātma*. The base frame of Gurudeva's prowess is Ātmic gorgeousness. He saw and studied the world in the scientific temper of His self-revelation. His vision is the majestic guiding line for transforming life into a pilgrimage to the realisation of the self. That vision leads us to the scientific process of purifying worldly life in the furnace of modernisation (reformation) and self-sanctification. It was not to negate worldly life that Gurudeva had undertaken a spiritual messenger's task. What filled in all His movements was a manoeuvring dexterity to tactfully guide earthly life to a gratuitous vision of truth through a path which keeps scrupulous watch on virtue and maintenance of continuity. His approach to the abjuration of liquor, activities aimed towards eradication of caste outlook on the untrammelled co-existence of religions and the ceaseless exhortations for the promotion of education are all psychological contrivances to offer a hand lift to invest temporal life with the air of spirituality.

What glistens in Gurudeva's visions and messages is an all embracing outlook to offer man a new life path and new fangled sense of direction by a constitutional, basic and resonant shift in individual life. At the root of our individuality is an uncanny admixture of history, geography, heredity and social legacy. Gurudeva had always kept in mind an awareness of the reality that it is impossible to subvert human character shaped out of an intermixture of intricate ingredients. He has given us the spiritual and temporal inspiration and light which are propitious in regenerating and turning subjective, everyone's individuality which is being annihilated by the pressure of variegated circumstances. When we look at and see Gurudeva's messages and actions as the never ceasing call for subjective existence and the never swerving right-path-pointer, we receive fairly good insight.

What is simply desirable for us is to evaluate in the context of its unbroken character, the action phase of Gurudeva's life, pregnant in achievements and profuse in events and His vision germane in cosmopolitanism and rife in international appropriateness. To reach its depth, diversity and amplitude, is not smooth sailing. That is why varied analyses and appraisements of Gurudeva and His visions are taking place continuously. What we should do is to perceive and accept these as complete or partial undertakings to discover the greatness of Gurudeva and the *par-excellence* of His visions. We will perforce have to approach every factor as incentives to know more and more from what we have known already.

It is with a new burning wick in his hand which points to us an exhaustive and rich zone of study of Gurudeva that Dr. Vijayalayam Jayakumar has entered the fray with this book, *Sree Narayana Guru: A Critical Study*. More than basic intention, the book provides us with the ineluctable practical sense. Not only an overall survey of Gurudeva, His poems and *modus-operandi* but also authentic information about His spiritual-cum-material projects have been brilliantly expatiated upon and presented in the book in integrated form. I am happy to point out that Dr. Vijayalayam Jayakumar has been able to mould out a style enriched by intense reading habit, an effortless narrative talent and unshakable faith in Gurudeva. This book is rendered all the more ornate with the wealth of experience Dr. Vijayalayam has acquired over the last many decades by the unrelenting effort he has brought to bear upon his study of Gurudeva. In this book is enclosed every material that could be known and that could be collected and so it is a tremendous contribution to the Sree Narayana Movement. There is many a fact in it, not unearthed so far. Many parts concerning the Dharma Sangham deserve special attention.

With the expectation that to those who desire to have a general idea about Gurudeva and the Gurudeva Movement, this work will shine as a guiding light, and with the prayer that it may credit itself with wide popularity, it is hereby presented to the revered public.

*Sivagiri Matom* **Sreemat Saswathikananda Swamigal**
*Varkala*
*08.12.1997*

# Preface

To attempt a fairly massive research work entitled *Sree Narayana Guru: A Critical Study* was my life's ambition. When its blue-print was ready the thought that its completion would require a five-year plan itself, did not escape me. As expected it was a result of five years of continuous work, that the research effort enough to study Guru comprehensively had fructified into a book.

The original work in Malayalam is framed in two Cantos viz., Canto of Genesis and the Canto of Redemption and in 25 books; the research study covers 500 pages. In the translation, this arrangement has been reshuffled to 15 Chapters; and much material relevant only in the local context had to be omitted for the sake of compactness and brevity.

Every effort has been made to examine all reference books which could be available to evaluate diversified expert opinion minutely and to include relevant portions from rare treatises available in the collections of Kerala University, Kerala Sahitya Academy and the Thiruvananthapuram Public Library. It was but great luck that it has been possible to trace out and examine scrupulously, almost all books written in Malayalam, Sanskrit, English and Hindi about Sree Narayana Guru and detailed commentaries, translations and critical studies of Gurudeva's works. The miracles attributed to Gurudeva in some of these biographies have been left out of this work as they appear super-normal. It was by creating a new horizon of love that Guru had rejuvenated a vast collection of people branded as *avarṇas* and leading an oppressed life in the lower rungs of the Social Strata, cursing themselves.

In chapter 1 the socio-historical background of Kerala before the birth of the Gurudeva, the life history of Guru, the reforms and progress which took place in the social sphere of Kerala after Guru's birth, have been dealt with.

In the next chapter are included epitomised studies of Gurudeva's poems and their critical discussions. Herein are contained subjects headed the Inner Currents of Spirituality, Hymns to Goddess Devī, Lord Subrahmaṇya, Lord Viṣṇu and Lord Śiva, thoughts on Advaita, Sanskrit Poems, Translations and Tamil Works.

In the remaining chapters a variety of topics, such as the influence of Guru's literary works on the Malayalam language, the social reforms sponsored by Guru, the preceptors of Guru and his disciples, are covered. Guru's conceptions on Education and organisation, and how these conceptions had their impact on the social set-up, have been examined. The later chapters describe Guru's humour and sarcasm, His creation of a permanent arrangement for the implementation of his scheme of social reforms, and finally the quantum leap of the social frame- work achieved in consequence.

Another matter that requires special mention is that many Gurudeva *bhaktas* have by now written and published exhaustive commentaries on Gurudeva's works. Prominent among them are Prof. K. Balarama Panicker, Dr. Nataraja Guru, Prof. Balakrishnan Nair and Guru Nitya Chaitanya Yati. All of them are extremely learned scholars who have known Guru's spiritual greatness and imbibed the eternal magnitude of the Vedas and *Itihāsas* preserved by the *ṛṣis* of Bhārata as their own heritage. Hence in their commentaries and interpretations there will be an abundant stream of the ideas engulfed by the Vedic-Itihāsic works. But it is by standing apart from all of them that I have attempted interpretation of the doctrines subsumed by Gurudeva's creations, my reason being that these should be assimilated by the common man. Even though Gurudeva's tiny stanzas are in simple Malayalam the spiritual profundity they reflect is like the richness of idea conveyed by the dew reflecting a whole woodland. The Gurudeva *Gītā* is not susceptible to ordinary pen because of the deep philosophical ideas they encompass. Yet those works, I felt, should be comprehended not only by the learned, but also by the layman. Hence my aim was to reveal in simple form their ideas, meaning and spiritual intensity to the extent possible. If Gurudeva *bhaktas* are, through this effort, able to absorb an overall idea of Gurudeva's works, I consider that my work shall not have been in vain.

Gurudeva's motive was to create an one caste, one religion society from the Kerala society of earlier days, already disrupted by the ruinous diversities of castes and religions. In short Gurudeva was through his messages, creating an atmosphere suited to the peace and happiness of the modern world. The sages of the cadre of Nataraja Guru and Guru Nitya Chaitanya Yati endowed those messages with planetary publicity.

There are many learned friends of mine who have helped me wholeheartedly in the fulfilment of the daunting task I have herein undertaken to swim across the inestimably deep and vast ocean Divine Grace that is Sree Narayana Guru. I hereby express my heartfelt love and respect to all those magnanimous, gentle hearts. On this occasion I enduce with extreme gratitude the names of my close friend and reputed literati Prof. G. N. Panicker who has carefully gone through this research work and made necessary corrections, and Sriharsha who has extended sincere cooperation to my undertaking. I am also indebted to Smt. P. Jagadama, Sarvasree D. Sanjeeva Ghosh, K. Swaminathan and Artist Gopal in the completion of this book.

This is the first book of Sree Narayana Research Centre. I record here my hearty gratitude and love to well-known litterateurs Prof. S. Guptan Nair, Dr. K.M. George, Dr. N.A. Karim, Sri. E.M.S. Namboodiripad and Prof. M. Krishnan Nair who have provided it with valuable and informative appraisals.

*Thiruvananthapuram* **Dr. Vijayalayam Jayakumar**

# Contents

# Appraisements

## I

THIS immense book namely *Sree Narayana Guru: A Critical Study* by Dr. Vijayalayam Jayakumar is an intense endeavour to install the name of the universally revered Sree Narayana Guru against the real background. Numerous works on Sree Narayana are available to us now. Through treatises written in English by great souls like Nataraja Guru, Guru's greatness is at present shimmering across the whole world. But Vijayalayam's book follows a hitherto unknown path. The author's attempt is to enfold in one shell as it were, the last hundred years' social, spiritual and literary history of Kerala. That this creative effort enshrining a streamlined annotation of the main works of Guru, will greatly benefit the common people, is undoubted. The story of Guru's spiritual and householder disciples doing services to mankind at the time, is also available from this work. Rich with the fruits of elaborate research and enquiry, this book can be expected to receive deserving encouragement from the intelligentsia.

*Thiruvananthapuram* **S. Guptan Nair**
*08.12.1997*

## II

In the history of Bhārat's Renaissance the one gift which Kerala can ever remember with pride is Sree Narayana Guru and His message. Though the Keralites are aware of Him, they do not evaluate Him properly. The saying that familiarity breeds contempt can be said to be relevant here. He is familiar to us in time and space. For that very reason His life and message do not press in upon us. Outside Kerala too Gurudeva is not known adequately. But there are a few who know Him. It is they who are estimating Him in proper perspective.

I have said this with the memory of a particular experience in mind. The research institute named Indian Institute of Advanced Study, situated in Simla had organised a seminar of all India importance in 1977. The subject of the seminar was 'Resent, Protest and Reform in Indian Civilization'. More than forty intellectuals took part in it. As a visiting fellow I also got an opportunity to participate and present a paper. This discussion group was one which afforded a break to see and make acquaintance with many who were well versed in the social sciences. The one individual to whom I was drawn from among them was Dr. M.S.A. Rao, the then Head of the Department of Sociology in the Delhi University. He was interested in me because I belonged to the land of Sree Narayana Guru, with knowledge of Malayalam, Guru's language. Dr. Rao was engaged in learning Malayalam at the time. The main aim of this endeavour was to study and understand Guru's teachings in the original language itself. So far as I was concerned, this was a curious experience. Rao asked me many questions about Guru. In the thesis submitted by him there were a few paragraphs about Guru's teachings. Besides, he remnisces about Guru in many of his essays. There are a few enlightened ones like Rao in every group of people in the world. They are able to grasp Guru's sayings fairly well through certain works in the English language. Not only in English but in all prominent languages in the world authentic and inspiring works on Sree Narayana Guru should come into existence.

So many books on Guru have come out in Malayalam. Several of them are no doubt beneficial. But no work can claim comprehensiveness as the one now presented by Dr. Vijayalayam Jayakumar. In this, two special features have attracted me. (1) The research thrust underlying its compilative process. That Dr. Vijayalayam has already demonstrated his knowledge and capability in literary research, is well-known. In studying and appraising casteism through an analysis of historical material, this strength is well explicit. (2) The dexterity with which he has amalgamated the traditional approach and the modern *modus-operandi*. When a personage of the greatness of Sree Narayana Guru is the subject of study, this feature is especially relevant. Like Sree Ramakrishna Paramahamsa, Sree Narayana Guru is one of those great men who, after stabilising their stances in the foundation of Bhārat's Dharmaśāstra (morality), have created new tracts of their own in our philosophical territory, through their meditative enterprises. As to those tracts it is known that they are extremely relevant to modern life. This approach of Dr. Vijayalayam is manifest even in the material zone up to an extent. What I have indicated here is the compartmentalisation of the body of the treatise into Cantos, and Books.

This thought-provoking, knowledgeable and comprehensive work can on the whole be undoubtedly a blessing to the readers of Malayalam.

*Thiruvananthapuram* **K. M. George**
*08.12.1997*

## III

Among the several books on Sree Narayana Guru in Malayalam and English only a few are really outstanding ones in the sense that they alone throw new light on the uniquely multifaceted life and personality of Guru. The rest of the writings treat the subject in the conceptional biographical or hagiographical style. However there are a few definitive biographies which will be extremely useful for future students of Guru or the researchers who would like to probe deep into his social and spiritual relevance.

Dr. Vijayalayam Jayakumar in his new book on Sree Narayana Guru makes a meaningful departure from the trodden path of his predecessors. This comprehensive work is the product of long study, serious research and deep reflection on the life, works and activities of Guru. As he was a saint, philosopher, poet, social revolutionary all rolled into a perfect but largely inscrutable human being whose teachings laid the foundation of modern Kerala, Dr.

Jayakumar, in order to make his study of Guru a holistic one, had to use the tools of a biographer, historian, social scientist and literary critic. And he has succeeded in this difficult task, and the result is an eminently readable and extremely valuable study of the saint-reformer.

Dr. Jayakumar has made the backdrop of his subject as wide as possible. It is against the appropriate social, religious, philosophical and literary background that he has placed the achievements of Guru with the result that the assessment of the magnitude of his achievements becomes easier. Considerable time and energy might have been spent for the reconstruction of the picture of the period of Guru but they have not gone waste. This is particularly so in the case of the fairly wide historical canvas provided by the author in order to impress upon his readers the magnitude of the social revolution Guru brought about in so short a time. Historical facts are well supported by extensive quotations from standard works on relevant aspects. He has cast his net very wide and many historical facts and social truths have been gathered in it. Dr. Vijayalayam's observations on them are keen and his conclusions are valid.

Particular mention is to be made of the remarkable critical acumen with which the author has studied the philosophy of Sree Narayana and evaluated the poetry of that philosophy. Sixtytwo works of Swamiji have been dealt with in detail in more than three hundred and fifty pages of the book. The study is complete and rewarding.

What perplexes any student of Hinduism is the seemingly irreconcilable contradiction between its sublime philosophy and the narrow social outlook it propagated. In the matter of belief it is tolerant and eclectic but imposed upon people several unjust practices. Swamiji's epoch-making achievement is that he successfully fought against those entrenched social evils by using the philosophical weapons of the very same Advaita philosophy in the name of which many of the abominable things were perpetrated on society. Guru was inspired by a vision of an egalitarian society the guiding principles of which was unity of God and universal brotherhood of man. This book of Dr. Vijayalayam Jayakumar is undoubtedly a valuable addition to the now considerable rich Sree Narayana literature.

*Thiruvananthapuram* **N. A. Karim**
*08.12.1997*

## IV

The Caste System creates darkness. Cultural decadence too is a cause of darkness. It was Sree Narayana Guru who erased out both these darknesses. What disposed of that want of light was not exclusively his activities or his messages. Sri Kinikkara Padmanabha Pillai and Sree P. Kesava Dev who had seen Sree Narayana in flesh and blood, had told this writer that his very presence had evoked illumination. Sree Narayana had sprinkled not merely by the light of spirituality. He had shown us the path towards the acquisition of knowledge and the shaping of human character. He thus became instrumental for a Renaissance. On that count Sree Narayana is our preceptor. We are his disciples. This preceptor-disciple nexus is alluringly brought out in the work *Sree Narayana Guru: A Critical Sudy* by Dr. Vijayalayam Jayakumar. This writer has read many works on Guru. But Dr. Vijayalayam's work has outstripped them all by the analytical skill and objective evaluation demonstrated in it. This is the life history of a great Guru: the story of His noble actions; reverential appraisement of His highly esteemed literary works; and over and above, the history of the period covered by His life. The book has also brought to light the picture of a forgotten culture. At the same time it is also a reference book.

A great Guru and a versatile genius that he had been, we know that He was an accomplished poet too. The author of this book is able to enlarge upon that knowledge.

While dealing with spiritual matter, spirituality gets percolated. When the same spirituality dons the role of poems, poetry gets percolated too. All these have been logically expressed by Dr. Vijayalayam.

It was not in a mechanical trend that the culture of Bhārat had taken form and shape. That culture and civilization has enriched itself, through machines, in the line of thinking adopted by the Occidents. Our civilization and culture are premissed on the messages and philosophies of the Preceptors and their spiritual perspectives. Sree Narayana who was the proponent of Bhārat's culture with a religious and spiritual bias, had written Sanskrit works also with the same predilection. Prominent among such works have been taken out and annotated in the book for the sake of readers not conversant with Sanskrit. Was that great *ṛṣi* a philosopher alone? No. He was a social reformer too. That the social reforms presented by him had a thread of spirituality running through them, was the special feature of those reforms. I am happy to quote a passage in the book where the synchronisation of the two has been made clear.

> The Second quarter of that night was bright with the fine moonlight and soothing by a pleasant breeze. Swamy was sitting in the vicinity of the Manakkal temple in solitude. The village slumbered in long silence. In that atmosphere, he gave himself up to repeated contemplation of the momentariness of Maya or illusion stricken human life. The universe is subject to change. I have become lonely with the departure of my mother; in one sense it has set me free. What is now needed is to reach a zone of peace not susceptible to change. Some power unknown is beckoning me up to that. If I reach there, the Supreme Truth of Unity in Diversity would be realised by me. Then it should be possible to revitalise Human values and mould up a real human society. So I implore Devi in my search for the Self and Truth.

Thus Sree Narayana prayed to Devi to bless Him. How that prayer was fructified, is exquisitely driven home by Dr. Vijayalayam in this book.

*Thiruvananthapuram* **M. Krishnan Nair**
*08.12.1997*

## V

In the preface to the first edition of this work, the author Dr. Vijayalayam Jayakumar says:

> This research study extends to 750 pages. Every effort has been made to examine all reference books which could be available to evaluate diversified expert opinions minutely and to include relevant portions from rare treatises available in the collections of the Kerala University, Kerala Sahitya Academy and the Thiruvananthapuram Public Library. It was but great luck that it had been possible to trace out and examine scrupulously, almost all books written in Malayalam, Sanskrit, English and Hindi about Sree Narayana Guru, and detailed commentaries, translations and critical studies of Gurudeva's works. It was by creating a new horizon of love that Guru had rejuvenated a vast collection of people branded as *avarṇas* and leading an oppressed life in the lower rungs of the social strata, cursing themselves.

That this claim is fully justified, anyone who reads this book at least once, will be convinced. From that standpoint I have great pleasure in congratulating the author. The link between the reform movement sponsored by Śrī Rāmakṛṣṇa and continued by Svāmī Vivekānanda in Bengal and the Sree Narayana movements in Kerala, has been made clear in the book. Of a series of Indian Renaissance movements, the one which first devoted itself to the regeneration of the lower castes was that inaugurated and proliferated by Sree Narayana Guru. It was because that the significance of this was grasped, that Svāmī Vivekānanda and later Mahatma Gandhi had looked upon the Sree Narayana movement with respect and regard. To repeat, Sree Narayana was the first to array members of the oppressed classes in the peaceful struggle to achieve their rights. Even the Ambedkar movement which originated in Maharastra and subsequently gained all India momentum, was a continuation of the Sree Narayana movement in Kerala.

The two followers of Sree Narayana Guru who had upheld His

teachings and gave them a revolutionary dimension, and whom the author has specially mentioned, are Swamy Anandtheerdhar, a brāhmin and Sahodaran Ayyappan. The latter moulded the Sree Narayana's dictum 'One caste, One religion, One God for man' into a new dictum viz. 'no caste, no religion, no God for man'. He arranged joint eating by all castes in his native village and incurred the wrath of the upper classes.

*Thiruvananthapuram* **E.M.S. Namboodiripad**
*08.12.1997*

## VI

Of the sages modern Kerala has had the privilege to produce, Sree Narayana Guru occupies the most prominent place. The research work *Sree Narayana Guru: A Critical Study* by Dr. Vijayalayam Jayakumar with the life and vision of Guru as its theme is, as its name indicates, a work which enfolds within it everything that is to be known about Sree Narayana Guru. Guru's literary works and their annotations constitute the main subject-matter of this massive work. Such topics as the Kerala Society before Guru's birth, the life of Guru, the beneficial transformations which had accrued to the Kerala Society and Malayalam literature taken in by Guru's messages, the accounts given by his preceptors, His great contemporaries and His disciples, His utterances, the reminiscences of reputed personalities of the preceding generation — all are included in a single work. It presents the impression of many books. The author's approach is descriptive throughout. It is but natural that this book, which is a rendezvous as it were, of the rules of the academic research theses, has more than the required allusions. One thing deserves special notice. It is the intensity of the effort behind the preparation of the work. Further, the author says that it was his life's ambition.

The division of the work into Canto and Books gives it an epic stature. The divisions deal with besides such other topics as Guru's life history, His messages and philosophy, His literary works, the influence of Guru's literary works on Malayalam literature and umpteen other subjects associated with the life and works of the great social reformer. These tend to endear this book to the reader considerably. Guru's humour is worth reading. The book of Smṛti is thought-inspiring.

The book leads humanity to the path of *śānti*, peace, fraternity and co-existence by popularising the word of Guru. It is prayed that it may achieve success in this sacred endeavour and with that, attain fulfilment.

*Thiruvananthapuram* **Raja Raja Varma**
*08.12.1997*

## VII

The book *Sree Narayana Guru: A Critical Study* by Dr. Vijayalayam Jayakumar is a tremendous work which has triumphed in deleanating with truthful exactitude and visionary expertise, the life and work and the literary creations of Sree Narayana Guru. It is impossible to bring into fruition a work of this dimension without sustained effort, protracted study and thought. For those who aspire to know about Guru, it is an ideal torch bearer, and for those who desire to study him, it is a perennial source of reference. It serves the purpose of a compendium of three or four works that could be written on Sree Narayana Guru.

The study is an emulative guide for the seekers of the Sree Narayana thought. I heartfully congratulate Vijayalayam Jayakumar for having brought out such a remarkable work and the Keralite readers for having read and have it restated into the English language, thus paving the way for its accessibility to a world-wide readership.

*Viyyoor* **Dr. Sukumar Azhikode**
*15.12.1997*

# Translator's Note

THE research work on Sree Narayana Guru authored by Dr. Vijayalayam Jayakumar is a massive one of 750 pages in print. In the original are contained details parenthetical to the main theme relevant only to the local context. For the sake of brevity these details had to be left out. Further the structure of the original, framed through Cantos and Books, has been changed and they have been reshuffled and categorised as chapters with a view to invest the work with more compactness. These alterations in the overall arrangement of the treatise have been effected with the consent and concurrence of the author.

The translation is not by any means word by word or sentence by sentence. Such an endeavour in a large work as this one, is neither practicable nor achievable. So the translation has been based idea-wise. Every effort has been made to conform scrupulously and strictly to the ideas and facts as narrated by the author.

For the translations of the poems, dependence has been placed on those of Nataraja Guru, Guru Nitya Chaitanya Yati and P. Damodara Panicker. I am very much indebted to these great souls.

I hereby express my heartfelt gratitude to the author for having given me the opportunity to undertake the work and Smt. G. Janaki who had extended to me all help in scrutinising the manuscript.

Sree Narayana Guru is one of the greatest philosophers and social reformers India has seen. To have had the opportunity to translate a work on Him of epic grandeur, is a rare privilege. By

Guru's blessings it is hoped that the English version of this research study would be a welcome presentation to the illustrious readers.

In humble submission to Guru.

*Thiruvananthapuram* **K. Sadanandan**
*1.12.1997*

# Transliteration Chart

| a | ā | i | ī | u | ū | e | ai | o | au |
|---|---|---|---|---|---|---|---|---|---|
| अ | आ | इ | ई | उ | ऊ | ए | ऐ | ओ | औ |

| ṁ | ḥ | ṛ |
|---|---|---|
| अं | अः | ऋ |

| k | kh | g | gh | ṅ |
|---|---|---|---|---|
| क् | ख् | ग् | घ् | ङ् |
| c | ch | j | jh | ñ |
| च् | छ् | ज् | झ् | ञ् |
| ṭ | ṭh | ḍ | ḍh | ṇ |
| ट् | ठ् | ड् | ढ् | ण् |
| t | th | d | dh | n |
| त् | थ् | द् | ध् | न् |
| p | ph | b | bh | m |
| प् | फ् | ब् | भ् | म् |

| y | r | l | v |
|---|---|---|---|
| य् | र् | ल् | व् |
| ś | ṣ | s | h |
| श् | ष् | स् | ह् |

| kṣ | tr | jñ |
|---|---|---|
| क्ष् | त्र् | ज्ञ् |

# 1

# Kerala — Before the Advent of Sree Narayana Guru and After

SREE Narayana Guru, the philosopher saint of modern Kerala, was the architect of a peaceful, yet sprightly social revolution which eventually lifted the lowly and downtrodden in that part of India to the status of respectable human beings. His *modus operandi*, though premissed on spirituality, had that incisive edge of rationalism which cut through the debased and beleaguered social order of His day, like a knife galvanised with the sharpness of cold reason. Renascent Kerala is indeed synonymous with His name. He has rightly been compared to, or even identified with, Lord Buddha for His unflinching dedication to the cause of social equality.

Just as Bengal can take pride in having given to the world Śrī Rāmakṛṣṇa Paramahaṁsa[1] and Svāmī Vivekānanda[2] so does Kerala stand glorified in having given birth to two champions of Advaita Theory (Monism), viz. Śrī Śaṅkarācārya[3] and Sree Narayana Guru.[4] It is a fact however that while the one propelled the theory, the other realised it through an august life.

There was nevertheless a marked dissemblance between the two in the context of their social backgrounds. Śrī Śaṅkara was born in the brāhmin community sheltered by the protective fortress of antiquity. But Sree Narayana Guru was born in the Ezhava community whose members, along with members of other communities similarly placed, were driven to suffer the humiliation of being untouchables, branded so by the society held under the fist by brāhmin domination. Guru's greatness lies in having achieved a rewriting, from a human perspective, of the history of Kerala's social life which had been corrupted through the ages by the tyranny of man-made caste and religion benumbing the life of the helpless human beings categorised as of society's lower strata.

If one were to grasp in full the long and blurred social history of Kerala, one has to ponder over the struggles waged in the name of caste and religion. In doing so one should keep an open mind and be very particular about a discrete and objective approach to the problems.

There is consensus among scholars that of the two great religions, Buddhism and Jainism, which had more or less contemporaneously emerged in Bhārat and captured her social arena, the former had a decisive edge over the latter in carrying the popular mind along with it. Buddhism was born two thousand five hundred years ago. Christianity with a history of two thousand years and Islam of over one thousand four hundred years, had their origin in the Asian subcontinent. Further, we may legitimately felicitate ourselves that our region which forms the eastern part of the globe, is the fountain spring of all the great religions which have flourished in the world over the centuries.

It is a fact of history that Buddhism impregnated as it is, with profuse knowledge of virtue, of social awareness and with spiritual thought to spilling point and premissed on truth, virtue and non-violence, embodied in the values adumbrated through *pañca-śīla*, has caught the imagination of the world in no time. When the flame of Bhārat's ancient greatness blazed across the world, what really dazzled everywhere was nothing but our glorious cultural heritage in its diversified forms flashing its inner core at the same time; the heritage we have been at pains to conserve through the ages. Not only in India, but also in China, Japan, Malaysia, Indonesia, Singapore, Sri Lanka and a host of other countries, had Buddhism spread spiritual lustre for more than ten centuries. Even today, at least in 15 countries Buddhism is the dominant religion. Because Buddhism is posited on human love, the people of various countries were captivated by its powerful sway. But after some centuries this great religion had its setback on the lanes of history. The Āryans who occupied northern India had, for their survival, founded the caste system of the Hindu society, an effective weapon against the humane teachings of Buddha, and directed it against it (Buddhism) to uproot it from Indian soil. The stroke served to resurrect Hinduism. It is a truism that in the ordinary course it is from the debris of one project that another sprouts up.

So far as Kerala was concerned, the Namboodiris who were the legatees of the Āryan brāhmins tried their utmost to bring about the fall of Buddhism. What acted as a catalyst to that endeavour was the revival of Hinduism embarked upon by Śaṅkarācārya. Their conspiracy to exterminate not only Buddhism and Buddhist precepts, but also believers in and sympathisers of that religion and expropriating them of their movable and immovable properties, resulted in the reconstruction of Hinduism. The convert and overt evidences strayed on the pages of history bear ample testimony to this. A religion which in a few centuries had cast its magic spell over the entire world, was in this sinister design and manner swept out of this subcontinent, if slowly. At least the process of destruction was successfully launched by the Namboodiris.

Ādi Śaṅkara's concept to resuscitate Hinduism was the greatest blow inflicted upon Buddhism in India.

Buddhism and its philosophy had been deeply rooted in Kerala soil. Yet it was in this soil that the Namboodiris succeeded in projecting the cursed caste system under cover of *cāturvarṇya*, or the division of humanity into four castes. Under the shade of that very perverse quadraforcation of mankind they got into their side a very minor though powerful section of society which was included to join them for privileges, and with its complicity, effected a deliberate division of human beings into privileged and unprivileged classes. This was followed by the surfacing of untouchability by which a member of the unprivileged class was regarded as impure and as such, should be treated as an untouchable. If he touches a member of the privileged class the latter is rendered impure.

Making use of untouchability as a means of oppression, the crafty Namboodiris, by the wily exercise of their intellect, successfully kept these ordinary, hard working people at bay. This gave them the opportunity to establish their undisputed supremacy over the Kerala society and thus authenticate permanance of their inveterate status as lords of the land. This paved the way for their dependents, the śūdras also being won over to their fold, so that the Namboodiris' power became absolute. But the śūdras did not realise then that the bargain had resulted in loss for them. It is every one's birth right to learn and put what is learnt to practical use. Denying that right to the śūdras, the Namboodiris proclaimed that if a śūdra were to learn the scriptures (Vedas), his sense of hearing should be sealed off with melted zinc. Was it not a paradox that in spite of this malignant stance of their overlords towards them, the śūdras should have wholeheartedly cooperated with their evil designs against the downtrodden? The struggle between the two sections of society, though spread over many centuries, failed to yield positive results. At last when those discarded as coloured fled to the forests, and by the hard sweat of their brow, cleared them and converted them into fertile agricultural land, the upper caste ones lost no time in declaring them as untouchables and keeping them away from their society.

> Before *cāturvarṇya* was ushered in, the social set up in Kerala was not subject to the caste system. Opportunity for growth and expansion lay open equally for every one. There was no higher or lower caste. It was with the establishment of brāhmin supremacy that,that social organisation was destroyed and the caste raised its head.[5]

As misfortune would have it, superstitions, irrational customs and caste differences had imprinted themselves deeply into the society and are remaining there even today inflicting shock waves to social consciousness.

The prominent history researcher Sri. V.R. Parameswaran Pillai has given an account of the brāhmin supremacy in Kerala and of the Ezhava and other depressed communities whose members here had been Buddhists. In this context it would be relevant to quote him:

> The Namboodiris of Kerala were a powerful lot. Such works as the "Birth of Kerala" were caused to be written up by them only to eulogise their deeds. When they had established *cāturvarṇya* on a firm footing, Kerala was converted into a lunatic asylum. Temples became the instruments of fortification of the caste structure that had been carved out. Though the kṣatriyas are said to have ruled Kerala from the tenth to the sixteenth century AD, the Namboodiris were its *de facto* rulers. Crafty and tactful as they were, they could easily secure the goodwill and obedience of other minor coloured sections and thus make themselves impregnable. And with that the propagators of *cāturvarṇya* could successfully chase Buddhism away from this soil. It is a fact that Kerala which had been free from caste differences was made a playground of caste with no holds barred by the Namboodiris. When in later times the rites like worship in Buddhism were accepted in Hindusim too *in toto*, the two religions became almost indistinguishable. The Namboodiris labelled those who stood by them as *savarṇa*s (fair coloured) and the others as *avarṇa*s (dark coloured). They achieved relationship with the former, closer through matrimonial alliances. The hard working *avarṇa*s kept themselves apart from them. Consequently the Namboodiris declared the *avarṇa*s ineligible for such privileges as temple entry and connected freedoms. The rulers were puppets in their hands dancing to whatever tunes they played. What Buddhism gave to Kerala was universal education. The savants and preceptors who were originally non-brāhmins and who had converted into Buddhists, were profound scholars in Sanskrit and Pāli. There were numerous *avarṇa* followers of Buddhism who had acquired through heredity vast knowledge of Sanskrit, medicine and astrology. That they had earned admirable scholarship in all branches of knowledge was

their success.[6]

There is ample evidence that like elsewhere in India, Buddhism had achieved immense popularity throughout Kerala from the third century BC to the eighth century AD. The *Saṁgham* works have disclosed that those Jaina-Buddha *vihāras* which functioned as joint entities throughout the length and breadth of Kerala during Śaṅkarācārya's time had been transformed into Hindu temples. It is said that the Sri Padmanabhaswami Temple at Thiruvananthapuram and the Sri Krishnaswami Temple at Guruvayoor were Buddhist *vihāras* once.

> A picture of a bronze Buddha received from Ceylon is appended to Monier-Williams' book *Buddhism*. In this picture the Buddha is shown as reclining in meditative pose upon a huge serpent shaded by its enormous hood. The whole figure resembles the idol of Sri Padmanabha reclining on Anantha.[7]

From these instances it can be seen that during the various stages of Hindu resurrection the influence of Buddhism was decisive.

> The old temples and churches that are seen in Kerala today were either Buddha *vihāras* or Buddha *vihāras* converted. Though the Namboodiris had transformed Buddha idols into idols of Śāstha, the fact Buddha idols are found in various parts of Kerala today cannot be refuted.[8]

> The Śāstha Temple prevalent in Kerala today are signals of the popularity Buddhism had enjoyed here. Idols of the Buddha are found in Mavelikkara, Bharanikkavu, Maruthoor-Kkulangara, Krishnapuram, Pallikkal, Ambalappuzha (Karumadi), Paruvassery (Thrissur), Pallippadikkal (Neelamperoor), Kiliroor (Kottayam) and other places. Several Buddha idols of old are worshipped even today as Śāstha idols. As is known the word Śāstha is a synonym of the Buddha. Sri. T.K. Krishna Menon has come to the conclusion that the Kettukazhcha (a rite associated with the Buddha) of the Chettikulangara Temple

> at Mavelikara reminds one of a ceremony connected with Buddhism, viz. *Bouddholsava.*[9]
>
> In ancient Kerala numerous small and large temples were found close to one another in all the villages from Cape Comerin to Gokarnam. Every one of these was a Buddhist *vihāra*. The fact that elephants, horses, chariots and the like were received as festival offerings by these temples, reveals unmistakable evidence of Buddhist influence.[10]

They are referred to in Aśokaśāsanas.

> During the infancy of Buddhism, the Ezhavas and other unprivileged classes of Kerala had faith in and lived as, Buddhists. This process extended to over several centuries and brought about tremendous growth of the religion (Buddhism). Stunned by this development, the Namboodiri brāhmins, at their wits end, joined hands with the privileged class followers of the Hindu revivalist, Śaṅkarācārya, to attack the Buddhists in a bid to achieve the downfall of Buddhism in this soil. The means adopted by them in the name of Hindu regeneration were through such monstrocities as murder, arson, loot and vulgar songs. Even when with such manoeuvres they could not send the backward people packing, they resorted to the heinous tactic of declaring them as untouchables and consequently as outcastes. When that attempt also failed to yield the desired result, they took hold of the śūdras to their camp and banged upon a phrase of their own creation namely *brāhmaṇa śāpa* (the curse of the brāhmin), applying which they appropriated the properties of these helpless people. They suffered these persecutions without resistance and ascribing all sufferings to fate, lived with them through generations without realising that their superstitions were at the root of their misfortunes, yet with self-confidence, that freedom and justice would find a breakthrough in their lives one day.[11]

The Namboodiris who had been in absolute control of the social, cultural and economic spheres of Kerala for centuries before the birth of Sree Narayana Guru, had taken refuge behind the shadow thrown up by the fictitious story of Paraśurāma. With the time of Śaṅkarācārya when the situation was more favourable to the fulfilment of their schemes, they found themselves unquestioned masters of Kerala society. With the aid of other coloured minor classes they were able to keep the kṣatriyas also under their thumbs. As already pointed out, it was as a result of this that the Namboodiris could effectively capitalise on the martial power of the kṣatriyas to subdue the unprotected sections of society.

From the Buddhist perspective, man is basically of the same creed. This approach to humanity struck at the very root of Brāhmaṇical thought, and formed a part of a revolutionary movement set afoot in India during the sixth century AD. But Buddhism could not effectively and convincingly hold under check the rising tide of brāhmin insurgency. The Buddha had only argued against the practice of caste differences. He had not evolved a scheme with the motive of eliminating the caste system. He believed that when *dharma* (righteousness) was established caste would automatically disappear.[12]

The Vaiṣṇava Āḷvārs and Śaiva Nāyanārs whom Śaṅkarācārya had created, were able to easily root out Buddhism which had established itself deeply in Indian soil. With that, Brāhmin domination which had been founded on the bed of *cāturvarṇya* raised its tentacles with a vengeance. Yet, even under their subjection, the chieftains, Kulaśekharas and Perumakanmars had made valiant attempts to achieve self-sufficiency at the time. Even while tension between them was at its deepest, there was no alleviation at all of the great sufferings endured by the backward classes. A history researcher has given the following account of the existing social organisation and its endemic slavery:

> The adversities faced by the poor man in the name of Hinduism defies description. Not only did the Namboodiris brand the people who did not abide by their commands as

> untouchables; but they made bold to keep them at a call's distance from themselves. It is stated that the śūdras were empowered to kill at once any Ezhava or member of the lowly placed communities who had polluted by his physical touch, a Namboodiri, a kṣatriya or a śūdra. If it was a Pulaya who had so polluted a śūdra, he should digress from his path and run away into hiding upon realisation of his crime. If he broke that unwritten law, it was incumbent on the śūdra to cut his throat. But the śūdra had the right to go before a Namboodiri, though not touch him. On the other hand a young śūdra woman was entitled to touch and sleep with a Namboodiri according to the legal code contained in the work called *Manusmṛti*. The lower classes though Hindus, were untouchables. But if they embraced another religion, they ceased to be untouchables and the Namboodiris would have no hesitation to accept them on equal footing and pay respects to them. How such degeneration had crept into the Eternal Religion (*Sanātana* religion) is impossible to explain. . . .[13]

From this it can be seen that the Namboodiris were masquerading as the flag holders of Hindu priesthood, thus directly promoting conversion of Hindus to other religions on a profuse scale.

Sheltering themselves within the framework of the code of laws written up for their own protection, the Namboodiris had dealt utter havoc not only upon the underprivileged, but caused untold damages to some of the privileged classes too.

> If a śūdra happened to hear recitation of the scriptures his ears should be turned deaf with melted zinc. That was the brāhmin oracle.[14]

If Buddhism during its hey-day in India had given due reckoning to human values, during the period of Hindu hegemony such values were trodden under foot. Cultural history has the following account to furnish about this injustice:

> To elevate the brāhmin section of society to the unchallenged

> summit of the Hindu hierarchy, the chief role was played by such works as *Manusmṛti* and Kauṭilya's *Arthaśāstra*. When the code of laws prepared by the brāhmins for the brāhmins themselves was available at their disposal to operate intelligently and effectively, the golden chance to exploit society was offered to them on a platter. But, for the lowly placed Hindus it was not possible even to understand that those codes were meant for the brāhmins only.[15]

This was the outcome of the cultural sphere of Kerala having been tactfully misappropriated by the high and the mighty.

> When the Namboodiri could render the *Mahābhārata*, the main pillar of Indian mythology, in such enthralling manner as to appeal even to the ordinary people, it hit the mark. In the guise of showering encomiums upon the childhood friendship of Kṛṣṇa and Kuchela, the then king was consciously and premeditatedly cementing the already established brāhmin ascendancy. When rulers themselves worshipped the brāhmins, how could the common people avoid following suit? It is subjection to this line of thinking that promoted Ezhuthachan, the author of the celebrated bird songs in the Malayalam language namely *Adhyātma Rāmāyaṇa* and the *Mahābhārata*, to euologise the brāhmins as the Lords of the earth. If the poet Cheruserri prevailed over the common folk who once repeated the Buddhist prayers, to switch over to the word 'Kṛṣṇa', Ezhuthachan, succeeded in laying stress on repeating the word 'Rāma' in prayers. He crowned himself with glory in upholding the paramountcy of his patrons, the brāhmins. His creations were permeated by his adoration of and fear for, his masters. Ezhuthachan had even driven home to the common folk the baseless notion that worshipping brāhmins and giving away cows as alms to them, were sure paths to the acquirement of exceptional creative ability. "The brāhmin, if his child died, did not hesitate to declare that the death was brought about by the penance of the śūdra. Consequently under pretext of the "Ramakrishna culture"

> and in the shadow of the terror so created, the sorrow imposed upon a large section of the population for a considerable period of time, was beyond endurance.[16]

How cursed the period was, was reflected in the poet Kumaran Asan's lament,

> Man is an impure thing even to man
> And walk on earth is regarded as sin
> By atmospheric pollution of man.
> The hell itself is here, alas, O' God.

> There is a temple for Nairs in Vellamanal at Mayyanad. The priest there at that time was a frenetic adherent of untouchability. Normally he looked as if possessed when he came to the temple after the morning bath. One day we were walking along the path towards each other from opposite directions. He shouted at me. "Hoy, get out of my path". I shouted back at him equally possessed. "You hell, I will not". The episode refers to an untouchability problem cited in the autobiography of an illustrious son of Kerala.[17]

According to the *cāturvarṇya* law, the human being classed as *avarṇa* is an untouchable. Separate distances from the *savarṇa*s should be kept by members of each community to preserve untouchability intact. For the Paraya the distance was 64 ft, the Pulaya 54 ft and Ezhava 36 ft. Another perversion was the touching act.

> If a Tamil brāhmin touched a Namboodiri, the latter was made impure. The stringency with which these practices were observed rendered travel for the lower classes miserable with terror. While walking along if they hear the alarm about 'Hoy' from the privileged, these unfortunates had either to turn back and run, or jump off the path into knee deep marsh for the privileged class walker to pass along. If the touching actually happened, the toucher and the touched were equally punishable. It was the blind faith then that the touched would contract incurable diseases.

> Everyone was required to be ruthlessly strict about letting this evil practice survive in an unmitigated state. The privileged had the power to punish the unprivileged, found guilty of violation of the established practice. No evidence or court of justice was to be sought after. When a *savarṇa* was sighted, the *avarṇa* had to reveal his identity by removing the clothing on the upper half of his body, irrespective of whether the *avarṇa* was a man or a woman. The *avarṇa*s were denied the right to use foot-wear, umbrella, good clothes or ornaments. Even in the rain the Namboodiris alone had the right to use umbrellas. If the temple tank or house was polluted by touch, the impurity could be erased out by a special rite called *Puṇyaham*, to be performed by the Namboodiris only. The expenses required should be footed by the guilty person himself. If the latter refused, the offender would be visited with an adverse court order. Mr. M.K. Narayanan, Excise Inspector, on a trip to inspect a tobacco shop as part of his official duty, had perforce to go close by a Koṅkiṇī brāhmin's hotel. His case gained notoriety when the court before which it was filed, fined him three hundred rupees as compensation for having polluted the food kept ready inside the hotel for the upper castes.[18]

Till the commencement of the Malayalam Era the Ezhavas of the *avarṇa* class held the original rights of the lions share of the land. But when the fabricated story that Paraśurāma created Kerala rapidly gained credibility with popular imagination, the Namboodiris were quick to grab all those lands with its support. Thus they became the real landlords of the Brahmaswom, Devaswom, and Sreepadam. That class of land the yield from which went direct to the brāhmins was Brahmaswom, to the Temples, Devaswom, and to the rulers, Sreepadam. By virtue respectively of the trusteeship of temples held by them, the consort-ship of princesses thrust upon them and the special rights conferred on, or acquired by them, the Namboodiris were assured of a steady and fat income from all these classes of lands. At the lowest rung of that unprincipled financial arrangement stood slave like, the underdogs of society such as the Ezhavas and others. These people implicitly believed that they were fated to suffer only poverty and other drawbacks, without even the remotest chance to taste the good things of life.

> Actually a nether world had been created in Kerala by the untouchability practised in the name of caste. The *Savarṇas* never shunned keeping the *avarṇas* apart from them. If a Pulaya happened to touch a śūdra, the śūdra should bathe in seven tanks and shed a few drops of his own blood into water to expurgate himself of the impurity caused.

So says Edgar Thirston in his travel accounts.[19]

While untouchability and the horror of wilfully imposed impurity humiliated and weighed them down in the one side, the exploited suffers were faced with another repressive measure on the other. Over taxation. As if to add insult to injury they were suffocated with heavy taxes imposed on them by the brāhmin priests with the consent and connivance of the ruling chieftains. In the *cāturvarṇya* gradation of humanity those down to the śūdras were exempt from these taxes. What all injustices were not perpetrated by these Namboodiris who once reigned supreme in Kerala, with the aid of their own improvised and reprehensibly cruel laws, framed to suit their expropriative purposes!

> The hard-working farmers belonging to the privilege denied classes were duty bound to cultivate the land and surrender the yield to the Namboodiris who became landlords through muscle power. But they had no right over the land. They were a totally exploited lot without the right to voice their grievances, let alone protest. Even to the extent of ruining the future generations, the Namboodiris and their aides kept education and independent thinking beyond reach of these helpless people.[20]

In Kerala especially Travancore, the rules in vogue permitted honourable life only for the *savarṇas*. Neither the rulers nor their Namboodiri advisers condescended to treat the *avarṇas* as ordinary human beings at the least. Even if permitted to eke out a bare existence, they were burdened with heavy taxes. For how many centuries had this perverse set up pervaded and maligned human life! The *avarṇas* were compelled to pay taxes in the name of caste, profession, human organs, the addresses worn and of innumerable items and swell the chieftains' coffers. To cite some of these: *anikkaram*, *thalavari* (tax for the head), *valakkaram*, *tharikkaram*, *noolkaram*, *thiruva*, *padappanam*, *vivāhakkaram*, *thalakkaram*, *mulakkaram*, *azha*, *Kozha*, *kāzhcha*, *pizha*, *ponnarippu*, *menipponnu*, *chethupattom*, *panthallkaram*, *mechilkaram*, *kottupattukkaram*, *ābharaṇakkaram*, *ankakkaram*, *adimakkaram*, *vannarappattom*, *thallarappattom*, *rupavari*, *rājabhogom* and so on. The punishments prescribed for the *avarṇa* defaulters of these taxes were inhuman to say the least. Is it not said that the law survives on sword point? It should not also be ignored that taxes of these diverse varieties were never in force in any country at any time. In short it was an administration of the *savarṇas* and for the *savarṇas*.

Women who belonged to the Ezhava and other castes of the *avarṇa* section had by law to pay *mulakkaram* (breast tax) on keeping with their pedigree and status. That they had paid such taxes on their bodily organs for tens of years might appear incredible to the up-and-coming generations.

> There is a story that at the locality called Shertallai, a young Ezhava woman to whom a Nair official approached for collecting *mulakkaram* chopped off her breasts and threw them before him and roared, from henceforth atleast save me from *mulakkaram*.[21]

The plot of land where that heroic woman lived is known by the name *Mulachipparambu* (the compound in which the owner of the chopped breasts lived).

> *Achippudava* (the cloth meant exclusively for the *savarṇa* women) was the monopoly of the *savarṇa* woman. The *avarṇa* women were not permitted to wear it. Their clothing

should not come further down the knees. They were also not given the freedom to wear dress to shield their breasts from exposure. The Nadar women of south Travancore had launched an agitation to establish their right to cover their breasts. When the *savarṇa* rulers found that these women were determined to secure their birth right even at the risk of their own lives, they had no alternative but to grant it. Having been exposed to unheard of persecution through taxes, oppression, threats, torture, insecurity to life and property, and all other subjugatory pressures imaginable, it was evident that the *avarṇa*s found themselves thrown between the devil and the deep sea. The fortune to be born into the *savarṇa* community having been denied to them, they would well have preferred to have been not born as human beings at all, so they must have wailed.[22]

Such inhuman laws found their worst and most atrocious expression in Travancore compared with their operation in other States in India. To cite an instance.

In Paravoor, Kollam, while a road was being built, an Ezhava landlord had evaded the responsibility to feed the elephant with coconut leaves. A village officer caught, and chained him, placed a heavy stone on his back and made him stand in the hot sun for two hours.[23]

To gauge the intensity of the injustice the chieftains had perpetrated upon the people who lived by sheer hard work, one need only know how the tax system operated at the time. Brāhmins to śūdras were completely exempted from the taxes. At the same time there was a series of taxes ranging from tax on head to tax on breast for the *avarṇas*.[24] Discussions of the kind appearing in the celebrated work *Jeevitha Samaram* (the battle of life) are worth attention.

Says Rev. Mettiar in his travel notes:

For prosecuting war, a kind of tax counting heads was imposed on the *avarṇa* section and another variety of tax was levied from a certain sect of Christians.[25]

> The taxes imposed in Travancore then were so heavy that the ordinary people found it almost impossible to earn a hand to mouth existence. But those revenues were squandered on the luxuries lavished upon the brāhmins and the annual festivals of temples.[26]

Members of the Ezhava and other communities belonging to the *avarṇa* class who presented *andu kazhcha* or yearly gift to the ruling chieftain were conferred such titles as Thandar, Panicker, Pilla, Kaimal, Kartha, Kurup, depending on the volume of their wealth. Through superior status in caste so also flowed large wealth into the treasury. These amounts were spent on the ostentatious and luxurious lives led by the rulers. For the loud noices like *kurava* and *ārppu* required to be produced in connection with marriages and other ceremonies those concerned should obtain consent by submitting the fee on betel leaves before the ceremony was actually performed. *Avarṇa* males from the age of sixteen to sixty should pay tax on their heads. For women to wear ornaments, for obsequies to be held after death in the family, etc., the *avarṇa*s should remit into the treasury the amounts fixed by the rulers and obtain proper receipts. One hundred and five varieties of the taxes on this type were withdrawn in Travancore in the year 1865. To the reference made of these matters in the *State Manual*, Mr. Nanu Pillai, the contemporary Dewan, had responded as follows:

> By having to withdraw these taxes the government had to lose heavily in revenues every year.[27]

Since royal pleasure alone was the concern of our historians, they pretended not to have noticed the enormous luxury indulged in by the powers that be. How could they, blind as they were, to justice and righteousness?

If the virtue innate in the Hindu religion were to blossom, the laws ordained by the *Manusmṛti* and other texts should be followed in full; that was the belief the Namboodiris had succeeded in infusing among the common people, *Manusmṛti* says for instance.

> A brāhmin who commits murder cannot be hanged. Only

> tonsuring of his head is enough. If very particular, he may be banished from the land. If an *avarṇa* is murderer he should be tortured to death. A red hot long nail should be driven into the mouth of an *avarṇa* who abuses a brāhmin. If any *avarṇa* attempts to preach the scriptural texts in emulation of the brāhmin, his tongue should be plucked out. With whatever organ of his body does a non-brāhmin harm a brāhmin that organ should be cut off. The farmer should surrender without receiving compensation, the rice and other grains he gathers from the land through his labour. The sex-organs of the non-brāhmin who has sex with a brāhmin woman should be cut off. Every beautiful woman of whatever caste, is the property of the brāhmin. A young beauty whoever she may be, refusing to give herself up to the brāhmin can be put to the sword. The rulers can be converted into brāhmins through a ceremony known as *Hiraṇyagarbha*.[28]

Several rulers of Travancore are on record as having undergone *Hiraṇyagarbha* and become brāhmins and thus swelled the wealth of their brāhmin accomplices. However, the money required for the performance of that function was extracted from the toiling *avarṇa* classes.

The long and short of it was that in society, brāhmins alone enjoyed the right to live like human beings.

> *daivādhīnam jagat sarvam,*
> *mantradhīnam tu daivatam*
> *tan mantram brahmadhīnam*
> *brāhmaṇo mama daivatam.*
>
> The whole world is under the power of the Gods,
> The Gods are under the power of *mantras*,
> The *mantras* are under the power of brāhmin,
> The brāhmin is therefore our God.
>
> —Manu, IX.314, 316.

The modes of punishments then prevailing in Travancore were not only very cruel, but like the tax laws in operation, crude and shocking to the human heart. So there was no end to the sufferings of the *avarṇa* castes. The cultural history of Kerala of the time throws ample light on the system of punishments enforced in contemporary society:

> The brāhmin domination was conspicuously evident in the strange crime detection system current in feudal times. The examination of the truth meant for proving innocence of the accused was of four kinds: Trial by water, trial by poison, trial by fire and trial by weighing. Trial by water involved swimming in a crocodile or alligator infested water reservoir. Trial by fire required of the accused to dip his hand in boiling oil. (The hand dipping at *sucīndram* is well known). In trial by poison, the accused was to insert his hand into a pot wherein a poisonous snake was imprisoned. If the accused was a brāhmin these tests were not applicable to him. For brāhmins the test prescribed was trial by weighing. First the accused was weighed in a balance. Then the allegations against him were written down on sheets of paper and the sheets tied together and added to the weights. The accused was again weighed. If his weight remained unchanged, he was declared as not guilty! Logan has indicated in the *Malabar Manual* that the English East India Company had, at the instigation of the Zomorin of Calicut, accepted the system of proving guilt by trial by fire. The procedure was that a coin was dropped into boiling oil and the suspect was to take it out with his bare hand. The hand was then lightly bandaged and sealed. After three days the seal was broken and the bandage undone. If it was found that the hand remained without damage the suspect was innocent. Otherwise cruel punishment would be awarded to him. The atrocities committed on those embroiled among the dark chambers of superstitions without deliverance! Even the mildest crimes were visited by the severest of punishments. The common punishment was hanging in the gallows. Such inflictions as chopping off head or organs, enslavement, giving hundred

> and one strokes after being tied to a tripod, heavy fines and excommunication, were prevalent. The guilty were killed in diverse ways. To kill the guilty inch by inch was a cruel entertainment those days. Other modes of carrying out death penalty were: peel off the skin alive and the body upside down until death; elephant trample, grinding the body in a mill, smashing off the head by firing cannon ball, throwing before a hungry tiger, tying hands and legs, felling head long and then placing a red hot ten kilogram heavy iron piece upon the chest until life expired, boring out the eyes and then stoning to death, cutting off organs such as hands, legs, ears, nose and tongue and then chopping the head off, forcing poison into the mouth, causing poisonous snakes wind round the body and bite, slashing with thick whips, beating recklessly after being tied to a tripod and then applying chilli paste on the wounds so created, and so on without count. The punishments were exclusively meant for the *avarṇas*. Brāhmins alone had the right to excommunicate. Mettian has in his travel notes recorded that for having stolen a coconut from a Nair's tree, a Channan was sent to the gallows. The event took place at Kollam. He has also recorded an incident in which five *avarṇas* were hanged on the allegation of having killed a cow. The priest Visher has in his notes written about some *avarṇas* having been forced to eat salt-concentrated rice for refusal to donate sugar for a public purpose. Among the punishments meted out was an inhuman one known as Citravadham or causing death by a horrendous process by which a red hot long iron bar was forced into the body of the accused through his arms at such length as to thrust his throat and then hang him by his leg, head down from a tree branch. The intention is that he should die only after suffering agonising pain in that position for three days.[29]

These are, to say the least, mentally paralysing.

Historians, social historians especially, should be motivated by a sense of justice towards society, and objectivity in the presentation of their material. If those who wrote the history of ancient Kerala were imbued with at least a semblance of sincerity, they would not have embellished this part of India — a segment of land in which the *avarṇas* were subjected to repression, unknown in any part of the world, for the convenience and luxurious living of the *savarṇas* — with the title *Dharma Rājya* or Land of Righteousness. It is when one probes deeper into these mind battering exemplifications of dastardliness that one encounters the callousness and hypocrisy of our rulers whom we have adored and worshipped as our benevolent kings.

Was actually righteousness reigning here while Mārthaṇḍa Varmā was expanding his kingdom by annihilating and annexing his neighbouring kindgoms and Dharma Rāja was ruling it without much wars? That the welfare and well-being of the *avarṇas* were not their lookout, is a fact of history. On the other hand they were ruling to please and pander the *savarṇas*. Perhaps these two rulers were complying with the dictates of their Dewans in carrying out the administration in conformity with the selfish interests of the ascendent brāhmin power. The action of Mārthaṇḍa Varmā and his dewan Rāmayyan, both renowned as great warriors, in having imposed unbearably heavy taxes upon their *avarṇa* subjects in the name of improving the State's finances, was beyond endurance by the taxpayers and hence indefensible. Like the *jaziyā*, the special tax thrust upon the Hindus by the Mughals, how many unjust impositions were not forced upon the *avarṇas* by Mārthaṇḍa Varmā! It was Mārthaṇḍa Varmā who first introduced taxes like *thalayara*, *thalappanam* and *thalavari* in Travancore.[30] How lightheartedly had Rāmayyan exempted his *savarṇa* brothren from those taxes! Either the historians had not noticed the partial attitude of the rulers towards the *savarṇas*, or they had turned a blind eye to it.

> The story of Mārthaṇḍa Varmā's 'Dedication' of the state to Sree Padmanābha is well known. The huge amounts required for the function were made available through such taxes as *thalavari*. They were spent to meet expenses

> connected with the running of *Ootupuras* or free food centres for the Namboodiris and distributing *sarvaṇi* or gifts to them, besides other purposes. Many do not know that this money was squeezed out of the toiling *avarṇa* class from Ezhavas to Parayas.[31]

Kārtika Thirunal, known by the colourful title of Dharmarāja or the righteous king, in collaboration with his Dewan Keśava Pillai, the 'famed' *Valia Devānjī* or Great Dewan, had burdened the *avarṇas* with numerous unjustifiable taxes. They renamed the tax *thalavari* as *roopavani*. What was the purpose for which the blood of the poor, extracted in the form of coins, was spent? For the luxurious living indulged in by members of royal families who fled from Malabar and took refuge in Travancore on the eve of Ṭīppu's invasion. Instead of spending the amount collected through taxes for the welfare of the people, spending them wastefully and irresponsibly on providing luxuries for the royal personalities of outside states, was the *dharma* or righteousness practised in the then state of Travancore!

Because Balarāma Varmā who succeeded Dharmarāja was weak and incapable, the stage suitable for intriguers, and ear poisoners to gain their selfish ends, was well and truly set. It was then that Velu Thampi whom history has honoured with the title *Deśābhimānī* or Patriot, marched into the capital with a set of followers from Southern Travancore. As the gang approached the gates of the palace, the terrified Balarāma Varmā greeted Velu Thampi with an unconditional surrender. Velu Thampi was appointed as the *dalwa* or Dewan straight away. Even he, donning the title of 'protector of the subjects' from misrule, levered upon the mantle of authority to let loose financial oppression on the already exploited *avarṇas*. It was by placing human beings upon the sword point of the strict letter of the law that Velu Thampi carried out this tyrannical administration; that was his achievement, say some historians. For theft he introduced death penalty besides amputation of the organs. It is not true to say that Thampi had kept the people as a whole under the dark shadow of terror. What is true was that the terror he had unleashed was only among the *avarṇa* groups. In his Kundara Proclamation he had enjoined that "no one should cause any trouble to the brāhmins of Travancore".[32] What was evident behind this exhortation was the brāhmin love of Thampi, himself a *savarṇa*.

As the right to lead and control the mob came into the hands of the Namboodiris, their right to property and administer the temples multiplied their power several fold.Their status as landlords and guardians of the chieftains as their advisors in matters of administration fortified their status as unquestionable masters of the land. Now they were in a position to turn their attention to temple administration without hurdle.

> When the temples gradually emerged as the pivotal centres of social life, there began to thrive under their shade a collection of beautiful and lascivious *devadāsīs* with their dances and songs. This development enhanced the income of the temples considerably. But the temples and their suburbs became the active fields of prostitution. And the temples were converted into centres of activity for pleasure seeking and aesthetically inclined Namboodiris. The temple compounds once held sacred became terrifying land blocks for prostitution, murder and robbery. So along with temple culture, another culture that had evolved was the *devadāsī* System.[33.]

Even though the Namboodiris had converted a section of the *avarṇas* into slaves, slave trade was not in existence then. But with the passage of time slavery became widespread and established itself as a trade. With that heavy taxes and cruel punishments found their way upon the slaves. The flow of money into the public coffers reached the maximum when slavery was carried on at the largest scale.

> . . . For every Namboodiri, kṣatriya ruler and śūdra landlord of Kerala, there was a slave collection for toiling on agriculture. The children of these slaves also continued to be born slaves and lived and grew up as such. Though basically they lived as members of diverse communities,

> functionally they were of a class or group. Their masters could kill, torture or sell them at will as animals. There was no law which forbade it.[34]

So records Canter Visher in his travel accounts.

That slavery as a trade continued uninterrupted in Kerala till the end of the eighteenth century, is borne out by travellers who visited Kerala at the time. The work *Adimarekhakal* or records of slavery, and the book *The Slaves of Kerala* by Dr. Kusuman throw enough light on the issue.

> It is stated that there were one lakh and sixtyfive thousand slaves in Travancore, forty thousand in Cochi and about one lakh and sixtyfive thousand in Malabar. Of the total population of Kerala an estimated one-fifth are slaves.[35]

So says Buccanan. In another account of his it is recorded as follows:

> Of the slaves in Travancore, those who were forced to do government work without remuneration known as *Oozhika Vela* came to fifty thousand. Their work included construction of roads and canals, carrying the copper coins in the treasury, taking out the tobacco bundles in the warehouse and labouring for the construction of Sirkar buildings, etc. All these slaves belonged to the *avarṇa* classes. They had to work mostly in semi-starvation. The Namboodiris had succeeded in infusing in them the belief that they deserved no sympathy at all and that what they suffered during their present lives was the consequence of their misdeeds in their previous lives. The combined price of a slave youth and his woman was rupees fifty. For a child the price was rupees fourteen. The *savarṇa*s could obtain slaves either through purchase or on rent. Two *edangazhi*s (small measures) of rice were given to a slave every week, for food. For old people and children the quota was one *edangazhi* each. An yearly supply of cloth was being given to every young slave at the rate of sixteen and fourteen small measures respectively for male and female. For a

> young male slave the yearly rent was one rupee and for a young female slave half a rupee. The law permitted anyone to buy or sell slaves. For exporting slaves to foreign countries also there was no legal inhibition. The foreigners who came to Kerala for trade used to purchase slaves from here at runaway prices and sell them at exceptionally high prices in Europe and America. Good looking slave girls, well built slave youths, and smart and sturdy slave children meant for export to countries abroad were seen in the Portuguese fort at Cochi, their legs tied to wooden stumps and kept in the burning sun. Christian priests were noticed as purchasing slaves and letting them free after convertion to Christianity.[36]

Even though the Government of India had prohibited slavery by law with effect from 1843, slave trade continued unabated till 1862 when the Indian Penal Code came into force.[37] Those humane souls who came forward against slave trade were the Christian priests. It was they who raised their hands to wipe off the tears of the suffering on considerations of humanity. To have released the slaves from bondage and thrown open free lives before them was their ever laudable deed. A large number of slaves, who had been suffocating in the stench filled atmosphere of the deterioration caused by the untouchability and other inhuman practices which reigned free and supreme in Hinduism, were freed and released into the magnanimity of Christianity. They had been kept at a distance hitherto as untouchables. But the Namboodiris now received them with open hands in their newly acquired status as Christians.[38]

That Hinduism is a debased religion is evidenced by the fact that numerous outrageous customs had crept into its ranks during the several centuries of its existence. Perverse practices such as *bhreṣṭ* or excommunication, *mannappedi* and *pulappedi* or keeping people away from society by attaching their names to evil gods, have contributed immensely to the growth of slavery. On the ground that caste rules have been violated, many *savarṇa*s were pushed into the grade of *avarṇa*s and their numbers swelled.[39]

Under directions from the Namboodiris, the kṣatriya rulers rewarded the Christian and Muslim religious men who came forward for conversion work, by granting them permission to freely buy the Hindu slaves. As a result the number of slaves in Travancore was reduced considerably. The fact that the Christian priests had represented to the authorities for the protection of the just and reasonable rights of ordinary people can never be erased from the walls of history.[40] The chief demands in the petitions presented by the priests Baily, Baker, Malt and Charles Smid, were: end slave trade, ban export of slaves to foreign countries, grant them right to own land and banish by law all remnants of slavery. The petitions of these lovers of humanity served to open the eyes of the authorities to the horrors of slave trade practised for centuries. Slavery ended in Travancore through the efforts of colonel Munroe. Ironically in the land of Śrī Buddha and Śrī Śaṅkara, the help of Christian Missionaries was required for that good work.

As the Namboodiris touched the pinnacle of social status in Kerala, they plunged into unscrupulous pleasure hunt. With that their faiths and conceptions underwent a change for the irrational and unrefined. In keeping with their heritage they stuck themselves assiduously to indolence and luxuriated in pleasures of the senses. In the process they forgot to reckon the rust contracted by their inborn intellectual potential and diligence. Their invaluable time was now being spent on ostentation and perverse indulgence. Similarly they began to pay scant respect to moral values. Their youth was wasted upon sexual excesses and prostitution. Under the shield of *savarṇa* superiority they had succeeded in arrogating to themselves too much power upon the kṣatriya rule. As a result the rulers remained under their thumb without reserve. So that in their brains were evolved more devises to exploit the *avarṇas*. They never hesitated to do whatever was possible within the existing lead framework for the realisation of their selfish ends. Their downfall was precipitated by the loose morality they practised through the avoidance of matrimony from their own caste and preference for brides from other castes with little numerical restriction. Any number of brides from the Nair community could be taken through the simple ceremony known as *muṇḍukoḍa* or cloth giving just for the enjoyment of sex, and without matrimonial obligations resulting therefrom. This excessive indulgence accelerated the process of their fall. The free food and other means of satisfying sensual longings afforded by the authorities served to pour oil into the fire of physical passion burning in them.

Another naked truth must be remembered here. Only the men were afforded the facilities to submerge in these pleasures and sexual abnormalities. The lot of the Namboodiri women was worse than the slaves of the *avarṇa* class. Under the impact of the repression, they were suffering mental and physical disintegration by the hour. In that orthodoxy-ridden community which looked askance at modern education and cultural regeneration, the sufferings to which the women folk were thrown, beggar description. They had to lead a life akin to a mixture of slavery and imprisonment inside the dark interiors of their *illams* or residences, as if in mute submission to a kind of social ostracism. Despair piled up in their lives which held little scope for hope. For a young Namboodiri woman even to see a young man of her own community was forbidden. So utter misery filled the atmosphere of the *illams*. A female child was born as the very object of hatred. Harsh and stringent restrictions simply paralysed their mental stance. A reason for that was the unprincipled living of their men folk. The eldest male member of the family alone married from the community. The others would have relations with Nair families. As a result there would be Namboodiri women remaining as spinsters. At the same time a practice of sending a Namboodiri girl along with an old Namboodiri before she attained puberty, also began to increase in the *illams*. If, before she reached womanhood, her husband died, she would be doomed to permanent widowhood, her head tonsured to mark her as a widow. Due to the strong sexual urges characteristic of youth the possibility of many of them drifting wayward could not be ruled out. If it was discovered that a Namboodiri woman had illicit connection with a man, the ever alert watchdogs of the community's orthodoxy would spot her as a criminal and send her out of the *illam* publicly and shut its doors on her as an outcast under a show trial known as *Smartha Vicāram*.[41] After that her only refuge was suicide apart from joining the *avarṇas*. She might continue among them as the wife of a healthy young man too. By and large the fate of a Namboodiri woman was to remain a spinster, or a co-wife, and often as a widow. Nothing more than these. The result was that the Namboodiri community faced depletion in its numbers over the centuries. It was reduced to a minority. What the orthodox Namboodiri succeeded in accomplishing was to drag the emerging generations from the plenty of landlordism to the frying pan of starvation.

In modern times the regeneration work of the community was intiated by progressive-minded stalwarts like V.T. Bhattathiripad, Kuroor Namboodiripad, Bhavathrathan Namboodiri, E.M.S., M.R.B. and C.K. Namboodiri. The marriages of maidens adorned with gold ornaments to grooms of the community began in right earnest. Remarriage of widows, monogamy, marriage from the community, and *makkathāyam* of succession of son to father, were enforced. With these changes the women hitherto thrown into the dark corners of the *illam*, uncared for and neglected, were transformed into human beings. The practice of hiding their figures either with umbrella or by using veils was given up. Following the message of Sree Narayana Guru, to organise and get strengthened, the Yogakshema Sabha or welfare society was born under the leadership of V.T. Bhattathiripad. Through his works *Marakkullile Mahanarakam* (the hell behind the screen), *Ruthumathy* (The mature woman), and *Adukkalayil Ninnu Arangathekku* (from the kitchen to the stage), the efforts of V.T. to transform the Namboodiri women into humans were epoch-making. In addition, regeneration of the community was contiuned through magazines such as Sudarsanam and Unni Namboodiri. The part played by the Yogakshema Sabha and English education in later times to lead the Namboodiri community along lines of change motivated reconstruction, was not at all negligible. It was the progressive thinking of modern times that provided the incentive for the renaissance of the Namboodiri community.[42]

Before the birth of Sree Narayana Guru and Sree Chattambi

Swamikal the Nair community of Kerala was passing through a pathetic phase. Embroiled in social malcustoms the community ceased to have an organised existence, and was struggling in the grip of superstitions which held aloft pernicious practices as ideal. With unnecessary and expensive ceremonies such as *muṇḍukoḍa* (distribution of cloth on a vast scale during marriages), *thiraṇḍu kalyāṇam* (elaborate celebration of occasions when girls attained puberty) and *pula kuli* (lavish feastings after deaths), the community was pushed to the verge of economic ruin. Although lived by the velvet carpet of *cāturvarṇya* extended by the Namboodiris to include them and prided in the *savarṇa* status thus gained, the Nairs had to contend themselves as the servants of the Namboodiris who were actually in command of the affairs of society. Having been compelled to function as their *kāryasthāns* or the managers of their affairs, they were obliged to play second fiddle to the fulfilment of the out of the way desires of their masters.

> Despite being deputed to share the beds of Namboodiris and kṣatriyas, the Nair women had no right to the property of these men who virtually held the position of their husbands in all respects.[43]

So if they had not been provided with any property by other means, they were thrown inescapably to a life of poverty and starvation. It is relevant in this context to quote what K. Bhaskara Pillai has to say about such miserable plight of these women.

> The Nairs who had taken the lands of the Namboodiris for cultivation had no permanent right over those lands. But the Namboodiris had the right to have sexual relationship with young virgins of their families through a sort of marriage. The Nairs considered such marriage as an honour. That period of history during which the Nairs considered the Namboodiri's relation with their daughters or nieces as a status symbol, was indeed a shameful one. The truth was that the children born from those marriages had no right at all to their fathers' wealth. A Nair had no right even to touch a Namboodiri. He could only stand at a distance from

> him in humble submission, and talk. Ironically the Nair women could touch their Namboodiri husbands without any right to inherit their wealth. A redressal of the situation was brought about through the concerted efforts of Changanassery Parameswaran Pillai, T.K. Velu Pillai and Mannath Padmanabhan.[44]

About the fact that for subsistence the Nairs received abundant support from their brāhmin landlords, there can be no two opinions. The Namboodiris were easily irritable and equally easily pleaseable. Because of these susceptibilities they often behaved stupidly. Their Nair minions no doubt found in these frailties of theirs an easy axe to grind. But western education, progressive thought and the renascent contemporary culture built up the rungs of communal upliftment. The resistance from the conservative wing of the community to the tide of progressive thinking on the part of the rising young generation could not last long. The reformatory movement thus ushered in weaned away the people from vanity, conservatism, superstitions and crude social customs to which they had been indoctrinated, to the enlightening aura of a new life. It was the flair for action exhibited by the Nair youths in downright defiance of the deep-rooted and ruinous customs that so strengthened the community with vigour and hope.

When the Namboodiri and other communities took the cue from the message of Sree Narayana Guru to organise and strengthen, the Nairs also conceived of an organisation for themselves. Under the leadership of Mannath Padmanabhan, men like C.K.P. Nair, Changanassery Parameswaran Pillai, K. Kelappan, and C.V. Raman Pillai entered the communal arena. Not long afterwards the Nair Service Society was founded at a meeting held in Mannath House with K. Kelappan as President and Mannath Padmanabhan as Secretary. It started community reform work straightaway. A rare combination of enthralling oratory, untiring energy for action and insatiable thirst for reform, Mannam epitomised unmatched zeal for selfless and dedicated service in the cause of the community. The first field in which his attention was concentrated was the reformation of the community. It had reached rock bottom level of survival because of the expensive *thālikettu kalyāṇam* (a sort of infant marriage), *thiranḍu kuli* (function connected with the puberty of girl), *puḍavakoḍa* (lavish distribution of clothes) and marriage of Nair girls to Namboodiris. When these undesirable practices were eliminated, a new social framework naturally took shape. Mannam's services helped decisively to tone down the power of communal differences and narrow the gulf that had existed between the high and the low. With the abolition of the marriage of Nair women with men of other communities, the Namboodiri *sambandham* (marriage of Nair girls to Namboodiris), disappeared. Because of that the rising generation had the opportunity to breathe the air of freedom. That accelerated the process of reclamation of the Nair community.

Though men and women have equal rights, it is the woman who holds the reins in the Nair family. In those days her married brothers had no place in the family. Their place was in their wives' houses. From this it is clear that the senior female member was the pivot of the family. The Nairs had been following this practice for a long time. As the outcome of the Malayali memorial presented for grant of adequate representation in Government Service, the men and women of the Nair community got the opportunity to lead orderly family life. Because of the many faceted reforming operations of the Nair Service Society, the community had achieved tremendous progress in the social, economic and educational zones.

> The Nair Regulation paved the way for the resurrection of the Nairs. Marumakkathāyam gave way to *makkathāyam*, i.e., descent came to be traced through the sons and daughters instead of through nephews and nieces as of old. Restrictions were imposed on marriages. Rights of Nair women over the wealth of their extra communal husbands were established.[45]

That the reasons for these welcome changes lay in the efforts of Mannath Padmanabhan and the Nair Service Society cannot be refuted.

Sree Kunjan Pillai Chattambi Swamikal was one of the

> greatest spiritual souls Kerala has seen. The Swami's goal was to eradicate the caste based deformities and build up in Kerala, a society based on the ideal of equality. The Swami declares in his work *Vedadhikara Niroopanam*, that Vedic education is not forbidden to the śūdra. Similarly in His book *Prācīna Kerala* (Ancient Kerala), it is established that the right to the ownership of Malayala land belongs to the Nairs.[46]

It has been recognised by anthropologists and historians alike that the Uzhavas mentioned in the *Saṁgha* literature were cultivators of land and that it was as their successors that the Ezhavas had appeared in Kerala.

> In the beginning the Ezhavas were a set of physically robust cultivators. They are referred to as Uzhavas in the *Saṁgha* works, says Logan[47].

Edgar Thirston has recorded that

> the chief occupation of the Ezhavas was agriculture and that there were rich land owners among them.[48]

> When the Uzhavas named as cultivators of Kerala of the *Saṁgham* age and prior to it, became Ezhavas through the path cleared for agricultural expansion under Buddhist leadership, there arose landlords among them. This can be seen in Kerala History.[49]

With the advent of Brāhmaṇism, *cāturvarṇya* made its appearance in Kerala. The caste name Ezhava is seen first used in the *Tharisappally Śāsana* of the ninth century and that of 'Nair' in the *Thrikkodithānam Śāsana*," says A. Ayyappan.[50] From this it is clear that the caste system had not taken shape in Kerala till the ninth century.[51] The above observation of Prof. Elankulam is relevant in this context.

> During the revival process of Hinduism a section of the Buddhists became śūdras under pressure from the

> Namboodiris. Another section which continued as Buddhists were treated as barbarians. It was the latter who came to be known by the name Ezhavas. During the period when Buddhism flourished in Kerala by the attraction of its insistence on righteousness, the Ezhavas thrived with enough right and authority over the agricultural land and with as high a social status as not to be counted below anyone. But as Hinduism gained power, they began to be trodden down socially and economically. As they were constrained under pressure to surrender their landed properties to the brāhmins, kings and temples, their decline also commenced.[52]

The Ezhava-Thiya section of the people which held high rating in society and which along with the others constituted the majority in the populace, had slipped into the depths of decline in status by the ninth century AD.

Another matter worth reckoning here is:

> The Ezhavas were unmatched in the art of weaving with thread made out of cotton, nice as well as wrought clothes. That the cloths woven by them should be sold to the *savarṇas* at cheap prices was the unwritten law. Violation of this law involved such brutal punishments as those ranging from cutting off the fingres to possible death. And they had no right too to wear cloths woven by themselves. As the community lived through centuries, bearing and enduring everything, the young members of the emerging generations began a crusade against these oppressions. Not only to men, but to women also the right to wear clothes down to the knees, had been denied. And for women even to cover their breasts with a small towel was unlawful.[53]

When the authorities turned a deaf ear against the legitimate rights of the Ezhavas and others of the *avarṇa* group, the voices of discontent began to echo from their ranks. When agitation broke loose from the Nadars of South Travancore against the breast exposure law imposed on their women, the eyes of the *savarṇa* administration were opened. Yet as a last stroke came the proclamation. "It is unlawful for the others to imitate those women who have the right to cover their breasts. The agitators will be suppressed."[54] But before the invincible surge of that agitation the authorities succumbed. It was when they had no alternative but to concede all rights to dress respectably that the royal proclamation appeared. That was a new start: the first success of the *avarṇa*s struggle for their rights.

There were two *rānī*s (woman rulers) in Travancore whose reigns gave a semblance of hope and expectation for the ordinary people. They were Rānī Lakṣmī Bāī and Rānī Pārvatī Bāī. It was during their period that on the recommendation of their Dewan, Colonel Munroe that slave trade was abolished and a start was made in English education in Travancore. This was as a result of the establishment of British rule in India.

Not even when the great music maestro Swathi Thirunal was ruling Travancore which gloried under the ornate name *dharma rājya*, had the *avarṇa* sections received any kind of justice. They had to continue with their allotted quota of suppression. But the *savarṇa*s too had suffered a setback in their illusion of superiority because of their slavish mentality although their luxurious pleasure filled life continued unabashed. But having given himself up unreservedly to music and courtesans, the ruler could neither see the increasing misrule of the *savarṇa* officials nor apply restraint on it. He was interested only in entertaining and honouring musicians. The administration was drifting along the same old beaten track uninterrupted. What came out of the set up was to burgeon the haves by intensified expropriation of the have-nots. In short it was a situation in which social life was reduced to a shambles.

As time passed on, the struggle for the acquisition of rights gained momentum.

> Mass agitations broke out under the leadership of Arattupuzha Velayudha Panicker in mid Travancore and Pandalam over the prohibition of *avarṇa* women wearing

> upper clothes and nose rings. It was Velayudha Panicker's towering personality and his influence over his followers which ignited the struggles and evoked favourable response from the authorities. It is unforgettable that he supplied upper wear for a thousand women at Kayamkulam and nose rings for another thousand women at Pandalam at his own expense.[55]

And on the heels of these happenings came the royal proclamation granting freedom to *avarṇa* women to wear *rowka*s or upper clothes and nose rings like *savarṇa* women.

For the *avarṇa* classes there were also embargos in the educational and cultural fields during those days. In course of time slight changes were noticeable in the system of education. But more time was required for such changes to materialise in the cultural atmosphere. The Ezhavas and other *avarṇa*s were denied the right to wear the *kathakali* attire or to take roles in its performance. A group of *savarṇa*s petitioned to the Dewan to forbid Arattupuzha Velayudha Panicker from conducting *kathakali* under his auspices. Nairs were the petitioners.

> We are śūdras. Caste Hindus. The Ezhavas are untouchables. They are permitted to stay only sixteen feet away from us and thirtytwo feet away from brāhmins. Violation of this restriction in distance to be kept between the communities is punishable. Śūdra has the right to sword down the *avarṇa* who touches a brāhmin.[56]

Velayudha Panicker explained his stand in a more refined manner.

> I am an Ezhava. What the śūdras say about *kathakali* namely that it is a reenactment of the stories in the *Rāmāyaṇa*, *Mahābhārata* and other Purāṇic works for entertainment only, is true to fact. The performers appear on the scene duly attired as the respective characters. It is requested that the Sirkar may not ban this entertainment. We are also Hindus. What is presented in the Purāṇas in the form of episodes is what ought to be observed in every-

> day life. What the petitioners say is that we should not enlighten ourselves by pursuing those ideals.[57]

After examining the claims of both sides the Dewan gave his verdict in favour of Panicker.

Behind the inspiration of Sree Narayana Guru to install idols in temples, the decisive influence of temple construction work associated with Velayudha Panicker cannot be ruled out. It is however a fact that in the temples built by him, the Namboodiris performed the *pūjā* (worship).

> In northern Kerala there were Nair and Thiya families with identical names. Rights associated with births or deaths were mutually performed by the Nairs and Thiyas. Such families are known to me as well. The practice of wearing chits (a kind of ornament) before marriage was prevalent among Namboodiris and Thiyas. But chit was not available for Nairs. Probably it was because of the informal nature of the relationship contemplated (*sambandham*), that the symbol of a regular marriage was dispensed with. The Thiyas and Nairs worship the same gods. Their mode of worship is also identical.[58]

In the opinion of Moorkoth Kunjappa the Ezhavas and Nairs, two most powerful communities of Kerala as they are, are connected with each other like the two sides of a coin.

Mannath Padmanabhan's autobiography makes it clear how the śūdra community liberated itself from the crushing hold of the Namboodiris and secured the capacity to stand on its own legs . . .

> the religious practices of the Nairs, the lamp carrying by the Nair women, management of festivals in every locality by the Nairs, setting fire to fireworks and giving feasts to brāhmins by them and other functions which devolved on them, became regular features in the society. But even in their own temples the Nairs could only remain as slaves. They were forced to leave the temples to the authority of the brāhmin minority and remain as just watchmen there,

> shouldering the responsibility of keeping the *avarṇas* as slaves into the bargain. With that the way was clear for Hinduism to remain immersed in ignorance and darkness. In turn they earned the name that the brain behind these developments was that of the Nair community and also thereby, the wrath of the *avarṇas*.[59]

Hinduism carrying the acclaim of *sanātana* or eternal religion was in reality a disaster for the ordinary people of Kerala. When the Christian and Muslim religious men arrived in Kerala for the propagation of their respective religions, the Namboodiris who were the Hindu priests and their coteries, the kṣatriya rulers expressed readiness to extend all help and support to them. What was achieved through those religious conversions was the liberation of a section of the untouchables and the deprived, dumped into the prison of suffocating social embargos, who constituted the majority of the population. But those *avarṇas* who were not prepared to abandon the religion they believed in, despite having to suffer untold hardships, and who had decided to continue as Hindus braving all the sorrows, oppressions and encroachments on their rights perpetrated on them by society, are to be looked upon as great sacrificers.

> The downtrodden section was not aware of the deterioration and fall which had crept into Hinduism what with its internecine strifes and countless groups and sub-groups and the about to be broken threads of customs which bound them haphazardly together. If so inhuman and horrendous was the set up which subsisted in Hinduism once upon a time, why should the dispossessed sections continue in it in awful environments instead of shedding off all spiritual attachment to that religion? 'That is the unresolvable puzzle.' It is another matter that a section of those capable of reasoning, broke away from the octopus grip of Hinduism and took refuge in the light of freedom held out by other religions. Yet is it not surprising that some poor people did not dare to take such steps, thinking that religious conversion was sinful and decided to continue to shoulder

> that evil fate? Be that as it may. How did the *avarṇa*s who till the eighth century had been holding the landlordship titles earned by them, for centuries and enjoying all privileges and power connected therewith, become the slaves of the Namboodiris? If it were not for sustaining their status as administrators why did the kṣatriyas court subservience to Brāhmaṇism? Why did the śūdras crave for the mercy of the Namboodiris who had meted out to them nothing but inhuman treatment? Were not *Manusmṛti* and *Arthaśāstra* the Vedic works written to defend and uphold the status of the Namboodiris? Could they at any time pay homage to justice or human values? Only if those outmoded value cults of the antiquity preserved through dried palm leaves are cremated in the blazing embers of modern-culture, can humanity be offered a social build up rooted in justice, resplendent with worthy ideals and holding human considerations aloft.[60]

Even for brāhmin priests who have taught generations that Hinduism is the eternal religion, it is impossible to shut their eyes against the naked truth that it has been afflicted with deterioration for centuries.

It was a good augury that the far-sighted Munore had considered that set-up as healthy which eradicated all social filth and superstitions and inflated human life with the cool breeze of self-confidence. He did not hesitate to impart education to the *avarṇa* children who had been denied admission to schools on the basis of caste. But when he found that opportunity for these children to enter schools would be lost due to opposition from the upper castes, he gave permission to the Christian Missionaries to run schools. With that all children irrespective of caste or creed, got admission into these schools. Yet the governing reality of the situation was that this *Dharma-Rājya* could not contain the ideal held high by the Missionaries. If it was not so, the kṣatriya rulers would not have reacted negatively to the demand for legitimate rights of the *avarṇa* sections of their subjects. In any case the educational activities of the Christian Missionaries proved to be a blessing for this native

State.

> The educational enterprise of the Christian missionaries was an accidental occurrence in Kerala. The Church Mission Society concerned itself with the spread of English Education and established a college at Kottayam in 1813. Baily, the author of the first Malayalam Dictionary was an illustrious soul who worked in that society. When the salvation army also started establishing English Schools, the Sirkar too entered the field. But only the *savarṇa* children were granted admission into the schools established by the ruling authorities initially. Government schools were established at Tiruvananthapuram in 1834 and Cochin in 1837. A college each was established at Ernakulam and Tiruvananthapuram in 1865 and 1866 respectively. The Basal Missionaries started English Schools in Malabar Area also. Doctor Gundert was a member of that Mission.[61]

From this it is clear for whose sake did the then Government introduce English Education.

It was as a result of the struggle the unprivileged classes had launched against the then authorities and carried it relentlessly for half a century, that their children began to get admission to government schools. An examination of the history of schools in Kerala from the beginning of the nineteenth century would reveal the frightening dimensions of the cleavage in the respective standing of the high and the low in society, and of the thrust of untouchability between them. The stories of the struggle of the unprivileged to extricate themselves from the irredeemable tangles created for them by superstitions and to set the stage for the victorious march of the future generations, by awakening the social conscience, fill the pages of history. Yet that there broke out in certain localities of Travancore, Nair-Ezhava as well as Nair-Nadar conflicts, is not ignored in this context. The fact that because of Ṭīpu's Malabar Proclamations there were momentous changes in the school customs of Kerala, deserves mention.Though he was tagged with the title 'Mysore Tiger', in reality Ṭīpu was an admirable ruler who stood for social changes with due respect for human values. Only he was a much misunderstood statesman.[62]

The commencement of the nineteenth century was marked by the inauguration of the decisive epoch in India, in Kerala especially. The new tides of thought generated on the social surface by Raja Rammohan Roy in Bengal through the Brahma Samāj and by Svāmī Dayānanda Sarasvatī in the Punjab through the Ārya Samāj, Ramaswamy Naikar in Tamil Nadu and Mahatma Jyotiba Phule in Maharashtra were transmitting fresh impetus to anti-brāhmin cults. The British administration of these days injected revolutionary outlook in human thought and ideals, social life and religious faiths. The waves created by these movements passed into Kerala too. With these the deep-rooted superstitions and inhuman customs began to shake. The English education which brought a sea change throughout India expanded the horizons of scientific knowledge and social ideas. Their influence brought about vast changes in the Ezhava-Thiya sections of the population. It was those changes which caused the decline of the power of the Namboodiris with their unlimited sway over the Hindu rulers.

The śūdra and Ezhava sections of Kerala held identical ideals and maintained identical ways of life. But the Namboodiris by including the śūdras among the *savarṇa*s and the Ezhavas among the *avarṇa*s, split them apart and created animosity between them. The Namboodiris used the śūdras for their selfish ends. The Ezhavas along with the other *avarṇa*s questioned the Namboodiri supremacy. They were thus declared as untouchables, and were in the peculiar situation obtaining then, deprived of even the facilities for education. It was probably because they could not acquire proficiency in literature and other arts. As a result of the brāhmin supremacy that remained unchallenged in Kerala till the final phase of the nineteenth century, the economic and social grievances and injustice created by the caste difference began to surface themselves. The thinking among the mentally and physically wounded Ezhavas could not put up with the inhumanities of the *savarṇa*s. It was at that accursed time that the birth of Sree Narayana Guru took place.

During that period when the society in Kerala touched the lowest ebb of deplorability, the withered debris of an obsolescent social structure hovered ominously over the Ezhava community, already in agony under the gruelling weight of superstitions and crude customs tangled in conservative ideology. Many among its members could see that all their social and economic disabilities were the outcome of the caste system. Such practices as internal compartmentalisation between the high and the low, primitive modes of worship, *muṇḍukoḍa* (marriage by giving clothes), *thālikettu* (tying the *tālī*, a small ornament symbolising marriage, round the bride's neck), *pulakuli* (ceremony after death) and the like which existed in the community pushed it to the depths of decline. To have turned the Ezhava community from the misery-filled existence in slavery, to the path of renaissance and, converted it into a self-respecting sect was no mean achievement. Nor was it a small success that Sree Narayana Guru had scored the liberation of the community from the ignoble customs by exhorting its members to gain strength through organisation. The creator of the modern age that he was, that great soul was, by founding SNDP Yogam, moulding out an ideal community. That was the incomparable success of the Ezhava proletariat.

What made Guru address Himself to the problem was the aloofness from every field of social activity, forced upon the community. The crusade for freedom of worship which was inaugurated by the installation of the idol of Lord Śiva at Aruvippuram and ended by the mirror installation at Kalavangodam, created the impression of a revolutionary explosion in human thinking. Another revolution in social life was achieved through the founding of schools for getting the right to education established. When this social revolutionary threw into oblivion the reprehensible customs which had gripped society in the name of superstitions, a new healthy mood of compromise rooted in friendliness took shape. Today the enlightenment seen not only in the Ezhava community, but in all the other communities — those stamped as low castes like Nadar, Kammalar, Arayar, Parayar, Kuravar, Vedar, Kannikkar, Pulluvar and a host of others — is the result of the successful efforts at social reform which Sree Narayana Guru had pressed into service. In short, Sree Narayana Guru who created for the suffering millions an atmosphere in which they could consider themselves as equals of the others who had hitherto been placed in a higher rung in society, and life with their heads held high, has even come to be regarded as an incarnation of God.

The contribution of Sree Narayana Guru to the regeneration of the depressed classes of Kerala is inestimable. At the time of His birth they had been victims of degradation and slavery, sacrificing their lives for the convenience of the social elites. They not only believed, but were also persuaded to believe that they were destined to work as slaves and hence were born for that purpose only. It was when the torture and exploitation by the high-ups which they had been enduring for centuries, had touched melting point that they saw the occasion to set themselves thinking about their plight in light of the message of Sree Narayana Guru, fated as they had been from birth to death, to be the servants of the masters, to be concerned only with their pleasure and convenience. The masters had arrogated to themselves, the right to kill or sell these unfortunates whose sufferings at their hands defy description. The *savarṇas* had believed that these people did not deserve even an iota of mercy. Other than being the constant companions of misery through the incessant shedding of tears, they could never for once show up a shining face. Through bitter experience they learned that life was meant exclusively to suffer pain. When the stage came that anyone at the higher rungs of the social order could do anything to them with impunity and when they had perforce to tolerate, like Mother Earth, the brutality inflicted on them, Sree Narayana Guru with his cosmopolitan theory appeared before them like God sent.

When the lower classes like the Ezhavas and others received from Guru the much needed light and leadership, the stage was set for a widespread social revolution. Without complaint or grudge, or without the ability to give expression to them in case they surged within, and accepting that inability as the penalty to be paid for having been born and pulling on the days resigning themselves to the situation, they were blessed with the spiritual inspiration from the messages of Guru to awaken from the stupor of inaction. Ayyankali accepted the spirit of Guru's message to get strengthened through organisation and formed the Sadhu Jana Paripalana Sangam (organisation for supporting the poor), and devoted his life to the cause of the oppressed classes. These people by their concerted effort could win their rights one by one. When they began to live and act in conformity with Ayyankali's advice, a consciousness of freedom and spiritual enlightenment dawned upon them; the incentive provided by Dr. Ambedkar whose activities stormed across the length and breadth of India, added courage to their convictions. In short the social changes enunciated by Ayyankali, K.P. Karuppan, K.P. Veloon and K. Ayyappan through such innovative measures as intercaste marriages, joint eating, etc., accentuated the attainment of success and freedom of the lowly.

Although there were, and are several religions in India, the *avarṇa* sections of Hinduism which claims to be the eternal religion, were denied even animal status. The undaunted and relentless struggle launched by Guru sounded the death-knell of that centuries old age of atrocities and heralded the welcome birth of a new age of equality and freedom. We shall now settle down to examine how Sree Narayana Guru was enabled to amend the title of 'Madhouse' Svāmī Vivekānanda had conferred upon Kerala.

## I

### SREE NARAYANA GURU — THE EPOCH-MAKER OF KERALA

The one event which had sent shock waves among the entire lot of conservatives in Kerala was the installation of Lord Śiva's idol at Aruvippuram by Sree Narayana Guru more than a century ago. That spiritual insight which sensed the presence of the supreme inside and outside, the beginningless and endless was blowing the trumpet for a total transformation. His messages impregnated with the instinct of human love and equality, took His metaphysical articulations to the deepest recesses of the human heart. As a result the utterances of Sree Narayana Guru have transcended all narrow boundaries and lie stamped upon the wide passages of universality.

What distinguishes Guru's contribution to human thought is that His rich philosophy and ideology based-messages cut out for social reorientation have settled down as integral parts of the ordinary people's lives.

Whenever *dharma* (righteousness) declines and *adharma* (evil) gains ascendency over it, the Lord will incarnate to redeem *dharma*, says the *Gītā*. As if to realise the truth of this pronouncement, it may be that, like the morning star of a long and dark age, beacons of light are born in this world. It is well-known that Guru was born at the time when India was engaged in a life and death struggle for the establishment of the spiritual and material freedoms of humanity, when the country was passing through the most fearfully dark period of its history. It was an evil period of crisis when Indian culture and social progress had touched a dead end through centuries of suppression, and threw human values into the unfathomable depths of deterioration. The period was certainly one full of misery for the labouring thousands of Kerala crushed as they were, under the extortionate treatment of them by the Namboodiris, who had cunningly appropriated their land and posed as their masters using the power so acquired. Because of the ruthless operation of the caste, the life of the so-called *avarṇas* had already been torn to shreds. Respectable life became a wild dream for them. When oppression rose to unendurable proportions one could see that true to the prophecy in the *Gītā*, *dharma* had declined and *adharma* held the field, and that it was time for the emergence of a great soul entrusted with the mission to save the situation. It was as if that the Supreme had intervened for the purpose and caused the birth of Sree Narayana Guru. It was the disclosure of historical truth, the silent inauguration of the birth of a new era.

The time was the festive occasion of *Oṇam* which the Keralites have been celebrating through the ages. A soul stirring evening in the golden Malayalam month of *Chingom*. As intoxicating atmosphere languishing the lap of indolence inspired by the sweet cool moon. The captivating glow of enchantment not yet dimmed out of the alluring lips of the evening nymph, appeared to be enthralling everyone. On the whole an aesthetic simplicity solidified environment. The time when that village stood mystified by the sweet songs emanating from the soft throats of young girls enjoying the swing, and the shouts of joy bursting forth from the young men inebriated by the festiveness of the occasion and spurred by inexhaustible enthusiasm and vigour of youth. It was the 28th of August 1856. The star *Chathayam*. What was heralded that day was one of those rare happenings in several millennia. With the birth of Sree Narayana Guru, the creator of an epoch-making age in the life of humanity, the village of Chempazhanthi near Thiruvananthapuram, blessed by the momentous event, was to be converted as the focus of attention of the external world in later years. In the ordinary course, apart from being treated as the birth of a male child, could anybody have looked upon that event as the precursor of a complete revolution in the social life of Kerala?

The centuries-old Manakkal temple and the Vayalwaram house there, had been the symbols of Nair-Ezhava cordiality. The descendants of Chempazhanthi Pillai of the historical Ettuveetil Pillai gang (a gang of eight from eight prominent Nair families which the ruler of Travancore, Mārtaṇḍa Varmā had to encounter and subjugate before his accession), and the heads of the famous Vayalwaram family had equal powers over administration of the Manakkal temple. Even the reinstallation of the idol of that temple was done by the great grandfather of Sree Narayana Guru, Kochasan who was a great scholar and a *brahmacārī* (one who abjures wordly life and lives a life of spiritual celibacy). Because he was an adept in scribing on palm leaves, he was known more as Achuthan Kochasan.

Kochuvilayil Madanasan was a brilliant young man and a scholar. He married the quiet and pious natured Kuṭṭiyammā during his tenure as a teacher in the locally run ancient type school known as Kudippalikkoodam (school for children of local families). She was the lone sister of the reputed physician Krishnan Vaidyar. Of the three offsprings of that union, the youngest was Narayanan. Though given the name Narayanan the child was known by the pet name Nanoo. It is said that the child did not cry at the time of birth as children ordinarily do. It is not to be wondered at if its near and dear ones got anxious over that extraordinary event.

Because he was noticed as deeply devoted to God, the boy was addressed as 'Swamy' (pious person) by all who knew him. While the caste distinctions were operating ruthlessly at the time, he used to play with the children belonging to the *avarṇa* communities and made himself impure by touching them.

Nanoo had to take a bath every time he touched an *avarṇa* to absolve himself of the impurity so caused in pursuance of an unwritten rule in vogue then.

Because of the love and sympathy Nanoo had extended to all other children with little concern for their caste, the household got slightly alarmed too. On the other hand it was wonder rather than anxiety that made the relatives uneasy on seeing the unusual behaviour and conversation of the boy. Devoted to God as he was, Nanoo while worshipping in the Manakkal temple, used to enter inside its sanctum-sanctorum and take out and eat the sweets which formed the offerings to the diety. If he was questioned about it he had the proper answer in readiness, "If I derive happiness it will be Devī's pleasure too."

Nanoo was initiated into the alphabet by the Karanavar or head of the Kannankara family of Chempazhanthi to which belonged Chempazanthi Pillai afore mentioned. Besides being the local village officer, he was a good astrologer as well. He along with vernacular alphabet, learned the children's lessons conforming to Sanskrit literature like *Siddharūpam, Bālaprabodhanam* and *Amarakośam*. After that Nanoo discontinued his studies for some-time. During that time he had lent a helping hand to his father in farming and also tended cattle in the nearby woods. He took regularly to prayer (both loud and silent), meditation, and fasting and other religious observances. He also assisted his father in the planting and nursing of betel vines. These activities he himself had recalled in later life. Kumaran Asan's accounts have thrown further light on Guru's early life.

The education in the Kudippallikoodam lasted up to the

> age of ten. In those days the facilities for higher education were few and far between. What is more, admission to schools had been forbidden to the lower castes. It was probably because of this that Ezhava children had pursued their studies through what is known as *gurukula* system in Sanskrit, astrology and *Āyurveda*, and achieved fame.[63]

Nanoo made use of that opportunity to learn Sanskrit and *Āyurveda* from his maternal uncle Krishnan Vaidyar. It was usual for Nanoo to sit in the shades or on the branches of trees during afternoons occasionally, and sing prayers or other songs. Krishnan Vaidyar chanced to read some prayer songs and stanzas Nanoo had written at that time. Impressed and elated by the artistic taste in his nephew, Krishnan Vaidyar decided to send him for higher education in Sanskrit. The Varanapally family which gave prominence to Sanskrit also came to his mind simultaneously.

Whenever he got the opportunity Nanoo used to go to the relatives staying in distant areas. The usual places of these visits included Kaikkara, Nadunganda, Anchuthengu and Thiruvanantha-puram. Prior to that he had shown interest in morning bath, smearing ash on his forehead, meditation and visiting temples and in performing other rites. So people started addressing him as Nanoo Bhaktan (devotee of God).

At that time the renounced Sanskrit scholar Raman Pillai Asan was running a teaching centre in central Travancore. It was by staying in the well-known Varanappally family nearby that Nanoo proceeded with his advanced education in Sanskrit. Kochukrishna Panicker of Varanappally was a lover of literature, a Sanskrit scholar and philanthropist. Under his patronage several students from various parts of Kerala stayed there and learned Sanskrit. In subsequent years many of them had acquired fame.

Those who had earned reputation as teachers in Kudipallikkoodams in Kerala were Kummampally Raman Pillai, Chavara Krishna Pillai, Aalappurathu Kunjuraman Pillai, Manarcaud Sankara Warier, Vayaskara Sankaran Moos, Pettahyil Raman Pillai and Thalassery M. K. Gurikkal. Of them Kummampally Raman Pillai ranked first.

Nanoo who had outstripped all his co-students and topped the class within a short time, became the teacher's favourite and was made monitor. Prominent among those who were his co-students then were Perunelli Krishnan Vaidyar, Velutheri Kesavan Vaidyar, Puthukkat Krishnan Asan, Manamboor Govindan Asan and others. Even though all the outstanding pupils of his were exceptionally brilliant, Raman Pillai Asan had a special esteem for Nanoo. For Nanoo alone had the talent to bring out the meaning of profound and thought-provoking portions of poems and to take in and merge himself with the ecstasies thrown up by the ideas ingrained in them. As desired by the literature -crazy Karanavar of Varanappally, Nanoo re-wrote the story *Gajedramokṣam* in the form of *Ammanappattu* (a particular poetic form). That was Guru's maiden literary effort.

It is stated in Kumaran Asan's biography of Sree Narayana Guru that within two years Swamy had earned proficiency in *kāvya, nāṭaka, alaṁkāra*, etc. (the various facets of Sanskrit literature), and terminated his studies at Varanappally after having duly performed the rite of *guru-dakṣiṇā* (reward for the teacher). But it is seen from Moorkoth Kumaran's book that Swamy had a four-year stint as a student in Varanappally. On the other hand in K. Damodaran's work it is clarified as two years. Though these three works are Swamy's biographies, the opinions of Asan and K. Damodaran appear more plausible. After two years of study Guru was afflicted with serious dysentery. With that he was constrained to give up his studies and return home.

The discussions and debates in the literary assemblies of Varanappally had maintained a high standard. Perunelli and Velutheri added a touch of romance to those assemblies and enhanced their attraction with the recitation of love poems composed by them. But Nanoo, pious by disposition that he was, was not at all drawn towards these distractions. While Nanoo desired to have a profound insight into life, the others gave importance only to the ephemeral pleasures easily derivable from a superficial view of it. Nanoo on those occasions was immersed in philosophical and Vedic thoughts. Probably because of that he had written songs in praise of Gaṇapathi, Viṣṇu, Subramaṇian, and the supreme Goddess (Devī).

To maintain contact with the ordinary people, Nanoo paid regular visits to the huts of Pulayas staying in his neighbourhood. As is well-known his life's mission was the search for the primordial and ultimate Truth. It was during that period of his life that he was presented with the opportunity to study comprehensively the epics *Rāmāyaṇa*, *Mahābhārata*, *Bhāgavata* and other great works, to wander alone in the sugary sands of Varanappally even in the odd morning hours, and to learn and contemplate on the superstitions and irrational customs which had embedded themselves in the depths of social life. To induce consciousness of freedom among the common people aggrieved by the cruelty of caste, was his set goal from early life.

After completing his education at Varanappally Nanoo returned home and started teaching Sanskrit to children in Kudippallikkoodams he himself had established at Chempazhanthi and Kadakkavoor. With that Nanoo Bhaktan came to be known as Nanoo Asan. During periods of rest he took refuge in solitude and immersed himself in matters connected with God. He discovered that human life was momentary and an illusion, being a mixture of happiness and sorrow, and hence it was imperative to give a suitable meaning to it. Nanoo Asan believed that it was meaningless for people to wail over deaths and births or material successes. He found out that untouchability and impurity associated with it were deadly scourges which had held society in dastardly grip, and realised that only through proper treatment could the sufferers be elevated to complete health.

During this period Nanoo Asan accepted an invitation to teach Sanskrit in a school in Anchuthengu. Bereft of any care in worldly matters he visited his own house very rarely only. The reason for that was his occasional preoccupation with reading, meditation and worship.

The expectations of his kinsfolk that the Swamy who had attained youth-hood, could be tied down by a marriage so as to ensure a systematic and ordered life for him, were totally misplaced. It was not in his interest to identify himself with worldly life. Even after having been convinced that his son's attitude towards marriage was in the negative, Madanasan decided upon a marriage for him. The prospective bride was Kaliamma, Madanasan's niece's daughter. In those days no one gave any value to the opinions of the would-be bridegrooms and brides on their proposed marriages. The full authority for the union rested with their guardians. According to the practice in vogue then, the bridegroom's sister had the right to take the bride to her future husband's house after presenting her with the symbolic clothes. So no one refused that right to Nanoo Asan's sister. But when the bride reached her husband's home, Nanoo Asan was found wandering in the woods near Chempazhanthi. The next day he reached home on his own. The happy relatives presented him with the bride. The beautiful bride Kaliamma approached him with a silver plate full of plantain fruits, and a glass of milk, and placed them before him and then stood aside obsequiously. With the least change of expression, Asan took one of the fruits and gave it to her in the attitude of blessing her. Then he said

> Every person is born into this world to accomplish a particular objective. You and I have one such objective each. I have my path and you have yours. So leave me to pursue my path.[64]

Seeking solitude, Nanoo Asan carried himself across forests, mountains, hills and valleys and reached the base of Agasthyakoodam Hills. He spent a few days there in meditation and recitation of stanzas in praise of the Omnipotent. When he felt anxious over his growing greed for knowledge, he came back to human society. He went to the shop of a Tamil bookseller at Chalai in Thiruvananthapuram. He was an early acquaintance. From there Nanoo Asan dug out a few spiritual books. He got enough time to read them too. Those works included such great ones as *Thirukkural*, *Thiruppukal*, *Thiruppavai*, *Ozhiviloduckam*, *Śivapurāṇam* and *Thirumandiram*. Within a short time the saint in the making acquired proficiency in Tamil. In later years he was able to write poems in Tamil because of the mastery in that language gained through assiduous coverage of those great works.

Several days had passed. Nanoo who had taken to a life of asceticism, travelled across many places in south India as a Swamy. He trudged on day in and day out. His aim in this facet of his life was to study scrupulously, social life, and the superstitions and inhuman customs which stood in the way of social progress. He would walk along the narrow lanes in country sides in search of Truth. When tired he would lie down in the tree shades or verandahs of roadside shops. He would eat what he got and accept if anyone offered something. Thus he spent his days by sleeping in out of the way places, thinking about what was to be observed, getting up and moving off before daybreak, probing into the secrets of the universe and relentlessly pursuing his search for Truth.

On one of these days Swamy took himself to the famous Pulivathukkal House near Neyyattinkara. This house had connections with his family at Chempazhanthi. The Karanavar of the House, Velayudhan Vaidyar, was a known Vedic scholar and Āyurvedic physician. Swamy stayed there for a few days. He came to know that Kuttiamma was in sick-bed. So he proceeded to Chempazhanthi. The mother saw her son. She poured forth her sorrow and complaints about him in tears. At last the son consoled her. He spent a few days there praying for his mother's recovery and giving her proper treatment. The Swamy who knew that this mother's end was near tended her for several days. One day her illness took a turn for the worse and she passed away. Swamy performed the last rites of the departed befittingly.

As Swamy had become convinced that it was time for him to bid adieu to his father and uncle, he did not feel hesitant to speak out to them about his future plans.

> Birth occurs on the basis of *karma* or actions in past life of man. Everyone of us has a set goal in life. To objectify that, is duty. No one, whoever it may be, can take leave of this life without fulfilling that duty. So I am going in search of my path.

Though Madanasan and Krishnan Vaidyar had heard those words, they only remained silent.

The second quarter of that night was bright with fine moonlight and soothing by pleasant breeze. Swamy was sitting in the vicinity of the Manakkal temple in solitude. The village slumbered in long silence. In that atmosphere he gave himself up to repeated contemplation of the momentariness of *māyā* or illusion-stricken human life.

> The universe is subject to change. I have become lonely with the departure of my mother. In one sense it has set me free. What is now needed is to reach a zone of peace not susceptible to change. Some power unknown is beckoning me to that. If I reach there the Supreme Truth of Unity in Diversity would be realised by me. Then it should be possible to revitalise human values and mould a real human society. So I implore Devī in my search for the self and truth.[65]

Swamy discovered fulfilment in a life of asceticism indispensable for one who had abjured all worldly encumbrances and taken to the search for the self; for a relentless hunt for witnessing and knowing about strange ways of life, customs and practices which discarded righteous values, and human beings carried away by the setbacks and successes in life, and above all for taking in, and identifying, experiences. Swamy set about on a long wandering mission to places far and near. At times He would, in those peregrinations, leave behind Him woods and rivers and seek rest in mid-forest; at other times the sojourn would be in the beach. During year ends when nature assumes a frightening posture, it would be on the expanse of sandy shores of the roaring sea that Swamy would find a suitable spot for His early morning meditations. The uninhabited land slices enriched with natural beauty were very endearing to Swamy. On certain evenings when hunger and thirst became intolerable, Swamy used to walk into the huts of the poor nearby, seeking succour. He would take the food offered by them lovingly, appease himself and resume his journey. Swamy was able to learn much, mainly about the daily life patterns of those residing in places familiar and unfamiliar. As everyone knows, sorrows and sufferings are unavoidable scourges, in human life. How to remedy them was the thought that occupied most of Swamy's time. His early wanderings covered such places as Veli, Kovalam, Vizhinjam, Neyyattinkara, Marthandom, Eraniel, Nagercoil, Kanyākumārī, Thirunelveli, Madhura, Coimbatore and several other places in southern India. He would take with relish the humble food offered by the fishermen, Muslims or Christians. During that period Swamy is believed to have not abjured non-vegetarian food.

It was when Swamy was trekking along in the Manacaud region that he chanced to strike acquaintance with Kunjan Pillai Chattamby, popularly known as Chattamby Swamikal. Having become close to each other, and known about each other very intimately, their journey thenceforth was undertaken jointly during which they shared and cemented their intimacy. In Kumaran Asan's biography of Sree Narayana Guruswamy, it is stated thus:

> During this period Swami met the author of *Prācīna Malayalam* and other works, and renowned ascetic, Kunjan Pillai Chattamby and through him came into contact with the great Subrahmaṇya devotee and Yoga stalwart and preceptor, Ayyavu of Thycaud, Thiruvananthapuram. From him Swamy received advice on the practice of *yoga*. Performing *yoga āsanas* in his native village and in the adjoining areas, Swamy built a hut at the Veli beach and spent sometime there. After that he stayed in an old idolless temple at Anchuthengu for yet another period. Swamy was not seen permanently at a single place in those days. It is believed that in the course of this time of his life Swami visited Palani and other great temples of South India. Stories are also heard that on one occasion Swamy had a brush with disaster, and escaped miraculously from it.[66]

Swamy was drawn towards Chattambi Swamy's profound scholarship of the Vedas. Similarly Swamy's intelligence, devotion to *dharma*, imposing profile and proclivity to silent social revolution, had attracted Chattamby Swamikal too. Both of them were happy to have had the opportunity to command Thycaud Ayyavu's love and respect, and also to pick up yogic lessons under him. Ayyaswamikal who had known that his spiritual disciples were great souls capable of lighting the torch of a social revolution in Kerala, blessed them with a full heart. It is possible that Nanoo Guru Swamy who had once been a Kṛṣṇa devotee was transformed into a devotee of Muruka, Devī and Śiva at the hands of Ayyaswamikal.

Chattambi Swamikal assumed the name of 'Shanmukhadasan (servant of Shaṇmukha) and Nanoo Guru Swamikal of Shanmukhabhaktan (devotees of Shaṇmukha). After their education in *yoga*, Shanmughadasan and Shamukhabhaktan began their journeys to several parts of southern Travancore together. On one of these days they were traversing along Manacaud. It was then that they met Perunelli and Velutheri and visited their homes. The friendly relationship so established lasted for a long time.

Shanmukhadasan who was the foremost disciple of Raman Pillai Asan of Pettah, was an undaunted adherent of action and an illustrious soul absolutely without touch of caste feeling. At a time when untouchability and caste distinctions, the bane of Kerala, were at their zenith, Chattambi Swamikal held himself fast to his ideals and stood a long distance away from those insane practices. His firm belief was that the man-made caste system was nonsensical, unwarranted and irrelevant. His pen had moved against it in the strongest of terms.

Chattambi Swamikal was an illustrious savant. He treated with contempt those aberrated social customs which kept man apart from his fellow beings. In this respect primarily his nexus with Sree Narayana Guru Swamikal was unbreachable and so they were bound together in life-long intimacy. On one occasion Swamy went to Panmana Hermitage to see Chattambi Swamikal who was resting there indisposed. The moment they met, Swamy helped Chattambi Swamikal to sitting pose and embraced Him before talking to Him.

Recently a grain of false prestige appears to have settled in the eyes of some people. As a result of that an opinion that Sree Narayana Guru was a disciple of Chattambi Swamikal came up. In Kumaran Asan's conviction they were friends. But Sahodaran Ayyappan has stated that it makes no difference whether or not Chattambi Swamikal was preceptor to Sree Narayana Guru Swamy. Let us have a look at the evidence presented by K.R. Bhaskaran about this.

> In the midst of these controversies, Amritananda Swamikal, disciple of Sree Narayana Guru, born of brāhmin parents, approached Chattambi Swamikal and enquired.
>
> Great soul, it is heard it said that you are preceptor to Sree Narayana Guru. What may be the truth?

Chattambi Swamikal burst into a laughter and said:

> He is a versatile savant. When He was Nanoo I was Chattambi. He is a real treasure of spiritual knowledge.

Another disciple of Sree Narayana Guru, Narasimha Swamikal enquired of Guru:

> Has Swamy learned anything from Chattambi Swamikal?
>
> No. When he got acquainted with each other I had noticed that his knowledge of Sanskrit was not fully doubt free. I had the privilege to clear some of those doubts. Chattambi is a versatile savant, replied Swamy.

From this it is clear that Kumaran Asan's findings fit in more appropriately than those of the others.[67]

After an interval Swamy resumed his wanderings. With the light of *yoga* knowledge lit from the blessings of Ayya Swamikal, the days he had wandered across woods, highlands, lake banks and sea shores like a long traveller were without number. One day, probably by an urge from past life he reached a hill called Maruthwamala in Kanyākumārī district. There in the heart of the sacred hill was a cave known as Pillathadam. It was this cave which Swamy selected for His lonely meditation. Standing on the verge of that mountain range resplendent in natural beauty, one could see the Arabian Sea at the slope of the distant horizon. Swamy spent numerous days in Pallithadam in meditation and search of truth.

For sometime Swamy did *tapas* (austerity) inside the cave without coming out of it. In these days Swamy appeased hunger with roots and juice extracted from leaves. Water from forest springs was available for quenching thirst. He spent about five years in Maruthwamala in quest of the revelation of spiritual light. As a result he got enlightenment like Buddha at the foot of the *bodhi* tree.

It was there that Swamy was able to realise the spiritual unity between nature and man. Along with the long *tapas* at Maruthwamala, Swamy perceived the path through which to discover the ways and means to ameliorate the miseries and sufferings of humanity, and to secure peace of mind for mankind. The night in which Swamy was blessed with Enlightenment. . . . The universe slumbering with a sense of loneliness and draped in cooling moonlight. When reeling in the exhaustion by the unendurable hunger and thirst, Swamy had a vision of a glittering tower of dazzling light standing before his eyes. It appeared to be a figure whose legs hung out of the body like those of a leper. At one look Swamy felt that in that manifestation of a *yogī*'s body, a frightening deformity was noticeable.

The hands held a pot of buttermilk and a goblet with water. The *yogī* sat himself on a nearby flat rock surface bathed in moonlight. Then with his dirty hands, mixed the rice in the pot and made balls of it, and invited Swamy also to partake of it. Swamy accepted the offer wholeheartedly. Swamy had stated in later years, that food excelled even Nectar in deliciousness. After a sumptuous meal both drank water from the goblet. At the glorious moment filled with unaccountable relief and spiritual contentment, that disgusting figure was transformed into an extremely well built and beautiful, heavenly personage. Transmitting bliss at the very moment of the transformation the figure disappeared from sight. It was then that Swamy understood that great *yogī* to be Lord Muruga Himself.

After that miracle, Swamy, the Muruga *bhakta* was known as Nanoo Guru as well as Sree Narayana Guru.

Swamy had stated on subsequent occasions that during the period of his meditation and *tapas* at Maruthwamala, he had two friends there. Who were those friends in the solitude? A cobra and a spotted leopard. Both are stated to have planted themselves during nights, as sentinels at the door of the cave when Swamy had been reclining inside it. Sometimes the snake, it is believed, would trek on Swamy's body and lie beside Him, completely coiled up. The leopard used to lick Swamy's feet clean and then rest at those feet. Even animals had great love for Swamy.[68]

The above words are quoted from the English biography of Swamy titled *Narayana Guru*.

Towards the end of Swamy's *tapas* at Maruthwamala some people from the outside world came in search of Him. Swamy was happily leading a life of total identity with nature. He was moulding the awakening He had acquired from there, like the Buddha at the foot of the *bodhi* tree, into practical application for the emancipation of the suffering. People from the outskirts of the hills, both poor and rich, started streaming into have a *darśana* of Swamy who by that time had come to be known as the *siddha* of Maruthwamala. Swamy began to make their acquaintance and advise them as to how to ease their grievances. Of those who came to Him the majority comprised those who spoke Malayalam, Tamil and other south Indian Languages. Swamy always talked affectionately to His visitors who were made up of various communities such as Nairs, Ezhavas, Channans, Vellalas, Pulayas, Parayas, Muslims, Christians and many others in the various sectors of life. In this He was not hindered by religion or caste. He was immensely popular with them. This might be because Swamy succeeded in curing their ailments and miseries miraculously.

The enlightenment which Swamy attained through His relentless search for the self, simultaneous with His endeavour for the discovery of truth, was the gift of Maruthwamala. When caste and untouchability were eating into the very vitals of the underprivileged, it was with the calculated look for a lead to save them from the aberrations to which the caste infected society had been prone, that Swamy confronted the evil. Probably it was during that phase of His life that he could assure himself with complete confidence in the success of His crusade for the regeneration of man; that he could awaken the feelings for release and liberation lying dormant in man. When the thought that all human beings are equal and belong to a common fraternity, had blossomed in Him, through His wanderings among people of different languages and cultures, He realised that the irrational customs and practices which ruled the roost in society could only pave the path for an unhealthy social life. That Swamy desired to eradicate these perversities is made clear in Moorkoth Kumaran's work *Sree Narayana Guru Swamikal*.

After the sojourn in Maruthwamala Swamy travelled repeatedly in and around the area covered by Thiruvananthapuram and Kanyākumārī districts with a few members of the Nair community who had held Him in esteem. Except the family of Doctor Palpu, no one in the Ezhava community had respect for Him. It is said that not only by this show of indifference, but also by openly insulting Him with the attribution of such qualities as insanity whenever they got the opportunity, they gave expression to their spite. But none of these imputations could shake Swamy's resolution, and sway Him from His path. He transcended all thoughts about caste or religion, and so loved all human beings on equal footing. Swamy had no opposition at all in the process of intermingling and interaction between Nadars, Muslims, Christians or any others.[69]

More than the journeys Swamy had undertaken among people of diverse ways of life after severing all family connections and attachments, the wanderings in south India after Maruthwamala had conferred on Him the benefit of rich experience. He was able to reap new and useful knowledge from what He saw at Kanyākumārī, Thirunelveli, Madura, Coimbatore, Selam, Kāñcīpuram, Pondicherry and Madras. In these places He had trodden as a lone-traveller, and gained additional advantage thereby in learning more objectively about the suffering thousands. He gave them relief from their sufferings and cured them of illness through the administration of wonder medicines known as *ottamūli*. When He cured insanity, epilepsy and other chronic conditions, people accepted Him as a celestial, and worshipped Him. There are instances in which barren women were given fruits or sweets, and they were blessed with children. How fast Swamy's reputation had winged across the country because of His wonderful deeds and the faith they had evoked among people in His powers! In short His humanity and kindness which offered succour to the needy, and His effort in the human cause were nothing but blessings for mankind.

Swamy had travelled by foot several times places like Bangalore, Mysore, Coorg, and Mangalore in Karnataka in addition to the Kerala towns of Kannur, Thalasserry, Kozhikode, Palakkad, Thrissur, Ernakulam and Kottayam. Even though the horrible impact of the brāhmin-created *cāturvarṇya* had ruled unchallenged all over India, it had never touched such bitter heights as in Kerala. Swamy witnessed human beings persecuted and exploited in the name of caste. He was convinced of the cruelty the *savarṇa*s had inflicted upon the *avarṇa*s for the simple fault that the *avarṇa*s were born as Hindus. Swamy held Himself steadfastly to the stand that those remaining as Hindus without looking for conversion were legitimately entitled to receive all those privileges which were lavished upon those Hindus who had converted to other religions. It was to avoid the persecutions and exploitations that Hindus took refuge in conversion. That was all the more reason why the non-converts should be granted the privileges going to the converts. But Swamy found that the time was not ripe to drive home at the inequity of the discriminatory treatment and so He had to wait for sometime more. Swamy had carried on His struggle not merely for the sake of a particular community but for the sake of all the communities of the world. Swamy decided to start His revolutionary activities with full self-confidence from Aruvippuram itself. When His imagination had materialised into action, the poisonous teeth of the caste demon and his attendant superstitions began shaking to their very roots and falling. As the response was seen favourable, Swamy with doubled confidence decided to work for carving out a new social order, ideal for, and respectful of, human values.

Swamy fixed His abode at Kodithookkimala which was without human habitation, but which abounded in wild animals and thick forest vegetation on uneven rocky surface. Flowing along its base, and washing the hills opposite is the mellifluous river Neyyar, the loving daughter of peak Agastyakooda. Legend has it that the famous Purāṇic sage Agastya who is believed to have drunk out the entire water of the oceans and drained them dry, had his *yajñaśālā* or sacrificial altar at the top of Agastyakooda, and that it was the *ghī* from the *śālā* fire that had flowed down as the river Neyyar. The river flows in tumultuous roar during the rainy season, but during spring time, pacifies into a mellow movement carrying along with it a mirror of crystal clear, tear-like liquid as if enabling the forest plants on its banks to see and beautify themselves through their reflections in it. During this season the river poured ecstatic delight into the eyes and hearts of onlookers. That Swamy had a wonderful innate sense of beauty, is evident from His predilection for such unexcelled spots as the Kunnum Para, Sivagiri and the area skirting the Advaitāśramam at Aluva. As to Aruvippuram, swooning in the lap of solitude, it may be that Swamy had seen through divine insight that it had been shedding lustre through the ages like a synonym of silence.

Standing on the rectangular plateau-like area at the summit of Kodithookkimala, if one directs one's eyes around, and at the landscape which extends up to the horizon, one would be frozen with delight at the sight. Swamy named the spot as the Palani of Kerala. On the southern slope of Kodithookkimala there is a deep cave swarmed with leopards and tigers. A fearsome area, difficult of access and covered with huge boulders. Even sun rays fear to tread here. It was here that Swamy had chosen for the performance of his spiritual rites. It was also this very moment that Swamy's unbounded love of humanity manifested though His dauntless efforts lasting endless, and numerous days and nights, to chalk out a proper plan of action for the amelioration of the privilege-denied *avarṇas*, had exteriorised into a honey sweet rivulet. The Neyyar river pursuing its course sometimes with restive guffaws, sometimes in mild turmoil eventuated by the effort to tide over the flat rocks on its path throwing up silvery drops in the process and looking up to the skies straight with sarcasm and everflowing like an artist, extended not a little pleasure to Swamy. Swamy relished taking rest inside the spot on the river bank called Thiruvazhi where rain water does not seep in, air and light do not penetrate, and which is sheltered by a rocky covering. He was contended with the suitability of the place as the seat of His activities to fulfil His mission because people rarely reached there and distracted Him. It is probably in accord with the will of incarnations like Swamy that nature prepares such settings for them.

When Kodithookkimala and its suburbs flip into the forefront of memory plane, we are driven to recapitulate the story of Swamy's journey braving insurmountable obstacles of passage, to reach the place Puliwazhi. Even today it is a feat to climb the hills covering a distance of about two kilometers from Aruvippuram and get to the foot of Kodithookkimala.

While the belief prevailed that even human voice could not be heard at Aruvippuram, three days after Swamy's arrival there, a boy who had been going about tending cattle along with others lost his way and came there as if by accident. He saw a shining figure at a small distance away. The boy stood wonderstruck, rooted to the spot he was at, for sometime. On Swamy's enchanting figure a halo of light was seen blazing. The boy summoned courage and approached Swamy and talked something to Him. Swamy called him to His side and asked him of his whereabouts. He was Ayyappan Pillai, Swamy's first disciple who came to be known as Sivalingadasa Swamikal.

Ayyappan Pillai decided that something should be obtained to entertain Swamy. He ran to his house, pulled out a topioca plant with plenty of roots, cut the roots to small size, peeled and steamed them, and made a condiment of locally grown small pungent chilly, ground with the required ingredients, and with these ran back to Swamy and placed at His feet. Swamy ate a portion of the offering with satisfaction and also gave some of it to the boy. This continued for some days. At the time some people nursed a curiosity to uncover Swamy's identity. It must be because caste was at its height that Ayyappan Pillai's guardians tried to dissuade him from meeting

Swamy. He had to suffer scoldings and even torture on that score. Ignoring all these he persisted with his endeavour to see and serve Swamy, and his guardians had to give in. In serving Swamy the boy had a particular adeptness. It was Swamy Himself who conferred the name Sivalingadasa Swamy on him, and taught him Sanskrit in which he achieved mastery. Several years later when Kumaran Asan came to Aruvippuram as Chinnaswamy, Sivilingadasa Swamy became his close associate.

Some of the leading natives of Aruvippuram approached Swamy and represented that the backward classes were denied entry in the temples controlled by the upper classes and that a temple for the former was required. Swamy informed them that before long facilities would be provided to them for free worship. But how to transform that undertaking into an accomplished fact, was the thought that occupied His mind.

Narayana Pillai, a high ranking official of the Forest Department, was staying in the vicinity of Aruvippuram. He had no children. One day he submitted his grievance before Swamy. Swamy blessed him, and in course of time a daughter was born to him. Swamy Himself named the child as Narayani. The girl was the future M.L.A., T.V. Narayani Amma, a leading disciple of Swamy and well-known public figure.

Some people devoted to Swamy, with the cooperation of the Pulivathukkal family and others, constructed a temple at Aruvippuram and requested Swamy to perform the *pratiṣthā*, i.e., install the idol. It was an epoch-making event which sent waves of exciting thrill along the lanes of history.

Swamy applied His mind in right earnest to the proposed project. He consulted several disciples and devotees and resolved to install an idol of Lord Śiva in the temple. It was an auspicious day of a hundred years ago, being the sacred Śivarātri day. Swamy entered the flowing waters of Neyyar and moved towards the deepest part of the river known by the name Sankaran Kuzhi. Reaching there He dived and disappeared into the depths. As Swamy did not reappear for a long time the devotees who stood on the river bank got anxious and even panicky. Then to their great relief and amazement, they saw Swamy, emerge on the water surface, dazzling in brilliance, absorbed in meditation and holding a stone shaped as a Śiva-liṅgam (idol). The description of the event by K.R. Bhaskaran is worth repeating here.

> It is a memorable Śivarātri day. Ayyappan Pillai has played the key role in the *pratiṣṭhā* ceremony at Aruvippuram right from the beginning. Before the *pratiṣṭhā*, Swamy walked into the flowing river water, went down in its depths and emerged, with a stone shaped like a Śivaliṅga. He moved with it towards the river bank and entrusted it into the hands of Ayyappan Pillai standing close by. On setting foot on the bank Swamy got it back and with it proceeded towards the temple accompanied by the devotees. Inside the temple Swamy held the idol with both hands close to His chest and stood in meditation for sometime. Then He installed it.[70]

Poet Kumaran Asan described this event in the following words:

> Swamy's intention is to imagine a rock on the eastern bank of the river as the *pīṭam* or base on which to install on Śivarātri day, a piece of rock approximating in shape to Śiva-liṅgam. Towards midnight Swamy had bath and entered the temple. Then he lifted the *liṅgam*, and holding it, stood still in meditation until 3 o'clock in the morning. On that beaming face tears were found flowing down. The spectators stood around sunk in deep devotion and sang aloud with absolute concentration, a particular hymn called *pañcākṣara mantram*. At 3 o'clock Swamy installed the deity and performed *abhiṣeka* (sprinkling of holy water on the idol).[71]

The contents of these two accounts are epitomised by M.K. Kumaran thus.

> It was Guru's *pratiṣṭhā* at the Aruvippuram temple that inaugurated the Renaissance movement in Kerala in such

> a manner as to be noticed by the world. Before that such an event had not taken place either in Kerala or anywhere in India. 'What authority has the low caste (Cāṇḍāla) Ezhava to install Lord Śiva?' Came the question loud and high. The answer was quite composed. 'What we have installed is not Brāhmaṇa Śiva. It is our Śiva only.' It was an answer which made the Namboodiri questioner think and which transformed him into a human being in the years to come. In every temple where the deity was installed by Guru a new idea also reverberated along with the sound of conch blowing. What Guru had done was to install a new God and a new religious faith in place of the old god and old faith, which imposed inequalities between man and man. Guru's religious renovation was a part of the social revolution.[72]

The repercussions to the Śiva-*pratiṣṭhā* were far more sweeping than Swamy had anticipated. Swamy's cutting answer to the meaningless question of the Namboodiri's, hitherto the undisputed masters of the social order, blunted the edge of their power. That silent revolution echoed not only across the length and breadth of India but also of the whole world. The heroic and action-oriented defiance of the centuries-old irrationalities in the social order which had drained out of the underprivileged their very life breath, by a young man, presented them with a new order holding out hope, and inspiration and freedom from a life which had till then been the very synonym of misery. Swamy blew the trumpet of change to make Kerala great with the momentous utterance. "This is an ideal place where everyone lives in fraternity with no difference between castes and no hostilities between religions."— This was the most daring feat when looked at in contemporary context.

After Śiva-*pratiṣṭhā* came the auspicious new moon day in the Malayalam month *Karkitakom*. On that day a meeting was held at Aruvippuram in commemoration, which became the precursor of *Vāvūtusaṅgham* of later years. At Swamy's instructions it was changed as the *kṣetra yogam* (temple meeting) from next *Karkitakom* onwards. But its aim was not confined to temple affairs alone.

Within its purview was also included the question of how to regenerate the backward sections of society. Swamy was the owner of a magnetic personality. He exuded a spiritual power capable of drawing towards Him all those who had the fortune to meet Him once or several times.

Swamy loved to travel because of His innate disposition to learn more about people. Once he was going by foot along places such as Kadakkavur, Anchuthengu and Kaikara in Thiruvananthapuram district. It was the day next to the third anniversary day of Aruvippuram *prathiṣṭhā*. Kumaran Asan's father Narayanan who met Swamy accidentally requested Swamy to visit his house. Swamy complied. During their talk enquiring about each other's welfare, the subject of Kumaran also cropped up. When Swamy came to know that the boy was endowed with poetic talents, He was extremely pleased. As for Kumaran (who was present there) he recited before Swamy quite melodiously some of the poems he had written. "Good. You have the talent. But do not write love poems. They are not worthy enough," was Swamy's reaction. Kumaran swore then and there that he would abide by Swamy's advice to the letter. It was that boy known till then as Kaikara Kumaru who later became famous as *mahākavi* Kumaran Asan (The great poet).

"Is Kumaran coming to Aruvippuram?" asked Swamy.

"I shall come Swamy" replied Kumaran with enthusiasm.

"I am taking Kumaran with me. Hope you have no objection," said Swamy turning to Narayanan.

"As Swamy pleases" was Narayanan's response.

Then without delay Swamy and Kumaran set out for Aruvippuram.

They were greeted at Aruvippuram by Ayyappan Pillai and Vairavan Santhi (*śānthi* is the name given to the person who conducts *pūjā* in the temples). Vairavan was staying with Swamy at Aruvippuram as the *śānthi* of the temple. Ayyappan Pillai who had knowledge only of Malayalam was studying Sanskrit from Swamy. Swamy taught Kumaran also such lessons in Sanskrit as

*Amarakośam*, *kāvyam* and *nātakom*. Before long Swamy decided to send Kumaran to the most outstanding Sanskrit college in India, to acquire proficiency in that language. Ayyappan Pillai was sent for higher studies in Sanskrit to Perunelli Krishnan Vaidyer and Velutheri Kesavan Vaidyer.

At that time, Doctor Palpu who was to play the decisive role later on propagating the movement Swamy had set in motion, was holding a high ranking status in the service of the then Mysore State, as the State physician and head of the Health Department. He paid supreme respect to Swamy's *pratiṣṭhā* act at Aruvippuram. He declared that what Swamy had perforned at Aruvippuram was the inauguration of a movement which gave hope and inspiration to the weaker sections of society. When he arrived at Aruvippuram thereafter for Swamy's *darśana*, Swamy sent Kumaran with him to Bangalore for pursuing higher studies in Sanskrit there.

The time was when Svāmī Vivekānanda visited the Mysore Mahārājā's palace as his quest. Doctor Palpu met the sage there. The sage had visited Kerala a few days earlier. He had seen Kerala as a lunatic asylum. He was very much pained at sight of the people of Kerala being held in the disabling grip of orthodoxy and its evils, and the inhuman social customs, and driven to the verge of insanity. He had also let out a warning that if this state of affairs could not suitably be rectified the repercussions would be disastrous. Doctor Palpu asked what his proposals were for a way out. Svāmī Vivekānanda's policy was:

> If the state in which a set of people, divested of mental power washing the dirty linen called *cāturvarṇya*, and which enjoys trodding humanity under foot, is to be extirpated, a Guru should be found from among the *avarṇa* classes under whose guidance to carry on social re-construction.[73]

That advice of the sage gave Doctor Palpu enough food for thought for a long, long time.

Not before long the Doctor proceeded to Aruvippuram. He

placed before Swamy the opinion given out by Svāmī Vivekānanda. Swamy listened to the Doctor with all attention. The sage's words comprised a fresh expression to the idea that had been originated long ago and striving for materialisation in Swamy's mind since then. Both of them were then seized of the necessity to evolve a practical manifestation of the proposition.

Doctor Palpu was the embodient of humanitarian sentiments. He was also a dexterous organiser and zestful man of action. Besides, he excelled in charity. He saw the brāhmins who had for centuries been sitting at the apex of the social ladder and exploiting the *avarṇas* by treating them as their hewers of wood and drawers of water. They held the śūdras and identically placed people under their tutelage, and made them willing and indiscreet accessories to their exploitation of the poor. The doctor realised this and was convinced of the need to indoctrinate these puppets, of their innate power and capabilities as indispensable for the all round growth of the social system. The daring to react strongly to the caste discriminations had also surged within Him. As a result he felt the necessity of a social organisation to work for the development and progress of the depressed classes. This synchronised with Swamy's perceptions on the subject. So there was smooth sailing for the idea to concretise. Just as the *Vāvūtu Saṅgam* was transformed into the *kṣetra yogam* (temple meeting), why not the latter undergo a further transformation and evolve into Sree Narayana Dharma Paripalana Yogam (SNDP Yogam) in response to the call of the time they were passing through? This was the proposal of Doctor Palpu which led to the momentous and historic decisions. SNDP Yogam was the child of this decision: an organisation, registered as a joint stock company and started functioning from the beginning of the twentieth century, encompassing within its fold the members of various communities living in different parts of Kerala. It took shape by the untiring efforts of Doctor Palpu and Kumaran Asan.

With Doctor Palpu's help Kumaran Asan carried out his higher education in Sanskrit at Bangalore and Calcutta. On his return to Aruvippuram, he took over as Secretary of SNDP Yogam with the blessings of Swamy. He held that position for sixteen years relentlessly working for the growth of the organisation. During that period of his tenure he succeeded with the cooperation of Swamy and Doctor Palpu, in stirring the Ezhava and other backward communities to cultural and social awareness. In His capacity as the spiritual Guru and the living symbol of the power acquired through *tapas*, Swamy was rightly looked upon and accepted as the source from which sprung all inspiration for action towards the upliftment of the suffering sections of society.

With the activities of the new organisation gathering momentum, considerable changes were in the offing among the *avarṇa* classes, especially the Ezhavas. Swamy concentrated His attention on eradicating the ruinous customs in the community expeditiously. He endeavoured to impress upon members of the community about the necessity to dispense with these customs and practices, as they not only infringed upon the community's self-respect but stood in the way of progress.

Swamy discovered that among these lower sections of the social structure, particularly the Ezhavas, there were numerous young prodigies, distinguished by unlimited potential who would touch the hitherto unreached pedestals, if only shaped and guided in the right direction. Prominent among them were the Sanskrit scholar and poet Mooloor S. Padmanabha Panicker, well-known journalist C. V. Kunjuraman, freedom-fighter T.K. Madhavan, the late Chief Minister of Travancore-Cochin, C. Kesavan (Swamy did not know him) and those who came to limelight in Malabar namely, Moorkoth Kumaran, Rarichan Moopan, Kottiath Ramunni, the editor of Mithavadi, C. Krishnan, poet Pallath Raman and others. Swamy knew them to be gems. If their services were made available to the community, it would have been a tremendous support to Doctor Palpu and Kumaran Asan labouring for the popularisation of Swamy's ideas. Those belonging to other communities who came to Swamy's notice were such outstanding leaders like Ayyankali, K. P. Vallon and K.P. Karuppan.

As the Secretary of SNDP Yogam, Kumaran Asan had travelled intermittently throughout Kerala under instructions from Swamy and enrolled members in the organisation. Asan's share in promoting within it, unity, enthusiasm and motive for action is inestimable. In addition, his knowledge of English language and the modern trends in Bengali literature when fully assimilated, enabled him to take in the Renaissance which had set in, in Malayalam literature, and the internal motivations which had permeated the newly evolved poetic genre, and equipped thus, he was able to open up a new poetic vista in Malayalam verse.

It was Asan in his capacity as the Founder Secretary of SNDP Yogam, who tended it into the first organisation in Kerala which stood for championing the cause of a community. But unfortunately, hardly had the organisation hoisted itself on its feet after fighting off the infirmities of infancy, than a section of the community started questioning his sincerety. But as if coining a befitting response to the allegations, and exposing their meaninglessness, Asan had perforce to compile a sonnet captioned 'Nightingale of the Village Tree'. The development in which Asan was subjected to unwarranted allegations had hurt Swamy very much. In any case the Yogam also became a torch-bearer to all those social organisations which came into existence in Kerala after it.

> Seeing Sree Narayana Guru's spiritual utterances and the activities of Yogam, the other communities also moved step by step towards progress, like the Ezhava Community. As a result all communities in Kerala began to organise and go ahead with their activities on that basis.[74]

This opinion of Mannath Padmanabhan is relevant to the core.

As is known, the temporary headquarters of Swamy's social activities was Aruvippuram. He realised that to introduce certain vital reforms in the social life pattern of the Ezhava-Thiya communities of the backward sections, was indispensable for their healthy growth. For the success of this scheme it was necessary to objectify the ideals for which the Yogam stood. For this Swamy undertook travels to various places, and learned several things. To dissuade the community from blindly following the crude customs rooted in coarse inheritances, it was found imperative to frame stringent rules. How the ceremony of *thālikettu* (tying *thāli*, round the girl child's neck), known as *kettukalyāṇam* (it was celebrated as a marriage though it was not actually a marriage), was stopped, is stated in Sree Narayana Guru's *Āścarya Cinthakal* (Surprising Thoughts) in the following words:

> When Swamy came to Karumkulam he usually stayed in the *pūjā* room of our old *tharavād* (family house). (It is as the experience of Vasudevan, retired District Judge, that Gopalan Thantri describes that episode). I used to partake of the rituals conducted by my grandfather. I had the opportunity to perform *pūjā* before the portrait of Guru installed in the *pūjā* room. It was in our old *tharavād* that Swamy performed the last rites of the unwanted custom of *kettukalyāṇam*. What was taking place there then was the *kettukalyāṇam* of my father's two younger sisters. For decades that uncivilised custom had been in vogue and hailed as noble, respectable and symbolising richness of heritage. It had been held in universal acclaim and absolute esteem by an outstanding community. Its abolition downright was a master stroke exemplifying Guru's power of command. It was a remarkable achievement and a decisive forward step at that.[75]

The stoppage of *kettukalyāṇam* is described in greater detail in the biographical work *Sree Narayana Guru Swamikal*, thus:

> Preparations in all pomp were afoot for the *thālikettukalyāṇam* of the only daughter of a prominent and trusted devotee of Guru, and immensely rich landlord of Karumkulam near Neyyattinkara, along with that of a few other young girls. Having got wind if this, Swamy reached the spot at the exact moment of the function. Inside the vast pandal erected for the purpose by wastefully spending considerable sums of money, were seated on spots set apart for them, the girls for whom the ritual was meant, decorated profusely in ornaments and silk. The

> deafening noise of musical piper and drums rent the air. People of different religions and castes were present there on invitation. Because of the elaborate nature of the feast the house and its compound were packed with people. Swamy's arrival there like Lord Kṛṣṇa in the Kaurava Assembly at that juncture, evoked mixed feelings in those present. Swamy summoned the girl's father to His side and said. *Kettukalyāṇam* is not a necessity. We have informed people accordingly several times in the past. Yet you are not paying any heed to it. It is for your benefit that we are saying this. If you have faith in our words you should dispense with *kettukalyāṇam*.[76]
>
> The landlord replied humbly,
>
> Whatever is Swamy's command, will be obeyed. *Kettukalyāṇam* will not be held in our family henceforth.[77]

Swamy continued:

> That is not enough. This *kettukalyāṇam* itself is unnecessary, meaningless. Why can't you prevent it from taking place? By preventing it no one is going to be harmed.

The landlord again said with humility,

> I am willing to comply with Swamy's command.

Swamy then called the girls designated for the function, gave them plantain fruit and flowers, and sent them inside the house. Then He said these words,

> We have put a stop to this *kettukalyāṇam*. It is our desire that in future none of our people should conduct this unwanted function.[78]

That was inviolable mandate. With that *kettukalyāṇam* and connected perverse customs made their exit not only from the Ezhava community, but also from other communities. In continuation Swamy ended such superstition-based practices as polygamy, and animal sacrifice.

People from various places in Kerala streamed into Aruvippuram. They requested Swamy to install idols in temples in their places in order that they might be bestowed with freedom of worship. Accordingly several temples were built in different parts in the land. Prominent among these in which Swamy had done the *pratiṣṭhā* were the Jaganātha temple at Thalassery, the Śrī Kanteswaram temple at Kozhikode, the temple at Murukkumpuzha and the Kalavankodam temple at Sherthalai. On the whole Swamy had brought into being, about fifty temples all over Kerala. In the last among the lot, the Kalavamkodaṃ temple, was installed a mirror as the deity giving a new dimension to the worship of God.

Of the many places pronounced for their natural beauty, which Swamy had visited, the one that attracted Him most was Śivagiri at Varkala. Swamy felt that more than Aruvippuram, Śivagiri was suited for the concourse of people. So after the establishment of SNDP Yogam, Swamy accepted Śivagiri as His permanent headquarters. A hermitage was arranged to be built there for His stay. It was on that occasion that the desire to install the idol of Śāradā, the goddess of learning, with a view to transform Śivagiri into a centre of worship, sprouted in His mind. The truth was driven home to those who came from different parts of Kerala for Swamy's *darśana*, as well as for seeking Swamy's advice on social welfare schemes undertaken in their villages, that Swamy's choice of Śivagiri as the centre of his activities was perfect. The construction of the octagonal Śāradā temple, a novel structure, for the benefit of Guru's devotees was a great event of the time. What Swamy had intended by the *pratiṣṭhā* of Śāradā, was to afford an opportunity for all to worship the Goddess of Learning. Swamy's work *Jananī Navaratna Mañjarī* (a poem in praise of the Goddess) was written as the concluding part of the *pratiṣṭhā* ceremony.

Not long afterwards Swamy reached Aluva and founded the hermitage named Advaitāśramam. It is not surprising that the coolness extended by the river Periyar, the breath taking natural beauty of the area and the vast sandy landscape famous for the time honoured Śivarātri festival, had held Swamy's attention. To provide a new interpretation to the intermixture of happiness and sorrow that is life and thus enrich humanity, was the creative aspect of Swamy's work. As a result of the assistance and unflinching cooperation of the devotees, the Advaitāśramam assumed shape there. During the period of His stay at Aluva, Swamy undertook journeys to various parts of Tamil Nadu for some time. He had acquired adequate scholarship in Tamil. Making use of it he began to compose poems in that language on spirituality, philosophy and the Upaniṣads. During that interval Swamy had also brought out praiseworthy works premised on the immortal creations of great Tamil scholars and poets like Agastyar, Thiruvalluvar and Nalvar. Swamy knew every nook and corner of Tamil Nadu. In the midst of the peregrinations Swamy was able to embark on preparations for the establishment of hermitages and *maṭhas* at Madura, Kumbhakonam, Karakkal, Pudukotta, Karakkudi, Thirunelveli, Thanjavoor and Madras. These *maṭhas* and hermitages were born because of the wholehearted cooperation of Swamy's devotees. They flourish today as prominent centres of worship, influencing the lives of ordinary people.

Returning to Advaitāśramam at Aluva, Swamy took rest there for a time. The *āśrama* was vibrant with discussions and seminars by social reformers, freedom-fighters, educationalists, poets and thinkers from all over India. In this atmosphere of intense intellectual activity, Swamy chalked out His plan of action for the eradication of the retrogressive system of caste. His actions and pronouncements administered a sort of shock treatment to the poor by promoting in them the much needed self-consciousness, self-confidence and the faculty for positive response to situations. For the benefit of those denied of opportunities for growth and expansion, Swamy had established centres of worship and schools, thus fulfilling His life's mission. To realise His aim to mould a society in which people did not ask or talk or even think, about caste, Swamy had with remarkable sagacity and farsightedness, worked out a time bound programme. He entrusted the implimentation of this programme into the hands of His leading followers namely, Kumaran Asan, Mooloor, Ayyappan, T.K. Madhavan, Moorkoth Kumaran, C. Krishnan and others. This accounted for His theories and ideals crowning themselves with universal acclaim.

Swamy had deputed certain outstanding personalities for popularising His *dharma* among the ordinary people with the aim of accomplishing the demolition of the superstitions which had wrought havoc on the smooth functioning of society. What those invested with the work of social reforms were to handle, were such subjects as selected by Swamy and pregnant with the prospect of being beneficial to society, like religion, morality, industry and education. As a result of perseverent effort, it was made possible to awaken the hitherto drowsing community to leap into action.

> Swamy who had believed that without differences in status, it was impossible to create difference in caste, laid particular emphasis on the manner in which Ezhavas were to behave towards members of other communities. In all the temples in which He had performed the *pratiṣṭhā* He made it a point to induct the Harijans also for *pūjā* work. Swamy was not content with the issuance of instructions alone to that effect. He mingled himself with the people, advised them, prevented the unwanted practices in person and satisfied Himself that the instructions given by Him were put into practice. He spent His time thus for the benefit of society. In addition Swamy had insisted that SNDP Yogam should take the initiative in putting His directions into practice.[79]

Besides people from His own community, Swamy had among his disciples few well-known persons from other communities as well. Prominent among them was Sathyavratha Swamikal. A member of a Nair family of Changanassery, he was known for his purity of heart and absolute freedom from caste feeling. Swamy's other disciples namely Sivalinga Swamikal, Chaitanya Swamikal, Dharmatheerdhar and Anandatheerdhar were of the *savarṇa* class — great souls who had awakened from the myth of orthodoxy, and swore themselves to the ideals of equality and human love. Anandatheerdhar outstripped the others in his devotion to the cause of *avarṇa* upliftment and progress. For the reason that he had participated in the brāhmin feast at Guruvayoor, the *savarṇa* group which monopolised the activities of the temple had manhandled him in the mid-eighties taking him as a non-brāhmin by mistake. That a brāhmin disciple of Sree Narayana Guru was exposed to the horrors of caste makes one thing certain: the truth that the menace of caste is even today masquerading as the servants of God inside the temple. Anyway with that event the brāhmin feast at Guruvayoor also came to an end.

At Śivagiri there were four or five Pulaya-Pariah boys doing kitchen chores for the whole *āśrama*. Swamy arranged for their proper education to foster their intellectual growth. The effort bore fruit and they reached high position in later life. A child's birth into this community or that, does not bear his knowledge or consent. For that reason it is meaningless to assign him a higher or lower status. He should be seen as a human being. That was how Swamy looked at the ludicrous concept of caste. But how could the caste fanatics stomach those great words? Yet it is consoling that today with the cosmopolitan outlook among people gaining ground, the tendency is to look at caste more realistically in the light of the equality ideal preached and practised by Swamy.

Even while preoccupied with the founding of centres of worship and charity homes throughout Kerala, Swamy found time to discover the diverse zones in social life, and spread the light of knowledge in them. At a time when transport facilities were too limited, Swamy had toured several times to all parts of Kerala by foot. Not only Kerala, but also to all parts of south India had He undertaken repeated tours. It was these travels which made Him the supreme sacrificer and social reformer of India.

Swamy's *ṣaṣṭhipūrti* (the ceremony on attainment of sixty years of age) was celebrated in 1916 as a great event in Kerala and the neighbouring areas. But in Advaitāśramam at Aluva where the day was observed in Swamy's presence, the programme was restricted to a simple ceremony. He had serious objections to ostentations and squandering of money for anything. The day after the celebrations, Swamy performed the *pratiṣṭhā* in the Maheśvara temple at Koorkancherry.

Swamy decided upon a pilgrimage to the then Madras

Presidency. On the day fixed He set out with a few adherents and covered Thirunelveli, Madura, Thiruchirapally, Kumbhakonam, Madras and other areas. After that He stayed for two days in Doctor Palpu's house at Bangalore as his guest. It was at this time and in Doctor Palpu's presence that Swamy had articulated his messages into immortal words and placed them before the temple of human mind. "One Caste, One Religion, One God for Man", "One process of birth, one form, no difference in this", "Liquor is poison, do not make, give or take it", "whatever the religion, dress and language of human beings, because their race is the same, inter-marriages and mixed eating can be adopted", "whatever the religion it is enough if man improves", "desire strength through organisation", "gain freedom through education", "what one adopts for one's happiness should be conducive to the benefit of others", and "ask not, talk not, or think not caste". These are the chief message of Guru.

The conference of all religions held at Aluva in 1924 was the first of its kind in Asia. "Not to argue and win, but to know and to be known." This was the message which Swamy had coined and caused to be exhibited at the entrance to the *paṇḍāl* of the meeting.

In the first such religious conference in the history of the world held in Chicago, Svāmī Vivekānanda took part to represent Hinduism. After that spectacular event in which the spiritual power of the eternal religion was brought to the fore in all its glory, the conference master-minded and brought to reality by Sree Narayana Guru was the second in the world and the first in Asia. The project was exclusively His brain child. No government had extended a helping hand for its execution. Praises poured in from all quarters, hailing Swamy as the triumphant mainstay of the historic conference. At a time when the waves of proseylitism were sweeping across everywhere, Swamy called up this conference of religions and cemented the individuality of the Hindu religion. The conduct of the conference was spearheaded by the stalwarts Bodhananda Swamikal, Sathyavrata Swamikal, Ayyapan, C.V. Kunjuraman, and T.K. Madhavan. Swamy was seated in the dais. The meeting was presided over by the Chief Justice of the Madras High Court Sir. T. Sadasiva Iyer. Pandit

Rishiram of Brahmo Samāj, Sadhu Sivaprasad representing Ārya Samāj, Muhammed Maulavi representing Islam, K.K. Kuruvila deputising for Christianity and Manjeri Rama Iyer and Manjeri Ramakrishna Iyer acting on behalf of Hinduism, took part in the conference. Sathyavrata Swamikal welcomed the conference. He said,

> It is universally accepted that through continuous penance, and austere celibacy, Bhagavan Sree Narayana Paramahaṁsa has by concentrating His mind on spiritual philosophy, become the greatest religious guide living in Kerala society today. He has enriched human thought with the immortal words that the essence of all religions is the same, and that to accept and honour his enjoinment of "one caste, one religion, one God for man" as a slogan is indispensable for the success of modern age.[80]

The welcome speech went on in that emphatic and impressive refrain for long. The conference lasted for two days.

Towards its close Swamy issued the following proclamation:

> As it has been established by the speeches held in this great concourse of religious leaders that the prime goal of all religions is the same and that it is unwise of the followers of different religions to quarrel among themselves over matters of religion. In the religious study centre which we intend to establish in Śivagiri, facilities for the study of all religions will be provided.[81]

The conference of religions at Aluva was a resounding success. It was a glorious confluence of religious heads, religious priests and religious reformers, and represented a milestone in Swamy's life. Swamy Himself was the author of the concept of discussions on religious cordiality.

The Sanskrit School at Aluva and the English Middle School at Śivagiri Swamy had established, marched towards progress from day-to-day. (The latter was elevated as a High School and in its suburbs flourishes a first grade college today).

Swamy had never for once worked for any particular religion or community. His entire activities were motivated towards the collective onward march of humanity as a whole. Will the author of the great epic *Mahābhārata* standing like a colossus in the human intellectual arena, be denounced on the basis of caste by any knowledgeable person because, he was the progeny of a fisher-maid? Similarly will it be possible to assume that because Swamy had been born to an Ezhava woman, anyone may cry down His imperishable visions and philosophical utterances with the lapse of ages? What Swamy had pronounced, written and enjoined was for the good of mankind. There can be no two opinions about the truth that Swamy had been labouring for the eradication of narrow thinking and avaricious states of mind.

Swamy was the living symbol of religious cordiality. The love and respect He extended to the other religions and religious priests was beyond acclaim. On one occasion Swamy happened to take part in the reading of the *Koran* and rendering of explanations on what was read. Swamy was requested to give out His opinion. He said that the essence of all religions is one and that therefore one could pin one's faith in any religion. The words of Swamy were happily received by the Muslim religious scholars. The irrefutable truth is that the paramount goal in founding religions is the upliftment of man.

On another occasion a few Christian priests from America visited Swamy and made an attempt to convert Him to their religion. They requested that He should embrace Christianity as the benefactor of mankind. Swamy replied that He stood as the well-wisher of mankind as a whole including Christians. They could not absorb that reply in its entirety. In the end they deputed a priest named John to teach Him the *Bible*. He started his teaching accordingly. Days passed. At last in Swamy's acquaintance John underwent a transformation to cosmopolitanism without affiliation to and susceptibility to be influenced by, any religion in particular. Till the end of his days he spent his entire time in the service of Guru, as a real Christian. Guru's vision makes it clear that irrespective of one's religious faith, to live as an ideal human being is the stepping stone to life's success.

Swamy had never believed in speeches. His motto was to achieve whatever one could through action. As a prelude to the creation of a casteless society, He started in His hermitage itself the schemes for its realisation. Many of His leading disciples were representatives of diverse communities. In the hermitage, Hindus, Christians, Muslims and Buddhists lived in a sort of assimilated fraternity. This fraternity encompassed in its fold a wide range of devotees from brāhmins to Pariahs. The Dewan of the then State of Travancore, Rajagopalachari visited Śivagiri one day. The Dewan gave expression to his views on caste on these lines:

> Caste is a phenomenon endemic in society; differences in status are nature's projections; and persons belonging to different castes could be recognised by a mere look at them or by the manner of their conversation.

Instead of giving His verbal reply to this Swamy summoned the inmates of the hermitage and asked them to line up. And He made them recite a few hymns. Then He required of Rajagopalachari to say from which communities each of them hailed. The Dewan could not give a proper answer to this quiz. It is to be presumed that the Dewan took his leave of the hermitage entertaining the impression that caste was not an endemic phenomenon of society after all.

Swamy had insisted that all human beings should live together with a feeling of equality, and with a sense of unity fostered through spontaneous love for one another, and dispelling from the mind, all mean thoughts and jealousies through proper education. What lay behind this stress was the intense desire to found a society which assimilated within itself the creative potential owing its origin to humanism.

The interviews between Gandhiji and Swamy had tremendous influence in shaping the future programmes of Gandhiji. Of all the subjects covered by their discussions the one worth special mention was that concerning the status of *savarṇas vis-a-vis avarṇas*. Swamy was able to convince Gandhiji with examples that untouchability was meaningless and an inhuman practice adopted by the *savarṇas* for their selfish ends. It was only because of Swamy's influence that Gandhiji called the lower classes as Harijans thus imparting a semblance of respectability to them. Swamy however looked askance at Gandhiji's endeavour to rid the South African Indians of their political disabilities, instead of diverting his efforts to redress the grievances of the *avarṇas* of India who constituted the majority of the population, reeling under the weight of the injustices and inequalities of the Hindu society. Swamy did not give open vent to His objection. But Kumaran Asan had sensed it as is exemplified by the strong terms in which he gave expression to it in his work *Vivakodayam*.

The quarter of a century following the birth of SNDP Yogam was the most decisive period of Swamy's life. It is doubtful whether there was any other social reformer as much armed with the awareness and knowledge of the social life of Kerala as Swamy was. Swamy's attention was confined to, and concentrated upon inculcating among the suffering strata of humanity, self-confidence and consciousness of their rights without attempting to found a religion, and insisting at the same time that all were free to embrace any religion of their choice and that whatever the religion, it would be enough if only man had prospered. This mode of action yielded rich dividends. It was by strongly deprecating man's futile exercises in mauling and killing each other for trifling reasons that Swamy had dedicated His life for the emancipation of the aggrieved, and creation of a casteless social edifice.

The priestly class, the Namboodiri Brāhmins and their minions had been on the track to do whatever they could to weaken or even dismember Hinduism. Not only that. The encouragement they had given to the foreigners who had landed here for religions conversion was, to say the least, debasing. What harm had their own religion done to them to warrant such vengeful attitude towards it? This stance on their part defies all understanding. No wonder therefore that the intelligent among the *avarṇas* had decided upon conversion to other religions with an eye on sharing rights on a footing of equality with the *savarṇas*. The majority of the self-respecting people enjoying economic prosperity and covetable status in officialdom, seen today among the Muslim and Christian branches of society, are none other than the successors of those who had converted to these religions to save themselves from the cul de sac of despair they had been driven into by utter social humiliation. They had grown under the protective shade of other religions after escaping from the crude atrocities of Hinduism. Hoping for a similar escape from the boa constrictor's crush of Hindu priesthood, a section of right thinking people of the Ezhava community approached Swamy for permission to convert. Earlier, some had already converted to Buddhism and Sikhism and secured freedom from social disabilities. But to C.V. Kunjuraman and C. Krishnan, editors of *Kerala Kaumudi* and *Mithavadi* respectively, who had approached Swamy seeking permission for conversion, Swamy refused permission even for conversion to the casteless Buddhist religion. That the possibility for the gradual corrosion of Hinduism in Kerala, though not for its complete banishment from here, was writ large in the event of such permission being granted, was beyond question. Be that as it may, Swamy was against religious conversion. Just as Śaṅkara had destroyed Buddhism, Swamy could also have, if He wanted, made use of that opportunity and inflicted a deadly blow upon Hinduism. Hinduism was fortunate in that He did not embark upon such misadventure. Endowed as He was with remarkable foresight, Swamy did not visualise that any useful purpose would be served by conversion. What Swamy desired was to remain inside Hinduism and seek redressal of grievances from within. That desire was fructified in the not too distant future.

> Religion means opinion. It is to aim at living together in complete identity of opinion that is wanted. What is called for is not the perpetuation of caste differences, but their total extermination. So what is expedient is to refrain from conversion.[82]

Swamy's opinion posed a problem of self-respect to one and all. So they agreed with Swamy. Thus in a sense Swamy had saved Hinduism from disaster in Kerala to start with, and thus held in abeyance the escalation of the declining trend to other parts of the country into the bargain.

Swamy's *ṣaṣthipūrti* of which mention has been made earlier in this work, was celebrated not only in Kerala, but also in places beyond its frontiers where His adherents abounded. Singapore and Ceylon out-smarted the others in this respect. After the enthusiasm over it had cooled down, Swamy decided upon a visit to Ceylon (the future Sri Lanka). It was on that occasion that Swamy took to wearing ochre robes. He preferred white clothes, but had perforce to take on the ochre in deference to the wishes of His followers. During that trip the group which had accompanied Him got sufficient opportunity to mingle with the people of Ceylon and spread among them the great ideals of Swamy.

The two weeks' visit afforded Him the occasion to establish acquaintance with prominent citizens, administrators and intellectuals of the island: along with it the opportunity to partake of the receptions arranged in His honour. Swamy's blessings flowed into the Ceylonese in the form of extreme love. At the end of the tour, they gave Him a tearful farewell. At Thrikkannamalai and in all centres of Buddhism, thousands had converged to bid Him born voyage. The stamp of affection for these simple people imprinted upon His mind, had shone as the symbol of eternal human love.

SNDP Yogam was without doubt Swamy's vehicle for the popularisation of His imperishable ideals and for the eradication of the deleterious superstitions which had tarnished the social body. But when a section of the community motivated by the desire for wealth and power, was led astray on that account, that selfless lover of humanity felt His heart burning with pangs of pain. But when not only the activists in SNDP Yogam, but even some of those who had embraced asceticism, were found attracted by the lure of money, Swamy for the first time felt wanting in mental strength to remain four square against the impact of an outrage on His ideal. As a solution He decided to stand aloof from all those organisations and individuals who stood with daggers drawn at each other in the name of wealth and positions.

Despite His spiritual and material activities being centered in

Kerala, their awakening power had spread throughout south India. In the course of His journeys in Tamil Nadu He had prevailed upon His followers to construct *āśramas*, or temples, or at least buildings with facilities for the needy to stay, at Papanasam, Madura, Ooty and similar places where He had visited and rested. The Sree Narayana Sevasram at Kāñcīpuram, the Sree Narayana Matom at Madras, the Sree Narayana Gurukulam at Ooty, the Pillayar Coil at Kottar near Nagercoil and the Śiva temple at Bhavani near Erode, all bearing testimony to the power of this very name, are growing from strength to strength day by day. In addition there are centres of worship on His trail functioning at Sri Perumpathoor, Pollachi, Salem, Thiruchendur, Karakkudi and Vikramapuram. It must be mentioned that the Illathu Pillais stand in the forefront of these activities in Tamil Nadu. The origins of the Ezhava-Thiyas of Kerala, the Villavars of Karnataka and the Illathu Pillais of Tamil Nadu are traced to the same lineage.

A few happening before Swamy's second visit to Ceylon may be recounted here. The first of these is the talk Swamy had had with the poet Rabīndranāth Tagore and then later with Mahatma Gandhi at Śivagiri. That Swamy could earn the love and respect of eminent personalities with whom He came into contact, such as Sraddhanandaji, Andrews, Rajagopalachari, Vinobaji and Ramaswamy Naikar, is authentic proof of His greatness as a spiritual leader who dedicated His life for the emancipation of the suffering.

Rabīndranāth Tagore had expressed his impressions about Swamy in the following words:

> I am on a travelling mission to different parts of the world. During this venture I have had the rare opportunity to visit many saints and sages. But I could not see any one greater than or even equal to, Sree Narayana Guru of Kerala. I will not forget those *yoga* powered eyes stretching their looks into the unknown far away, and that refulgent face which exuded divinity.[83]

Here are Mahatma Gandhi's words:

> I consider as my greatest fortune to have had the opportunity to visit the richly beautiful land of Travancore and the great saint Sree Narayana Guru Swamikal. I also had the great fortune to stay in the sacred *āśrama* of Guru Swamikal (Śivagiri) for a day.[84]

No annotation of these opinions is needed as evidence of the magnetic power which Swamy's individuality had wielded.

Another important happening before the second visit to Ceylon was the well-known Vaikom Satyagraha of 1924. Its chief architect was T.K. Madhavan who entered the arena with Swamy's blessings and best wishes. The *satyāgraha* had for its goal, the removal of the untouchability boards which signalled the denial of temple entry to *avarṇas*, and the establishment of their right to move freely along the temple's precincts. Prominent among those who actively took part in it to reinforce T.K. Madhavan were K.P. Kesava Menon, Mannath Padmanabhan, E.K. Ramaswami Naiker, C.V. Kunjuraman, Sohodharan (Brother) Ayyappan, C. Krishnan, Swamy Brahma Vrathan and Swamy Ramanandhan. Mahatma Gandhi had also arrived to offer his blessings for the success of the *satyāgraha*. Swamy visited the place and donated one thousand rupees for the cause. Though the struggle could not present T.K. Madhavan and his associates with complete success, it was without doubt an epoch-making undertaking.

The Sree Narayana Dharma Sanghom was registered at Trichur in 1928. It was formed by twelve ascetics including Bodhananda Swamikal. More than one hundred and twenty-five *saṁnyāsīs* had enrolled themselves as its members. Swamy's total assets can be estimated to touch the twenty-five crores mark today. Since the conversion of the Sanghom into a Trust, its management and activities have gone forward smoothly and systematically.

Swamy had lauded T.K. Madhavan profusely for the invaluable and daring services he had rendered in his capacity as the Secretary of SNDP Yogam, at a meeting held in Śivagiri. In that meeting Swamy reiterated that the supreme goal of the Yogam was the progress of humanity, in the following words:

> No community can gain strength and progress without proper organisation. It was for that reason that the Yogam was established twenty-five years ago. The 'Caption' Ezhava specifies no religion or caste. So members can be coopted to the organisation without reference to caste differences. We wish that many may join the Yogam.[85]

The last function in which Swamy had participated was the special gathering of SNDP Yogam held at Kottayam. That was at T.K. Madhavan's request. It was there that Swamy gave out the message of the Yogam:

> It should not be the purpose of the organisation to enlist as its members, a particular group of people alone to create a community. Our social organisation should be one which brings within its fold all human beings as a single entity. Religion should permit freedom of faith and guide people towards illustrious ideals. The only path open to communities to escape from untold disabilities is organisation. This truth should be imprinted ineraseably and presented in our memory.[86]

One event which deserves special mention here is the birth of the movement 'Sivagiri Pilgrimage' at Kottayam after the great meeting. Swamy gave His permision and blessings to the idea while taking rest in the Nagambadam temple. This was in 1928. It was mooted by Vallabhasery Govindan Vaidyar and T.K. Krishnan, writers who jointly presented the scheme at Swamy's Feet. Accordingly the pilgrims could undertake the sacred journey at the termination of every year and the commencement of the next, in yellow attire, and in all purity of heart and body. The five purities formed as *pañca śuddhis* are those of the word, mind, senses, action and body. In addition Swamy insisted that every pilgrim should observe non-violence, truth, devotion to god, celibacy and avoidance of liquor.[87]

In this context we should remember with pride that P.P. Raghavan of Elavumthitta who had participated in the Pilgrimate (1991-2) was a member of the first batch of 1928. The pilgrims converge on Śivagiri on the 30th and 31st of December and the 1st of January every year.

As a result of the dauntless and perseverent efforts of the Yogam, the material progress of the backward classes in general and the Ezhava-Thiya group in particular, registered a forward trend. Many undesirable customs and practices disappeared. The services of the Yogam in fostering schemes for the organisational resurgence of the backward, their education, and their industrial and economic progress and all round development are inestimable.

> Sree Narayana Guru is a burning tower of light not only of today but for all time to come. As an action motivated social reformer, a farsighted luminary of the ages and a visionary with a heart spilling over with human love, He has earned unblemished reputation. In the spiritual field He stands in the front rank of his peers as a great thinker, a refined humorist and a remarkably endowed poet. Treading His feet along the motivated path bound for human good, and reviving and resuscitating the human species from the state of inaction and backwardness into which they have been pushed by the social injustices, He, by His spiritual power, animated them to action. Swamy was such a divinely endowed genius and intellectual marvel.[88]

In short Sree Narayana Guru was one of those wonderous and rare phenomena of the age which rose in the darkness-dominating-periods of time to illuminate them with the rays of hope and enlightenment.

Swamy was able to acquire mastery of Sanskrit, Malayalam and Tamil because of His spiritual prowess. This spiritual prowess transmuted itself into the powerfully flowing current of the poetic Gaṅga. That flow generated waves of spiritual awakening in human hearts. The especial quality of Guru's poetic creations was that they could capture in tiny stanzas with spectacular dexterity, the pristine splendour embodied in the Vedic hymns. He had engulfed in His poems those process of action which served to promote the moral progress of the human mind.

Swamy had abandoned outright the accepted theory that, asceticism, philosophy and spirituality are means which stand apart from the burning problems faced by the social animal that is man. He was a theist with faith in religion, who taught and subdued the brāhmin priests who had kept God in their custody for centuries, and upheld His ideal, that whatever the religion it is enough if man prospers. With that, religious fundamentalism founded on *cāturvarṇya* began to shake. That cleared the way for a new vision, and along with that, the work towards the material and spiritual welfare of the ordinary people. Swamy held for Himself the analogous status of being the visionary and the social reformer at the same time. However the movement initiated by this great lover of humanity has proved to be the harbinger of a resurrection of the Indian Renaissance movement inaugurated in the previous century, but lay dormant since then. Sree Narayana Guru is thus one of the foremost captains of this ancient country's Renaissance Movement.

Sree Narayana Guru's life covered a span of almost three quarters of a century. How crowded and extensive were His achievements which an ordinary individual would have required several lives to accomplish! That was the aim of His incarnation. How that His mission had been completed, he knew that it was time for Him to take leave of this world. Even for the journey to the Lotus Feet of God also a cause is necessary. It is an ordinary truth that the last days of all great men who had enriched their lives through services to humanity and stamped the imprint of their personalities upon the social fabric, were periods of considerable physical suffering and pain. To the transformations inherent in the vicissitude-filled life, even the *avatārs* (incarnations) also are not exempt.

Incessant travels, mental exercise of detachment, endless and intense philosophical manoeuvres required for toiling through worldly life to the effulgence of spirituality, had not only borne in on His figure with immense mental and physical exhaustion, but also contributed adversely to His life as well. He was afflicted with urine blockage due to postrate disorder in the first instance which later on was compounded by other symptoms.

When the ageing Guru's illness took a turn for the worse, He reached the Advaitāśramam at Aluva for a few days' rest. From there He went to the Velloor Maṭha at Vaikom. But His weak physical condition remained unchanged. His health deteriorated by the hour. His bodily pain was aggravating. Yet His face remained pleasant. So from there Swamy's disciples and the inmates of the Maṭha, took Him to the well-known Doctor Krishnan's hospital at Palakkad. As the expected result did not materialise, Swamy was taken to Madras to be examined by the renowned physician, Doctor Pandalai. Neither of these steps served either to cure the illness or at least give some relief to it.[89]

The best treatments that could be given from within or without Kerala, proved inadequate to tackle the illness successfully. From Madras Swamy returned to Palakkad and was subjected to treatment again by Doctor Krishnan and by two Āyurvedic Physicians, Kakkanad Mama Vaidyer and Cholayil Mami Vaidyer. When a slight relief was felt Swamy returned to Śivagiri. There, Thycatt Moss, Doctors Raman Thampi and Palpu continued the treatment. But the illness only worsened. As directed by Swamy someone read *Daivadasakam*. Swamy lay listening to it. And that too the following last stanza

> In the ocean of your Glory
> Of Great profundity
> Let us all, together, become sunk
> To dwell therein everlastingly in Happiness

was being read.[90]

It was a cursed day, for all mankind, in short — 19 September 1928 (Kanni 5, 1104 ME). Clouds had crowded and blackened the atmosphere. As the clock ticked past 3.30 p.m. tiny rain drops fell to the earth's surface as if nature was shedding tears. Like Her taking deep breaths, a gentle cool breeze blew. A pal of gloom seemed to have settled on Her countenance. With sighing hearts and tear filled eyes, thousands streamed towards the *āśrama*.

About Swamy's demise certain details from the work *Sree Narayana Guru* are quoted here:

Time was nearing 3.30 p.m. The atmosphere remained

veiled in dismay. As desired by Swamy, Mambalam Vidyananda Swamy was reading *Yogavariṣtam Jīvanmuktiprakaraṇam.* Swamy's prime principles like Bhodananda Swamy, Sungunananda Swamy, Dharmatheerdhar and others were present close to Guru. In fulfilment of His wish Swamy was seated in the *padmāsana* pose. Immediately Swamy desired to hear *Daiva Dasakam* read out. He was listening closely to its melodious rendering. The moment when recitation of the last stanza ended, Swamy's eyes were closed.[91]

News of the *samādhi* spread like forest fire inside and outside Kerala. Swamy's devotees, on hearing of the Demise, streamed towards Śivagiri. Within no time the whole area was converted into a vast sea of humanity. Insufferable sorrow and endless tears were borne in absolute muteness.

At the appointed time the rites connected with Swamy's *samādhi* were performed in the presence of the unprecedented crowd ever witnessed at Śivagiri. The spiritual presence of Sree Narayana Guru, by then accepted as modern Buddha, permeating the entire atmosphere there as blessings, was consoling to the lakhs of mourners waiting with their feet rooted to the ground in anguish. As Balarama Panicker has wished,

> May Sree Narayana Dharma be instrumental in lighting the lamp of peace and contentment, and diffuse its luminance everywhere.[92]

The passage of years saw a *samādhi mandiram* — rare monument of architectural perfection, standing atop the Śivagiri Hill. It is the contribution of M.P. Moothedath, a great devotee of Guru, as a humble expression of his reverence for the Master.

It is no small matter that SNDP Yogam, a brain child of Swamy, could wipe out of existence the undesirable customs which dominated social activity for centuries. Besides, when marriage ceremonies and modes of worship were simplified and had assumed new patterns, the rays of freedom were reaching everywhere. That marked sowing the seeds of a new social order, promising a situation in which man can thrive as man with equality of opportunity for one and all. In short, after the advant of Sree Narayana Guru, the face of Kerala gleamed in new light, until then unknown.

## II
## KERALA AFTER THE ADVENT OF SREE NARAYANA GURU, SOCIAL REFORMS

Human life is but a speck when viewed against the endlessness of time. Time guides and tempers it. Yet those great souls like Sree Narayana Guru who have made their impress by illuminating it, will remain refulgent in social memory for ever. Not only that. Along with the inexorable passage of time, their remembrance gets more pronounced in the human mind.

Guru's life had exerted a decisive influence on the course of history. It was a life of epic magnitude and it forges into the forefront of the memory plain as the voice, torch and mirror of a particular age. The daring with which Guru had set on a plan of action to duck off the destructive customs and superstitions which held society to ransom, and achieved remarkable triumph, was indeed phenomenal.

> Any way it was in the atmosphere of a storm of social transformation which Sree Narayana Guru had ignited by the *pratiṣṭhā* at Aruvippuram that the rays of a social Renaissance were manifest across Kerala.[93]

That historical event was besides declaration of a life's vision which upheld and popularised the legitimacy and irrevocability of the birthright of the deprived classes.

The Centenary Committee of *Malayala Manorama* decided to spot out the greatest individual from among those who had lived in Kerala during the one hundred years from 1888, as a notable personality. Who had not only encompassed within his hold a period of time but also wielded tremendous influence upon its course, and in the process, made memorable contributions to the social history of this part of India. The Committee constituted of

N.V. Krishna Warrier, C. Achutha Menon and A.P. Udayabhanu, after comprehensive study, came to the unanimous decision: "Sree Narayana Guru: by all counts,"[94] who stood out amid those one hundred years blotted by the bloodshed of the holocausts of two world wars, 'as the tower of light'. It was a challenging task for the Committee.

The world beholds Sree Narayana Guru as a phenomenon which became the revolutional inspiration to collective progress in thought and action of the ordinary people. His every meaning filled word and well thought out move opened the flood gates of transition from one age to another. Guru's footsteps are imprinted indelibly upon the vast expanse of world brotherhood.

> . . . The greatness of Guru rests on the fact that He evolved the magnificent ideal of humanitarianism, and provided moral leadership to the organised move for its realisation in Kerala. It may be remembered that Svāmī Vivekānanda, the apostle of modern Indian Renaissance, had conferred on Kerala the title of 'Lunatic Asylum'.[95]

Apart from being a visionary, thinker, scholar and poet of no mean proportions, He adorns a conspicuous status as a connoisseur of art too. The first article in the centenary issue of *Malayala Manorama* captioned "The eternal symbol of human greatness", expatiates on who Sree Narayana Guru was and what his messages were.

The following statement contained in the above article points to a correct view of Guru.

> Of the rare great personalities incarnated in the modern age, to reclaim India, from being the happy hunting ground of evil customs born out of ignorance and envy, into a civilized and proud, independent nation, Sree Narayana Guru occupies the top place.[96]

This assertion points to Guru's great visionary status.

> Even Śaṅkara had given his stamp of approval to keep śūdras and cāṇḍālas outside the walls of priesthood. Sree

> Narayana Guru was born at a time when the material and spiritual existence of the Hindus in this sub-continent was suffocating under pressure of the accumulated waste discharged from the time of Vaivaswathu Manu to that of the creators of the 'sixtyfour' in human customs in Kerala, namely the Namboodiris. As an independent person unbound by worldly encumberance of any sort, it would have been enough for Guru to seek salvation by doing *tapas* somewhere in the Himalayan suburbs, had He given importance to His personal liberty only. If, on the other hand, he wanted to win the allround freedom of His fellow men he could have, like Bruno, challenged all self-styled leaders (though the Western religious priests had burnt Bruno to a painful death, that would not have happened in India). If none of these, He could have like Nietzsche, Kamus and Sartre, declared His independence by keeping aloof from society, and redeemed the oppressed classes from the grip of exploiters and cheats, by rearing their organisational potential. The realisation of His personal vision through the materialisation of their class triumph could thus have been an accomplished fact. Yet what Sree Narayana Guru had done was none of these, and all of them at the same time.[97]

This philosophical reasoning of Guru Nitya Chaitanya Yati brings to light the objective of Sree Narayana Guru's incarnation as well as how its necessity fits in with the modern era. The ordinary man who had come to the conclusion that the superstitions which defrauded his life was the inevitable externalisation of an irremediable curse, had been living in helpless misery in the name of the caste into which his lot was cast. Guru, aware of the poisoning influence of religion and caste, upon life, was bent upon rooting them out from society. While Raja Rammohun Roy, Dayananda Sarasvati, Mahadeva Ranade and others had tried to tie down the suffering classes within the confines of religion, Guru was breaking new ground with a hitherto unknown ideal "whatever may be the religion it is enough if man improves his lot", thus weaning him away from the clutches of religion and uniting him into one fraternity through the bond of love. It was therefore by diverting social thinking towards an explosive scenario that Guru had drawn human consciousness into Him.

> There is a reason for Sree Narayana Guru having concentrated his activities upon social and religious subjects to the exclusion of the agitation for political power. For it was Guru's belief that when the Indian masses had acquired the much lacked social awakening, the British would be constrained to transfer power to them. That, to what extent this belief proved sustainable and true, is substantiated by subsequent history. If one probes slightly deeper into this aspect, one would find that Guru had worked out a silent, constructive revolution which encompassed the entire social order from head to foot. Comprehensive advancement not of one particular community but of all sections of peoples residing throughout the world, was Guru's aim.[98]

Enlightened by the penance at Maruthwamala, Guru unlike other sages, travelled and lived among the common folk during the phase as *avadhūta* (a particular type of mendicant) and studied their life. In the period spent as *avadūta*, Guru is said to have plunged into thinking disposition and travelled throughout south India several times. On one occasion in answer to a disciple's query, Guru had alluded to this phase of His life in the following words which Dharmatheerdhar has recorded:

> Railways were not available in those days. He wandered in Tamil Nadu for many days. Once He reached Coimbatore via Thirunelveli. From these to Pollachi and then to Palani. Next He returned to Kerala. All these journeys were by foot. That too alone. Ate the food loving people gave, and slept at places without human presence. The period of *avadhūta* was spent ignoring rain and sun and the journey interspersed with walking and sleeping. Stayed with fishermen and Muslims and took their food. So continued the real search for the real man in society.[99]

Guru was considerably pained at the sufferings of the *avarṇas* inflicted on them in the name of the hated *cāturvarṇya*. How to emancipate them from the inhuman torture and extortions of the Namboodiris and their minions, was the one predominant thought in His mind. Slavery had transformed them into phantoms with initiative and power of response destroyed. So whatever cruelties came from above they bore mutely having lost the capability even for silent protest. Guru's aim was to rescue them from this atmosphere of servitude and enable them to breathe the air of freedom. So, for the creation of an atmosphere of such freedom it was imperative to set them thinking in terms of liberation and positive action. They were stirred into an awakening. Yet they knew that even a feeble murmer to organise would be fraught with fatal consequences. However, it was not long before the autocratic atrocities of the *savarṇas* were consigned to banishment. So Guru formed in mind a time bound plan of action giving top priority to the education of the community.

> If few at least of those in the Ezhava community who had received English education were encouraged with government jobs, the new generation of that community would have imbibed greater impetus for English education. The criterion that entitles an individual for government job is educational qualification. But in the native State of Travancore, communal rank used to be treated as the criterion. Conversely, since the position in Malabar area was otherwise; the Thiya community achieved progress in official status. Had the government here shown the same magnanimity as the British Government, the official status of the Ezhavas here would also have risen.

This opinion of Doctor Palpu cannot be ignored. As an excuse for refusing Government jobs to Ezhavas, Dewan Sankara Subbaier, in his reply to the *Malayali Memorial*, had pinned the entire fault for the situation upon the community itself.

> The Ezhavas in this State are an uneducated lot. Instead of going for English education which renders them eligible

> for government jobs, they are contented with their hereditary occupations like agriculture, coir yarn making and toddy tapping.[100]
>
> How lightheartedly that problem had been tackled! While the responsibility for providing the facilities for admission to schools rests with the government, is not the reason 'not educated' advanced to justify the dereliction, a ploy invented to evade granting a right? Even the protection given to the Hindu converts to Islam and Christianity was refused to the Ezhavas whose ties with Hinduism remained intact, because some spiteful individuals in the *savarṇa* segment did not want to grant it. The government should reconcile itself to this truth at least at this late hour. It is the duty of a government to provide relief to those in dire straits at the lowest rung of the economic and social ladder. We are humbly recording here that most of the *savarṇa* Hindus of Travancore are superstitious and stricklers for the preservation of the existing social order. They are hostile to, and spiteful of, any progress of the Ezhavas. To take cognisance of such caste hatred to dispense social justice is not becoming of any civilized government, nor will that approach be in keeping with governmental obligations and duties.[101]

What is quoted above is the relevant portion of Doctor Palpu's memorandum, submitted to the government with the knowledge and consent of Sree Narayana Guru. The services in the cause of the material advancement of his own community while remaining in a high post with renown in the Mysore State Service, are innumerable. In this memorandum even in the context of denial of admission to schools, there was detailed treatment of the birthright for English education.

For the information of the up and coming generation, the story of the refusal of government jobs to Doctor Palpu and his elder brother P. Velayudhan in the name of caste in spite of their being in possession of adequate educational qualifications, is recorded here. Having been refused admission in the colleges in Travancore, even in the English schools, P. Velayudhan had his education in Madras and secured B.A. Degree with distinction. After that, as the first Ezhava degree holder he returned to Travancore and applied for a government job. He saw the then Mahārāja of the State and submitted his grievance in person. The ruler not only showed his scorn but also directly asked the petitioner, "Why can't you convert to Christianity?" When Velayudhan heard this, he felt his self-respect wounded. He retreated without replying. Shortly afterwards he was given a post in the Madras Government Service. He later held the post of Deputy Collector in the Revenue Department and retired as a departmental head. When it is remembered that it was this type of Mahārājas who ruled this *dharma rājya*, the future generations would feel ashamed.

> After this incident Sundaram Pillai who had arrived with a Masters Degree was received at the Railway Station and taken to the palace with all fanfare and ostentation, and entertained there. The next day he was appointed in the government service. This instance of naked caste prejudice will remain in public memory for ever as a blot on the reputation of this State committed to *dharma*.[102]

How many prodigious gems have ended their days in misery and despair by the deadly bite of the communal serpent remaining entwined in the *savarṇa* mind!

The government had placed hurdles in the way of Doctor Palpu's education as well. Not only that, but he was driven away without complying with his request for a post in the Health Department after he had earned the required qualification. Ignoring the hurdles he had completed the course in F.A. But notwithstanding a resounding first rank pass in the entrance examination for the course in medicine, he was refused admission to the medical school outright.

> If Palpu became a doctor the *savarṇas* would be constrained to consume the water in the mixture given by him, and that would infringe upon their accepted customs. So he should not be admitted to the medical school. That was the vein of their argument.[103]

The authorities rejected his application for admission without assigning any reason therefore. But the real reason was known to everyone. Except to suffer in silence whatever injustice committed by this *dharma rājya*, none of the *avarṇa*s of the day could raise his voice of protest.

"When the government and the *savarṇa*s jointly, thwarted his attempt to study Alopathy, Palpu's resolution to study it only hardened."[104] He joined the Madras Medical College and came out in flying colours as a top ranker. But the Travancore State Government rejected his application for a job. By dedicating his life as an experiment as it were, to subject government to bitter criticism for its action in refusing jobs on grounds of caste, and to prevail upon it to recognise genuine eligibility, he joined the then Mysore State Medical Service as a doctor. Rising by sheer efficiency and hard work to be its head, and standing at the pinacle of glory in that position, he worked for the upliftment of his community. There were innumerable cases of denial of opportunities to deserving candidates in the name of caste, thus demoralising and ruining many a brilliant job seeker. All of them glaring testimonials to the unrighteousness of a State donning the robe of righteousness!

It was the British administration which had plucked out the poisonous teeth of the *savarṇa* supremacy in this part of India. It was also that administration which showed itself capable of injecting at least a modicum of humanity into the ignorance and superstition infected, narrow-minded conservative elements in the *avarṇa* group. English education proved itself as the instrument for the liberation of man from the dark chamber of caste. With that were sown the seeds of a shake-up in the social fabric by the disappearance of the age-old Nair infantry, and ushering in of the educational services of the Christian missionaries. When Sree Narayana Guru was convinced of the reality of the miserable plight to which the job-rejected *avarṇa*s were exposed, He found the occasion to open wide the door to social reform. It was fructified by the relentless labours of Doctor Palpu and others with the silent concurrence of Guru. In a sense that also was one of those happenings which made possible the straightening of the path of this *dharma rājya* towards virtue.

Because Ezhavas and others were kept out of reckoning for the grant of rights with the brand name 'depressed class' tied to them, it was a time when all *avarṇa* children had been divested of educational facilities. Though the deprivation of Doctor Palpu had created minor expressions of protest, the iron hand of the *savarṇa* government succeeded in suppressing them to mute silence. After that, Kadakkavoor P.M. Raman was refused admission to the Attingal English School. The *savarṇa* Sirkar had caused the memo to that effect to be issued to him through the Inspector of Schools. Prior to him, the first Ezhava District Judge M. Govindan had also suffered the same experience as that of Raman. He too had his High School Education in the English School run by Christian priests at Chirayinkil. It was the time when Ezhava children began getting admission to schools through the efforts of Guru and Doctor Palpu. Govindan joined the college and passed the B.A. Degree Examination with a first class first.

Before long he was appointed as Inspector in the Excise Department. Later he took the B.L. Degree and enrolled as an Advocate. He then adorned the posts of Munsiff and District Judge.

The entry into government service, of M. Govindan, a staunch devotee of Guru and contemporary of the poet Kumaran Asan, heralded the elimination of hurdles for the Ezhavas and other backward classes to their triumphant voyage to that hitherto forbidden zone.

The irritatingly narrow-minded thinking of contemporary *savarṇas* is brought out by K.N. Prakasan in the following words:

> The Ezhavas who had held high status and respectable positions in Kerala in virtue of their numerical strength and social superiority till the eighth century, began to decline thereafter for historical reasons. The protracted conflict which took place in the ninth century between Hinduism and Buddhism ended in the decline of Buddhism. Together with that the fabricated stories extolling the past of the Hindu religion, framed and popularised by those interested in preserving brāhmin supremacy, accelerated

the process of completing and stabilising the victory of Hinduism. As a result, the artistic creations filled with a series of laws necessary for their survival, together with their hold on the government, had considerably aided in the degradation of the Ezhavas from their high social stature, to the status of untouchables. Simultaneously the higher-ups also triumphed in bringing about the all-round suppression of the Ezhavas who comprised the major chunk of the agricultural sector of the population. And during the lapse of the next thousand years either because of some inscrutable social code, or because of some unknown change, resisting social regulations, the Ezhavas were, to say without doubt, pushed further down into the depths of darkness. It is true that stray families are found with their original wealth and power undiminished like green trees in a fire devastated forest. But when the high caste Hindus forced the Ezhavas into the category of low castes, the Ezhavas and other *avarṇa* classes like them, were compelled to take their imposed untouchability for granted. In due course the *savarṇa*s could keep the *avarṇa*s out of centres of worship in their entirety. Further, the Ezhavas were driven out of temples in which they had special rights and privileges, by the tactful use of rules and force. The *savarṇa*s planted 'untouchability boards' on several public roads with the inscription in bold letters 'entry prohibited', so as to prevent the Ezhavas and other lower caste Hindus from traversing along these roads. Admission to the courts and Anchal Offices was denied to the Ezhavas. The Ezhavas were not permitted to perform the *kathakali* dance with the prescribed crown on their heads like the *savarṇa*s. The social framework of the times forbade the *avarṇa*s from wearing pure gold ornaments. Even Doctor Palpu's mother had perforce to wear ornaments made of gold diluted with silver in order to preserve the caste symbol. Confrontations erupted in various places because the Ezhavas had cremated their dead, and went on horseback for the immersion of dead bodies. It is pointed out that in north Parur, Doctor

> Palpu and his companions were asked to move out of the path to give way to a Namboodiri's dead body, by the porters who took it by procession. The Ezhavas and other backward classes had not been granted admission to Sirkar schools. "It is not possible to admit children of your community to the Kayamkulam English School" was the reply of the authorities to a memorandum submitted by the Ezhavas. A year later with the government's permission, Ezhava children were admitted to schools. That let loose a series of infamous communal riots at Haripad and Parur. Doctor Palpu's father had not been given permission to join the pleadership examination because of the cruel operation of the caste rules. If school admission was so prohibitive, how beyond reach the entry into government service must have been, may be left unsaid. The Malayali Memorial, and the petition signed by thirteen thousand Ezhavas and submitted to the Mahārāja under the leadership of Doctor Palpu alike, had catagorically stated that there was not a single Ezhava in the Travancore Sirkar service receiving government salary. Despite being in possession of the required educational qualifications, Doctor Palpu and his brother P. Velayudhan had the humiliation of seeking employment elsewhere. From this, how horrendous was the mad play of caste, could be imagined. Even after that how much oppressions Ezhavas and others had suffered! It was with the activities of SNDP Yogam founded by Sree Narayana Guru gathering full momentum, that the social injustices and inequalities were shattered to pieces.[105]

When He returned after completing His education at Varanappally, Guru saw the disruptive forces and fateful tendencies which were eating into the very vitals of the community into which He had been born. A spasm of pain swept across His being. He then assessed the disabilities of His community straightaway. All the great figures who could lay milestones in social history, had started their activities at the grassroots from family and from there, by steps, proceeded along society and nation, ending in a world-view. Sree Narayana

Guru was no exception.

After completing the *saṁnyāsa* phase of His life, Sree Narayana Guru ascended to the heights of solitude and from there surveyed the Kerala society over and over again. That survey finally targeted itself upon the Ezhava community and those placed in identical situations. In those days, because there was no freedom of worship in temples, the affected people rejected *savarṇa* gods and accepted such primitive deities as Mādan, Marutha, Cāthan and Cāmuṇḍī as their gods and worshipped them. This they were forced to do by the pressure of circumstances. In all probability, superstitions thrust their roots deep in society because of the compulsions of situations. When one is stricken ill, the patient is treated by the sorcerer consistent with the prevailing practice, instead of by the knowing physician. So that when the sickman died, the superstition possessed relatives did not grieve. By playing ducks and drakes of the money earned through agricutural occupations for unnecessary and ostentatious ceremonies, they held themselves on tightly to bad customs. Morality was jolted. Progress was halted. Human values eroded. Lack of education formed the fodder for the growth of crude customs. As the *savarṇa* supremacy over them reigned unchallenged, the *avarṇa* classes were down to despair. Guru saw the Ezhavas and suffering communities only as automatons living in dependence, despondence, and ignorance. Guru's aim centered round the idea of resolving this social stalemate.

Before embarking on the action in fulfilment of His life's mission, it was on setting the required background in the collective consciousness of His followers, that Sree Narayana Guru concentrated attention. The epoch-making *avatāra* found time to study along with the lives of the refugeless and the aggrieved, the realities in the lives of the wealthy and mighty as well. He saw that the Mahārāja of Travancore had run the administration of this *dharma rājya* with arbitrary authority by running roughshod over the conscience of the *avarṇa* branch of his subjects. Guru found himself a helpless witness to the ruler ensuring constant flow of money into his coffers through ruthless torture and extortion of the hard toiling depressed classes, creating a terror-spilling atmosphere in their trail. He was pained not a little by the *savarṇa* supremacy ingratiating itself to the Mahārāja's favour through tale bearing and flattery and poisoning his ears in the process, and through the advantage so gained, appropriating absolute hold over his person, so that key offices as also the power to lash the horse whip of oppression upon the backs of the lowly placed with impunity to complete their suppression, found a smooth passage into its hands. To find proper solution to this intricate social situation, Guru was evolving a plan of action.

> To counter the argument that if the untouchables were granted entry, the temples would be polluted, what Sree Narayana Guru first attempted was to secure for the depressed classes, the freedom of temple entry.[106]

It was a time when even the very thought of opening the *savarṇa* temples for *avarṇa*s was dreaded. Guru spent days in comtemplation about a scheme to open wide for the *avarṇa*s, that threshold to the paradise which promised them freedom. That originator of revolutionary thought must have conceived of such a metamorphosis as tantamount to an atomic explosion inside the conventional stronghold held on to tenaciously and guarded jealously, by the *savarṇa* hegemony. On the appointed day itself the explosion took place, sending shock waves ripping across human consciousness. However, only after the passage of a hundred years had the impact of that great explosion detonated at Aruvippuram, found its way to the common man's sensory experience.

The national renaissance movement which had sprouted throughout India stopped short at the reformation of the *varṇāśrama dharma* or observance of the four states of life commencing with *brahmacarya* or celebacy. What Guru attempted against this background was to bring together all those labelled as untouchables, and thrown into the wayside of the social mainstream, and mould them into a new society. But it was not a craze for the creation of a new religion that had vibrated behind that endeavour. It was daring expression of a mighty vision incarnating the far-reaching messages of "One caste, One religion and One God for man", and "whatever may be the religion it will suffice if man achieves progress". The Hindu priesthood was wanting in the intellectual apparatus necessary to probe into its indepth meaning. How could they have had that insight, interested as they were, only in carrying on exploitation in the name of religion and enhancing their comforts? Even Mahatma Gandhi had reservations about stomaching the import of those great messages. This was evident from a conversation between Guru and the Mahatma during the latter's visit to Śivagiri. When Guru had argued out the irrationality of caste, Gandhiji responded with this question: "Just as leaves of the same tree are of diverse forms and shapes, are not the differences in caste among human beings a recognition of the legitimacy of *cāturvarṇya*?" Swamy replied: "It is a fact that leaves of the same tree are of different forms and shapes. But if they are plucked, taken together and crushed, the resultant juice is of one colour and one taste." Swamy's reply must have set the Mahatma thinking. Anyway it had had its impact on him no doubt.

The brāhmins who had arrogated to themselves the dictatorship of religion never believed in human progress. It was a declaration of freedom against this, that Guru had achieved.

> The economic and social inequalities which were the creations of the caste system, and the princely rule, had survived for hundreds of years because of their firm fealty to brāhmins. Some who had achieved wisdom through education only stood with bowed heads in obeisance before the brāhmin priesthood. It was then that a progressive minded *avarṇa* who had no English education and who had learned Sanskrit in the ancient *gurukula* style, rang an awakening call to the Kerala conscience, challenging the till then uncontested brāhmin hegemony, which freely rode upon the social brain. The awakening so administered by Sree Narayana Guru in later years escalated every where and benefitted all irrespective of *savarṇa-avarṇa* distinctions.[107]

There are two faces for the scheme of serving humanity, social and spiritual. He who had consecrated temples, once said:

> Hereafter it is not creation of temples, but creation of schools that people want. The prime temples should necessarily be schools.[108]

How pregnant with meaning Guru's words were, time testified.

Guru's enjoinment to get fortified by organisation and enlightened by education when crystallised, a new awakening was born among the *avarṇa* class. To a certain extent it influenced the *savarṇa* classes as well. It was the Nagasundrar community of Bengal that gave birth to Svāmī Vivekānanda. Svāmī Vivekānanda could bring fresh awareness to that community. So also Guru believed in the indispensability of a well-knit community among the Ezhava-Thiyas, and other backward classes to foster in them an assurance of mature freedom and equality of opportunity. That farsight and foresight proved meaningful. His ultimate goal was to awaken through the instrumentality of SNDP Yogam, the great power which lay dormant in the discarded sections of society. That determined sage could bring His project to fruition for the most part during His lifetime itself.

> The *Devaswom* reforms implemented by colonel Munroe, helped the *savarṇas* to establish their political power in another way. In those days Ezhavas had no temples with universally acknowledged deities installed in them. Velayudha Panicker who was a devotee of Lord Śiva had a Śiva temple consecrated at Edakkad in 1856. The ceremonies followed in *savarṇa* temples were adopted there also.[109]

That this temple was established in the same year as Guru was born, may be a coincidence. Yet it was when its thirty-second anniversary was being celebrated that Guru had consecrated the Śiva temple at Aruvippuram. This fact is probably not known to many. But Guru had not only not imitated *savarṇa* temples in the performance of the rites and other practices, but also put aside the outmoded rule that only Namboodiris were entitled to consecrate temples and conduct *pūjā* therein, and instituted new arrangements in their stead. That was the personal impact of Guru.

> Establish birth rights through organisation and get enlightened through education, were the catchwords of Guru which were rendered practicable through the labours of SNDP Yogam. This fact should not be lost sight of.[110]

Whether historical backgrounds are recognised or rejected, the fact remains that the *avarṇa* communities trodden under foot for centuries, took in the self-confidence and moral power that SNDP Yogam had passed on to them. By then they were all set to draw enough inspiration to recover step by step, their lost social, cultural and financial rights. The words Guru spoke to the first anniversary gathering of the Yogam at Aruvippuram sum up his philosophy. Guru who believed only in action, and not in speech, let out His key messages there, which pointed to the progress of the community. The maxims "freedom through organisation," "enlightenment through education", "One caste, one religion, one God for man" and a host of others bore the torch to awaken the collective conscience from its long torpor.

The second anniversary of SNDP Yogam was held at Thamarakkulam in Kollam in the year 1905. Addressing the gathering, what Doctor Palpu, the very life breath of the organisation, had said was that we should objectify Guru's teachings and messages in our lives and do away with all superstitions and barbarous customs. Along with that, he repeated Guru's exhortation that members of the community should achieve progress by resorting to industrial undertakings.

The third anniversary meeting held at Alappuzha in 1906 was presided over by the reputed lawyer and public figure of Thalasserry, Kottiath Ramunny. In his presidential address, he said:

> Whatever might be our former state, however independent we may have been in ancient Kerala, our plight today is pitiable. I therefore believe that you can acquire the ability and expertise to achieve educational and economic

progress.[111]

His speech was inspiring. The succeeding anniversary gatherings were chaired by such eminent personalities as Raarichan Moopan of Kallingalmatom, Kozhikode, P.G. Govindan, of the Bombay Government Secretariat, Oithi Krishnan, Municipal Chairman, Kozhikode, M.R. Kelappan, C. Krishnan, Editor *Mithavadi* daily, the well-known literary figure Moorkoth Kumaran, P.V. Ramunni, Accountant General, Patiala, P. Sankunni, Principal Victoria College Palghat, M. Govindan, the first Ezhava Judge of Travancore, Sahodaran Ayyappan and umpteen other outstanding individuals. They were not merely vehicles of Guru's messages but torch-bearers of their real significance and implication. As the leading light behind these tremendous movements, Kumaran Asan stood out as the fountain spring from which all activities originated, bringing out in the process, his exceptional organising capacity as the secretary of the Yogam as also his remarkable oratory, which kept the mobs in thrall under his magnetic spell, and carried them with him to the field of action.

> Our Yogam is born at the time when the solitary austere life of Guru enters the stage of transition to the service of humanity. The caste set up of the Hindu religion has placed constraints upon the bounds of His sphere of activity. It is natural that Swamikal, the great *yogī* that He is, has assigned top priority to the reform of religion. Guru who had installed deities to provide facilities for worship to His own class of people, has stopped the *thālikettu kalyāṇam* and reformed and simplified the existing intricate and expensive marriage functions, with the intention of promoting community's healthy growth. These are by no means without significance. The Yogam's exigent attention fell upon matters like temple entry rights, prohibition, admission to schools and others of identical character.[112]

It was in this refrain that Kumaran Asan had, at the twentieth anniversary celebrations of SNDP Yogam held at Kollam, evaluated Guru's service to the community through that organisation.

> The agitations for rights which were practically absent during the first stage, and which found conspicuous expression during the second stage, when T.K. Mahadevan was Secretary, went into full gear at the next stage, reckoned as the C. Kesavan stage. It is when one reminds oneself of the inner urge the Yogam has engendered in one to carry on the struggle relentlessly, that one is struck by the core of the power that the community has acquired to itself during these past thirty four years.[113]

This is a relevant extract of Sahodaran Ayyappan's presidential address at the Yogam's thirty-fourth annual gathering.

During the lifetime of Guru, twenty-five annual gatherings in the name of SNDP Yogam had been held at various centres in Kerala. It is a fact that these annual assemblages had tended to awaken and plunge into action the Ezhavas, who constituted a very prominent community of Kerala. Later, outstanding personalities such as C. Kesavan, K. Ayyappan and R. Sankar took up the thread and led the community to greater heights.

Sree Narayana Guru's messages bear the relevance of international adoptation. Their very facial ensign is a superhuman accomplishment to annotate profound visionary thoughts in the simplest terms. They have served the supreme purpose of activating multitudes rendered barren of action and dumbed into the bottom-most layer of the social heap. The Yogam's inner core was the essential impetus it provided for a powerful cultural revolution.

The Upaniṣads were instrumental in popularising the Advaita Vedānta or the non-duality wisdom as the common heritage of all mankind. Was it not by imbibing also the ideas expounded in the Upaniṣads which stand rightly defined as the granary of oriental thought, that Lord Buddha had given shape to His august wisdom. His opposition was not to Vedic thought but to Vedic priesthood. But Ādi Śaṅkara, the retriever of the Advaita creed, has accepted the creed by recognising the Śruti-Smṛtis which don the title Hindu Epics. However, it should not be forgotten that it hampered social progress. What he had endeavoured was to tie down humanity within the fortress he had built with Śruti-Smṛtis, by the promptings of his metamorphosis as the guardian and the protector of *cāturvarṇya* and brāhmin supremacy. But Śaṅkara must have ignored the truth that Buddha by reducing the orthodox strongholds to rubbles, let the nectar of equality flow into all minds. As for Sree Narayana Guru, He had grasped it in its totality, and so had broken to smithereens, the caste system reared up by Śaṅkara and his followers, not by any intellectual gymnastics, but by the application of cold reasoning born out of His own social background. "Śaṅkaran had flown with his intelligence, to feed the caste to stabilise it",[114]so said Sree Narayana Guru with a touch of sarcasm. He proceeded with His task by holding high the ennobling power of human love. In a short while, Lord Buddha's love instilled mission marked the emergence of a golden age in India, Śaṅkara's annihilating enterprise of Buddhism was creating a dark age here for the protection of the *savarṇa* class. And that dark age continued to shed its dismal shadow here for centuries. But Guru's social reform launched after a thousand years' intermission, incited the dying groan of the dark age. That gave relief and joy to the people at large and the *avarṇa* classes in particular. That basic divergence could be noticed in the exposition of the *Advaita Sidhānta* by the two spiritual stalwarts. It is when this divergence is understood in full, that the tenability of the opinion of those who argue that the *Advaita Sidhānta* of the two is identical, tumbles to the ground.

It is as a social organisation evolved out of the thought process of Guru that SNDP Yogam claims its worth. That it owes immensely to Doctor Palpu and Kumaran Asan for its growth into a guiding spirit of a great national plan of action, cannot be too strongly emphasised. When the peculiar state in which the *avarṇa* castes were sidelined and suffering untold setbacks, as if "bound by some illusory dictates, to the depths of darkness", had driven itself to the pinacle of its inglorious existence, the two had stepped in for serving the community at the wish of Guru. Guru's messages created a vibration in *avarṇa* hearts. With the lapse of time superstitions and unwanted customs were shown the exit passage. That period was accredited with the encomium, "the age of Doctor Palpu, Kumaran

Asan", and earned name and fame. In a word it was these towering figures who laid the foundation for the successful achievements of SNDP Yogam. Seeing Kerala as one indivisible whole, and coopting Thiya leaders to key positions in the Yogam, helped to strengthen it and gain greater range for its activities.

N. Kumaran, T.K. Madhavan, C.V. Kunjuraman, C. Kesavan and K. Ayyappan who had steered the Yogam during the second phase of its life, had all accepted as their guiding principle Guru's exhortation to gain strength through organisation. C. Kesavan who had emphasised that only through agitation and aggressive courage can success be achieved, and K. Ayyappan, the rationalist who had assessed the worth of Guru's teachings in the simmering glow of cold reasoning and mature thought, represent the second phase of Yogam's growth.

The one versatile genius who shines like a silver star in the mental horizon of the trampled communities was R. Sankar, the very living image of action-based public life, who led the Yogam for a considerable period of time. While in its infant days Yogam approached the authorities for the grant of rights with a begging bowl, rights were demanded during the next phase with the proclivity for direct action held inside clenched fists. It was a legendary struggle that was launched to get hold of the rights held by the *savarṇas* for long with an assumed claim of legitimacy for inherited property, as it were. Without waiting with the begging hand outstretched before anyone, without hoping for anyone's goodwill, it was a struggle to possess the power to rule. But when it came to the period of R. Sankar, Yogam's leadership had the opportunity to remain in power and had the privilege and fortune to lay hands on rights indisputably and legitimately due to the deprived classes. Actually it was those privileges and fortunes which gave the required strength to the members of Yogam. Sankar was able to consummate his work with unqualified success by remaining at the helm of authority. For this he had Guru's blessings in ample measure. The Sree Narayana colleges which stand with their heads held high like the community's victory towers, are not only memorials to R. Sankar; they are also memorials to the oppressed classes' victory. Unfortunately for those classes, during the period of a strenuous effort for the establishment of a Sree Narayana University, had death laid its cruel hands on this great son of Kerala. That was really a grievous blow for the community.

> It was not a time akin in any way, to that of Sree Narayana Guru or of K. Ayyappan and others who had laboured for preparing the ground for, and given leadership to the agitation, seeking relief to the grievances of Ezhavas and other backward communities, when R. Sankar found himself thrust into public life. He was actually moving to the social sphere from the political field. His admirable brain found its proper hunting ground not in the endeavour to reforming the community as such; on the contrary, to the more complex field of education where to work our schemes for founding educational institutions and expanding them. When the imbecile social consciousness, which might have dug cleavages in society's body constitution and weakened the country's body politic itself, was awakened with creative vigour, time was ripe for the emergence of Sree Narayana Colleges. The sole credit for the rise of that creative spirit rests exclusively with the now sixty years covered R. Sankar, starting life with an invaluable wealth of experience.[115]

This opinion of Panambilly Govinda Menon is worth recall in this context.

The facts which R. Sankar records with legitimate pride in the first Annual Report of the Sree Narayana Trust cannot but strike us with wonder.

> The S.N. College established in 1948 grew rapidly and earned the top place among the colleges under the University. This is the largest college born in the State in the last fourteen years. Not for the largeness in the number of students; but because of the profusion of courses conducted as also of the diversity of the postgraduate studies held, that the Sree Narayana Colleges stand in the fore-front.[116]

From this it will be seen that his educational expertise enters a new zone.

We may now have an idea as to how the mature scholar M.K. Kumaran estimates the intelligence and accomplishments of R. Sankar in the following words:

> That great soul who has brought about an educational revolution in Kerala is R. Sankar. His work in education has benefitted not the Ezhava alone. Members of all communities have gained from it. Even students belonging to the scheduled castes were encouraged with admission to the postgraduate courses and accommodation in hostels. Bright students received encouragement indiscriminately without regard to their communities. Narrow communal feelings were foreign to him. He followed this attitude in the appointment of teachers as well. Qualifications and efficiency took precedence over all other considerations. To recognise competence and capability wherever they were found was inborn quality in him. It was during his tenure as the Minister for Education in Kerala, that the colleges which stand throughout Kerala with their heads towering in dignity and which could with justifiable pride, be regarded as the property of all communities, were established. . . . That the facilities for higher education which were concentrated in cities alone, had spiralled into the hearts of villages, was the enviable truimph of Śaṅkar's individuality; actually that was the educational revolution planned and executed by him.[117]

There are few in Kerala endowed with such magnanimity and envy exciting capabilities as Sankar.

It must be admitted that the British rule in India had contributed immensely to diluting the power of the brāhmins and others down the social ladder who had held sway over Hinduism socially and spiritually, and melting away the blind communal injustice, through passing on the radiant rays of equality across society.

> Our aim is to retrieve the great Hindu society which has fallen into the abyss of mistaken notions and hateful slavery, to correct such sordid social practices as polyandry, and engender in them the affinity for public duty and citizens' rights.[118]

These words of Tipu Sultan are memorable. It must have been grasp of the same ideas which had prompted Sree Narayana Guru to give first priority to the social reform of the *avarṇa* classes. Because of that, the occasion arose in the Kerala after the birth of Guru, for hope and enthusiasm in the lives of the ordinary people. That was a blessing in every respect.

## References

1. Śrī Rāmakṛṣṇa Paramahaṁsa (1833-86).
2. Svāmī Vivekānanda (1863-1902).
3. Śrī Śaṅkarācārya (825-58).
4. Sree Narayana Guru (1856-1928).
5. *The March of Social Reforms in Kerala.*
6. *Kerala and Buddhism*, V.R. Parameswaran Pillai, p. 203.
7. *Buddhism*, Monier-Williams, p. 187.
8. *Beginning of South Indian History*, Dr. S. Ramaswamy Ayangar, p. 144.
9. *T.K. Krishna Menon,* Bulletin V, p. 77.
10. *Ancient Inscriptions*, V.R. Parameswaran Pillai, p. 120.
11. *Kerala and Buddhism*,V.P. Nanoo, p. 258.
12. *The Modernisation of Kerala, the Majesty of Sree Narayana Epoch*, T. K. Ravindran, p. 325.
13. *Lands of Perumala*, Francis Dey, p. 68.
14. *The Religion of India*, Max Weber, p. 131.
15. *The Cultural History of Kerala,* P. K. Gopalakrishnan, p. 278.
16. *Ibid.*, p. 348.
17. *Jeevitha Samaram* (The Struggle of Life), C. Kesavan, p. 97.
18. *Ibid.*, p. 108.
19. *Notes* (Edgar Thirston), Vol. I, p. 162.
20. *The Cultural History of Kerala*, p. 405.

21. *Mooloor, the Inlightful Poet*, 248.
22. *Jeevitha Samaram* (The Struggle of Life), p. 115.
23. *Ibid.*, p. 118.
24. *Ibid.*, p. 119.
25. *The Travel Notes of Mettier*, p. 128.
26. *The Cultural History of Kerala*, p. 422.
27. *State Manual*, p. 260.
28. *The Culture of and Reform in Ancient India*, Kosambi, pp. 15-20.
29. *The Cultural History of Kerala*, pp. 418, 419.
30. *Jeevitha Samaram* (The Struggle of Life), p. 153.
31. *The History of Travancore*, R. Narayana Panicker, p.10.
32. *Jeevitha Samaram* (The Struggle of Life), p. 182.
33. *The Cultural History of Kerala*, p. 266.
34. *Travel Notes the Dutch Traveller Canter Vishir* (wherein reference to the slaves in Kerala is made for the first time).
35. *Travel Notes*, Buccanan 1912 (Documentary Evidence on slavery).
36. *Ibid.*, p. 410.
37. *The Cultural History of Kerala*, p. 427.
38. *The History of Travancore*, R. Narayana Panicker, p. 293.
39. *Travel Notes of Barbossa* (In the Malayalam months of Makaram and Kumbhom, if *avarṇa* youths happen to see *savarṇa* women outside their house, they could be taken away by these youths; so said the existing laws. They were named as *Mannappedi* and *Pulappedi*).
40. *The Darkened Pages of Kerala History*, p. 146.
41. *The Majesty of Sree Narayana Epoch*—'Renaissance in the Namboodiri Community, p. 354.
42. *The Renaissance of Nairs*, K. Bhaskara Pillai, p. 364.
43. *The Cultural History of Kerala,* p. 268.
44. *The Renaissance of Nairs*, K. Bhaskara Pillai, pp. 361-2.
45. *Ibid.*, p. 364.
46. *Ibid.*, p. 363.
47. *Logan*, Vol.I, p. 117.
48. *Castes and Tribes in South India.*
49. *Kerala History,* Padmanabha Menon, p. 968.
50. *Social Revolution in Kerala Villages*, Dr. A. Ayyappan, p. 120.

51. *Some Problems of Kerala History*, Ilamkulam, p. 121.
52. *Kerala History*, Padmanabha Menon, p. 977.
53. *Platinam Jubilee Momorial*, Vaalath p. 351.
54. *Kerala History*, Vol. V, Ulloor, p. 326.
55. *Sree Narayana Epoch*, p. 69.
56. *The Ezhavas and Kathakali*, Kunju Panicker, Jubilee Publication, p. 203.
57. *Ibid.*, p. 204.
58. *The History of Thiyas*, Murkoth Kunjappa, p. 67.
59. *Remininces*, Mannath Padmanabhan, pp. 39, 40.
60. *Souvenir on Kanaka Jubilee*, p. 232.
61. *Native Life in Travancore*, p. 168.
62. *The Cultural History of Kerala*, p. 376.
63. *The Biography of Sree Narayana Guru Swamy*, Kumaran Asan, p. 2.
64. *Ibid.*, p. 38.
65. *Ibid.*
66. *Ibid.*, p. 5.
67. *Sree Narayana Guru Swamikal*, K.R. Bhaskaran, pp. 30, 31.
68. *Narayana Guru*, M.K. Sanoo, p. 48.
69. *Sree Narayana Guru Swamy*, Murkoth Kumaran, p. 21.
70. *Ibid*, p. 24.
71. *Biography of Sree Narayana Guru Swamy*, Kumaran Asan, p. 10.
72. *The Indian Renaissance*, M.K. Kumaran. *The Majesty of Sree Narayana Epoch*, p. 317.
73. *Torch Bearers*, C.R. Kesavan Vaidyar, p. 12.
74. *Narayana Guru*, Mannathu Padmanabhan, p. 337.
75. *The Striking thoughts of Sree Narayana Guru*, K. Golapan Thantri, pp. 54-5.
76 *Sree Narayana Guru Swamy*, K.R. Bhaskaran, p. 70.
77. *Sree Narayana Guru Swamy*, K. Damodaran, p. 60.
78. *The Cultural History of Kerala*, P.K. Gopalakrishnan, p. 529.
79. *The Majesty of Sree Narayana Epoch* (The path of the Guru), p. 14.
80. *Sree Narayana Guru Swamigal*, K.R. Bhaskaran, pp. 108-10.
81. *Ibid.*, pp. 108-10.

82. *The Majesty of Sree Narayana Epoch*, p. 168.
83. *Sree Narayana Guru Swamigal*, K.R. Bhaskaran, p. 148.
84. *Ibid.*, p. 143.
85. The Message of Sree Narayana Guru on the occasion of the '*Sammelan*' at Sivagiri. *The Platinum Jubilee Memorial Work*, p. 153.
86. *Platinum Jubilee Souvenir*, M.K. Narayanan, p. 164.
87. *Sree Narayana Guru Swamigal* . . . p. 191.
88. *The Cultural History of Kerala*, p. 550.
89. *Dharmam Magazine*, (Sivagiri) Medical Report, p. 213.
90. *Sree Narayana Guru Swamigal*, p. 20.
91. *Sree Narayana Guru*, Sankaran Karipayi, p. 128.
92. *Sree Narayana Guru Through Accounts*, Balarama Panicker.
93. *Malayala Manorama Century Special* (1988), p. 7.
94. *Ibid.*, p. 23.
95. *Ibid.*, p. 24.
96. *Kanaka Jubilee Memorial Work 1953*, Statement, p. 24.
97. *The Majesty of Sree Narayana Epoch*, Guru Nitya Chaitanya Yati, p. 288.
98. *Majesty of the Epoch*, Fr. T.K. Ravindran, p. 324.
99. *Sree Narayana Darsanam* (Vision), Swamy Dharmatheerdhar, p. 67.
100. *Dr. Palpu*, T.K. Madhavan, p. 98.
101. *Ibid.*, p. 99.
102 Sundaram Pillai was the father of P.S. Nataraja Pillai who was a Minister in the State Cabinet of Pattom Thanu Pillai.
103. *Dr. Palpu*, T.K. Madhavan, p. 29.
104. *Ibid.*, p. 30.
105. *The Kanaka Jubilee Memorial Work*, K.N. Prakasam, p. 185.
106. *Sree Narayana Guru, Biography*, Kotukoikal Velayudhan, p. 137.
107. *Indian Renaissance*, M.K. Kumaran, *Majesty of Epoch*, p. 177.
108. *The Cultural History of Kerala*, p. 545.
109. *Arattupuzha Velayudha Paniker*, P.O. Kunju Panicker, p. 232.
110. *At the Feet of the Guru*, C.R. Kesavan Vaidyar, p. 52.
111. The Presidental Address of Kottiyath Ramunni in the Third Anniversary Meeting of SNDP Yogam.
112. *Presidental Speeches*, The Presidental Speech of Asan, p. 145.

113. *The Presidental Speeches of the Anniversaries of SNDP Yogam*, K. Ayyappan, p. 151.
114. *Sree Narayana Guru, Biography*, Kotukoikal Velayudhan, p. 224.
115. *R. Sankar*, M.K. Kumaran.
116. *Ibid.*
117. *Ibid.*, p. 242.
118. *The Cultural History of Kerala*, p. 473.

# 2

# The Inner Currents of Spirituality

## Hymns to Gods

### I

### CURRENT OF SPIRITUALITY

MANY biographies of Sree Narayana Guru have come out in Malayalam, English, Hindi and other languages. But the Malayalam language had not been presented yet with an authentic study or annotation of his spirituality resplendent works, in a style simple enough to be intelligible to the common mind. Most of our biographers have not been able to detach themselves from the halo of Guru's spiritual and material eminence. To understand the inner core of the great sage's imposing individuality we will have to delve into the depths of his visionary creations dropped out of his opulent poetic imagination.

The intention in this humble attempt is to present a research based expanded exposition of the currents of thought running through the entire fabric of Gurudeva's works. The author however is not unaware of a mild challenge thrown up to his confidence by the daunting nature of the task he has undertaken. This is because to enable the ordinary people to grasp His meaning, Guru has clothed his poems in simple language, sweet syllables dexteriously aligned in perfect, magical rhythm. The author's task is to bring out the effulgent spiritual power curdled in, as well as permeating, them. Hence the susceptibility to doubt.

Nevertheless the author is also conscious of the reassurance available to him in adequate measure from Guru's ever present Grace. Hence the confidence to go ahead.

### Daivadaśakam

Non-dual vision, ancient India's gift to the world of thought, is acknowledged as the greatest among the philosophical concepts of mankind. Indian culture is a conglomerate of Vedic, Upaniṣadic and Purāṇic ideologies. The works expounding these ideologies are in the nature of hymns. Grasping their significance in full, man has in the light of the teaching in the Vedas and Upaniṣads, assigned sanctity to humanity in the modern age, by abjuring all religious animosities. So to suit the taste of all those prone to faith in one God it became necessary to compose a prayer of cosmopolitan character. Gurudeva's *Daivadaśakam* was the outcome of this need.

Sree Narayana Guru has literally taken for granted the love permeating all living beings. The secret of that life lies in the victory achieved through a silent struggle launched against the injustices and inequalities which pervaded society with ruthless aggressiveness. When that is understood, one will experience *Daivadaśakam* as a vision, hymn and science at the same time. Though there are several hymns in the *R̥gveda*, Gāyatrī alone is the song in praise of One God. It was only several centuries after the Vedic period that a universally acceptable, philosophically conceived hymn, akin to Gāyatrī came into existence. It is a fact that man finds well-being only through prayer. The universal prayer *Daivadaśakam* (ten stanzas) which starts with the invocation "O God, keep watch on us" and which leads to God realisation, actually confers *ānanda* or supreme happiness to the devotees. Here is the English translation of the poem followed by its commentary stanza-wise:

**1.** O God, as ever from there, keep watch on us here,<br>
Never letting go your hand!<br>
You are the great Captain<br>
And the mighty steamship on the ocean<br>
Of change and becoming is your foot.

2. Counting all here, one by one,
   When all things touched are done with
   Then the seeing eyė remains
   So the inner self in you attain rest.

3. Food clothes and all we need
   You give to us unceasingly,
   Ever saving us, seeing us well provided
   Such a one, You, are for us our only chief.

4. As ocean, wave, wind and depth
   Let us within see the scheme
   Of us, of nescience,
   Your glory and you.

5. You are creation, the creator,
   And the magical variety of created things
   Are you not O God,
   Even the substance of creation too!

6. You are Maya
   The agent thereof and the Enjoyer too:
   To grant the limitive State!

7. You are the Existant, the Subsistant and the
   Value factor supreme.
   You are the Present and the Past,
   And the Future is none else but you
   Even the spoken word, when we consider it, it but
   You alone.

8. Your state of glory that fills
   Both inside and outside
   We for ever praise!
   Victory be, O God, to You!

9. Victory to you! Great and Radiant one!
   Ever intent upon saving the needy!
   Victory to You, perceptual abode of joy!
   Ocean of Mercy, Hail!

**10.** In the ocean of Your Glory
Of Great profundity,
Let us all, together, become sunk
To dwell therein everlastingly in Happiness!
(Translation: Nataraja Guru)

COMMENTARY

**1.** O God, the one light which out-shines and stands atop all other lights, do not forsake us, encumbered as we are in worldly attachments, and stranded in the misery-filled *saṁsāra sāgara* (ocean of life). Just as the passengers in the ship cannot see its captain, so we cannot see You. Yet we may always be graced with Your blessings. As a matter of fact because of the intermingling of births and deaths, of joy and sorrow, our life is placed in a difficult state. You are the Great Captain, the God of the ship which carries us across this *saṁsāra sāgara*. It is not a ship which is guided by the wind. On the contrary You are its powerful Captain who leads, controls and guides it. As for that ship, it is but Your Lotus Feet. If sought refuge at those Feet, Chanting God's name, every devotee will undoubtedly receive protection. You take us across this ocean of life and bless us with permanent liberation from the cycle of births and deaths and grant us ultimate peace. You are embodiment of everything that is great and noble. You alone are the Almighty which guides us.

If for effacing sorrow and for realisation of self, devotion is the proper medicine; the devotee who has embraced complete renunciation, should first shed his ego and strive for God Realisation. Gurudeva depicts the world as misery-ridden *saṁsāra sāgara*, the devotee as the helpless being trapped in it, God as the mighty Captain who helps him across it and the Lotus Feet of the Lord as a steamship. These beautiful images which Guru's rich imagination has conjured up, are thought-provoking. Here the logic involved in treating God as a captain is rendered all the more sweet by the sheer appropriateness of the metaphor. Only a captain conversant with the sea route is competent to lead the ship sailing in mid-ocean along the correct route and ultimately to safety. So also only the

Omniscient God who knows all secrets of the Universe can lead the devotee struggling amid life's travails to the other side of *saṁsāra sāgara*. It is there that Gurudeva's analogy calls for deeper probe.

Just as the preceptor destroys the darkness of ignorance enveloping the disciple's self, so God liberates the devotee from the fear of *saṁsāra duḥkha* (worldly sorrows) benumbing him. The God who extends the kindness to free man from *saṁsāra duhkha* is the Lord of the World, *bhakta-priya* (Lover of the devotees) and the Great Guru.

To indicate one more fact here, may not be out of place. The word *pādam* (feet) Gurudeva has used here, has several meanings implicit in it such as feet, name, word, sense and *oṁkāram*. *Pādam* can be interpreted as feet or *pādam* as well as that the steamship is the Lord's Feet themselves. *Pādam* can also be taken to mean *nāmam* or name. Even those who cannot attain the Lord's Feet through the route prescribed in the scriptures, can reach God through the repeated utterance of His name. The meaning of *pādam* immediately understood is word. Your Feet (*nin pādam* in the original) can also be taken as Lord's command. The directives to enrich worldly life and to make it joyous are entrusted to us by God in the form of commands. Those commands are mutually interpretative. Finally, the word *pādam* can be extended to mean sense or meaning and *oṁkāram*. The very birth of the Universe is from *oṁkāra nādam* (sound). *Brahma pādam* or Final beatitude is nothing but the Great Illustrious Meaning. Thus the essence of the first stanza of this poem is that by identifying himself with the Great Meaning the *bhakta* (devotee) can claim eternal Bliss.

**2.** When we take one by one and analyse the things, we can see in this world first one, then another, and after that a third and so on in this manner classed one by one and each visible thing taken separately and observed — our eyes cease to function for a moment. It is because that the things already counted are again subjected to scrutiny that the eyes become still in that manner. This can be made clear with the aid of an example. Small children make bread and other things with sand, and play with them. When asked how many breads there are they will direct eyes towards the breads made. Their young eyes can be noticed as shifting gaze from one bread to another. When the counting is completed the vibrations of their eyes will also come to a stop. That stillness may not be lasting long. Yet it is a stillness surely, albeit momentary. From this one thing will be made clear. Counting of separate articles is naturally done one by one. It is also natural that while counting, the eyes switch from one to another; when all are counted out, because there is nothing else to count, the eyes naturally stop functioning. When viewed in the light of this fact it is at the Vedic level that our thoughts ascend. When probed deep into the knowledge gathered from visible objects, the visible objects would prove themselves to be mere symbols. By that time the eyes hovering over those objects would be withdrawn for a moment. With that the eyes seeing the reality of visible objects will discover that reality in themselves. Consequently these organs touch an infinitesimally short period of inactivity. The *bhakta*'s eyes which yearn to see God in all dead objects, when get convinced that God resides in none of them, will also derive the conviction that the eyes are *ātmā* itself which is still, which stillness only is reflected in the eyes. Thus through the stillness of the eyes the mind reaches God.

This may be made clear further. Human mind is restive and oscillating from one thought to another unceasingly. This proneness to movement is an artistic taste innate in human nature. Even bringing the mind to subjection and absolute concentration upon one activity, involves a sort of rich resoluteness. Yet when one's mind is subordinated to concentration the advantage reaped will be inestimable. If real concentration is to be achieved, the mind should be pinned down firmly on to a single goal, that is say, God. Once mind is rendered capable of merging itself in God, the door is open to everlasting happiness. But to get that door open God's Grace is the indispensable qualification.

Identification of articles is possible because of the sense-organs. If seeing an article creates the awareness that is not the one looked for, repeated search for the real one lands a seeker to the knowledge that *ātmā* alone is real, and, such a journey towards God will cause stillness of his eyes. Object is visibility, and sight the eyes. That is to say eye is visibility, and mind the perceiver. The eyes see large and small objects without being able to differentiate them. As a result the moment when knowledge of the inner core of *ātmā* propelled by discretionary perception dawns on the seeker, is also the moment when all the visible objects disappear and the eyes in stillness merge with *ātmā*. In short along with the eyes the *ātmā* also merges with God. In like manner O, Lord, bless me to fix my mind also in stillness in You.

**3.** You are our Saviour who gives us food, clothing and homes and other articles needed for our daily consumption, in the required measure punctually and without default, and thus protect us. In this manner you enable us to lead honourable lives. You alone are therefore our Master, O, Lord of all worlds!

It can be seen that even while Gurudeva was composing *Daivadaśakam*, the different sects in Hinduism namely Śaivaites, Vaisnavaites and Śāktheists were worshipping the Gods and Goddesses accepted in their respective faiths. Gurudeva who had denounced the multiplicity of Gods approved by the Hindus had however recognised the practice of each sect worshipping the deity adopted by it. As a result of that outlook of tolerance the Composing of *Daivadaśakam* enclosing in it the "One God for All" theory in a manner acceptable to all religions and communities, assumed meaningful significance. "Lord give us tomorrow also the bread thou giveth today." The truth echoing through this prayer of the followers of Christianity is worth remembering here. On the other hand, in this stanza of *Daivadaśakam*, it is not for giving food, but because of the inspiration derived from devotion to the giver of food that the Lord is praised.

God has also devised the means for our sustenance along with our birth. He puts them into operation through parents. He is interested fully in furnishing the food, required from time to time in accordance with the needs of the child's growth. It is because of this, that even when the child is able to stand on his own legs, and after that he pays attention to prepare the ground for his success in life. The Provider of our means to live, He is elevated to a formidable spot in human consciousness in the memorising of His name. Gurudeva has made this fact clear here. Because of this God stands above as the means giving Saviour.

Gurudeva has also included in this stanza an aspect brought out through implied meaning. There are two indispensable vital bases in human life. The instinct for experiencing the spontaneous freedom of *ātmā*, and the provisions for the body's growth. If food and clothing are not available, man's desire and the happiness therefrom will dissipate. Without food, life cannot be sustained; and without life, food is rendered redundant. So all living beings, because they thrive on food, the blessing of the Lord who provides it, is essential for existence. Gurudeva explains this in this stanza.

**4.** We who inhabit this world are like the ocean, the waves in it, the wind that generates them and the ocean deep. *Māyā* is akin to the wave and the greatness of God to the Wind, and God indecipherable like the depths of the ocean. O Lord give us the non-dual wisdom to enable us to get enlightened of this spiritual secret.

The ocean, waves, wind, the ocean's depths and we alike, and along with these, the mysterious *māyā*, the Lord's Grandeur and the Lord Himself should reside within me, O, the Supreme Being. In short I may be blessed with the awakening of the insight endemic in me that I am embodiment of everything that is. The knowledge that gleams in the *māyā* enamoured intelligence is individual in nature like the waves. But there is a truth which pervades equally in the individual and the entire whole (particular and general) of God's Power. Just as how the depth is symbolically reflected equally through the waves and the ocean, so is God existent in infinitesimally reflected manifestations in the entire universe. Guru has brought out with remarkable spiritual astuteness the above idea which exudes absolute metaphysical wisdom.

For a person who sees the ocean for the first time, what impresses upon his mind is the waves in it. He will go satisfied that he has seen the Ocean. It is water that makes up the ocean. The waves are congenital to it. Even while they ceaselessly come forward towards the shore one by one and smash themselves into death by hitting their heads against the sand, they do not remain isolated from the water. It follows that water is waves themselves and waves are water itself. It is in similar manner that the ocean is seen as analogous to the universe and the waves to *māyā*. But *māyā* is not visible to us. What is visible is only the individual. Individuals constitute society. But the prospects of the individual, his success or failure, do not constitute society's problem. As for the ocean, what countless waves arise and disappear! It is only a phenomenon there. Our relation with *māyā* is identical to that between the ocean and the waves. Thus Gurudeva has presented comprehensively the mutual relationship between society and the individual in this stanza.

As is known, it is when the wind blows that the waves rise in the ocean. Their force increases in accordance with the increase in the wind's force. This is in the very same proportion, as exists between *māyā* and God's Greatness. It is because of that greatness that *māyā* is born. In a sense wind and ocean are not separate. The earth and its atmosphere get hot because of the sun's heat. When the wind which has gathered heat rises skywards, the wind which has not, enters the space rendered vacant thereby. The land gets hot faster than water. But even in water, shallower areas are heated more quickly than the deeper ones. As the deeper one goes, the colder it will be. The atmospheric pressure will be more intense in those areas. That aggravates the force of the wind. As the wind flows abundantly towards that area in consequence it can be seen that its origin also is not anywhere else. The reason for the movement of the wind is also the depth of the ocean. Like that O, Lord, the power caused by Your Greatness becomes operative from You only.

**5.** Let us examine how the mysteries of the universe are explained in this stanza. You are God! the Omnipotent, Omnipresent, Omniscient God. Because you perform the great task of creation, You have become the Creator.When your Creations are thought of, wonderful secrets come to our minds, our hearts are full with bliss. By having created the universe You have become not only the Creator but the Instrument of creation too. In short, You are the

Creator, the Instrument of creation and the Creation as well. O Lord, it is none else who created all the moving and unmoving objects in this universe. Although there is diversity in the process of creation, the Creator, the God is a single entity. The pot which the potter has moulded and the picture to which the painter's imagination has given shape, are the means of creation. But they are seen as apart from their creators. On the other hand, the creations of God do not have their existence as separate from Him. That is why the glory in creation not within reach of the potter and the painter, is found in God's creations. The truth that the originator of everything that exists in this universe is God Himself, is known to us. At the same time God can also generate activity in everything, that the potter or painter or any other creator is unable to accomplish. It is there that God's Greatness is visible in its spectacular fullness.

O Lord, You are the Created, the Creator, the Known and Unknown objects in the universe created, and the instruments for creation. This great secret of the universe is beautifully presented here.

**6.** The universe is ephimeral. It is like a magical contrivance. But the separateness which exists between the art of magic and the magician himself is not manifest between God and His creations. O Lord, You are *māyā* and the *māyā* wielder, the adept in the art of magic who creates through *māyā*. That being so, we believe that you are the Almighty God who removes *māyā* and confers Salvation.

What the magician exhibits is a trick whereby the illusion of the existence of an object which in fact does not exist, is created. The world seen in dream is only the product of mind's imagination. The mind alone can enjoy it. Similarly the universe which is only the objectification of God's conception, is rooted in the sport He indulges in through His magical manipulations. The Lord is *māyā* itself. He is also the entertainer in *māyā*. Not only that, "You are at the same time the Saviour who rescues us from the incapacitating grip of the knot of *māyā* around us and blesses us with salvation."

*Māyā* renders life unhappy by projecting before the senses what is not real. But isolating Truth from untruth, and refuting that Truth as well, is also done through the instrumentality of *māyā*. It is a contraption to identify Truth from untruth. God is the One without a second, who is at once *māyā* and the enjoyer of *māyā*. In a word, Gurudeva makes it clear that the one who creates and destroys *māyā* and gives salvation to man through *māyā,* is God Himself.

This can be clarified a bit further. We experience happiness and sorrow at magical performances. But at the end of the performances the objects created thereby disappear into oblivion. In reality the magician creates non-existent objects. After sometime the objects he has created vanish. We do not then treat those objects as real. They engender in us a sense of unreality only. One thing becomes clear from this. The objects which did not exist before the magical act, and which ceased to exist after that, were also not in existence during the act. This universe itself is transient, like those things that appear and disappear in magic. Gurudeva imagines as a work of magic, this world which was not in the beginning, and which will not be in the end. The world (universe) is *māyā* (magic), *māyāvī* (the magician), the one who ends in *māyā* and destroys *māyā* and Guru who uncovers the Truth are all God. So Gurudeva explains here.

**7.** O the Most Merciful. You are the *sat* (absolute truth), so too are the past, present and future which subject life to transformations. Further you are even the word which we use for our salutation of You. O Lord, You are the unshakable, permanent, everlasting, and the Truth and everything else immanent in the universe. You are the knowledge which knows the truth. The bliss of knowledge is also no one else. The fountain of blissful experience that is *sachidānanda* (truth, awareness and bliss) is you alone. We are fully aware that You are what was, is and will be. Are you not even the very word with which we praise You. Word also means what is said or argued before a judge. It is also extended to many Vedas or hymns. So God, whatever word we say, is addressed to none else than You. In short to those thinking of You, You are Truth, You appear as *sat* or the essence, are known as *cit* or awareness, and experienced as joy. Gurudeva has indicated in this stanza that God is *sacidānanda*.

**8.** O Lord, You are the symbol of Omnipresent Greatness. We praise that Greatness. Victory to you O the Creator of the universe. If real knowledge is split into the Enjoyer of the senses (*viṣayī*) and the subject (*viṣaya*), He who resides in the temple (*kṣetrajña*) and the temple (*kṣetram*), the knower (*nijatavu*) and the known (*jñeyam*), the eye (*druck*) and what is seen (*dr̥śyam*), the consumer (*bhoktāvu*) and what is consumed (*bhoktam*), then the enjoyer of the senses, He who resides in the temple, the knower, the Eye, the Consumer are interpreted as internal and the Subject, the Temple, the Knower, what is seen and what is consumed as external. But *Jagad-Guru*, the author of the universe permeates in conceptual state, the entire space and time in radiant splendour without these differentiations. Your resplendent feet (*brahma-pāda*) we praise. May you be exalted in all glory. You are the Great Omnipresent one who fills the universe without distinction between the inner and outer, the above and below. We adore you in our praise of you. You are the origin of everything that is. May You victoriously lead the universe. O, the Saviour of the suffering!

**9.** O, the Source of all light — the self-shining Supreme Light, that alights all else — You are the benefactor of the victims of poverty and illness and other miseries, living in despair and desperation. Victory to you, O, the Omnipotent God! You who are the Giver of the honey drops of bliss through Knowledge, are Knowledge itself and Bliss Incarnate. The Ocean of Love and compassion that You are, may You don the crown of victory and emblazon the universe. You are the Almighty who liberates us from sorrow and desire; who blesses us with guidance to cross *saṁsāra-sāgara* (the ocean of worldly life). Victory to you, the Embodiment of knowledge and Bliss. Gurudeva, the very image of kindness has reminded us of the Lord's eternal power and compassion through his compositions *Jīvakāruṇyapañcakam*, and *Anukambadaśakam*, just to give expression to the Supreme Being's virtue of mercy. How boundless that mercy is, Guru successfully demonstrates in this stanza.

**10.** O Lord, we may be blessed to merge in totality in the mysterious, inestimably deep and vast ocean of Divine Grace and remain there forever in enduring bliss. Unfathomably deep, inexplicably mysterious, and enigmatically unresolvable is the expansive ocean of Divine Grace. Gurudeva is striking us down with wonder by picturing to us here the spectacular feats of the supreme architect. Even by the widest stretch of imagination, it is impossible to gauge the Almighty's eternal, marvellous might! At the same time even to get lost in that might is blissful in its impact. We pray that immersed as we are, in the inescapable tangled web of *saṁsāra* and struggling helplessly to tide over it, we may be led to its terminating end where to take in the nectar of ecstatic experience till the end of time.

The prayer *Daivadaśakam* commences with the portrayal of humanity as the children of suffering because of their being trapped in *saṁsāra-sāgara*. After that, God is drawn as the depth of a huge ocean, and we are presented as the waves on its surface. Then God is represented as an unsurveyable ocean of kindness, and we appear as the devotees who sing in praise of its incomparable Greatness. Finally we are conceived as stepping into the vast and deep expanse of Divine Grace, then attaining oneness with God by merging in Him.

By epitomising to tabloid dimensions, the great ideas enshrined in the Vedas and Epics thereby making explicit what successful life and salvation are, Guru has, through this prayer, brought to light in simple terms, His scheme of thoughts adumbrating man's taste for *karma* (action) and the passage which leads him to salvation. Happiness is only short-lived. When that is shattered, knowledge of self gets jolted. As a result, love and kindness resurrect. With that the way is paved for the blessing of God for attainment of lasting happiness.

## Vināyakāṣṭakam

Among the earlier poems of Sree Narayana Guru, *Vināyakāṣṭakam* written in Sanskrit has the pride of place. In it, Gurudeva has expressed a sense of oneness with the Absolute, the Supreme Truth about the creator of the universe, in symbolic language in a style enlivened by emotion, bliss and bewilderment. This short poem confined to eight stanzas brimming with spiritual beauty is in praise of Lord Gaṇapati. Like other great poets Gurudeva also commences his worship of poetry by extolling the mighty Vināyaka, who removes impediments which appear in the form of darkness and spreads the light of knowledge in its stead. For, He is Vighna Vināyaka, the Destroyer of all hurdles to human endeavour. Gurudeva has written only this poem dedicated to Vināyaka though the descriptions befit Śiva more than Vināyaka.

A summary of the Poem follows:

> O Lord Vināyaka, the son of Śiva-Śakti, You are the seat of all virtues. The Vedas emanated from you. You are the beauteous crescent moon on Your crown. You are the object of veneration by all Gods including Viṣṇu, and the very embodiment of the entire spiritual might of *ādi parāśakti* (the primeval Supreme Goddess). Your inherent state of solemnity emblazons the primordial power which is *sat-cit-ānanda*, you are the mighty One who keeps all human sorrows at bay and instates happiness in their stead. You are the very expression of magnanimity and the destroyer of all evils. You wear the garland of snakes around Your neck, the trident-shaped sacred ash mark on Your forehead. You are knowledge. You destroy all hurdles to human endeavour for the attainment of happiness and peace.
>
> You confirm that the union of Śiva and Śakti leads to the emergence of the universe. You happily give salvation to the devotees. You save them from the dangers they have perforce to encounter in their struggle to live.
>
> You are the incarnation of Truth objectified as the everlasting form of Bliss. You are the source of creation. You wield the ever vibrant trident, cut down all ties and annihilate egotism. You bless the enlightened with success. With your head, shaped as that of an elephant, You reveal Yourself in very resonance in the universe and illuminate the entire space and time with your in-dwelling incandescence.

O the supreme preceptor of the universe, the very solidification of Lord Śiva's love, the one God with the lotus face of the tusker adorned by the beautiful trunk, I prostrate at Your Feet in absolute surrender and supplication.

God is One although known by various names. That is the absolute truth. Whether in dew drops, or the tiny grass plant or the ant or the philosopher, the one power we witness is the power of God. The enlightened never long for worldly pleasures. Their aim is lasting bliss. It is Gananadha, the all-pervading God who is realised in the *ātmā* that they surrender to. Where there is a wish, there also opens up wide the thresholds of possibilities. This is an acknowledged truth. It is because Sree Narayana Guru is an undiluted non-dualist that he is transmitting to human hearts his visionary surmises through this eulogy of Lord Vighneśvara.

## Arivu (Knowledge)

Although the poem *Arivu* (containing fifteen stanzas) is written in simple Malayalam, it is rich in wisdom. One can edge one's way along the banks of those rivulets of ideas only if equipped with imaginative caution. Any thought of delving into their depths may not often yield desirable results. The idea contained in the poem is expressed in outline after the text.

1. This which is known, on reflection,
   Is Knowledge itself:
   And as Knowledge is one amongst it,
   Naught else but Knowledge is everywhere.

2. Sans Knowledge, exists not the reality of what's known:
   Still, if knowledge itself be wanting,
   What knowing could be there of what Knowledge is,
   What Knowledge is not?

3. Whatever's is known outside knowledge's measure,
   That too as Knowledge shines everywhere,
   As the fancy that Knowledge inheres.
   Is here turned into Knowledge.

4. If Knowledge be all-inclusive,
Where could Non-knowledge abide?
Where shall it here survive,
On knowing what Knowledge is?

5. By knowing no ill comes, that itself
Is Knowledge, but where shall it descend?
Knowledge is not known,
And when known both become one.

6. Prior to knowing, whatev'r it be,
Exists here nothing sans knowledge:
What bounds has to that beyond knowing?
Still no Knowledge is here to be seen.

7. We know and know not
Which is which that we here know;
Looking at us we cognise,
That though we know, that is not Knowledge.

8. This too was so from the day Knowledge was,
And where can this stand if Knowledge is there?
There is naught else from Knowledge
Except Knowledge, and then what exists?

9. For Knowledge there is haven none,
Else from its being known;
In this swelling counting of what is known,
Where is that which is Knowledge?

10. On that day unknown is aught,
Though there's that quite known and Knowledge;
In the rest of it is whichever unknown,
And then whence Knowledge comes?

11. It is as the Knowledge of Knowledge
Which informs, that we do become here:
When told what the categories of Knowledge,
How known and whichever art they.

12. Thou art Knowledge, that which is known,
Free of Your Own Knowledge;
And what is known is two-fold:
One that knows and the other knowing not.

13. Knowledge too likewise goes to the knower,
Transformed and is again known;
One amongst it, split five-fold,
By Knowledge's spark comes to be known.

14. If it's that one knows he knows
And knows that it is Knowledge,
To the knower of one knowledge,
In working one includes six and eight.

15. Corresponding to what's known,
That Knowledge to seven plus one make eight;
Split up thus, Knowledge too
Will separately be known.

(Translation: Nataraja Guru)

COMMENTARY

The universe is the very embodiment of knowledge. There is nothing but knowledge in it. This world is the subject of knowledge. At the same time it is not apart from knowledge. For the thinker the world is a heap of knowledge. There is only one spiritual essence in the universe and that is Knowledge and Knowledge alone. By stretching one's thoughts a bit further on, one would find that Knowledge is Truth. What is contained in Knowledge is the known world alone. If there is no Knowledge? Even the known will not be available. That is why those enlightened by the scriptures say that the world does not exist in reality and that the feeling that it exists is engendered by *māyā* or illusion. One may recall here the very same idea Gurudeva has given expression to in his *Jananīnavaratna Mañjarī* and other compositions.

The world which draws sustenance from knowledge is not separate from it. Even when that belief prevails, if there is no proper

Knowledge of it, what is felt as real will be rendered unreal. That is to say that when one admits having no knowledge, what emerges is the knowledge that there is no Knowledge. But that kind of knowledge is free. Whereas the world which has knowledge as its substratum, is unfree. In those who have attained complete spiritual consciousness knowledge sparkles in glory.

Knowledge which cannot be fathomed, remains as real knowledge. Its state is akin to the knowledge which the dream arising out of knowledge is transmuted into. Because the dream world seen in sleep is just a deflection of knowledge, it merges back into knowledge itself. In short, the dream that emerges from knowledge is also knowledge only. It too is absorbed in knowledge. It is like this that the objects seen in this world, sink into oblivion in knowledge.

Knowledge has the attribute of comprehensiveness. It is Omnipresent too. As such where is the space for that bereft of knowledge, for its niche? The knowledge resulting from authentic deliberation on a subject is consummated into real knowledge. Which means knowledge and the subject known become one.

Knowledge is the corpus of nourishment for the world. That experience of the world exists as a conscious one. (Absorbed into the universe). But where does this universe get absorbed into? When truth is realised it is not possible for that knowledge to comprehend knowledge in its fulness. Because knowledge and the object known coalesce and acquire a single identity.

If it is examined what exists prior to knowledge, it will be clear that it is nothing else but knowledge. That is, the charming feature of knowledge is knowledge itself. As such, supposing it is known that ignorance is want of knowledge? No, there is nothing in this world to be regarded as wanting in knowledge.

We are unable to categorise specifically the measure of greatness inherent in the objects of the universe as known and not known. The seers do not recognise the knowledge as known knowledge.

To accept knowledge as that which recognises knowledge as

self-radiant may be fallacious. So to conceive of a state of no knowledge is to acquire knowledge of knowledgelessness. What enters our mind may not be perfect knowledge. Real Knowledge, if known as not knowledge will be no knowledge at all.

The universe has always co-existed contemporaneously with knowledge, never independent of and separate from it. Knowledge is without beginning or end. Knowledge alone is perpetual. It is without an equal, and above everything else. So as the universe is ensconced in knowledge.

Although the objects known are legion, Knowledge is one only, a single indivisible entity. Therefore all that is known is not Knowledge. Knowledge that exists as one alone is real Knowledge.

We never know anything even if we exhaust ourselves by relentless search. If it is what is known? It will submerge in Knowledge. But what is it that is not susceptible to be known in the universe? Even though Knowledge is undisputed, wherefrom does it reach us?

What exists as the Knowledge of all Knowledge, the source (the informer) and we, are all one. But it is impossible to say to which category does that kind of Knowledge belong. To understand how it came about is also difficult.

You are Knowledge, you yourself. It can be stated in two ways, viz., that it is your Knowledge and that you know it because of your Knowledge. Similarly what is known is of two categories, viz., that it is known and that it is not known. That is the mysterious characteristic of Knowledge.

The one who is the genuine knower is in possession of knowledge. That knowledge consciously reaches the knower as well. Then a spark from what is known fell and rose in five tongues (the five sense-organs are the five tongues the spark of knowledge has forked into).

He who knows will become conscious that he has Knowledge. He who knows that he has Knowledge will also receive that consciousness. Therefore three instruments emerge namely,

Knowledge, the person who knows and the object that is Known. Looked at from here, when with the five senses and Knowledge are joined, the knower and what is known, the power of Knowledge will be seen to open from its substance into eight petals.

Inclusive of what is known and the self, Knowledge has eight countenances. In that light when Knowledge and what is known are subjected to analytical evaluation, it will be seen that they shift in implications one by one. From this Knowledge alone will reveal itself as Truth. The world that is known will then become one with Knowledge.

Thus Gurudeva makes it clear in this poem that there is nothing in this universe other than Knowledge. This is accomplished in the halo of spirituality, alien to temporal attachments, and with the risk of engendering the dreariness of repetition. Yet Gurudeva crowns himself with success through the application of his ingenious artifice for fraying as it were, into the unexcelled reaches of Knowledge to impart its exceptional glory to His followers.

## Anukampadaśakam (Scriptures of Mercy)

This is a poem in ten stanzas. Its theme is kindness. Compassion, grace or mercy and love. The central current which runs through this small piece is premissed on these sentiments. It is a direct prayer to the Almighty. Here is the text of the poem followed by the summary:

1. Give to my core, O Compassionate One,
   Mercy, which brooks no harm
   Even to an ant, and thought that stays not
   Afar from Thy holy presence.

2. Grace brings, delight and from a bosom
   Bereft of love disasters galore come;
   Darkness ousts love, acts as sorrow's core,
   And is seed to every ill thing.

3. Grace, Love and Mercy — the Trio
   Have the same basis, which is life's staff

"A living thing is One who loves." Always repeat
This nine-syllabled message.

4. Bereft of Grace, One is nothing
But a stinking carcass of bone, skin and vein;
Such one is, like a stream in desert, lost,
A fragrant flower sans fruit.

5. In six phase do emotions manifest,
And wisdom equal to this does not confront now
In good name's from Mercy survives
Even after leaving the human form.

6. Who this merciful one be? The Reality
That after telling the Truth drives the chariot?
Or compassion's earth and ocean? or Guru
In simple, non-dual way expounds?

7. Is He God in man's form or the Law
Incarnate in divine human guise,
Or the Sacred Son of the Supreme God,
Or Compassionate Nabi, pearl and gem in one?

8. Is he that deity who with holy ashes
Curd fever and wonders worked of yore?
Or the Realised Soul, distressed by illness.
Slaked his ventral ague by song?

9. Or that great sage by writing Hara
Managed to illustrate a scripture sublime;
Or the Value Conscious devotee of the Supreme
Who, his body intact, ascended Heaven?

10. Is it the all giving Kamadhenu
Stalking this earth in human form?
Or is the one endowed with Mercy
That wondrous gift-tree of Heaven supreme?

Envoi

The meaning that the sacred scriptures give,

The meaning Guru tells and the Sage teaches:
All to the same kind belong, and same too
Is the essence of all wisdom words.
(Translation: Nataraja Guru)

COMMENTARY

The poem runs as a direct prayer to the Almighty in the following form:

O the Ocean of Mercy, such compassion and kindness as do not brook any harm even to an ant and which do not stray away from that Mind, I beseech thee that it be vouchsafed to me.

When thought of God and mercy combine what glorious power results from that union?

When kindness caused bliss and cruelty disaster, it may be ignorance that keeps kindness away. Real knowledge leads man to kindness and contentment.

Grace, Love and kindness when subjected to analysis, it will not be difficult to discover that their basic factor is one. They help man to reach the farther end of *saṁsāra-sāgara*. "He who loves is the one who really lives." Repeat these nine syllables perpetually, abjuring all other charming verbiage.

Man not blessed with the gift of Grace is but a body of bones, skin and tissues, emitting foul stench. He is like water disappearing in desert sand and the barren fruit, smell-less flower of the jungle. A man's life bereft of Grace is without meaning.

For every object passions usually arise in six phases like passions rooted in creation, decline and extinction. None of them touches sympathy. Conversely what is real is Knowledge. A sympathetic person even after his departure from this world leaves his reputation behind, unscathed for ever.

The real dispenser of sympathy or Mercy is the Almighty Himself, Lord Kr̥ṣṇa, the Deliverer of the message of *Gītā*. Or is it Śibi, the seat of endurance and love for fellow beings? Or again is it Śaṅkarācārya, the celebrated exponent of the non-dualistic creed.

Gurudeva also indicates that the really merciful can be Lord Kṛṣṇa or Prophet Muhammed or Christ.

God in human form may be regarded as the source of mercy; or it may be *dharma* or righteousness in human form. Who are Christ, the embodiment of love and Prophet Muhammed, the incarnation of sympathy, but personifications of Mercy?

Is it that those great souls who are blessed with divinity and those who have thralled the world with miracles who are known as Merciful? Or is it those who have cured human pains by singing in praise of Lord Śiva?

Who was the really Merciful? Was it the great sage Agastya who went about singing in sweet melody the Holy Script whose authorship belongs to Lord Hara? Or was it Nandanar, the peerless Śiva devotee privileged to be elevated to paradise in his earthly physique? All those illustrious souls unexcelled in perfect knowledge and unadulterated in devotion to the Lord, are incarnations of Mercy.

Who is the Merciful in truth? Is he the Kāmadhenu, the all bountiful, treading the earth in human form? Or is it that wonder tree of the world of celestials, the *devadāru* which bestows gifts in abundance to one and all?

That the essence of the Vedas, the word of Guru and message of Sages constitute real wisdom, is beyond doubt. In short everything coalesces into Mercy. Where there is mercy there is also humanity and human greatness. That echoes the spiritual message.

It is established in this piece that he who leads a life of piety without causing injury even to an ant, believes that it is not necessary to hunt for happiness anywhere else and considers the extinction of the physical form as not meaning the termination of the form of reputation. The seeker can find in *Anukampadaśakam*, the great ideals and pure dispositions of Sree Narayana Guru. Swamy conveys the message that all human beings should imbibe the virtue of Grace, Love and Mercy and that will be instrumental in bringing about life's success.

**Jīvakāruṇyapañcakam (Kindness to Life)**

This poem of five stanzas proceeds with an affirmation of the sanctity of all living things. It is also a theme on non-violence. Here is the text of the poem followed by its summary:

1. Shouldn't it be avowed
That all are part of one vital fraternity?
How then take life unmindful of it.
And with pity least eat living things?

2. The vow not to kill is best
And nobler still is the vow not to eat:
Musing on it, O righteous ones, shouldn't we admit
That this forms the essence of religions all?

3. If it is you that kill, it please you,
But whom will that fate delight?
Shouldn't it be declared, ye wise ones,
Justice same to all should exist?

4. There would be killer none,
If one kills, and himself alone has to eat:
A bigger sin than killing is to eat
And thereby making another kill.

5. He is a man good who doesn't kill;
Else to brute he is equal:
Refuge none the killer has,
Though other goodness in full he has.
(Translation: Nataraja Guru)

COMMENTARY

Like *Anukampadaśakam*, (Scriptures of Mercy) which lays stress on the virtue of Mercy, this composition also focuses on the need for compassion on the part of man for living beings. Here is its substance:

In a sense, all beings belong to one fraternity. As such how can one think of killing them and swallowing their flesh? The very thought is detestable.

If the vow not to kill the beings is noble, how much nobler is the observance not to eat their flesh. Upon deeper contemplation will it not become clear that the very essence of all religions is the insistence on such mercy? Is it not the same thing, that the followers of all religions have said?

No one relishes being killed. Hence the very idea of being killed is unthinkable. O, great learned men, just ponder upon this virtue embossed concept, and decide whether it is not worth adopting. The fear of death is endemic in everyone. No one is prepared to die of his own accord. Nevertheless such uncalled for deaths occur during certain unavoidable situations. There lies the mystery of the world of *māyā*.

When there is no one to eat, then there will be nobody to kill. If there is no one to eat, the killer himself should eat his kill. To abet killing is a much greater sin than eating. It is the person who is an accomplice to the act of killing who deserves greater punishment than the actual killer.

The killer is ruled by animal instinct. Therefore he persists with his cruel pursuit. It is made clear here that he who does not kill is virtuous and he who kills is animal in human form. Even if one has numerous virtues to boast of, if one attempts the cruel deed of killing, he should be branded as a monster.

The one spiritual thread that runs through the inner fabric of *Jīvakāruṇyapañcakam* is but the substance of Advaita Vedānta (Non-dual wisdom) that You and I are not two, but one.

## Ahiṁsā (Non-violence)

In this composition of ten lines, Sree Narayana Guru makes it clear how Lord Buddha's *ahiṁsā* theory (Theory of Non-violence) when put into practice, serves to be an essential ingredient to a successful life. While bringing out the greatness of *ahiṁsā*, Guru not only records emphatically his views about *ahiṁsā*, but also sets us thinking on its ramifications.

Here is a summary of the poem:

The person who kills and eats the harmless dumb animals which do nothing but good to society, will never be blessed with happiness in this life. Nor will he attain salvation after death. A kind-hearted person who does not catch these harmless beings, tie them down and mercilessly down the sword on them, will be elevated to the world of eternal happiness and peace. There will be purity in the nobility of thought, action, and wisdom of that person who does not kill with premeditated intention. Along with that he will attain fulfilment. It is impossible for a lover of meat diet not to kill animals. Is not killing sinful? Why commit such sin deliberately for the satisfaction of a selfish craze? Therefore the ideal path for man is to give up meat eating, and draw away from sin. It is possible for a person to feel aversion for meat if he ponders over how that meat reaches him. To kill animals by torturing them and inflicting death on them through slow painful process, does not at all become humanity. If it is given due thought, one will be convinced that to kill is criminal, and therefore it is only conducive to human mercy to abandon being a carnivore. The seeker will be able to grasp comprehensively Guru's considered views on the theory of *ahiṁsā* in this composition.

## Bhāryā Dharmam (Wifely Virtues)

This poem has special significance in that, it deals with the oriental conception of an ideal wife and how she shapes the fortunes of her household.

A brief summary of this poem follows:

She who possesses the virtues befitting a housewife, spends not more than her income. That lays foundation for an ideal life. Otherwise the lady of the house, however rich she is in other adorable qualities, cannot subscribe to the family's well-being. She will in consequence be a misfit. Every housewife should bear in mind that it is the virtues in her that bring lasting comfort, happiness and contentment in the family. If she is good and chaste, she will be the luminous radiance. Chastity of the housewife is the fountain spring of the family's welfare and felicity, which implacably grow step by step, day by day. The pious woman wakes early in the morning, offers prayers to God in bed itself, and then humbly salutes her husband before starting on her household chores. If such a lady prays for rain, it will come down in torrents. That is the power of chastity. A real lady is one who will have the courage of her ideals. Such a one protects not only herself but also the good name and fame of her spouse. She alone deserves the title of ladyship. It is absolutely essential that young ladies confining their activities within the house interiors should observe chastity with unflinching resolution. That will enable her to stand four square against all encroachments on her virtue. Wives who pay respects to their husbands and lavish extra love and munificence upon them, receive in return blessings which hold out divine bliss for them. An unvirtuous woman causes disaster for the family and for herself. The woman's goodness implies prosperity of the family. Her offspring will be an embodiment of benevolence.

**Sadācāram (Good Customs)**

Birth as a human being is a rare privilege. Without trying to understand what that is, without grasping its significance, it would be inflicting irreparable damage to life itself if one looks down on life. Therefore what is required is to discover ways and means to cut the proper path for life, and to initiate moves accordingly for its success. This is what Guru has to offer through his poem *Sadācāram*. It is a short poem in eight lines. Its main idea is summarised here:

> If any one tries to ignore or hide whatever has been done by an individual, for the good of the society, that is not at all

justifiable. On the contrary, the ideal procedure is to highlight them. Such undesirable predisposition to befog a good deed and obscure its potential is not at all justifiable.

This universe is predicated on Truth; *dharma* prevails and Truth smiles. Never commit *adharma* and allow untruth to have the upper hand. They may hold the fort for a short while. But truth and *dharma* will have the final say.

The water meant for paddy will often serve weeds as well. But if the water heading for paddy is diverted along other channels, it will be rocks which it reaches to. Supposing some good is done to an individual. It is possible that a portion of what is so done may benefit other individuals too. But if any one hampers the performance of a good deed, it will end up without being beneficial to any one.

Good-minded people will only endeavour to benefit by the name, fame and pedigree they have inherited and not discard them. But bad-minded people will be averse to that kind of approach. While the good people may be philosophically inclined, the bad ones can only cause harm to others thus rendering their existence meaningless.

**Dhathapaharam (Plunder)**

Sree Narayana Guru had a bitter experience of plunder which had given him a mild mental pain. Alumootil Channar (a rich aristocrat in Central Travancore) had through a will transferred the title to a building and its compound he owned in Madras to Guru's name. But after Channar's death, his heirs got the will nullified through Court. Guru's feelings, when He came to know of it, though trifling, galvanised themselves into this small piece titled *Dhathapaharam*. A short poem of six lines, its main idea is as follows:

> There is one thing in this universe that stands in agreement with Truth and Righteousness. But that thing is not real; it is illusion or *māyā*. Taking that fact into His reckoning what Gurudeva enjoins is that man should follow the paths

of Truth and Righteousness. Life is transient, and life's duration still more transient. They do not exist for ever. Therefore what man should aspire for is to preserve Truth and Righteousness and to desire for their final merger with the Ultimate Truth.

Whether it is property or wealth, once it is given should not be taken back. That is unethical. It is ruinous not only to the perpetrator of the act but to his family also. Perhaps this may be citing a proverb. Nevertheless it is true. How poor is the person who takes back what has been given for a good cause and thus satisfies his selfish end! In fact, a poorer person than he may not be traceable anywhere in the world. His mind should aptly be referred to as mean or leprosy stricken. To put it precisely, the man who commits such plunder, whoever he may be, will be visited upon by poverty during his lifetime itself. Undoubtedly.

### Jāti Nirṇayam (A Critique of Caste)

In this poem of twelve lines, Guru anatomises the caste structure and declares how irrational it is, as also how antagonistic of the intrinsic physical homogeneity of the human species. Here He establishes His point with absolute logical assurance. Here is the English version of the poem.

1. Man's humanity marks out the human kind
Even as bovinity proclaims a cow.
Brahminhood and such are not thus-wise;
None do see this truth, alas!

2. One kind, One of faith, and one God in man;
Of one womb, of one form; difference herein none.

3. Within a species, is it not, that offspring truly breed?
The Community of man thus viewed, to a single caste belongs.

4. Of the human species is even a Brahmin born, as is the

Pariah too,
Where is difference then in caste as between man and man?

5. In bygone days of a Pariah Woman the great sage Parasara was born,
As even he of Vedic-aphorism fame of a virgin of the fisher-folk.

(Translation: Nataraja Guru)

COMMENTARY

While His thoughts were running through the man-made cruel caste set-up, what suddenly shot into Gurudeva's memory was the *Manişa Pañcakam* of Śrī Śaṅkarācārya. One day when the Ācārya was returning with the disciples after bath in the Gaṅgā, a Cāṇḍāla (a low caste Hindu) came towards him. His disciples produced the usual '*Hoy, Hoy*' sound requiring him to divert his course to the way side of the Ācārya's path. Then that erudite Cāṇḍāla asked Śaṅkarācārya certain relevant questions based on his (the Ācārya's) *Advaita Siddhānta*. The Ācārya was unable to give proper answers to these questions. The Cāṇḍāla's queries can be epitomised as follows:

> O Great Sage, is it body from body or *ātmā* from *ātmā* that you are endeavouring to isolate to the wayside by this cry of *Hoy*? What is the criterion to decide whether an individual is Brāhmaṇa or Cāṇḍāla? What is the difference between the Sun's images reflected in the waters of the Gaṅgā and in those in the Pariah street, or between the sky reflected through water in a golden pot and that in a clay pot? Whether it is Cāṇḍāla or Brāhmaṇa, in whoever is stirred the consciousness that the wisdom (knowledge) which blossoms out of intuition, and which transfuses the entire gamut of life ranging right from Lord Brahmā to the tiny ant in the lowest stratum, is he himself ('I am') — if such a consciousness is inbred in a person, who else is he but a Guru? Is he not Guru himself who has confirmed wisdom in the pleasant, ever pure and blissful substance, whether

> he is Cāṇḍāla or Brāhmaṇa? Is not that great soul Guru who is worshipped by those, who, based on the knowledge that the universe is transient, meditate constantly upon the brāhmaṇa, incinerates the ill deeds of the past, present and the future in the fire of wisdom, and dedicates his own body to the rituals enjoined upon by the scriptures? That great *yogī* who meditates upon the effulgence matching the brilliance of Sun shaded by the clouds — is he not Guru himself? *Hey* Śaṅkarācārya, can you deny that he is Guru who having become one with eternal bliss, has not only become *brahmanical* (knower of *Brahman*), but *Brahman* Himself, worthy of being bowed to even by Devendra, whoever He is?

Unable to give proper answers to the posers of the learned Cāṇḍāla, the Ācārya gratified himself by accepting the intruder as his Guru. Similarly, Sree Narayana Guru who was convinced of the unsoundness of the logic behind the man-made caste, had, through his piece *Jāti Nirṇayam* set the stage for the creation of a new social order. How this was accomplished, we may now examine.

This small poem is an ideal example of how a Guru, who is a meditative *karmayogī* (one who acts without desire), and an enlightened visionary, evaluates a subject totally embroiled in social customs, and premissed on obligatory fulfilments. The poem contains the following idea, rooted in the ensuing four lines:

> Man's humanity marks out the human kind
> Even as bovinity proclaims a cow.
> Brahminhood and such are not thus-wise;
> None do see this truth, alas!

What bovinity is for the cows, so is humanness for the human beings. In the light of this reality, sub-sections like brāhmins do not at all exist. But this indubitable truth no one recognises.

The concept of caste differences which thrives in society as a heritage, had taken shape in the Sanskrit language. It may be because of this that Guru starts the poem *Jāti Nirṇayam* in

Sanskrit. The myth upon which the origin of caste rests, is the child of *cāturvarṇya*. It was because of the illusory distinction between brāhmin, Pariah and so on, that caste sprung out as part of the social code. All human beings belong to a single caste. Only the impression of the diversity of caste within caste had been created because of the diversities and inconsistencies prevalent in the social arrangement. Historical, social and economic factors may have contributed to the emergence of the intricate caste system. But there is nothing to justify its survival through the ages. At the same time any sort of custom or practice can only point to the indisputable, incontrovertible reality that the human race is of a single caste.

The line of argument tied on bovinity is not only logical but scientific too. The path of wisdom which stands to reason, is built upon foundations of being. It was as a consequence of the integration of the conceptual factor having their roots in the Ārya-Draviḍa cultural backdrops that the caste structure revolting against reason or rhyme, had assumed form here. Sree Narayana Guru has by accepting the spiritual Yogic reasoning as the criterion, exposed that untenability, and restated the concept in its entirety. To pluck away from the human mind those erroneous theories about caste which have found their abode there through misinterpretations and arm twisting tactics, and thus to adopt the reasonable theory formulated to suit the requirements of the age, is what Gurudeva is exhorting here.

The one ideal which man can reliably accept and adopt in social life is the ideal of "one caste, one religion, one God". This ideal has been accepted unanimously by the adherents of diverse religions. The universally acknowledged visionary's finding can be accepted as the guiding wand to life's triumphant goal. All people are born in the same womb. All have the same form. There is absolutely no difference between them.

Gurudeva who proclaims the supreme identity among the entire human race premissing himself upon the zones of humanness —of spiritual essence and wisdom—, is examining the social values in the light of the *yoga*, science and spiritual enlightenment. Although there may be conspicuous dissimilarities between individuals, humanity has on the whole, only one concrete, visible form. Inherited deviations form the general pattern, often cause evolutionary transformations. Yet the caste that is seen among humanity is based on the inherited occupations for livelihood. But there is absolutely no ground to decide caste based on occupation. Therefore all human beings are equals in society. As to the aberrations of the stratification of people into castes, they are the fabrications of selfish people, imposed by them upon the defenceless, through their muscle power to serve their own vested interests.

Looking at one caste basis, man belongs to a single indivisible group. It is the fundamental belief held out by all religions. It may be called God or Faith, but the basic value is the same. That procreation is possible only by the same species, cannot be disputed. From that it is clear that all human beings belong to the same caste. Worth quoting here is Kumaran Asan's famous question: "Is the Cāṇḍālī woman's body barren ground for the brāhmin's semen to go waste?" Religion is an institution which regulates man's social relations. Its basic function is to fulfil social and individual obligations. For historical reasons religion may acquire a special status. But when religion is seen separate from that status, its function can be seen to conform to the pattern outlined above. Religion which guides and regulates society provides simple happiness to mankind. So in the context of such inevitable inter-connection between man and religion, the irresistible conclusion that progenies arise only from the same species, follows.

Both brāhmins and Pariahs are born of the human species. Does any one have any doubt thereon? If so the reason is not far to seek. It is the sorbid tendency to keep human beings isolated from each other on the flimsy pretext of the prevailing social and religious incompatibilities. At times circumstances of life may be responsible. Though physical appearances may vary, there is no difference between brāhmins and Pariahs in respect of their mental equipments. In both what projects itself is the one fundamental attribute namely, the human core, though there might be divergences in their individual characteristics.

Even though Śaṅkarācārya was through his *Maniṣa Pañcakam*, constrained to accept Cāṇḍāla as his Guru, in his annotation of *Brahmasūtra* and *Bhagavad Gītā*, he had recognised the caste set-up endorsed in those scriptural texts. He had effected only a mild and vague questioning of the śūdras' right to study the Vedas. On the other hand, he had divested the Pariahs, even of the menial status of servant at the lowest stratum of the vast structure he built up upon the bottom floor of the social organisation. So by deliberately manoeuvring the Pariah's isolation from the brāhmin, Śaṅkarācārya was taking the role of accessory to the malignant project to glorify *savarṇa* supremacy and thus whittle down the *avarṇa* sections. In spite of the truth that all human beings are of the same caste, the distance between the brāhmins and the Pariahs persists.

Having discussed the dialectics of caste in all its conceivable material ramifications and theoretical inconsistencies, Sree Narayana Guru proceeds to substantiate His theory from the stand-point of historical evidence. As for example it is the case of two great spiritual personalities with unquestionable and unmatched excellence in *yoga* backed Vedic and philosophic wisdom, that He has cited. Sage Parāśara was the father of Veda-Vyāsa who compiled the epic *Mahābhārata*, enclosing in it, one of the most authentic philosophical works, the *Bhagavad Gītā*. The history of that Veda-Vyāsa, the codifier of the Vedas, is ample testimony to the meaninglessness of caste. Sree Narayana Guru makes it clear that Brāhmaṇahood is not the one reached through tastes and inclinations cultivated through inheritance. On the contrary, he is *Brahman* who identifies, knows and realises *Brahmam*.

Veda-Vyāsa, who assimilated the Vedic essence and presented it as sutras, was the outcome of the union of Sage Parāśara with Matsyagandhi, a consorted low caste woman. So the historical background of this great sage clearly weakens the case for *savarṇa* supremacy so emphatically held out by its proponents. He was not born in the brāhmin class. Gurudeva's exposure of the truth that he was not a brahmin, carries considerable implications. He was born in the lower community, a much abused, misunderstood and oppressed section of the human race. The brāhmin accepting a Pariah as *guru*, and giving recognition as brāhmin is a tale abounding in gross contradictions. Gurudeva surmises convincingly and conclusively that, in the light of that tale the concept of caste already proved as untenable, and built in the mask of superstitions, and along with it, the blatant inequalities sanctioned by it, should be exterminated from society. He achieves this in his poem *Jāti Nirṇayam* effectively.

About *cāturvarṇya*, the age-old system of social stratification then in vogue throughout, mention is made in the *Gītā* through the following declaration of the Lord:

> I have created *cāturvarṇya* based on the inherent internal attributes and action proneness of each individual. You may comprehend me as its creator as well as its cosmic non-creator.

This is the substance of the above declaration:

> The author of *Cāturvarṇya* is the Lord Himself. But he is also not its author at the same time. The sharp sighted should see this contradiction clearly. This is the time to rectify this anomalous division of the social animal on the ground of his occupation. If the author of the *Gītā* had a vague value reappraisal in view, Sree Narayana Guru is evaluating that reappraisal from a well defined and clear-cut angle. Human stock is one single whole. It is not susceptible to bifurcation on caste basis. Not all levels of social and intellectual existence are amenable to diversification. Even on subjective considerations, caste is bereft of sense; its survival unscientific too to boot.

## Jāti Lakṣaṇam (Caste Mark)

Does any one have a congenital mark to signify his caste? The question itself is silly and meaningless to warrant an answer. In this poem of twenty lines however, Guru deals with the question in all seriousness although with a hidden touch of sarcasm. Here is the idea contained in the poem:

All people, whether born by copulation with embrace or without embrace, come without exception, not under different species, but under a single one with identical physique and voice. Hence what are to be taken cognisance of, are just three things only, viz., name, place and occupation. This being so, Gurudeva points out that since identity is revealed by the body itself, special mention of it is rendered redundant. Gurudeva clarifies through this piece that just as distinction between male and female is made, so it is possible to identify all varieties in similar manner, that the materials that could be gathered in respect of all varieties would form an ocean of knowledge, and that by reminding oneself that one's categorisation is the work of the wisdom which is the creator Himself, one should be able to realise that they would continue to be subject to transmutations and that without diversity nothing can be permanent. This clarification is much beneficial to the future generations. *Jāti Lakṣaṇam* or the mark of caste has to be explained further. The first to question the justification for caste was Lord Buddha. The basic tenet of Buddhism namely castelessness proved to be the target upon which the axe raised by the Hindu revivalists under Śaṅkarācārya's supervision, was to fall. But Sree Narayana Guru was the one preceptor to have exposed the illusory premises of the caste arrangement.

Since procreation results from the mating of man and woman, it points specifically to a single caste. Children are born because the oats are sown consequent on their mutual embrace and copulation. Man and woman belong to the same species. Those which do not embrace and copulate are not of one species. Pairs are of identical class or group only. For each group or species, sound, smell, taste, temperature, both high and low, and shape of the body conform to the same pattern. Hence it is not difficult to recognise those belonging to the same class. To distinguish each individual from identical groups, there are certain common features. Those in possession of such common features can be understood as belonging to a single group. Why should the caste of a new acquaintance be enquired into? By seeking the name, place and occupation of a person, it should be easy to determine his caste. After that, it is unnecessary to ask him to reveal his caste. "If by sight the caste cannot be known, how can it be found out from word?" So Guru is on record to have asked an inquirer. That was why he had laid down: "Ask not, say not, think not caste." The body coming under a single group itself discloses its caste. So persons who have the intellectual powers and capabilities to perceive, do not ask for the caste. Some people who think that to disclose their caste, is below their dignity, do not hesitate to lie about it. No caste has any denigrating quality. It is a known truth that all are of the same caste. That being so, the inferiority complex in the name of caste is unwarranted. Just as there are specific marks to distinguish between male and female, so there are symptoms to know the class. By the same token the race can also be marked out. If human beings have caste, Gurudeva asserts that it is male and female only.

All those groups which rise from the ocean of wisdom have the variety of water as their soul waves. Each one is itself as its base. (Variety is the water in the Ocean of wisdom. Each one is itself as its base). Deeper thought will reveal that the material that is moulded out by the wisdom of creation is the variety. (As is known creation is a non-stop process. As such new varieties may also arise). In short, it is the crucible of the smith that is wisdom. It is because every group is described as with such and such features, that the nomenclature of variety has come into being. But for the existence of variety, there would have been no identification process of anything at all. From this, Gurudeva is able to substantiate His stand that the specification and attributes of caste conjured up among human beings, is illogical.

## Criticism of the Poems

Compiled as a common prayer for the followers of all religions is Guru's *Daśakam*. It is the most outstanding of his poems. The following stanzas of this poem written with the objective of assigning primacy to sense values of the spiritual aspect, are competent to bring out the beauty of import enshrined in it:

Food, clothes and all else we need
You give us unceasingly,
Ever saving us, seeing us well provided,
Such as one, You are for us our only Chief.

You are creation, the Creator,
And the magical variety of created things
Are you not, O God,
Even the substance of creation too?

You are the Existent, the Subsistent and the Value factor Supreme
You are the Present and the Past
And the Future is none else but you.
Even the spoken word, when we consider, is but You alone.

In the ocean of Your Glory
Of great profundity,
Let us all, together, become sunk
To dwell therein everlastingly in Happiness.

By using simple, purely beautiful and unadulterated Malayalam words, Guru is building up a spiritual empire in the human consciousness.

A prayer to Lord Gaṇapati captioned *Vināyakāṣṭakam* is the launching pad for Gurudeva for His journey into the poetic firmament. This may be ascribed to his propensity to emulate ancient Indian poets. *Vināyakāṣṭakam*, a piece rich in beauty of language and profuse in meaning, is moulded in the Sanskrit genre. Yet its persistent alliteration and figure of speech characteristic of Dravidian poetry, are arresting.

Guru has written the poem *Arivu* or Knowledge in charming and simple style. Knowledge permeates the whole universe like God's Omnipresence. But the meaning encompassed in every stanza is so profound that it is not easy for the common folk to grasp it. The following stanzas may be seen:

If knowledge be all inclusive

Where could non-knowledge abide?
Where shall it here survive
On knowing what knowledge is?

For knowledge there is heaven none,
Else from its being known;
In this swelling counting of what is known
Where is that which is Knowledge?

Plodding along these lines one might feel the weariness of the ideas, but the blaze hidden in them cannot but come out like flash of lightning.

In *Scriptures of Mercy* (*Anukampadaśakam*) and *Kindness to Life* (*Jīvakāruṇyapañcakam*), Guru insists that it is man's duty to show kindness to all living beings, animate as well as inanimate.

Such mercy that even to an ant
Would brook not the least harm to befall,
O' Mercy-Maker to vouchsafe with contemplation
Which from Thy pure presence never strays.

Grace, Love, Mercy — all the three
Stand for one reality — Life's Star.
"He who loves is he who really lives." Do learn
Those syllables nine by-heart in place of lettered charm.

In this manner Guru asserts that among the duties to be observed by human beings, mercy stands in the forefront. Similarly the following stanza in *Kindness to Life* will set us thinking:

Not killing makes, a Human good —
Else an animal's equal he becomes.
No refuge has the takers of life,
Although to him all other goods accrue.

Guru has accepted unreserved, the cult of non-violence as preached and practised by Lord Buddha and declared that it should be accepted as a must in our lives.

In the poem *Bhāryā Dharmam* (Wife's Duties), Gurudeva says

that a woman who properly cultivates a wife's duties prospers from day-to-day. Here He asserts that if the lady of the house is chaste and lovable, she will be the luminous lamp shedding radiance in the family.

Through the poems *Jāti Nirṇayam* (Critique of Caste) and *Jāti Lakṣaṇam* (Identification Marks of Caste), Guru scorns at the inhuman practices which, for historical reasons, have bound the Hindu religion with caste. The following lines in *Jāti Nirṇayam* declare what nonsense does caste make:

> One kind, one faith and one God in man
> Of One womb, of one form; difference herein none
> Within a species, is it not that offspring truly breeds?
> The community of man thus viewed, to a single
> caste belongs.

The modern world should pay particular attention to what Guru makes clear in these poems namely only by extinguishing the hypothesis upon which the nefarious social structure of religions and castes are built, that an ideal society can be moulded into being.

## II
## HYMNS TO GODDESS (DEVĪ)

Among the early works of Sree Narayana Guru those in praise of Goddess (Devī) carry considerable importance. *Mannanthala Devisthavam*, *Kalinadakam*, *Jananīnavaratnamañjarī*, and *Devistavam* are written in the Malayalam and for *Bhadrakalyaṣṭakam*, Sanskrit is used as the medium. Of the hymns dedicated to Devī, *Jananīnavaratnamañjarī* is the last.

Gurudeva had cleansed the Universal Consciousness of the stain time had inflicted upon it, and gave shape to a new ideal social order by restoring virtue in the human mind. He is therefore the refuge of modern human race. His goal was to uproot the inequalities and slavery which had established themselves in society through the centuries. Man has created religions. He then created Gods under cover of those religions, and arbitrarily took over as their minister and custodian. As a result, religion has, to conserve and preserve the interests of the custodian, been turned into a weapon to engulf humanity within the darks walls of the social prison. So Guru has composed these hymns with the calculated intention of liberating it from the tangle of religion and caste into which it had been trapped to suffer endlessly, and transform it into real human beings and lead them to the atmosphere of freedom, by awakening in them the prerequisite of spiritual power. These hymns also induce the growth of devotional disposition in man through the spiritual channel by revealing to him the ephimerality and meaninglessness of the materialistic approach to problems.

### (i) Jananīnavaratnamañjarī

As a prayer directly addressed to Devī Śāradā, the Goddess of Learning, *Jananīnavaratnamañjarī* has an added glory. It is a rare garland embellished with nine gems dedicated to Her as an ornament on Her Divine Neck. It was written on the occasion of the *pratiṣṭhā* of the Devī at Śivagiri. The distinguishing feature of this poem is that it highlights in enchanting style, the philosophy of man's *māyā* bound life. Here is the English version of the poem and an epitome of the perceptions enswathed in it:

1. From that unitive mind-stuff, all encompassing,
A thousand tri-basic rays (of knowledge-knower-known)
    come and, to and anon,
Self-consciousness gone,
There awakened love of food and such;
Fallen thus into the ocean of need and lost altogether,
Say, when, O Mother, shall my inner being
    regain that path of hope
To be merged within the domain of pure word import,
    bereft of all tri-basic prejudice
And, within the core of the radiance outspread
    of reason pure.
Reabsorbed in communion cool, ever remain.

2. This variegated display by *māyā* wrought —

Itself nothing-is no other than awareness pure;
Air, stone, sea or fire, and the void too,
Are all but prime awareness alone!
The rightness of such a view, if one should praise,
No scriptural confusion can come;
Rival claims of action shall not vie;
Such goodly gain would suffice itself alone;
O Mother of the Wisdom that all seek, easy and
exalting at once.

**3.** Knowledge that comes but to go again
Has come from times of yore; on each vision such
The limbs and the inner Self are swayed;
Filled with varied import and darkened by each.
Contracting, all within the Great Unknown is
reabsorbed again!
Even seeing thus, again and again. Wisdom comes not!
The learned man of good deeds is but a bee
Fallen into lotus core, drinking there the nectar
Of the unlimited experience of bliss supreme.

**4.** Thought, applied to waves, reduces them to water;
The snake as rope is known; the pot into clay resolved;
Likewise the world. Only when penetrated by thought
Has nothing here reality at all.
Your feet are the root for all this that I adore.
Bestow on me this boon which you alone can grant;.
Become as the Real to me; refuge there is none other
Thank You, O Mother of the Royal Yoga Way!

**5.** O Mother who, within the encircling veil
Of the prime mind of high, ever dwells,
Whose free dance it is that impels here below
This clamorous medley of water, air and fire
As the world manifest — when all is but name alone!
With that delicate yarn of time and so on,
A fancy vesture overcovers your form
So none do know your true appearance,

O, One that takes Your stand where all the Vedas end.

6. You became the deer, and the fish too.
The snake, and the heavenly bird alike,
The firm earth, and the river also. Woman as well as man,
Even the word on high and inferno, within your name-form couple.
Assuming varied natures, cognize here,
As the 'I' that too is even you!
O' One of word content alone, all is comedy indeed!

7. That wisdom's arrow that can smite my sin
In your flowery feet resides
My love, it is the bowstring, and an iron will the bow;
The ego-sense is the Victorious one.
While you the Mother it is, who victory gives;
My sin-stained self, thereupon is transformed
In terms of awareness, with the mightily heavy body too
The world and all else into awareness leaps!

8. As existing and then as subsisting ever,
And into a pearl combining both conscious of all the three,
As the heart, whose seed it is, that the sky and wind
With all the ramified expanse of sense-interests
Such as the eye projecting, and even as the eater of food
In glory abides, such are you.
O Mother, most high, unattainable even to psychic powers rare!

9. The earth and the other elements here
No basis they have, semblance only,
Specific expressions in awareness merely;
Whatever reality they have in this world
Is by you alone conferred!
In that exalted region where tongue or taste
Has no place, is where your glory abides.
Who is there to know your greatness, O Mother?
Words are weak, even for praising you, alas!

(Trans.: Nataraja Guru)

COMMENTARY

There are three branches of wisdom to which the human brain is responsive. These are known as Thripudies by which what is adumbrated here are the three aspects of spiritual knowledge. If the gross visible facet of wisdom is annotated as the knower, the known and knowable, there will be no end to these Thripudies in the worldly interactions of the intellect. As a result of the mental preoccupations with them, man gets lost in the pleasures of worldly life. I am one such, whose heart craves for release from the worldly entanglements created by Thripudies. You are the one power which can grant me release. O, Mother Supreme, the very pivotal Grace permeating the macro-micro manifestations of the universe! In your all consuming splendour, the Thripudies will be incinerated, and the way made clear for a vision of the ultimate Truth. Bless me Mother, with that vision, and the final release.

*Māyā* creates the illusion of the real out of the unreal. But *māyā* is the original truth as distinguished from the visible and root cause. The *māyā* that we seek and which, though devoid of spiritual essence, creates the contrary impression, is wisdom itself. The very same wisdom is unveiled by the five elements. O Mother of all worlds, grant me that wisdom.

The awareness that the universe bears witness to the emergence and extinction process is fugacious, is not engendered in man. Infatuated by the attraction held out by visible objects, he is running after them. When the ideas sprouting in him drop away in the barrenness of fantasy, they assume the final form by the impact of the self and become one with the *ātmā*. It may be that by the passage of time when such instinctive tendencies project themselves in the consciousness, the awareness that the secret of creation lies within the sphere of the unknown, is born. Yet real wisdom is hard to come by. The genuinely virtuous knower is like the black bee that lands upon the lotus flower blossomed in supreme bliss and enjoys the ecstasy of its honey. O Mother Goddess, You have made known to me that the world is an illusory phenomenon which manipulates the notion of reality in-between what is without beginning or end.

The wave in the ocean is born from water, though it is nothing but water. In twilight a piece of rope may at one look be seen as snake. But the next moment that belief is changed. Similarly the utencil made out of sand is sand only. The same is the case with the world. I am aware O Goddess of Learning, that you are Supreme Power revealed in space and time, the Sole Reality. Bless me Mother with devotion to reach *Brahmasatya*, the Ultimate Reality.

O Goddess of Knowledge, from Your Grace arises Divine Vibration. In tune with that vibration the five elements combine to generate the riotous Omnipotent motion plunging the world into a state of unceasing activity. You are draped in the soft attire of space and time, and rejoice in the oblivion of artistic deeds. Yet you alone are the Knower of the ultimate Reality. I pray, bless me with knowledge of that Reality.

O Mother, You are at once the infatuating *māyā* and the manifestation of *Brahman*. You take shape as every object in the universe. You are the original sound incarnate. I am armed with the arrow of spiritual knowledge with which to undo sin, and the bow of unshakeable devotion with which to reach You. Yet it is You who are to grant me victory. At times egotism may raise its head inside me. This may be because being tainted as I am with sin, my ego is solidified into this body of mine. You are the Ultimate Reality that is *saccidānanda*, and hence the Omniscient *ātmā*. The Pole star of the universe that you are, You wear the visage of the five elements and the five senses as one unified entity. This is the mysterious attribute of that grandewe of the Supreme Being which is inscrutable even to the most spiritually enlightened. Yet, the objects like the earth are not real. It is all a false impression engendered in the mind; it is only *māyā* or illusion, the objectivisation of Devī's sport. The greatness of Devī is beyond human comprehension.

O, the wielder of the *māyā* device, Supreme Mother who enraptures the universe with Your unrecountable games and baffles, the *bhaktas* with mysterious power, bless me with knowledge of the ultimate and release from worldly encumbrances.

### (ii) Devīstavam

This poem which has nine four-line stanzas and one two-line half stanza, is a restatement of Guru's belief that the devotee embroiled in the sufferings innate in life, can secure release only through Devī's Grace. Here again the prayer is addressed to the Goddess direct. The idea of the poem is given here in a nutshell.

O Devī, You are the *Brahman* incarnate of the original sound. Your organs are infatuating and vivacious. They defy description. Your silent posture is more eloquent than the most vociferous words. You are the ocean of kindness, and the most magnificent expression of Divine Femininity I have come across during my meditations.

My heart murmurs over and over again that everything in this world from wealth to woman that is visible to the naked eye, and attractive to the senses, is nothing but illusion. So, Devī, bless me with sanction to merge in the glory of your Divinity. Because the body is transient and the *ātmā* eternal, I nurture the longing to merge in Devī. Therefore, O, The most precious gem in my heart, bless me with the effulgence Your Divine body exudes. Along with that, extend to me knowledge of life's meaning. I pray in humility that while I use my physical body as the vehicle for crossing *saṁsāra-sāgara*, the sea of material existence, give it strength and have mercy on me, so that I may reach my goal.

Devī, You are the portent to well-being. I bow in devotion to you. O, the ever Bountiful, why this hesitation to call this devotee, engaged in your praise day-in and day-out, to that consoling and enchanting Divine Presence? I am unceasingly struggling to swim across the sorrow and torture filled sea of worldly life in the bid to gain entry into the zone of eternal bliss. Unstoppable tidal waves block my tread across *saṁsāra-sāgara*. I fall exhausted into the depths of misery. I am struggling in that vast ocean in utter helplessness. Give me a single niche to hold on to. Will you not save me from this suffering? You alone can bless me with the shelter of relief, drowning as I am into fathomless wretchedness.

O, Mother of all worlds! You guide and control the entire objects in the universe, animate and inanimate; bless the devotees with liberation; shower the nectar of bliss upon the human mind as the Goddess of Learning that You are; and pour forth in torrential abundance the milky moonlight of Divine Love to fill the universe with perpetual peace and *dharma*. I salute You, Devī, in supplication with palms joined. Have the mercy to confer kindness and contentment on this *bhakta*. If only Devī is gracious enough to bless one, born as a human being owing to my misdeeds in previous births, and swimming with tiring limbs and aching heart in the sea of life, bearing the torments inflicted by it, as also all the devotees along with me!

### (iii) Mannanthala Devīstavam
### (Hymn dedicated to the Devī of Mannanthala Temple)

This is a hymn Gurudeva wrote in praise of Devī whose idol He had installed more than a hundred years ago, in the temple at Mannanthala near Thiruvananthapuram. In this he has adumbrated the guidelines for a priest to conduct the worshipping ceremony (*pūjā*). The poem has nine stanzas and is addressed to the Goddess. Here is a summary of the piece:

The *kuṇḍalinī* (the snake which is the linch-pin of spiritual consciousness) is passing through, with its expanded hood towering as an umbrella over the wheel *maṇipūrakam*, shaped like a lotus.

The *maṇipūrakam* wheel blossoms, and sprays sweet smelling flowers around; the fragrance emanating therefrom is dissolved in Divine Grace, and then converted into worship itself; and finally the *pujārī* (Priest) himself after rising to Godliness, disappears into that radiance. At last when this *bhakta* (the author) yearns to reach Devī's proximity after transcending the Ocean pregnant in the virtue conglomerate of the three attributes of *sat*, *rajas* and *tamas* (truth, sin and ignorance), O Goddess, bless him.

O, Goddess, You wear on your sacred head the crescent moon and the Gaṅgā of the heavens, and hence you excel with a face more beautiful than the full moon. Having appropriated a share of Lord

Śiva's Body for yourself, you symbolise everything that is great and noble. Preserving the image of Your Lotus Feet in my mind for ever, not to permit egotism to gain ascendency over it, not to allow the extermination of wisdom and thus deprive life of meaning — O, Mother, have mercy to grant me the boon to achieve that end.

Mother of the world, Your form dazzles in divine brilliance. The very thought about the diversity of Your glorious features is enough to fill the *bhakta*'s heart with bliss. With that in mind, he is freed of cares and anxieties; and contentment will reign in their place. Devī, bless me to reach that state.

O Mother, You bless all beings by giving them everything their hearts crave for. With unbounded magnanimity bless me too with Your perpetual presence in my heart as my leading light. I am aware that the only way to escape from the eternal cycle of births and deaths, is to suppress all sensual longings and carry on by fixing the mind upon Your form. Bless me not to be trapped into, and stranded about, in the misery filled physical life so that I may be enabled to suppress all sensual desires and lead a virtuous life.

Mother, You are the very embodiment of the good and noble. I am not at all strong enough to reach Chidambaram by making use of intelligence whose whirling power puts to shame, even that of a top. Having taken refuge at Your Feet for a bit of kindness, I sing in Your praise in deep devotion. Lead me O Mother. Along with that, bless me with the boon to merge at those tender Feet.

However clever one individual may be it should be possible for him to be cheated by the allurements of the five senses of eye, nose, skin, tongue and ear. Mother, You have no affection for such an individual. On the contrary, if such people become interested in You and transform themselves into Your devotees, that every moment forgetting everything, unhesitatingly You grace them with Your blessing. Knowing all these I fall at the Feet of the Mother of all worlds in absolute devotion, by accepting Her as my Supreme Goddess. This body is to become food for vultures and kites. Will you not abstain from putting me to suffering at least from now on. My prayer is that Devī's pleasure be lavished upon me. O Devī, the half of the moon wearing Lord Śiva, give me the boon to diminish all my sorrows.

Devī of Mannanthala, You carry soil on Your Divine Crown. You are undoubtedly the Guardian and the Protector of the universe. It is something to feel proud about. You bear the fitting name, Mannanthala Devī. You carry the sand which is the very embodiment of everything that is worldly. While Devī protects all beings why does Devī occasionally attempt to destroy them? This contradictory attitude of Your mind is a wonderous phenomenon which passes understanding for mortals.

### (iv) Bhadrakalyaṣṭakam

This is a hymn of eight stanzas addressed to the Goddess Bhadrakālī (the terrorsome aspect of Goddess Durgā). It describes her horrifying form so picturesquely that the *bhakta* on reading it, is struck dumb with awe and devotion at the same time. Here is an unpruned version of the poem.

O, Goddess Bhadrakālī, You are magnificent in that adundant, thickly growing ivy tresses. When beetles attracted by the perfume emanating from the floral garlands worn on those tresses, raise noisy clatter, love-stricken Lord Śiva softly passes his palms with the allurement of the light touch, and you delight at the sight of the beetles flying off helter-skelter. You unhesitatingly pour out sweet honey, rain like, through the endless waves of the ocean of mercy. You abound in the freshness of girlish purity, and blaze in absolute lascivious attractiveness. I worship you.

O Devī, You broke the demon Dāruka's head and got intoxicated by gulping voraciously the blood which gushed out of it in torrents, Your lips horrifyingly scarlet with the thick stain of it; Your breasts smeared with sandal and saffron exude exhilarating fragrance. Your might like that innate in mares and Your magnificent figure manifests Your inherent power and stateliness, blazes in the majesty of ever preparedness to launch the war of annihilation. I worship You.

You wear the gold crown afire with the dazzle of a hundred billion suns, on Your aesthetically carved head; You flourish in the beauty that puts by the shade even the incomparable attractiveness of the fragrance carrying heavenly lotus; You impart ecstatic experience through your magical performance on the *vīṇā*; and You are the peerlessly lustful embodiment of feminine charm. I worship You.

You wear the baby elephant on your ears and add lustre to the animal, Your sweet words outdo even the sweetness of honey; You carry out the creative, preservative and destructive processes by just a flashing flick of the outer corner of Your eyes and momentary movement of Your eyebrows; You are the proud possessor of the ideally-shaped greatness enshrined lotus like palm; and You are Lord Śiva's consort and the demon Mahiṣāsura's annihilator. I worship You.

You are the mother of Lords Gaṇapati and Subrahmaṇya; You have the walking gait of the elephant; You possess attractive bodily beauty; You adorn Yourself with such beautiful eyes as those of sole-fish; You are the power that destroyed the evil demons Śumbha and Niśumbha; You are worshipped by Lord Brahmā; and You bless all with progenies and prosperity. I worship You.

You flow as the sole rivulet of ecstatic experience; You are the hen swan for the lotus and pure hearts; You are the owner of shapely, high and round breasts; You glow in beauty with the smear of sandal and perfumes of other sorts; You revel in the ringing of the bell in the girdle worn on Your waist veiled by silken costume; and You have the face as beautiful as the moon and eyes as attractive as the lotus petal. I worship You.

You appear dark because Your figure is as beautiful as the dark cloud and the flower with dark blue shade (*kayambu*); You wear a chain which shines over Your fatty round breasts, and which has pearls dangling from it; You glory in your beauteous, narrow waist, in the glazy infatuating hair line that rises from your naval; You are the owner of eternal brilliance. I worship you with the prayer to wipe off my woes.

Devī, in the act of beautifying Your figure, You have smeared Your shapely breasts with saffron. This has reddened Lord Śiva's Chest while embracing You. Thus You are glorified by having painted His Divine Chest in beautiful red; You are the precious gem among the galaxy of heavenly ladies, and worshipped by such celestial sages as Nārada and Sananda; You have long and lovely eyes like those of the dove; and You have profuse tresses which put to shame the long chain of dark clouds. I worship You.

*Bhadrakalyaṣṭakam* is a hurricane which blows away the dark clouds of sickness and sin. Those reciting it regularly everyday will be blessed with name, fame and prosperity.

### (v) Kālīnāṭakam
### (A hymn to be recited at the dance drama dedicated to Goddess Kālī)

In the piece *Kālīnāṭakam*, Gurudeva is unveiling the boundless prowess of Devī Bhadrakālī, the Creator, Protector and Destroyer of this universe. Simultaneously through the picturisation of Devī from head to foot, Devī's unexcelled beauty is also given expression to. With the imaginative genius of a beauty adoring master poet, Devī's frightening and genial aspects are also brought to light. Though the start is quiet, the hymn assumes a course gradually towards a vibrant climax. That is how Guru has planned and executed its theme. It is a direct address to the Goddess. Its one hundred and twenty-three lines are paraphrased here:

I prostrate before You Devī. You are the incarnation of the melody of sound. You are eternal; You are the luminous fountain spring of the four Vedas; and You are the Goddess whom the three Lords of the universe Brahmā, Viṣṇu and Śiva pay homage to. Like oil in the sesamum seed so is the eagerness to eradicate the miseries of devotees and grant them liberation inherent in the mother of the universe that You are. Devī blesses the devotees by showering on them the ecstasy of nectar in diverse ways. She enjoys revelling in acts of creation, protection and destruction. At times sporting and lusting, and at other times roaring in frenzy, she indulges herself in Your heart, upon those seeking shelter at Her Feet. Devī lavishes her blessing with relief from misery. So for those who are fortunate to earn Devī's pleasure will be free from sorrows. Life for them will be a synonym for happiness. In short, the glory of the Omnipresent, ever resonant Devī is beyond description.

Now Gurudeva is embarking on a eulogy of Devī's beauty from head to foot.

The abundance of Devī's tresses is so stocky as to receive with abandon the Heavenly Gaṅgā which descends into them with such impact as to cause frightening quake and carve depthless hollows where it falls if it is on the earth. Here Devī is pictured as the object of meditation, blazing with the golden crown adorned with the crescent, and infinite variety of veritable diamonds.

It is not easy to describe the beauty of the saffron mark on Devī's forehead. Even the full moon is relegated to the shade by the splendourous brilliance of that mark. What is planted in its middle is the ocean enfolding the seven Seas. That Ocean, Devī wears round her divine waist. Slight consideration will reveal that even the *trimūrtis* or the God Trio engaged in the creative, protective and destructive activities bow to the commands of Devī. From this, the might of the world's Mother is apprehensible.

After having described the beautiful divine forehead and the mark thereon, Gurudeva proceeds to describe comprehensively Devī's eyebrows, eyes, earrings, cheeks, sweet and full lips, and the superbly aligned teeth.

Devī's eyebrows put to shame Kāmadeva's sensual bows which let fly his arrow of flowers. Their voluptuous vibrations throw even Kāmadeva into utter despair. The honey of kindness that fills Devī's eyes, helps obliterate *bhakta*s' tears. As the tears of love flowing out of Devī's eyes collect into river and flow, those who sit and recite Vedic hymns on the other shore of the sea into which that river flows, can see Devī's burning cheeks. What about Devī's thirsting lips? Their redness dims even those of the hibiscus (shoe flower). Devī's well arranged teethline holds out a challenge to glass pearls; besides it adds a shade of contempt for precious stones.

Gurudeva reminds us that, it is not smooth sailing to describe artfully Devī's face, neck, breasts and other organs. That lotus face dims even the beauty of the full moon's face. But it is not possible to say that that face guarded by the two canine teeth is not terrifying. The hands shine with bangles ringing like bells. Devī attended by hobgoblins, wears spear, conch, sword and skull. Devī's fierce roar meant for scaring the enemies away, enfeebles the roar of lions. Devī's guffaws echo into, and shake the horizons. Ball-like breasts standing up challengingly, are beautified by saffron paint. Glass like second cloth is picturesque with the images of pearls. The garlands Devī wears, made out of flower bunches, make Devī's narrow waist and broad torso extremely attractive. The silken attire that drapes Devī's buttocks are as alluring as Kāmadeva's carriage. The perfectly shaped thighs which slide down from their source are not wanting to stand comparison with the elephant's trunk.

Devī's Lotus Feet are so graceful as to thwart Kāmadeva's attacks. Their base side gives the tortoise a run for a plunge into the waters' depths to do penance. Sweet singing Goddesses revel in exhilaration by taking in the honey emanating from those Feet. Devī enjoys artistic performances such as singing, *vīṇā* playing and dancing of the heavenly beauties. To the Gods who approach the Divine Presence for *darśana*, Devī extends blessing through kind and sweet looks, and makes them contented. The devotees crave for Devī's blessings. In short just one condescending look from Devī is enough for the devotee to get himself liberated from the miseries of earthly life.

O Mother of the world, O the embodiment of Mercy, to cross this sorrow filled sea of life, I find no means except the vessel which is Your Divine Feet. Show me Your mercy which has unsparingly given everything wished for by Your devotees. What throws man into the depth of sufferings are soil, woman and wealth. So Devī, bless me to be free from desire for them. I pray to Devī that I may be liberated from this evanescent universe into which I have fallen to suffer because of the loss of virtues and blessed to attain self-realisation and reach ultimate spiritual peace. O Lord Śiva's

Consort, Mother of the universe, Bhadrakālī, I prostrate at Your Divine Feet again and again for Liberation.

CRITICISM OF THE POEMS

Sree Narayana Guru's conception of the Goddess is impregnated with great ideas which readers of His poems can easily reach. Goddess Sarasvatī, the Goddess of Learning fills the universe with the original sound, *auṁ* and bears the name *Nāda Brahma Svarūpinī*. According to the Śaivite theory, man has to transgress the four stages of one worldliness (*sālokya*), nearness (*sāmīpya*), identity of appearance (*sārūpya*), and salvation (*sāyujya*) with the Supreme. Devī, as the symbol of the Śiva-Śakti communion, is the root of the Universe's creation, protection and destruction. It is the diverse countenances of that Devī that the devotee perceives in *Mannanthala Devī*, *Bhadra Kālī*, *Jananīnavaratnamañjarī*, *Kālīnāṭakam* and *Bhadrakalyaṣṭakam*. When one is in the crest of devotion, what one sees in Bhadrakālī is the very fountain spring of the universe in the inexplicate quintessence of Devī Pārvatī Herself. Even though Devī's sobre aspects are expressed in early *stotra* or eulogies, in *Kālīnāṭaka*, what is projected is Her ferocious and horrific form. In every *Devī-stotra*, Gurudeva has given expression to his poetic artistry in such thought-awakening, figurative and devotion filled style, and with refulgent spiritual conceptions as to attract aesthetic hearts to the utmost. It is true that Devī Bhadrakālī's head to foot description follows the pattern of the Sanskrit literati. Yet it follows the simple, but beautiful Draviḍa style, with its attractive word alignments, the spontaneous, incessant current and the poetic excellence rising in a quantum leap from the innermost recesses of the heart, and the inner current of utter devotion flowing through it — all will engulf the artistic mind in ecstatic reverie. The effortless simplicity of description, the poetic, ornamentative diction, and the magnificence and majesty of the macro power of Devī enshrined in these *stotras*, are all ensconced therein with such mastery as to stun even the greatest poets in Kerala into perplexity. There is no doubt that the imaginative genius of Guru exemplified in these *stotras* are so bewilderingly bewitching as to begger description.

## III
## HYMNS TO LORD VIṢṆU

### (i) Śrī Kṛṣṇa Darśanam

Sree Narayana Guru is generally regarded as a *bhakta* of Lord Śiva. But apart from his hymns to Śiva, Subrahmaṇya and Devī, He has also written three hymns to Lord Viṣṇu namely *Śrī Kṛṣṇa Darśanam*, *Vāsudevāṣṭakam* and *Viṣṇavāṣṭakam*. Of these *Śrī Kṛṣṇa Darśanam* is confined to a single stanza. In this stanza Guru soliloquises with contentment, about His experience of Realisation of Lord Kṛṣṇa through a dream. The following is a summarised version of the soliloquy:

By the merger of the world in *saccidānanda* that is the Supreme Being, the sweet voice proceeding from the nectar reserve of Paradise has ceased. Yet the Inner Light blazes enough to disperse around. It is then that the rare fortune of the image of blue black flower coloured Lord Kṛṣṇa is issuing forth into view, dazzling like the diamond in the inner alcove of a palace, and along with that the Kaustubha Jewel on the Lord's neck in all flaring glory. As a result of this sight of the Supreme, the veil of illusion enveloping my being has been lifted. What greater blessing for me than to thus earn God Realisation!

### (ii) Vāsudevāṣṭakam

Gurudeva in a direct address to Lord Kṛṣṇa, has in this Sanskrit hymn of eight stanzas, extolled His virtues. Significantly each stanza ends with a plea to the Lord to destroy the sorrows of the author. A summarised version of the idea of the poem is given here without altering its original pattern:

O Vāsudeva, You hold in Your hands the Lotus, the Conch, the club named Kammodaki and the fear eliminating Disc. You carry on Your chest the symbolic mole of Viṣṇu. You are the Saviour of all *bhaktas*. You have the most beautiful figure in the universe, with body as handsome as the clouds, and eyes as lovely shaped as the lotus petal. You are so great as to treat honour and shame with equanimity. You make the virtuous happy. You are the complete shield against *saṁsāra-duḥkha* (the sorrows of worldly life). You are all-pervading, the One without beginning or end. The *ṛṣis* treat You as the Sole Lord of their worship.

Such great One that You are, O Lord Supreme and the spouse of Goddess Lakṣmī, bless me by ending all my sorrows.

### (iii) Viṣṇavāṣṭakam

This is the last of Guru's hymns to Lord Viṣṇu. It is written in Sanskrit and has eight stanzas. Here too, the author addresses the Lord in unbounded devotion. Here is an abstract of the poem:

Lord, I seek refuge at Your Feet. You are the original Being, worshipped alike by Lords Śiva and Brahmā. You shine in the heart of the virtuous. I praise Lord Keśava, the conferrer of good to the World, the One who grants whatever is prayed for by the devotee, the Embodiment of mercy, the Destroyer of the sins of *kali yuga* and the One without beginning or end. I worship You Goddess Lakṣmī's spouse, the most beautiful in black beetle's hue and the Primordial Being. I worship You the Lord of all worlds who incarnates again and again to establish *dharma* and whose lovely countenance outshines all the most beautiful objects in the universe. I worship Lord Keśava the imperishable, who has Ananta the lord of the serpents, as His bed, and who lightens Palazhi, the Ocean of Milk. I worship Lord Keśava the asylum of the poor, the lotus eyes supreme Master. You confer boons O Lord. I prostrate at Your Feet in complete surrender. Let me again and again pay homage to those Lotus Feet.

Whoever recites *Viṣṇavāṣṭakam* with complete devotion will shed all sins and reach Lord Viṣṇu's Divine Feet.

CRITICISM OF THE PIECES

The two Sanskrit poems in this group are apt to attract the literary minded. In both *Śrī Vāsudevāṣṭakam* and *Viṣṇavāṣṭakam* the same idea is brought out although in different metres (*aṣṭākam* means a piece with eight stanzas). Even though both are equally enthralling and embellished with the synonyms of Lord Viṣṇu, what the admirer sees in them is not so much the profusion of ideas as their recurrence. Yet in these pieces which abound in the excellence of word structure, style and usage, the reader would be able to see the depth, expanse and adorability of Gurudeva's proficiency in Sanskrit. True *Śrī Kṛṣṇadarśanam* is limited to a single stanza, but Gurudeva's contentment in the rare opportunity he had been fortunate to get, of a vision of the dark lotus coloured Kṛṣṇa reflected in it, makes it a self-contained poem. These hymns to Lord Viṣṇu are ideal presentations of how deep a *bhakta*'s devotion can reach through those heart felt salutations to *Bhagavān*.

## IV
## HYMNS TO LORD SUBRĀHMAṆYA

After hymns to Devī and Viṣṇu, Sree Narayana Guru has sung in praise of Lord Subrāhmaṇya. These songs are seven in number as shown below. In each hymn what He does is to pluck one petal from the great flower that blazes in the effervescence of Subrāhmaṇya, and examine it. Of these *Guhāṣṭakam*, *Bahuleyāṣṭakam* and *Ṣaṇmaturāṣṭavam* are written in Sanskrit and the others in Malayalam. In these hymns Śiva's attributes are superimposed on Subrāhmaṇya.

### (i) Guhāṣṭakam

This is a poem in eight stanzas in praise of Guha who is Subrāhmaṇya. Here is a summary of this poem.

It enumerates and eulogises the great qualities of Lord Subrāhmaṇya. He is the son of Lord Śiva, the embodiment of Truth and the seat of all knowledge. He is kind and generous. Lords Viṣṇu and Brahmā worship Him. He imparts spiritual knowledge and self-confidence to His devotees. He is the complete Being, having His Divine sway across the universe. He wields the spear symbolising contentment and security. He exemplifies the most beautiful, and destroys the woes of earthly life. He practises detachment to show the way to His *bhaktas*. He is ageless, above and beyond time. He is joy incarnate. He pervades the entire universe and without any particular abode.

Let us praise Him with all our heart.

### (ii) Ṣaṇmukhastotram

This is a long poem in nineteen stanzas in praise of Lord Ṣaṇmukha who is Subrāhmaṇya. Here is a summary of the poem.

The Lord's form is presented comprehensively with its description from head to foot. That brilliance excels that of six suns shining simultaneously. The cool beauty radiated by six full moons shining together cannot put to shade the resplendence emanating from that form. Lord Ṣaṇmukha has the sun and moon as two eyes. Each of those six faces (Lord Ṣaṇmukha has six faces) shines like the moon. The splendidly shaped nose, the long beautiful lips putting diamonds to the background, the long thick curly tresses, the finely aligned teeth and the attractive beard — all stun the *bhakta* to surrender in absolute devotion. The broad torso, narrow stomach and the artistic naval are imprinted in the mind as symbols of purity. So are the shapely and long thighs, beautiful knees and the majestic ankles. His form has the power to keep the ever fluctuating mind in stillness.

God has divined that man born into this world has to fulfil three obligations. The one to the *deva*s is paid by *yaga*s, that to the sages through knowledge of the Vedas and that to the dead ancestors through progenies. But *yogī*s with absolute detachment can fulfil theirs without any of these. A true devotee of Lord Ṣaṇmukha will have no obligations at all to fulfil.

It is true that the rituals to ancestors can be performed only through progenies. For that, one has to marry. But even remaining unmarried one can turn ascetic, say the scriptures. Thus by devoting completely to the Lord, one can fulfil one's duties to ancestors.

Like the spider which weaves the net out of a material generated in its own body and then enjoys in it, so Lord Ṣaṇmukha creates this universe and rejoices inside it. And Ṣaṇmukha uncoils from human life the *kuṇḍalinī* snake which binds it into tangles and hinders man's deliverance. So Lord Subrāhmaṇya is the sole refuge for all. Like sage Agastya who learned the science of arms and war from

Lord Subrāhmaṇya and became preceptor to the world, so those unconditionally dedicated to Him can earn preceptor-hood. O Lord, Your mercy fills the world. One who repeats *praṇava* is rid of one's impurities, but one should repeat His divine name to be rid of unhappiness. Your place among the *trimūrtis* is identical to that of the moon among the stars. Just as the waves arising in the Ocean are submerged within itself, so the world which is born from You merges within Yourself. Those yearning with full heart for release from *māyā* or illusion will be favoured with that release. The Lord will never neglect His devotees in their struggle with *māyā*.

In every stanza, Gurudeva has included a prayer to bless Him with freedom from worldly misery, and release from bondage to ultimate Salvation.

### (iii) Ṣaṇmukhadaśakam

Here is another ten-stanza verse in praise of Lord Muruka. In it also attributes of Lord Śiva are superimposed on His son. Like the others, it too is a prayer addressed to Muruka. Here is a summary of the poem.

Muruka burns as the fire of knowledge. When knowledge is realised by the *bhakta*, he becomes one with the Lord. The splendid tresses tied into a bun at the crown of the head, and the crescent, the heavenly Gaṅgā, the snake, and the precious gem twinkling around that bun, the forehead which adorns a sandalwood paste dot, and the eyebrows which put the rainbow to shame — are all impressed upon the meditative mind in glittering colours. That captivating smile on the moon like face engenders unbounded devotion. Those earrings which reflect on the infectious cheeks and the nose which shines in resplendence are enthralling to the mind. The silver anklets, and the twelve magnificent hands, two of them each holding the flaring spear and the trident and two upraised and held in a finger-spread, hood-shaped, pose, symbolising the grant of boon and refuge respectively, are inviting to the devotee to play with the Lord.

O, Muruka! You embody mercy. Yet the *bhakta* is made to feel that that Heart does not easily melt to fulfil his yearning for salvation. Muruka's glorious ornaments tempt the devotee to complete surrender. The Lord will ride the peacock and reach him with blessings. How can he forget that magnificent figure of beauty and splendour? The real devotee will crave for serving those divine Feet. All of Muruka's sixty fingers outshine the newly blossomed lotus flowers in beauty. The *bhakta* expects that one day Muruka would come to him and bless him.

As in all the other pieces Guru is identifying himself with the *bhakta*.

### (iv) Subrāhmaṇyakīrtanam

This is one elaborate fifteen-stanza verse in praise of Lord Subrāhmaṇya. As in the others, the author in this case also identifies himself with the *bhakta* and solicits His blessings. Here is a summary of the poem.

The Lord wears on His crown glorious crescent moon of the evening. The Gaṅgā of the heavens is held beside it. He rides the world of darkness through the blazing brilliance of His third eye.

I am running hither and thither for release from this blinding illusion of the world into which I am pushed with a body, which is nothing but the solidification of my sins. I pray that I may be blessed with God Realisation. I am being drawn in this life by undulating movements of the forces of *kuṇḍalinī*. With God's Grace I will be able to cross the forces which hinder my progress towards salvation.

Because of attachment to worldly pleasures, the mind and brain go straying about. At the end of their wanderings, reality will have to be grasped. For this I am praying to you in absolute devotion with intense desire for discreet judgement between good and evil. Make my path free from hurdles, O Muruka. I am not a believer in meaningless words to please others or elicit sympathy. I have one *mantra* with me which I am happy to recite endlessly until I reach my goal. O Lord Subrāhmaṇya, You have twelve eyes, twelve ears and twelve hands. Don't you see my suffering? You can redress my agony with each one of these. My desire is to conquer the senses, awaken the *kuṇḍalinī* power and through that, experience spiritual bliss. Lead me Lord.

You are the fountain source of the sweet nectar of silence. You lead the *bhakta* through the mirror of knowledge. You have accepted as your consort a low-born woman. You do not consider that as an act of shame. Hence how can blessing me with Your Grace not become of You? With Your unfathomable knowledge, You have conquered time and space. Living inside my body which fastly succumbs to the infirmities of old age, is an ordeal for me. O the son of Lord Śiva, grant me enlightenment and lead me to salvation. Why don't You desire to save those suffering in *saṁsāra-sāgara*, yearning for Your mercy?

Because You did not direct me along the right path I am being dragged along the wrong passage with tottering steps to the doors of death. Are you determined to allow that to happen? Pardon all my faults and save me, O, Muruka. How can You abandon me Lord, in this manner when You Yourself are the son of Lord Śiva who was Himself a beggar? Can you not be kind enough to have mercy upon me who is another beggar. Lord Subrāhmaṇya, is not Your father earning His living by begging (because of a lie He had uttered)? Is there any end to the degradation into which His beggar's life has fallen? O, son of that Great God, accept me as one of your humble devotees and bless me.

### (v) Navamañjarī

This hymn to Lord Subrāhmaṇya has nine stanzas as indicated by the word *nava*. In this also Sree Narayana Guru assumes the role of a devotee and prays. Here is a summary of the poem.

Lured by the attractions of worldly pleasures, I cannot trek after them and render my life meaningless. I am not able to be privy to the perpetuation of acts of betrayals and deceits so rampant in this life, and to subject my youth to the infatuations held out by intoxicating substances. O Mind, instead of destroying yourself with inclinations, seek refuge with Lord Muruka for the attainment of Godliness, Greatness and Grandeur. O Lord, tell me a *mantra* by repeating which I can reach You. Plant Your Divine Feet upon my heart and wash away my sins. Give me the spiritual gift to slough off the darkness of ignorance enveloping me. Bless me with an unwavering mind. You are the child of Goddess Pārvatī, and I feel one with You in that capacity although I do not feel any justification for that. Give me the knowledge for the basis of this mysterious identity. My mind is a fugitive at Your Feet to quench my thirst for knowledge as knowledge bereft of Your blessing is like chaff. O Lord Muruka, bless me to merge at Your Lotus Feet.

### (vi) Bahuleyāṣṭakam

This is an eight-stanza verse in Sanskrit in praise of Lord Bahuleya (Muruka). In this piece, the author's manoeuvred Superimposition of Lord Śiva on Lord Muruka is loud and clear. A summary of the poem follows:

O Lord, I meditate upon Your majestic figure. You are the One who is the forest fire which burns away sin and death alike, and who is worshipped by the sages. I meditate upon Lord Bahuleya who protects the world from the wicked and confers knowledge to the virtuous. You are the dread of the enemies and the moulder of hell into paradise. You wield the Goddess of plenty, and crush the *asuras*. You are the Divine Principle upon which the universe exists. You are the Incarnation of all knowledge, and the enemy of all passions.

### (vii) Ṣaṇmaturastavam

Another verse of ten stanzas in Sanskrit in praise of Lord Subrāhmaṇya. It is the leading work among the hymns to the Lord, Sree Narayana Guru has compiled. Here is a summary of the poem.

O the Destroyer of all woes of the world, Lord Subrāhmaṇya, free me from the travails of worldly life. Grant me the blessing of salvation. Just as You bless Your lascivious consort, so bless me too. You are the one who incinerates desires, and sorrows. Lord, destroy my ego and attachment to worldly pleasures. You are the cynosure of all *bhakta*'s eyes and the terror to enemies. Bless me with an existence in Paradise. I am worshipping You in my heart to shower me with kindness. To those who merge with Your heart, You confer intelligence. You are so magnanimous. You alone are capable of annihilating my weaknesses. Grant me the favour of Your nearness till the end of the worldly existence. You are the seat of splendour and You enjoy killing sin as a game. I am praying for Your blessing for ever.

CRITICISM OF THE PIECES

These seven hymns show that Sree Narayana Guru was a complete devotee of Lord Muruka. At first sight most of them appear to abound in salutations; since the Lord's greatness and exploits are intermixed with them, the reader is not likely to be vexed with drabness. Yet more repetitions than are necessary, are not to be ruled out. The pleasant and refreshing thread of devotion which runs through the entire fabric of these works, is their redeeming aspect. Finally the poetic gift of Guru is outstandingly exemplified in these magnificent works.

## V
## HYMNS TO LORD ŚIVA

There are fourteen hymns in praise of Lord Śiva. They are discussed hereunder:

### (i) Kolathiresasthavam

This is a verse of ten stanzas in Malayalam. It was compiled on the occasion of reinstallation of the deity at the Kolathukara temple in Kulathoor near Thiruvananthapuram. The idea it underlines is that idols facilitate the *bhakta*'s concentration in worship. Here is a summary of the poem.

May Lord Śiva with three eyes, residing at Kalathukara, who receives and blesses those who take refuge at His Feet and who annihilates the perpetrators of evil deeds, bless me. May He who creates, protects and destroys the world in one look, bless me. May He the Omnipotent and Omnipresent, who corrects the devotee's mistakes, who dissuades me from committing evil deeds, who saves me from mental and physical illness, poverty and ego, who forgives my sins and who grants me the final refuge, bless me.

### (ii) Piṇḍanandī

It is the Lord who deposits the foetus (*piṇḍa*) into the mother's womb and blesses the being with birth. This poem of nine stanzas in Malayalam is an expression of gratitude of Him for the conferment of that Grace. Here is a summary of the poem:

When I was in the foetus state in my mother's womb, with how much care You looked after me, O Lord. Reminding myself of that Grace, I surrender at Your Feet my whole self. You alone are the protector of the child growing in the womb. Yours is the sole Divine Hand that took care of me growing there without being harmed for nine months. Hence You occupy the position of my parents. You opened to me the doors of the five senses through which I was able to know the secret of my birth. My mother had suffered untold pangs when she gave birth to me. Lord, forgive me for my share in it, though unintentioned. I gratefully surrender myself at Your Divine Feet, O, Lord of the World, in supplication and gratitude.

### (iii) Mananatheetham

This poem means beyond understanding. Written in Malayalam, it has ten stanzas. It points an accusing finger at the lust ridden human beings who in their thirst for physical pleasures, have failed to meditate on God. The author assumes the role of a *bhakta*. Here is a summary of the poem.

Because of my blind infatuation with women, I have forgotten Lord Śiva. With such unpardonable dereliction, what is my claim to live here. But there is cure for this state: Surrender at His Feet. I am doing just that. My frailty renders me unable to resist the approaching malevolent feminine beauty. O, Lord, save me from this craze for pleasure. I am a helpless prey to the attractions held out to me by these fair counterparts of the human male. As a result I have lost my heart, and suffer into the bargain. O, the Lord of all

Gods, come to me and drive away from me these evil carriers' blind lust. I fear and hate those vampires who lure me into the enjoyment of physical pleasure. O, Lord, save me from these destructive elements and take me into Your fold as You are my one refuge. A vivacious and sexy female has enslaved me with her erotic gestures. I am convinced that the pleasures obtainable from them are unreal. So Lord, I hereby surrender myself at Your Feet for liberation. O, the Omnipotent Master of all worlds, now at least save me from the attractions held out by those ephimeral pleasures.

### (iv) Indriyavairāgyam

Written in Malayalam, this verse contains ten stanzas. In this the theme is the necessity to keep the desire for wordly pleasures at bay. Here is a summary of the poem.

Lord, Your glorious form fills my heart in order that my senses, mad after enjoyment, may be relieved of that madness. To the one who seeks spiritual solace, Lord Śiva's form grants salvation. So God, bless me with a vision of that form. The agony is not for the sense-organs, but, for the person who experiences pleasure through their instrumentality. There is no end to that agony. Only Your blessing can save me from it. So bless me, O, Lord.

Your Body though smeared in ash, emblazons the entire universe. So, that body gives me the grace for salvation. I am struggling in the ocean of life because of my unceasing desires for pleasure. Save me Lord. You stay in Chidambaram encompassing within yourself, the five elements. But I am living in this earth encompassing within me, all the agony of life. Who else is there to rescue me from this state, O, My Lord.

O, the God of Destruction, show me the way to end my life with Your Divine name reverberating from my lips. I do not require anything else than the capacity to utter Lord Śiva's name both when life pulsates in my body, and departs from it. But I am engrossed in my struggle for existence in this world. This being so, where is the time for me to utter Your Name? Yet I am always uttering that Name for Salvation by surrendering myself at Your

Feet. So instead of brooding over my woes what is desirable is for me to narrate all of them to You.

O Lord, are You delivering me to senses which throb only for physical enjoyment? Because of that, my mind and body are alike weakened. Lift me to Your Feet, the Supreme Lord.

### (v) Śivaprasādapañcakam

A hymn of five stanzas in Malayalam, *Śivaprasādapañcakam* aims at directing the mind distracted by worldly pleasures, to Lord Śiva. The author as in the other pieces, is assuming the role of *bhakta* here. Here is a summary of the poem.

O Lord of the universe, I hereby surrender myself at Your Feet. Will You not bless me? You are the Power which saves me from the agony caused by my attachment to worldly possessions. My prayer is that my desires may be uprooted and I may be liberated from their clutches. Your prowess is beyond estimation or description. You strip my mind of all impurities and lead me to real devotion. I prostrate at Your Feet in complete surrender.

### (vi) Ardhanārīśvarastavam

This hymn of five stanzas in Malayalam pinpoints the irony of Lord Śiva holding the Gaṅgā on His crown, and yet denying water to the needy, gripped by smouldering heat and drought. Here is the gist of the prayer:

Lord, You carry the mighty Gaṅgā on Your crown. Yet the ordinary people face drought and are denied water to quench their thirst. Why this paradox? Are You not their sole saviour? Bless them, Great Lord. The inhabitable land and forest alike are in the hold of gruelling drought and the throats of beings have gone dry. Why this reluctance to extend Your Grace to them? Why when the world is being reduced to sandy desert by this sweltering heat, You, its only Saviour, is engrossed in *samādi* state as if unaware of this horrendous situation? We are unable to decipher the reason for this mysterious callousness towards the suffering of living beings. Is this God's justice? To whom else shall we submit our grievances for redressal but You? Yet You are deaf to our travails and prayers for reasons known only to You.

The idea contained in this verse can be condensed in a single poem. But Guru has rather wasted five stanzas on it, creating in its train a certain monotony of repetition.

## (vii) Cidambarāṣṭakam

This is a hymn in Sanskrit and contains eight stanzas. It extols Lord Śiva's greatness. Reading it one is reminded of Śrī Śaṅkarācārya's *Liṅgāṣṭaka* dealing with an identical theme. The author is the devotee here too. Here is a summary of the poem:

O the Idol of Lord Śiva at Cidambaram, save me. This Idol destroys the enemies of the world and protects it. It engrosses the might of the Lord. It grants boons to the *bhaktas*. It incarnates the fury of the forest fire and the splendour of the setting sun. It protects the virtuous and enhances its activities to cover the increasing refulgence of the Lord. It creates and sustains life among living beings. It is beyond human understanding and perception. But it manifests itself to the intelligent.

May such great images of Lord Śiva confer blessings on all things.

## (viii) Śivastavam

It is the poem in Malayalam and written in ten stanzas. Here again the Lord's greatness is extolled in eloquent terms. The author is the devotee. Here is a summary of the poem:

If the five senses are tamed to the meditation of the Lord, then spiritual enlightenment dawns upon one and one is drawn more and more to a knowledge of His prowess. From that understanding emerges real happiness. But very often the senses lapse repeatedly into the unreality of worldly pleasures. O Lord, save me from such pitfalls and consequent doom. You bless me to conquer the unreality of sensual pleasure and gain true knowledge. I hereby pledge myself to complete devotion to Your Feet. I have been fated to be born in this world and lured by the pleasures here, only to suffer into the bargain. What more misfortune can befall a human being? Indulgence in sensuality has rendered this life, a failure. So repeat the Lord's name with the aid of the rosary. One will then be endowed with real knowledge and be capable of driving away those evils and gain mental peace thereby. The Lord is not visible to the eye. But His manifestations like the sun, moon, earth, fire and the heavens are. Concentrate on them and recite the Lord's name to achieve salvation.

It is with gold that ornaments of diversified shapes are made. Similarly O Lord, all the different things in this universe are created by just one wink of Your eyes. To You I am only a flower. O, the all powerful *oṁ*, take me on to Your Divine Form. When knowledge emerges like the waves amid the turbulence of the ocean, the mind till then struggling in the turmoil of ignorance, achieves oneness with that knowledge. But till then succumbing to the demands of the body, men fight one another. Before this body of mine is broken, accept me as Your *bhakta*, O my Lord, and Master.

### (ix) Sadāśivadarśanam

There are ten stanzas in this piece, which is written in Malayalam. The author is the devotee. Here is a summary of the poem:

Even after all the sensual pleasure giving objects are erased out of this world, the mind continues to seek liaison with them. Lord Śiva alone can cleanse the mind of this bizarre inclination. He has unbounded affection for His *bhaktas*. When I am about to reach you after a tedious journey across the *saṁsāra-sāgara*, You disappear from my view. But you cannot disappear from my heart where You reign supreme. You are the Almighty God who fulfils all my wishes. The saviours of the world, the sun and moon, are just tools in Your Divine Hands. In truth, You and I are one — That thought alone pervades my being. I am convinced that while all other paths are pointers to misery and suffering, the only true path is the path of Śiva. Your brilliance outshines the dazzle of the golden lamp. You are the one God with the cauldron-like Form which can incinerate the universe. You are so magnanimous that in order to appease Pārvatī, suspicious of feminine presence on Your tresses, You prostrate at Her Feet. When am I privileged to prostrate at Her Feet? When am I privileged to prostrate in like manner at Your Feet, My Lord? It is the way to salvation, to worship that beautiful Form which engulfs the entire universe within itself. O the wearer of the crescent, perform the Cosmic Dance in the full splendour of Your Form. You are great. You are beyond comprehension even to Lords Viṣṇu and Brahmā who made a vain attempt to unravel Your mystery, one going down to the fathomless deep towards Your Feet and the other to the endless heights, towards Your Crown. They could not see Your spiritual Form. But You Graced me with a complete vision of that Form.

### (x) Chijjadachinthanam (Thought and Inertia)

As the title indicates, this is a thought on the *ātmā* (soul) and the physical body. Spiritualists believe that the concept of Monism is premissed on the relation between the *ātmā* and the physical body. Engulfing that concept and identifying the *ātmā* from the physical body is the theme of this remarkable piece of ten stanzas. It is also demonstrated here that the world is the result of the merger, of the two. The verse written in Malayalam is a projection of Guru's own wonderful experience of the realisation of this union. Here is a summary of the poem:

O Lord, may Your magnificent Form Shine within me for ever. O, the killer of all base passions, Your Form which embodies Truth, *ātmā*, and Bliss, blazes inside me. I will be freed of thoughts, about the body and able to deliver myself of it. O the Lord of Pārvatī, bless me to overcome the cravings of the body and reach the ultimate Reality. Awaken me to the isolation between the *ātmā* and the body. This truth is realised by all great souls including sage Suka. O, the Omnipotent Lord, save me from being submerged in the illusion surrounding the world. I bow before You, the Prime Destroyer. It is inexplicable how while remaining inside Your abode at Cidambaram, You have carried out Your task of Destruction. You are the embodiment of everything that is sweet and beautiful. Your Divine Feet alone are my refuge. You are my sole Saviour. Liberate me from the misery of worldly life and grant me Salvation.

### (xi) Kuṇḍalinīpaṭṭu (The song of the Kuṇḍalinī Snake)

Of Guru's musical compositions, the song of the *kuṇḍalinī* snake is the One which can be rendered in sweet melody. For richness of spirituality and profusion of ideas, it stands out as one of the most outstanding of His works. Singing it with heartfelt sincerity inspires devotion. It brings out the spiritual significance of a physical process by which a snake is lured to dance, and then seek out its hole. It discloses that *yoga* such as *bhakti*, *karma*, *raja*, lead to Salvation.

Written in Malayalam, the poem contains forty lines in stanzas of three lines each. Since it is of considerable significance to the spiritual seeker, its translated version is produced here.

*Refrain*

Dance, Cobra, dance!
Thy burrow seek and witness
The bliss of grace in wild display.
Dance, cobra, dance!

1. Keep close to the foot so lotus red
Sacred of the Lord who dons
The crescent moon and cassia bloom and
(repeat *refrain*) Dance, cobra, dance. . . .

2. Besmeared with ash and bright His Holy form shines.
Thy tears for Him in streams do shed,
And thus steadily (*refrain*)

3. Upon this burning ground
Where ghost and also corpse are born
United well with what subsists, its counterpart Supreme
(*refrain*)

4. That flute of flowery perfume
In shade it lies in shame
Besides this beauteous form, which view and
(*refrain*)

5. A spotted leopard skin surrounds
His form of tender bloom.
"Within the Self he dances" say and (*refrain*)

6. Upon the silver hill what gleams
As Vedic wisdom's quintessence,
Say "That in me is dancing too" and (*refrain*)

7. He for whom a sportive snake
An ornament becomes
His home it is in us; so (*refrain*)

8. No one has seen, not he of blossom's bloom,
Nor even that holy garlanded one,
This flower-form of thine, so (*refrain*)

9. Aum and all the rest that form
The essence of ten million charms
We now do know and so keep on, and (*refrain*)

10. To the One who conjures down,
Who all things here brings out
To His leaf-tender foot adhere, and (*refrain*)

11. From lettered charms of Siva-praise
To every formula of truth —
Even from sound do they come out, so (*refrain*)

12. Ten thousand millions
Of that Ananta snake art Thou:
Thy million hoods then open out, and (*refrain*)

13. This body here no truth it has;
Owner another in it resides.
Such wisdom do thou gain, and thus (*refrain*)

**14.** Uniting body and owner too,
Radiant, who abides as one,
Such there is to know, as well, so
(*refrain*)

**15.** What swallows all, with rival none,
Such is the omnipresent Word
Which swallow thou, and steadily
(*refrain*)

**16.** Consuming all the words there are
As the supporting wall for all,
Even on such do take thy stand, and
(*refrain*)

**17.** From very name this great expanse
And even earth as well did come,
As a presentiment in thought, so
(*refrain*)
(Trans.: Nataraja Guru)

Before Launching on to the full meaning of this poem let us try to understand what *kuṇḍalinī* is.

*Kuṇḍalinī* is a yogic concept. It refers to a snake lying coiled at the base of the vertebral column. It is supposed to represent a storehouse of nervous energy which irradiates upwards to the higher centres of the nervous system. It is psychic energy and is beyond the scope of scientific enquiry. Under systematically cultivated spiritual disciplines known to *yoga* the coiled up snake at the base of the vertebral column is capable of uncoiling itself, releasing immense power in consequence. That power then reaches higher and higher levels, touching or attaining successive plexes often referred to as lotuses or central points from which nervous energy of a spiritual order radiates. The swinging and swaying of the cobra with its hood lifted in response to music, release a sense of exultation to the *yogī*. Here, attempt is made only to bring out the meaning seen by the author in the process in so far as it is comprehensible to the lay devotee.

O, the knowledge incarnate snake, seeing you swing and sway to the music, one is made aware of the real value of life. The music symbolises the call to humanity to abjure caste and religious differences and live as members of a single family. What Kṛṣṇa, Buddha, Christ and Muhammed had given to the world was nothing but this message engulfed in music. So acceptance of the knowledge conveyed by the music as the guideline for life will lead to a vision of happiness.

The moon in the sky and the cassia on the earth are two illustrious flowers. Lord Śiva sports both on His divine tresses. Here the indication is that instead of chasing the ephemeral worldly pleasures and tiring oneself out, what is covetable is to search for and identify the Lord's Grace. The *kuṇḍalinī* power which gives salvation to man, goes up and merges with the highest plex known as *sahasra padma*. It is Lord Śiva who confers such salvation. O the snake which stands close to the Feet of that Lord, You go on with your dance in ecstasy.

Shed tear for Lord Śiva who burns off the three acts in the fire of knowledge and smears the ash all over His body, thus saving the world. It is accepted that tears are the symbols of devotion at its climax. O Snake, that dances for the blessing of that Lord, look at Him with tearful eyes and dance to His heart's pleasure.

You are the snake of knowledge. You are also the thousand headed, a thousand crores of Anantas (the bed of Lord Viṣṇu). It is the same knowledge that is endemic in all beings. In short, O Snake, you are the possessor of divine knowledge, who looks at all beings as identical to each other. So open your thousand tongues and dance with absolute contentment.

God is one and indivisible. The essence of all religions is one. God is the embodiment of that oneness. That oneness is realised by the primordial sound *AUṀ* which is the gist of all *mantras*. It can lead and restrain the world. Its essence is multi-million fold in its ramifications. Just assimilate the truth, O snake, that essence is no one but ourselves, and dance.

The spotted leopard represents five senses which hunt for

worldly pleasures. Lord Śiva wears its skin. By doing so He has shown that while outwardly He represents the material aspects, the external personality, internally, His personality maintains its divinity. So dance O Snake inculcating that ultimate truth about the Lord. Lord Śiva dances along with the devils and corpses in the cremation ground. That ground is the end of the journey for the body. Imbibe this message in the song and dance to its tune O, Snake.

Goddess Pārvatī is Lord Śiva's consort. She is so dear to Him because of Her devotion to Him. Her heart-thralling tresses which exude sweet fragrance of flowers and her body which excels in lascivious splendour has enraptured Him with desire. Look at that magnificent form and dance with all your thousand hoods spread out, O, Snake.

If the core of the universe can be traced to the Sound, the hymn *AUṀ namaḥśivāya* is energy thast pervades universe. Its origin, existence and destruction emanate from *Brahman*. The power of this *namaḥśivāya mantram* pre-existed the Origin of the universe. Taking this Truth in, you continue to dance, O, Snake.

Lord Brahmā is preoccupied with creation. So is Lord Viṣṇu with preservation. So the two could not realise Lord Śiva. O Snake, you perform your dance pretending not to have noticed this Truth.

Lust and desire have enveloped the world and stained its greatness. It is Lord Śiva who incinerated these evil forces. Repeating that Lord's Name, you go on with your dance. O Snake. Dance, snake dance, to pronounce that Lord Śiva resides in the heart of everyone.

With his novel ornaments like the serpents and skulls on, Lord Śiva is protecting the world. Know snake that He is our final abode and dance with that knowledge. It is Lord Śiva too who divests Himself of the burden of creation, preservation and extermination and takes over each work over again. Fix your heart on those Feet and go on with the dance.

All knowledge remains submerged in the atmosphere. It is

assimilated and experienced through the five senses; Dance snake, with the awareness of this truth. When all knowledge has disappeared from the physical world, real knowledge emerges and expresses itself as the word spoken through the mouths of great sages. Absorb that Truth and dance, the great snake. Consuming all words, the fire of knowledge enters the universe and remains and dazzles as knowledge of the ultimate. Bow to that mystery and dance, the benevolent Snake.

Know Snake that the body is not real and that what is real is the *ātmā* or spirit inside it, and dance. Though there are rural and urban people with different lifestyles and value senses, so far as spiritual truth is concerned, they are one. So what is required of the spiritual master is enjoinments equally appealing to both, and instilling God's name in them. With that belief you continue dancing.

It is true that the body is ephemeral and the *ātmā* is eternal. But remember that the one power which can swallow both is *Brahman* and proceed with your dance, great Snake. *Brahman* is indicated by the sound *AUṀ*. From *Brahman* could be seen everything in the universe, from the vast skies to the tiny sand grain. O Snake, dance with the motive of demonstrating this basic Truth. When the awakened *kuṇḍalinī* power has traversed along the seven plexes and entered the *sahasrāra padma*, all that is unreal in the self is shed off and the self remains in bliss. Know this Supreme Truth and continue that majestic dance O, the King of Snakes.

### (xii) Vilāsadarśanam (Vision of Virtuousness)

Sree Narayana Guru has written a poem captioned *Vilāsadarśanam* (Vision of Virtuousness). However a portion of it only has come to light. In that portion are traced three poems in praise of Lord Śiva, the first two in ten stanzas each and the third in thirty stanzas. They are:

(A) ANUBHŪTIDAŚAKAM

Here is a summary of the poem.

While Lord Śiva pervades everything in the universe let me worship His idol which remains in total detachment. Just as what is seen with the eyes lies dormant in them, so what is heard merges with the ear and what is touched blends with the skin. In like manner the experiences of all sense-organs fuse with each of the respective ones until a stage is reached when the sense-organs alone exist in passive state. When the rope which holds a person is cut the person falls to the ground. Similarly when the senses become inactive they become impotent and hence unreceptive to knowledge. There will be darkness only. In the darkness the illuminating *ātmā* remains and takes up the rescue act by uttering the word, 'I am your saviour'. With that sound all sorrows will disappear. What is the power of darkness before the dazzling sun? When relief is found, it is possible that indolence may set in. If we maintain a responsive stance to that light, bliss will be ours. This bliss interpenetrates everywhere. The enlightened sages consume it to their contentment. With the attainment of bliss, worldly longings will cease to exist, and eternal peace takes their place, without wasting life upon momentary thrills, and at the same time one loses oneself in that peace. A person who sees another as separate from himself is, whatever his stature, dominated by the animal instinct. When that feeling of difference is blotted out ecstasy will flow in.

(B) PRAPAÑCAŚUDDHIDAŚAKAM

Here is the poem's summary:

Before the brilliance of real knowledge, the crowd of rushing fearful objects disappear. The next moment the darkness of ignorance envelops the whole scenario. However the nectar of knowledge will re-emerge and loom large. What one should do is to labour hard to maintain it. (Light and darkness or knowledge and ignorance appear by turns). There is a riddle hidden in the elements like water and fire. If that is resolved everything will become clear like what is kept in the palm of the hand. There is a truth behind the phenomena of nature. This Truth is a riddle in the form of an ingenious artifice. How to unearth its mystery is the problem. Once it is deciphered everything becomes easy. Remaining in this life which is the fruit of deeds in previous lives, man is engaged in a mad hunt for worldly experiences. It is akin to a state in which one sees silvery moonlight before the Lord who dons his crown with the crescent. The cosmic dance of Lord Śiva represents actuated knowledge assuming frightful form and swallowing everything. (The cosmic dance symbolises the momentariness of the universe). If one is blessed to see that dance, calmness dawns upon one. On contemplation it could be seen that what overwhelmingly flows on the earth is beauty symptomised as bliss. This beauty is but the expression of the Omnipotent. This body is only cotton exposed to the fire of knowledge, and turned into ashes thereby. When the body is dead, all bodily functions cease, as the senses reach the stage of sterility. Then the power that rendered them so, appears as the indestructible *Brahman* which is immune to the onslaught of sorrow. It is the infinite truth and known as Salvation. Salvation in one stroke is unbounded benediction. The moment attachment to life is cut off, Salvation flushes in.

### (C) SVĀNUBHĀVAGĪTHI

In this piece the author takes on the role of the devotee. Here is the summary of the poem:

O Lord Śiva, is it not Your duty to bless me with Salvation? Grant me the power to describe You. Enlighten me with the intellectual artifice to remain detached to the fluctuating worldly experience. You stand above everything in the universe. How can I live without Your mercy. You create *māyā* (illusion), ego and *karma* (action). What a paradox! You fuse even the minutest object with *māyā*. When that *māyā* is burnt away, only the fire and fume which rise from it and You, remain. After all what else is the visible world but the fume or unreality? How mysterious are Your sports? You are my sole refuge. I prostrate at Your Feet. Save me from this *māyā*.

Your kind Eyes embrace the entire universe. May those Feet be placed on my head. Do not abandon me Lord. A devotee is proud to be the Lord's slave. My heart yearns to blend with You. All Veda is Śiva Himself as Vedic utterances are realities. Will you not bless me with deliverance? Unlike many who have failed to trace You out, I have found You and taken refuge at those Feet.

Swallow me O Lord, so that everything worldly will disappear, including the five elements. God is the single force seen in diverse forms and shapes. The real knower is the one who realises this truth. Do not unsettle me with the impression that God is more than one. Lord, You have enveloped the illusion that is me. And with that my travails are over. Are You bent on keeping me away? No, that is not possible.

Lord Candraśekhara, why don't you enwrap my entire consciousness, so that I shall attain blissful oblivion. I hereby pray for that complete fusion.

### (xiii) Śivaśatakam

Of the hymns Sree Narayana Guru wrote in praise of Lord Śiva, *Śivaśatakam* is the greatest and most massive. Contained in one hundred stanzas, this piece dwells first on exaltation of Gaṇapati, Sarasvatī and Subrāhmaṇya and then on a head to foot portrayal of Lord Śiva. The poem is rich in meaning and replete with the spiritual doctrine of Renunciation. It abounds in pure devotion as well. The author plays the role of the devotee. Here is the English version of the text:

1. The history whole of Bharat-war the great
   Was nicely written ere, on Meru mount.
   With the broken tusk of Lord "Ganapati"
   Had completely filled up distinctly well
   The word or 'Aum' the God who reconciled
   The mankind belongs to the sect low classed
   May kindly protect and bless willingly.

2. The four Vedas were once ere recited

Divided and did give to Lord Krishna
The rest was put on Sri Valluver's tongue
May save O, Bharathi sweetly perfumed.

**3.** Got on the golden peacock fine
    Bearing the weapon Vel
With piteousness and mercy much
    Whose eyes filled with hot tears
Who enters crematoriums
    And wearest Ashes enough
O! Subrahmaṇya, be piteous
    To protect and bless me.

**4.** Before the eternal sons of "Brahma"
Namely Sanath, and Sanantha
Spake advices to learned Sages ere
One sat under the shade of Kallaal tree
The Being who turned his face to the South
May kindly save and shower much blessings.

**5.** The holy name of "Lord Siva", well thought
Can find that there's no such else glorious names
I suffer much hard-ships of several kinds
Those knowingly in my heart here, Alas!

**6.** The movements of Lord Vishnu and Brahma
Had not been seen and known to me at all
Hara-Hara then who did know very well?
Thy dance and play, the idol in heart sees.

**7.** The crescent moon and matted hair brownish,
Having Ganga and fearful Serpent wreaths
And three-lined ash marks on thy broad forehead
Those seen above thy burning eye besides.

**8.** The eyes of Sun who wears the Crescent Moon,
And ears those worn the golden earrings
And golden flower of Sesamum plant.
That bowed down worshipping Maha Siva
And nose that breathes the "Pranayamic" deeds.

**9.** That which ruined the sins old committed
His fine lips that fought against Thonti fruit
That's known as fruit of "Bryoni a grandis"
The fair looking teeth like the well washed gems
And cheeks both seem like those of the full Moon.

**10.** The pleasing words that reach the heart of mine
Just like the nectar flows and fall in sea.
Of various sorrows of the birth and death
The piteous and kindest deeds of Mahesh
Have much cooled and comforted me enough
With gratitude and devotion I bow
In front of Lord and God Sree Maheshwar.

**11.** The coral mount new shines of country whole
And Moon rose up on laccous mount
That safely rubs the twinkling little stars
I humbly put my earnest prayers all
To protect and bless those who didst leave out.

**12.** The body wearing skull and snakes often
The dark clouds come and honour Śiva's neck
The four hands bearing Siva's favoured things
Such as Sool, Stag, refuge and granting boons
And four blooms, I want to see everfor.

**13.** So nicely combined Serpentine garlands
Fearlessly mix'd with horrid sorts of snakes
And body smeared with holiest "ashes"
And when can I see thy blessed body
With rows of black bees following Mahesh.

**14.** The flowing water of Akasa Ganga
A virgin maid, when taking her bath in
Likewise water then flown up as usual
The whirl at level of the wisdom centre
The tuft of hairs whole was supposed then bent.

**15.** The skin stripped off from thighs of an elephant
And wore it as His royal clothe and then

Did take the picture in one hand, with tail
When can I see them girded on thy belt?

**16.** Serpent Ananta, used as "Katchapram"
On cloth elephants skin, so much large and black
Covered with ashes much sweetly scented
And when can I see thy dance beauteous most?

**17.** While playing with the twinkling ornaments
Those put on two legs of the Dancing God
The kilukila Voice heard from Chilanka
When can I hear them in both ears of mine.

**18.** The top and bottom and the Central part
Those became one after being ruined
Seeing the lamp that stands up-right and shines
And expels all sorrows and afflictions
As the ocean goes off the shore in safety

**19.** The Supreme ruler of cosmos "Mahesh",
The Sun, Fire and Air, Water and the Earth
The well known five elements in the world.
And who dost know the tricks of Mahendra
The deep meaningful verses of great bards.

**20.** The golden pot that bearest the full Moon,
And being those interested in dramas,
The finest and most heartfelt dance and plays
Thine eagerness being seen expanded
The growing greediness in acts and plays
And all seen there may be happy and good
I was enforced to tell all what I saw.

**21.** Received and divided, the Mother Goddess
And gave the half, ere, to Lord Sree Krishna
A poor one likes to be with you "Goddess"
O! Mother Bhagavati, Pārvati, Sree-Bhadra.

**22.** O! Mahesh! be kind enough to save me
By destroying all sins I committed

Put off the tying chord of birth and death
And lift me up from sea of afflictions
You may not think that I'm a flesh eater
Pasupathi and coir are import,
Those please the Lord Maheshwar the great God.

**23.** A few days back I had been suffering from
A watery loose motion with great distress.
Bhagavan Siva did know it and well healed
After some months it had been forgotten
Forgetting and ingratitude are sins
I do suffer pains again and again
O! Maheshwar, be kind enough to save.

**24.** Medicines are gettable on this mount
There three snakes and a tiger to protect
Pulayan took the half he did eat
And have the rest for Omnipresent soul
To be kept for the future generations.

**25.** It's difficult to live on this world
I have no death here, if think over well
Have I done any sin great against Thee.
Have mercy upon me to save and bless
O! Maheshwar, the ocean of kindness.

**26.** To satisfy hunger or appetite
To eat enough food whatever I get
From anywhere are the occurrence of death
Get down the coir of pure devotion
And let me climb up to Kailas the Heaven
And save and bless me O! Lord Maheshwar.

**27.** The holy being who wears crescent Moon
And Akasa Ganga in the crown of his
Thou dost know all facts happen in this world
And thou art sea of kindness and pure love
Be kind to save and bless me O! Mahesh!

**28.** One who dost hold fast the stag in one hand
While after burgling bottom of full Moon
To take lot of gems bright and worthy most
And bears the river that flows to bottom still
I see e'er the stag and river Ganga
Through inner eyes given me by Mahesh.

**29.** To cure disease of birth and death e'er for
There's no medicine but effective Siva names
The world is again filled up all over
With this disease well mentioned just before
Forgetting events took place earlier.

**30.** The third eye of the Lord Sree Maheshwar
That burnt up Cupid Maran the devilish
With hottest fire emitted by Hara!
He comes and does much harm to devotees.
And deserves to be burnt again and 'gain.

**31.** When actions of the Senses five such as —
The eye, and nose and tongue, skin and the ears
And heart the chief sense of divine knowledge
And that of birth and some else connected
Are seen there being completely ended
Then nerve Kundalini begins to shake self
At its one end like very small round balls
And nerve Sushmna touches softly there
At the entrance hole way's opened to get in
At Muladhar the posterior and hips
Through which the Kundalini gets in the crown
At Sahasra Padma the goal important
By this time Atma's rebirth would occur
Otherwise, should bid farewell to the world.

**32.** Philosophical truth of Lord Siva
And Parvati the Sakti Holy most
And that of Voice or melodious sound
They became entirely nil by now,
Those all ruined were changed as the fuels

To sacrifice in worshipping Śiva.

**33.** The body is covered with skin having
Tiny and soft hairs almost all over
The death is sure for man who does own it
And man who being suffered from sorrow
Of birth and death and afflictions such as
The dry leaves those fell into cyclones great
Can't be expressed the rest stages of them
So be kind to save me O! Lord Śiva.

**34.** Had I been immersed in the sins very much
And groups of sins had I hid in my heart
Tho' I am a sinner great in thy presence
And Thou art the sea of kindness and love
I beg Thy pardon and to save me, Lord!

**35.** By mortifying all the chief senses
Or subduing the whole senses import
And when saint settled in meditation
Dost vanish his soul in the "Samaadhi"
Then th' saint can get the precious divine gift
The desired most blissful thing the nectar
And he can eat this food most excellent
And without having any objection
And if he does not fall in love with it
He can live shining just like sun the bright.

**36.** There is nobody in this world
To give necessary help
Excepting Thou who didst engage
In blissful "Taandava" dance
If Thou canst cast a kindly look
What anything more I want
To make happier much and more
No more blessings I want.

**37.** Thou mayest appear in front of
Mine, as soon as Thou canst

With Parvati who dost own thine half
O! Lord Maheshwar God
And let me worship foot of Thine
With devotion highest.

**38.** While seeing and enjoying all the charms
Of charming ladies all fairest and young
A sudden thought attracted me on Thee
That opened mine eyes, ears, both and the heart
So request I Thy pardon kind to save
Me from all the worldly allurements
And give occasions to worship Thy feet.

**39.** Due to tying with privities of girls
Young men do suffer much and more sorrows
And you may kindly save and bless me well
And may not I be ruined by women.

**40.** To fight against "Yama", known as "Kaalan"
Be Thou always with me, wasting no time
To suffer all troubles done by Cupid
Sent me not often O! Lord Maheshwar

**41.** Pleasure is not here and ne'er in heavens
But pains only in whole of outer world
And everything is thus; "Scripture admits"
And I didn't know e'er what's the day or night
O! Lord and God! great Master of Kailas.

**42.** Came once the Lord Mahesh the greatest God
Turned Divine face and kindly looked at me
When will you let me cross over the Sea
Of birth and death and afflictions such else
O! Lord the sea of kindness, and pure love.

**43.** The sacred most image of Lord Siva
That's seen in cosmos or in prapancha
In different forms are totally fifteen
As five forms on Earth, and four in water

And three in fire and two in air or wind
Excepting one in sky above the Earth.

**44.** Goddess Gouri who being Haimavati
Who stands e'er as a better, better half
Her shaken breasts here stored milk nectar like
The river flows from highest peaks of mount
That gives pleasure much to whole of mankind
And let it flow and fall on my head too.

**45.** Bearing Ganga and Smearing ashes enough
And wearing garlands of waves of Ganga
From topmost peaks of Himalaya mountains
And dec'rated with wreaths of horrid snakes
O Siva-Sankar, the ocean of kindness
And bless me Lord Siva-Sankar God the great.

**46.** Ne'er have I done or thought of doing sins
To any man who lived or living still
And thoughts of sins so as ne'er rise in me
Protect me Siva-Sankar O! my god
Will you make me holy expelling sins.

**47.** What sins had I committed in past life?
To dismiss not state of distress mine all
Thou hast to burn out past life sins of mine
Likewise once you burnt Muppuram to ash
Without delay, as soon as possible.

**48.** Most distressing misdeeds of Kamadev
Which you must push out of — my restless heart
If you could dwell e'er in my confused mind
I would have been saved from Kamadeva's troubles
Please get him out and stay in my abode.

**49.** The virtues give pleasure to senses five
Tho' very soon you went and bid blame the Moon
If you could turn thy favours all on me
The sorrows arose from the birth and death
Would have been excluded completely well.

**50.** O! My Lord Siva!
And all the senses mine have been fatigued
Mine eyes both are much drawnback to inside
And became completely out of focus
And eyesight is much lessened and thus' lost
To know the time of occurrence of death
The Atma or soul dost whisper always
The holy most charm "Namassivaaya"

**51.** O! Hail! hail my God Sri Sivasankar great
Who does not like the past and future lives
Be victorious whole Ruler of Universe
Who lives ever on Mountain Sree Kailas.

**52.** Be victorious O! Lord Sree Siva-Sankar
The greatest God who suppressed sinful lust
O! Hail! Hail! beauteous dancing God famous
And bless O! Lord Thy loving worshippers.

**53.** Don't You know and hear my cries sorrowful
Who awaits at Thy lotus holy feet
Desiring to be saved and kindly blessed
When can I get out of this pit so deep?

**54.** In days of yore Lord Vishnu did Pluck out
An eye of His own and adored it at
The divine Lotus Feet of God greatest
Lord Siva Sankar the ocean of Kindness
Kindly bless me by casting a kind look

**55.** Without saying any excuse to me
Who is being suffered from many pains
Like molten wax that's put in hottest pot
To make me under control of Thy will
Be kind to bless and direct me O Lord.

**56.** From the beginning state of Youthfulness, I had
To fight against misdeeds of Kamadev
The nature of his misdeeds was terrible
As a rock that rolls down from a mountain top

That's why I was obliged to forget Thee
Please save and bless me O! my God Siva.

**57.** Being fixed the sins of "Kali" in me
Just like the mountain known as "Kulagiri"
The strength or might, have been leaked out of me
Mine ability to fight Kamadev
Has much lessened, O! Lord Sree Maheshwar.

**58.** Became apart the caste like-wise family
Staying on mount, contemplating Mahesh
It's an art having much fearfulness
Being my fate let Thy will may happen.

**59.** One roams without discrimination I'm
When you like to bless, come here with Devi
Thy better half known as Goddess "Durga"
Protect me as no sins approach ever me
The heart if melt and joined with glory
Divine will would ne'er split by any cause.

**60.** To get not occasions to speak with girls
And make friendship and sinful attachments
That ruin my pure most life e'er for
Is the only humble prayer of mine O! Lord,
The greatest God known as Kailaasanaath!

**61.** If think over my life, I can well known
That Thou art my support and protection
All attachments except tie with Siva
Should be expelled from my heart is import
No space must be left without Siva Bhakti
Thus say the great men, having knowledge much.

**62.** O! Lord the sea of Kindness and pure love
When will You grant me leave to approach Thee
Going about begging controlling mind
And having with a thought in single end
And when will I get Sanyasic life good
Or the State having nearness of the same.

**63.** O! Hail ho! Lord Hara-Hara great God
Who burnt and killed all members of Muppuram
The Ganga concealed within matted hairs
May not it be flown out O! Maheshwar,
And be kind to save and bless me my Lord.

**64.** When I think, I have no one to help me
My sorrows become doubled O! my God
Except Thy holy Feet, and Thou alone
To protect and kindly save and bless me
And this become nil, all sins committed.

**65.** The waves of nectar flow from Thine eyes both
Will fall in channels, and flow to sea deep
From curl to curl, when will I reach Thy Feet
And when can I rise from there O! my Lord.

**66.** The falling rain like flowing tears of mine
Thy heart with utmost kindness did well melt
Seeing my sorrows and afflictions much
Thou hast blest me to get out of the sea
Of birth and death and many afflictions
Dissolved thy heart and So I became saved.

**67.** The difficulties those had been oft occurred
On ways of my life-trip disastrous most
Should all be expelled with the grace of God
And keep meat Thy holy Feet everfor
This desiring wish grows and grows in me.

**68.** As sorts of sins do rush into my heart
I humbly request You to protect me
I worship and salute You sincerely
For Thou art able to ruin all sins
And to do good all to Thy devotees
When fault is seen in my own heart confused
It seems butter melt on fire in hot pan.

**69.** Confounded with their eyes corner charming
The chariot Reti is built in beautiful style

Reti is drawn by five finest horses
Such as two eyes and one nose and two ears.
They are selected from the chief senses
The charioteer is well known as *Ātmā*
He has kept a fine image of his self
The haughty self interest in chariot fair
Desiring much and more of vicious sins.

**70.** Hair deftly dressed, ear lobes — diamond studded
Struts along the killer elephant mad
The breast's horn and head sky-ward raised —
Let these befudille me not, Oh Supreme Lord.

**71.** The greatest sin in the form of charming balls
Seen on breast of the teenaged female ones
Awaiting to pluck out the heart of mine
Throw not me in front of them, O my God
Who is well bound to keep and bless ever for.

**72.** If whole sea-water is drained and the rest
Being kept in a big tube for a while
And fill with sweepings, intolerable stench
That rise up make the odour more stinking.
Privities of girls kept so privately
May produce much of very bad smell strong
Yet bearing such worst stinking limbs, they do
Attract male persons tho' wisest and great
May not e'er consent me to go behind
The beauteous ladies the fearful sinners
O! Lord Siva-Sankar greatest God of mine.

**73.** The womb or uterus created in stomach
Is with the blood and flesh and the bones
The blood, puss, and water flow out in streams
From it with stench intolerable most
Without having charms in women's beauty.
Thou mayest protect me kindly with Thee
And be immersed in the sea of glory of Thine.

**74.** Unconditioned sinless and immortal
And beauteous most e'er lasting Lord Siva
Thou alone art my refuge ever for
Thy lotus feet both are my protection
When will I get Thy kindest permission

**75.** The pure most being and sin destroyer
And chief en'my of "Pura" the devilish
My hearty salute to Thee O! my God
Please give occasions to worship Thy Feet.

**76.** The Being who hath lotus like fair eyes
And being greatest en'my of Kamadev
And Over Lord of the whole Universe
May protect and bless me O! Lord Siva.

**77.** Never have I plucked fresh blooms to adore Thee
But mental worships only had I done
Is it the reason why I'm forced to suffer
O! my Lord and God great Sri Siva Sambhu!

**78.** O! Lord who beareth crescent moon on head
And holy river Ganga in matted hairs
My heart does not e'er become so silent
You may help me to keep it be so hushed
What must I do to keep my heart with Thee?

**79.** The fate settled by God can't be transgressed
By any one here in this present world
I do not know anything about it
Everything happens as the will of God
That's only I do know and nothing more.

**80.** Praising is pleasant to the whole mankind
Tho' fruit of flattery being bad or good.
As I don't like it I don't want at all
As I know not to boast Thee in true ways
I will not try to get good through boastings.

**81.** Overflowing with no bounds and limits

The waves of Thy greatest kindness and love
I request you humbly with devotion
To get in and come out from Thy kindness
Will you kindly save and gladly bless me.

**82.** The Moon the charioteer of Kamadev
Who owns only dimlight rays than others
Yet Moon stands in lily's field to muse
The Moon and lies try their best to defeat
Their foes with blessings of Lord Siva Sankar.

**83.** When do complete the daily changing scenes
Of Moon which shines with reduced dim light rays
Do You think that happen by actions self
Why dost Thou keep the pretty crescent Moon
Thine old enemy known Kamadeva and Moon
May not make sorrows to the crescent Moon
Seem on Thy head over Thy matted hairs.

**84.** Thou hast no timidity tho' beaten
With strongest waves countless of sky Ganga
And without making any different stage.
Why not thou keep the pretty crescent Moon
Thou liveth at Chidambaram, Tamil Nadu
Much and more reverence to Thee, O! God.

**85.** I wish to enter in a thick forest
To kill elephants and leopards to be stripped
As You like such skins as Thy divine cloth
Perhaps You would laugh at my foolishness
O! Lord and my God Sri Kailasanath.

**86.** To stay at home doing not any work
Desired and eating whatever You get
And become swelled like a pillow well filled
Thus You did mark on my head as my fate
O! my Lord and God Sri Siva Sambhu.

**87.** The Kaliyuga man comes like a tiger
Hiding and crouching slowly to catch prey

He comes from somewhere stands awaiting me
To cut off the head and legs of my prey
To take it as his prey that I did earn
Is the chief aim of that Kaliyuga man
He comes so horribly to catch myself
Kindly save me O my Lord Siva Sankar.

**88.** Just like the fragrance of good smelling blooms
The Arul pervades well in the three worlds
And reflects image in still sea waters
The Arul or Grace well reflects on the sea
Has it any connection with waters?

**89.** There are three kinds of seeds known Mummalam
Such as Aavanam, Karmmam and Maya.
There's much mountain water in this world
To be sprouted, and grown and to be reaped
The worldly men who engaged in farming
Do suffer much pain in their worldly lives.

**90.** The greyness, old age and death occur oft
Do come like a tiger to catch mankind
When will come there an end to this aspect?
O! Lord and God Sree Bhagavan Siva Sankar.

**91.** When devotion on Siva doth increase
And not to fluctuate the Divine thoughts
From Maya of the most powerful God
Sree Siva Sankar the mightiest Being
And shall it be seen alike ever for.

**92.** Please Save me from defeats and to do burn
All sinful uncleanness, O! my great God
With contemplation Thine O! Siva Siva
The shoe-flower coloured, most beauteous Lord.

**93.** By leading contemptible life in words.
The birth and death sprout and grow richly there
A fuel to the cremating fire or
A sweet meat for a tiger or lion.

**94.** A man dost born e'er singly in this world
Tho' he has mother, sire and the guardians
Moreover has friends and loving neighbours
And without Them he goes off singly last
So man dost live always a lonely life.
But man knows not that he lives really 'lone.

**95.** If Maheshwar who wears blooms of Erricks
Comes near me to spray blessings on me will
I would be happier than getting the presence
Of the late and respected mother and sire mine.

**96.** Would you be kind enough to grant me leave
To live doing thy servitudes ever for
Without suffering any sorrows henceforth
That helps to will fix devotion on Thee
Thy kind looks on me will end sorrows mine.

**97.** The waves arose from Sky Ganga, O! Lord,
The sorrows all will be frozen in them
But sorrows arose from the destiny
Can be cut out with Thy special sight 'lone
I pray humbly most for Thy kindest bliss.

**98.** Lord Maheshwar wearing the pompous dress
For the famous dance known as "Tandava"
With theatrical ornaments such as —
The leopard skin, Trishulam, and the stag
The crescent moon, over His matted hairs
And sky Ganges known as Akasa Ganga
And all else necessary apparatus best
Well belted with serpentine garlands fine
Let me see lotus face of Lord Nataraj.

**99.** The waves arose from the Akasa Ganga
Were seemed steered by hooded serpents much
Who lives on head and body of the Lord
And god the greatest "Being" "Sree Nataraj".

**100.** The full Moon bearing countless rays
And pervades the Moonlight
All over this world coolness with
Rose up the gentle Moon
Shone brightly in the Divine World
With likes blown in tanks
Especially in the Divine tank
Known "Sahasra Padma".
(Translation: P. Damodara Panicker)

COMMENTARY

1. The start is with a glorification of Lord Gaṇapati. The God with a broken tusk, who once wrote the great Epic *Mahābhārata*, stands for the humblest of the humble and the lowest of the low. May he bless me also. (The story is that Vyāsa dictated the story of *Mahābhārata* and Lord Gaṇapati willingly wrote it with his broken tusk as the *narayam* (pen) on the great mountain Mahāmeru which he used as his pad).

2. Goddess Sarasvatī dictated the greatest treasure of human knowledge namely the four Vedas to Vyāsa. After that she imparted them to Thiruvalluvar's tongue in the form of *Thirukural*, the great Tamil classic. May that Goddess of knowledge bless me.

3. Lord Subrāhmaṇya travels on the golden peacock throughout the world to shower kindness upon living beings. He dances in the burial ground which encompasses the process of birth and death, smears ash from it on His body to demonstrate the meaninglessness of physical existence. I pray for his blessings.

4. May Lord Śiva who sat countenance turned southwards on the granite platform around and in the shade of the banyan tree and imparted knowledge to the three great sages Sanakan, Sanandanan and Sanal Kumar, take care of me.

5. O Lord Śiva, when one contemplates on your name, one will realise that there is no other name to equal it. Even with this knowledge, I am struggling with this worldly life. What an irony!

6. Even Lords Viṣṇu and Brahmā are ignorant of your Divine sports. That being so, who else can grasp their meaning. Even if that Divine form dwells in one's heart in all its brilliance, no one can comprehend Lord Śiva's greatness.

7. (From now on, the author embarks on a head to foot depiction of Lord Śiva's mighty form).

   O Lord, enable me to see the Crescent and Goddess Gaṅgā on Your crown, the snake garland donning your neck, the three lines of ash marks on your forehead and the fierce third eye that had burnt to ashes Kāmadeva, the God of Lust.

8. O, the God, who has the sun and moon as Your two eyes, allow me to see Your Ears with the diamond set ringlets, Your golden hued nose which excels the sesamum flower in loveliness, bless me to bow before Your form in supplication, joining both hands.

9. I hereby prostrate before your glorious form with the most beautiful red lips which put the reddest of fruits to the shade and the sight of which extricates one from all sins of previous births. With the splendid teeth which outstrips the brilliantly shining, and freshly washed gems and with the cheeks dazzling in refulgence like the full moon.

10. I hereby bow before your sweet words which rush in like the waves of nectar and the look of kindness which emanates from those eyes and which cools down my heart smouldering in the woes of worldly existence.

11. I derive absolute contentment at the sight of that radiant smile which emerges from the pearl mountain and those beautiful beaming eyes which add lustre to that smile. Yet for self-protection as it were, I praise You Lord.

**12.** O the Great Almighty, permit me to see that lucent neck on which are worn the snake inter-spaced with bones, and those four hands each holding the power to gift, the might to grant refuge, the deer and the trident respectively.

**13.** Lord, bless me to see that wonderful chest embellished with garlands of snakes and flowers and that torso smeared with ash and with crowds of beetles enjoying its fragrance.

**14.** God Śiva's naval is like the middly swirling of the heavenly Gaṅgā river. The charming hair line on his stomach is as infatuating as the Yamunā river itself flowing upwards from that naval. Am I fated to see that my Lord?

**15.** When can I see Lord Śiva's Form, His nakedness covered with elephant skin girdled tight with the snake roped round.

**16.** When can I see that cosmic dance in full splendour with snakes as garlands and the body draped in holy ash?

**17.** When can I hear the reverberating sound of those anklets ringing in tune with the rhythmic leg movements involved in the cosmic dance?

**18.** The burning lamp which symbolises the fusion of the Beginning, the Middle and the End, boils the sea of unhappiness and reduces it to nothingness. So the journey to the other bank of *saṁsāra-sāgara* is made easy.

**19.** You are the Sun, Moon, Earth, the sacrificer and the five elements. Everything that is visible to the naked eye is nothing but you. Who can delve into the mysteries of Your poser and gauge its meaning? It is as intractable and undecipherable as the wonder strokes of the poet's imaginative creations.

**20.** O the Lord that wears the crescent! I yearn to realise the intellectual implications of the fantastic drama you are enacting. So whatever has sprung in my brain, I am speaking out. But everything I utter strangely befits you.

**21.** You have divided your body between Goddess Pārvatī and God Viṣṇu. If anything of it remains, lead me to dwell in it as my desire for that abode is beyond words.

**22.** You incarnate three aspects namely life, Śivan or ecstasy and the cycle of life. So you are the sole power to exculpate me from the woes of worldly existence. Save me. I have not rendered my being impure with unholy food.

**23.** In the recent past when I was afflicted with cholera and driven to desperation, You heard my wails and came to my rescue. But in the senseless indulgence in my well-being I forgot Your Divine Name. Consequently I am stricken with illness again. So cure me of this courage and save me Lord.

**24.** There are in the hill, cures for all illness, not temporary but enduring ones. They are guarded by three snakes and a leopard. (Swamy Vimalananda has defined the hill as the body and the medicines as *sat*, *cit*, *ānanda*). The spiritually enlightened took half of it and ate. The remaining half is preserved for the succeeding generations. The medicine is therefore actually knowledge. So as desired by the Lord, O the heart, take it. You will be rid of all ailments.

**25.** I am unable to suffer like this in this world any more. Why even death keeps aloof from me? What is my crime? O the Lord of Kailās, this is the time to show mercy on me. My only ambition is that you should come to me to free me from the worldly entanglements.

**26.** I have hitherto spent my life to fill my stomach with whatever I got and to dip myself into anything that satisfied my lust. I pray that before I die, give me the lift up to peace and salvation thereby.

**27.** You are Omnipresent and Omniscient, You are not unaware of what ails me, will you not bless me?

**28.** I pray that the resplendent Form of Lord Śiva, whatever of the Heavenly Gaṅgā and the deer, may bless me.

**29.** To put out for ever the disease of birth and death one has to incessantly recite Lord Śiva's name. Having forgotten that, I am being dragged into the never-ending circle of births and deaths and thus exposed to untold suffering.

**30.** Even Lord Viṣṇu who once incarnated as *Narasiṁha* (a form with the face of lion and the rest of the body, human) pays homage to you. With Your kind third eye you have destroyed the Lord of Lust. But the very same Lord of Lust chases me. Why don't you do away with him for ever?

**31.** After having inactivated the senses, spiritual and physical, *kuṇḍalinī* snake activates itself. As it moves towards the *sahasra padmam*, man reaches God realisation.

**32.** Remove O Lord, *śivatva*, *śaktitva* and *śabdatva* (the power of Śiva, Śakti and Sound) and convert them into the fuel to worship you and bless me to take the role of the worshipper.

**33.** This body is enveloped in the skin covered by tiny hair. Death is unavoidable for man. Just as the dry leaf swirls in the whirlpool of the wind, so man swirls helplessly in the whirlpool of *saṁsāra-sāgara* (the sea of life). To stop that happening to me, will you not burn away the worldly causes of my sorrows? (It is a prayer to separate body from the soul).

**34.** I am an ignorant man. I am hiding in my inside all my sins and hence full of dishonesty. You are the incarnation of kindness. Will You not save me?

**35.** At the height of meditation, the *samādhi* state is reached by the *yogī*. He then has the vision of light on the *bhrū madhya* (middle forehead). He enjoys that nectar to his heart's content. But if he gets infatuated by it that spells his ruin. Otherwise he becomes knowledge itself.

**36.** O the Lord that dances the Cosmic Dance. You are my sole refuge. What else do I require but Your blessings?

**37.** I pray Lord, come to me with Goddess Pārvatī and bless me.

**38.** Save me from the infatuation of sex held out by attractive women.

**39.** Do not leave me to ruin through blind attachment to the attractions of the evanescent body.

**40.** During my fight with the God of Death, keep by my side, Lord. Do not send me as a victim to the arrow of Kāmadeva (the Lord of love).

**41.** I do not experience anything in this life, but unhappiness. Because of this I have become immune to the reality binding the universe.

**42.** Come to me just once. All my sorrows will then disappear. When is it going to happen my Lord?

**43.** Your Form fills the universe. You are the five elements. You are visible as five on earth, four in water, three in fire, two in wind and one in the sky. These members five, four, three, two and one represent sound, touch, taste, form and smell respectively.

**44.** Goddess Pārvatī remains inseparably on your side. Her youthful tremulous breasts secrete the nectar of milk. When is that ecstatic flow from mount Kailās, the seat of rapture, going to lap on my humble self.

**45.** O the Lord that embellishes His Form with Vibhūti all over His body, the Gaṅgā on His crown and the snake garlands on His neck, bless me.

**46.** I have not thought ill of anyone in my life. If at all such thoughts have entered my mind without my knowledge, forgive me.

**47.** What sins have I committed to merit this unendurable suffering. With your power to incinerate evils, burn my sufferings to ashes, Lord.

**48.** If you install yourself within me after expelling Kāmadeva (the Lord of Lust), I would be able to resist the attempts of formidable enemies to beleaguer my life.

49. If your kind eyes spot me, all my sorrows will disappear.

50. To enable me to know the reason why the senses cease to function, with the eyes withdrawing into their sockets and giving up the power of sight, and death holding sway, may your sacred name remain imprinted in my consciousness.

51. O the Lord of all Worlds, save me.

52. Victory to you, O the Lord that fills time and space.

53. I have no doubt in my mind that, You are not deaf to my prayers. When is my struggle going to end?

54. Like Lord Viṣṇu, shall I be blessed with the power to pluck my eyes and place them at your feet to secure your Grace?

55. Why do you turn a deaf ear when I request for something specific? Like wax melting in fire, why don't you allow me to melt myself at your glorious Feet?

56. Ever since I reached youthhood, I have been struggling to keep my lust at bay. Just as the rock rolling down the mountain slope is uncontrollable, so my longing for life is unrestrainable. That is why I have forgotten you Lord.

57. Due to this attachment to life, my power of resistance has drained away. When is my heart going to be a repository of pure thoughts alone?

58. If only I could leave every worldly attachment behind, and go to the forests and do intense penance there, however fatal the consequence are, I shall face with contentment.

59. If you come to me with Goddess Pārvatī by your side and bless me, all my sins will be washed away.

60. I pray that my mind be free from strayed thoughts by being merged into You.

61. In this life I bear no thoughts other than about you. Knowledge dictates that every other thought should be kept away and thought of Śiva alone should dominate the consciousness.

**62.** O the Ocean of knowledge that You are, when are you giving me the boon to merge in You through a life of austerity?

**63.** Victory to you Lord, who killed the Mupara demons and burnt their city to ashes. I pray do not let loose the heavenly Gaṅgā You have hidden in Your tresses, but bless me.

**64.** When I realise that there is no one else but you as my saviour my sorrow aggravates. So give me the privilege to serve at your feet. Thus my sins be done away with.

**65.** Struggling among the waves of nectar which emanate from your kind eyes I will one day reach that Divine Feet.

**66.** When Your heart melted out of pity seeing my tears flowing in rainy outpour, You have condescended to give me liberation from earthly existence.

**67.** I have interblended myself in *bhakti*, concentrating all thoughts on tiding over any critical situation I may face in my life's journey. Consequently the longing to see and surrender myself at Your Feet burgeons within me amid unstoppable tears.

**68.** I prostrate at Your Feet being the only power in the universe to save me from sins which accumulate within me by the hour. When I feel that my offences are multiplying my heart is likely to melt like butter in fire.

**69.** Lord, do not expose me to the allurements of lascivious young women with inviting looks and fat breasts held out to trap me.

**70.** These friends approaching me with attractively made up bodies and full, liver penetrating breasts in captivating gait, and bewitchingly slow paces like the elephants, are out to destroy me. Give me the mental power to resist their power.

**71.** The sins that congeal in the chest of women in the form of heart piercing pointed breasts, approach to ensnare me.

Lord, do not throw me out, to the flesh-thirsty looks of these miscreations.

**72.** Draining the sea one will reach its bottom, full of filth. When filled into a pipe, it will rot and stench. The woman's reproductive organ is that pipe camouflaged in attractive attire to infatuate man's mind. Do not allow me Lord to be lured away by them.

**73.** The womb is made of flesh and blood. It spills dirt at intervals stinking horridly. Do not push me into that grisly hell, O the Great one.

**74.** You are the One without an equal, and my sole refuge. Therefore even if I am persuaded to do such deeds as to drag me to hell, do not hestitate to pull me back.

**75.** O the most Sacred Lord, the destroyer of all evils and the harbinger of the good, my *praṇāms* to You. When will you show mercy on me to enable me to have perpetual vision of your Feet.

**76.** You are the most beautiful with eyes as long and shapely as the petals of lotus, the dead enemy of Kāmadeva and the protector of all worlds., Save me Lord. I pray for Your undiminishing kindness.

**77.** I have never served You with garlands made out of sweet smelling flowers to deserve Your grace. Is it a punishment my Lord that I am subjected to this misery?

**78.** O Lord my mind never rests in peace. Help me to have mental tranquillity on an enduring measure.

**79.** People say Fate is irrevocable. I do not know this, though I believe that what is fated to happen will happen.

**80.** Everyone likes praise. But because of my ineptitude, I am unable to shower praises upon You, and secure my ends. Nor do I entertain any desire for it.

**81.** Bless me to souse myself into the depths of Your boundless blessings and then merge again in purity.

**82.** Even though the moon, charioteer to the God of Love (Kāmadeva), has lost his splendour, he still continues penance in darkness fixing his feet in the water lily pond. There is thus love nexus between the moon and water lily. I hate being entangled.

**83.** When the moon's charms become fully realised, do you think they will merge into nothingness? You carry him on Your crown, so he should not be made to suffer.

**84.** You remain unmoved even by the impact of the unending tidal waves of the heavenly Gaṅgā striking against You with force. O the wielder of such tremendous power, my homage to you.

**85.** I am prepared to enter the forest and kill elephants and tigers, present their leather for You to wear. But supposing You laugh at my foolish venture?

**86.** If it is my fate that you have marked on my head that I idle myself at home, eat and get fat, without doing anything worthwhile, I am extremely unhappy over that.

**87.** Like the tiger stealthily on the move to pounce upon its prey, so is the Lord of Kālī, to take me. Save me from the impending menace, Great Lord.

**88.** Like the ubiquitous fragrance of the flower, like the three worlds pervading sky, reflecting on the seas, O the Lord that permeates everywhere and everything, victory to you.

**89.** There is plenty of foul water everywhere for the sprouting of the three evils of ego, *karmam* and *māyā*. To see the people who sow into, and harvest from, the earth and thrive on the fruits of their effort, embroiled in life's setbacks and thus suffering, is indeed pathetic.

**90.** Decay and death very often approach to swallow me. Where is the end to this miserable state? May be, the Lord's game is without end.

**91.** As the meditation upon the Lord's form reaches the climax, a stillness of inactivity encumbers the mind. But often that state merges in the Lord's *māyā*. What I fear is whether there is frequent recurrence of the condition.

**92.** O the Lord, who is as beautiful as the rose flower, save me from failures and burn off my undesirable dispositions in the fire of Your power acquired through penance, and thus give me liberation.

**93.** Because of my evil deeds and as a result of having sown the seeds of births and deaths which have taken deep roots in me, the corpse like body is living by enjoying the pleasures provided by Nature. Will it be burnt in the fire or consumed by the lion.

**94.** Man who is born without the help of mother, father, preceptors, dear ones or neighbours, will be departing from this earth as well, without their help. So actually, living also is in loneliness.

**95.** The Lord who sports beautiful flowers on His crown, if blesses me with His nearness, then it will tantamount to my parents never leaving me. The all knowing Śiva, I am confident, will free me from all my sorrows.

**96.** Lord, will you bless me to be engaged in serving you single-mindedly throughout my life and thus fortify my devotion to You? Your commandments from the shade of the tree that yields every wish, are as inspiring and pure as the waves of the Gaṅgā of the heavens that you wear on your tresses.

**97.** Lord, all my miseries will be frozen in the wave garland of the heavenly Gaṅgā that You carry with Your person. But if the miseries arising out of *karma* are to be destroyed a vision of Your Divine Form is absolutely essential.

**98.** Bless me Lord, with a vision of your Face in all its ferocity as it manifests itself on the occasion of the Cosmic dance with those snake garlands entwined into the sacred beard.

**99.** May Lord Śiva, seated along with the snakes whose hoods pilot the waves of the sacred Gaṅgā, bless me.

**100.** The moon spreads his cool glow everywhere and gladdens the water lily thus proclaiming love's message. O' Lord, bless me with a vision of that flower blossoming into magnificence on receiving that message.

## A CRITICISM OF THE POEM

There is controversy over whether Sree Narayana Guru was a Śaivaite or had accepted the supremacy of any other God. But one thing is certain, namely that He was a sincere devotee of the Gods he had accepted as His favourites. But a majority of His works was in praise of Lord Śiva. The one thread running through all His poems is the Vedic philosophy of attachments wrought by births and deaths, and the external bliss achieved through self-realisation. The brilliance of His own vision about life and His messages, is fully brought out in them. But in the hymns to Śiva the monotony of repetition is evident.

One other feature of these particular hymns is the concept that man is drawn into the abyss of lives' woes by women only. This concept recurs in several pieces. When having to stress the transience of material life, the reader is surprised to see Guru's thoughts flowing into the social areas. Those objectively thinking may be tended to question the aptness of Guru even with His known disgust with worldly pleasures, wearing the veil of a woman hater. This attitude of Guru surfaces itself probably because of His having compiled these in his youth. Be that as it may, we may be guided by Guru's perception that Lord Śiva's grace alone can overcome our travails from attachments and take us to liberation beyond the entanglement of births and deaths.

# 3

# Poems Spilling Spiritual Vision — Advaita Dīpikā and Ātmopadeśa Śatakam

## Advaita Dīpikā (The Lamp of Non-Duality)

GURU was seized of the spiritual truth that human beings are being swallowed by the alligator of birth and death. *Advaita Dīpikā* is the outcome of kindness generated by this knowledge in Him. The role of Vedāntic creations like this, to eliminate the injustice found in society is unquestionable. This truth is absolute, it is indivisible and irrefutable. That is what is established in this poem. Here is its English translation followed by the idea conveyed by it:

1. One thousand names, one thousand forms.
   With whom, abiding therein, there
   are one thousand interests —
   such this world, uncritically viewed:
   It is real only until the dream is past;
   On waking, the awakened one is all that remains.

2. This visible world, it has not truth. Examined
   apart from the seeing eye.
   It is seen as having no status that is other;
   This universe is a mirage-like flux in awareness.
   What stands as effect
   Is none other than reality cause-based;

The wave is made of water indeed!

**3.** The cloth here is thread, which is but cotton
and which, in turn,
Is seen as elemental stuff again
thus speculated on and on.
To pure consciousness, as its source,
it could be traced.
Like a watershed found in desert land.
Consciousness is, indeed, the term ultimate.

**4.** In the active state of awareness
there is no universe at all,
Nor even ignorance, its seed. When the lamp has come,
There is no darkness thereabouts.
but if the wick is left behind
The lamp goes out — and to, darkness close in!

**5.** Critically scrutinised, the world is nought —
only nescience remains;
To a mind uncritical, by confusion, it presents
itself as the visible world
That, by virtue of which (scrutiny), while the
lamp is burning, gets abolished
Like the ghost; for him afraid of darkness
darkness is verily like the ghost.

**6.** As being and non-being, what is cognised either way,
Both are presentiments of the same
prime nature of nescience —
Both are not there when closely scrutinised; it is not
The snake that abides in a piece of rope, but
rope alone!

**7.** That which, as being, is established on itself,
and thus rising above all else stands.
That alone has truth; all else is false and transient.
All modifications of clay are false; but what
abides in each,

Such as clay itself here, when we consider, is
the existent Truth itself.

8. Even in a state of ignorance, one is not
without awareness
Of both Being as well as given Truth, and also
of a Value-factor as the third
What presents itself as snake having a rope-based
thisness, as given here,
Even for such a reality, if we consider, the
former constitutes the reference.

9. Though, in a state of positive understanding,
the world should be dissolved and lost.
It would still continue as given to the senses
and perceived as before.
To one who regained his space-bearings-once
confused or lost —
The wrong directions would persist for a long
time to seem the same.

10. The world is not over there as a verity;
everything, however.
In a wisdom-cancelled state, looms as before.
Even when one is convinced, without any doubt,
That there is no water in a mirage, it is
still seen as before.

11. To the wise man, the world has substance,
and mind-stuff represents the value-form
of delight —
Non-verity has no goodness in it for him;
the ignorant man
Is unclear herein. For one having sight, happiness
is a sun that exists,
While to the blind, the Sun's orb is a dark
and empty thing.

12. The seed is always one and the same, which looms,

in varied form;
Attributive adjuncts do not make for even a bit
of change to it by specification.
What owing to darkness presented itself to the
ignorant man as the snake.
How could it ever on critical scrutiny be seen
as other than rope?

**13.** When all component limbs are divided one by one
and so separated,
The World is null and void; such is the marvel
picturesque,
When again such parts thus divided are viewed
as given data,
Utter Nothingness results, and Self-consciousness
is all that is left.

**14.** Like thread in cloth, like water in brine,
By sheer nescience the world gets effected from view,
Even when thus lost into the varied magic
of speculative effect,
It is one's own pure consciousness
that alone there is.

**15.** Delight is what exists, and what in consciousness
looms, as one and the same;
Treated disjunctly from Self, it exists not,
looms not, as all else.
Mirage-water and sky-blue will have no existence,
While sky-flower and mirage-reflected sky reality gain.

**16.** The Self has no egoism; like a Yogi, through Maya
In sport, it is here engaged in varied ways,
Still established in Yoga, and never swerving therefrom,
Assuming hypostatic bodies, he keeps on
sporting hereunder, the Yogi.

**17.** The converse position to what is given to a state
of doubting puzzlement

Applies only to the case of the would-be seeker
of Self-knowledge — not in the least
to one established firmly therein.
The question whether a snake-presentiment be
a reptile or a rope,
Confusion of mind reveals; no sooner the rope,
is cognised, it ceases altogether to be.

**18.** Pressing forward, at every step overcoming each
item of sensual interest,
The function of the mind keeps banishing the veil
of wrong presentiments.
The awareness that still remains, following in the
wake of the light of intelligence —
As in the case of the eye — such a knowledge fails
to be cognisant of itself.

**19.** The eye it now sees when open; when shut,
The blind alone dwells within, as knowledge
doth not come forth.
By itself, knowledge cannot come out; it needs
the eye to do so,
In the same way that the eye, in turn, needs light.
(Translation: Guru Nitya Chaitanya Yati)

COMMENTARY

This universe has enfolded within itself countless names, images, peering endless reflections and numberless other objects related to them. To the thoughtless, it appears real like those seen in dreams till the dream ends. Viewed in this light the universe is only a myth. If the eyes which we see with are stymied, this truth becomes all the more evident. It will then be confirmed that this universe is not a reality but only a mirage in the desert of knowledge. Why this causal world which survives on the matter of which it was born is due to nothing else but the core of what actualised its being? As for example what else is in the waves but water?

Cloth is made of thread, thread of cotton and cotton of the

ultimate core of matter. This experience is born out of knowledge. It is simple like the mirage. But knowledge is the only reality. Knowledge is the creation of mental activity. From that knowledge it will also be clear that the universe is nothingness. The nucleus of the universe is ignorance. Ignorance too is darkness. If the light is put out suddenly, the darkness which had disappeared earlier, reappears. So long as the mind activates the universe has no reality. Once that activity stops, the appearance of its reality surfaces again. So the real world appears as real due to want of knowledge. For the thoughtless, the myth that is the world, presents itself as truth.

It is characteristic of the beginningless and endless *māyā* to appear first as non-existent and then as existent. When one is discreet enough to identify what is from what is not, one will be able to see that what is not is unreal. That is *māyā*. Where a rope piece is taken as snake, there will only be rope and not snake. For every object there exists the impression of it. That quality is the core of the object concerned. This is the state of all objects in the universe. The changed forms of soil like pot and pan, are unreal. But the soil innate in them is real.

Even in the state of ignorance, the two experiences of existence and sensation are there, and along with that the comfort. In the instance of rope being taken as snake in the dark, the form of the rope does not come to mind. Ultimately even after the truth is known the suspicion lingers. In the state of *māyā* also, when the affirmative "is" is sounded, what is stated is the condition of "being", of core. As one is awakened to knowledge, though everything disappears and discomfort sets in, as against the earlier experience, the sense will be able to experience the presence. Yet glimpses of the earlier experience will linger for sometime more. Realistically thinking, the universe will be found non-existent. Knowledge of the self destroys experience of the universe. Yet after that too the impression of its existence persists. Even after one is convinced that there is no water in the mirage, when it is seen again the belief that water exists in it, rises up. For one who has achieved God Realisation, it is easy to know that the universe is a fantasy.

Where the *puṇḍit* is concerned, this world is *sat-cit-ānanda*. It is not unreal. For the ignorant it is difficult to see that truth. The one who can see the truth can also see the sun encompassing happiness, existence and charity. But, for the blind, the sun is not visible. The diverse growth in the universe sprouts from a single core. When every part of objects is separated from the objects, it will be proved that there is no world composite with parts. If those parts are also split up? What remains is only one's consciousness. So everything is changed as consciousness.

Thread disappears in the cloth. Similarly water disappears in foam. So it will be seen that the entire world disappears in like manner. This is because of ignorance. When sufficient thought is bestowed to this truth, ignorance disappears, and what remains is knowledge only. Knowledge alone is truth. It alone is happiness and it alone blazes. What is not is what does not blaze. In the ultimate analysis therefore everything disappears except the *ākāśa* (sky) as the basis of everything.

The *ātmā* is free from ego. It plays in diverse ways through *māyā* like the *yogī*. The *yogī* in a state of inactivity, (like *ātmā*) manipulates in that stillness with different bodies. The one who longs for spiritual truth, experiences ignorance, doubt and hostility. For the one who has attained real knowledge none of these happens. The belief that the rope is snake (ignorance) the indecision whether it is coir or snake (doubt) and seeing rope as coir, all disappear and actual rope is seen.

## Ātmopadeśa Śatakam (Spiritual Knowledge)

*Ātmopadeśa Śatakam* is the greatest and most celebrated spiritual creation of Sree Narayana Guru. It transudes spiritual knowledge of the highest calibre in the simplest jargon quite comprehensively in an extravagant poem of one hundred stanzas. Here is the English translation of this masterpiece, followed by the annotations stanza-wise:

1. In and beyond the knowledge which shines
   At once within and without the knower

Is the KARU to that, with the five senses withheld
Prostrate again and again with devotion and chant.

**2.** The inner organ, the senses, the body,
The many worlds known by direct perception —
everything when contemplated,
Is the glorious embodiment of the sun that
shines in the sky beyond;
This should be known through relentless search.

**3.** Existing outside and, as specific modes seen within
The five elements, like sky, when contemplated,
Should become like waves rising in rows
From the treasury of the watery deep, without any
separate reality whatsoever.

**4.** Knowledge, the objectivisation of the value of the known
And one's personal knowledge are nothing other
than MAHAS;
Merging into that infinite supreme
Knowledge, become that alone.

**5.** Worldly people, having slept, wake and think
any thoughts;
Ever wakefully witnessing all this shines an
unlit lamp,
Precious beyond words; that never fades;
Ever seeing this, one should go forward.

**6.** One has to wake up, then go to sleep,
Has to eat food and embrace; thus in this way
Many ambivalent urges arise; therefore,
Who is there to comprehend reality's one
changeless form?

**7.** Do not wake any more, and without sleeping
remain as knowledge;
If you are unfit for this,
Then keep yourself in the service of those

contemplatives
Who live free from birth, awakened to AUM.

**8.** Enjoying the five fruits, such as beauty,
Mounted on a foul-smelling gun and evasively
flying back and forth
Are five birds; having brought them down,
through an inversion,
That radiant inner awareness should fill one's
entire being.

**9.** Growing on both sides, in a blossoming state,
Is the one Vine which has come, spread out
and risen to the tops of
A tree; remember that hell does not come
To the man dwelling in contemplation beneath it.

**10.** "Who is sitting in the dark? Speak, You!"
In this manner one speaks; having heard this,
you also,
To know, ask him, "And who are you?"
To this as well, the response is one.

**11.** "I, I", thus, all that are spoken of,
When carefully considered, inwardly are not many;
that is one;
As the receding I-identities are countless
In their totality, the substance of I-consciousness
continues.

**12.** See the skin, bone, dirt and inner urges which
end tragically
To which the I-identity is conjoined;
This which perishes is the other; O, grant the
cherished boon
That the great I-identity increases to perfection.

**13.** Having offered the flower of your mind to that Lord
Smeared with sacred ashes, the three GUNAS,

Having cooled down the senses, unwound everything,
and become calm,
Whenever the glory of aloneness has gone,
become established in MAHAS.

**14.** Going beyond the boundaries of the three worlds,
with all filling effulgence,
When the three-petalled knowledge has faded out
ever brighter shines that light;
A pretentious seer will never grasp this;
Thus, the Upanishad's secret word should be remembered.

**15.** To the blessed ones who sucked the milk of PARA
Ten thousand years is but a moment;
But if knowledge succumbs to APARA PRAKRTI
Half a second seems like a thousand years.

**16.** A very vast wasteland suddenly
Flooded by a river in spate — thus comes the sound
That fills the ears and opens the eyes of the one
who is never distracted;
Such should be the experience of the seer par-excellence.

**17.** Having two tires of five petals, whence pain arises,
Rotating, beginningless, hangs the lamp of the self
Burning as the shadow (of true being), with the oil
Of latent urges and mental modifications as the wicks.

**18.** The "I" is not dark; if it were dark we would be
in a state of blindness,
Unable to know even "I, I";
As we do know, the "I" is not darkness;
Thus for making this known, this should be told to
anyone.

**19.** The bottom, the top, the end, that is real, this is,
no, that is —
In this way people quarrel; the one primal reality
is all that is;

All this inertial matter is transient;
Except as a form of water could a wave ever arise?

**20.** Other than this the world has no reality;
"There is" — all such that people say is without reflection;
Even if to a numbskull it appears to be a snake,
Will a fresh flower garland ever become a serpent?

**21.** Endearment is one kind; this is dear to me
Your preference is for something else;
Thus, many objects of endearment are
differentiated and confusion comes;
What is dear to You is dear to another also; this
should be known.

**22.** The happiness of another — that is my happiness;
One's own joy is another's joy — this is the guiding
principle;
That action which is good for one person
Should bring happiness to another.

**23.** For the sake of another, day and night, performing
action,
Having given up self-centred interests, the
compassionate person acts;
The self-centred man is wholly immersed in necessity,
Performing unsuccessful actions for himself alone.

**24.** "That man", "this man" — thus all that is known
In this world, if contemplated, is the being of the
one primordial self:
What each performs for the happiness of the self
Should be conducive to the happiness of another.

**25.** What is good for one person and brings misery to
another
Such actions are opposed to the self, remember:
Those who give great grief to another
Will fall into the fiery sea of hell and burn.

**26.** Holding the limbs together, remaining like a bolt,
The limb owner envelops as vaporous being;
For this reason, "that man" and "this man"
arise in this way —
So that man believes, due solely to the weakness
of non-discrimination.

**27.** Sitting in the dark, that which knows is the self,
What is known then assumes name and form,
With the psychic dynamism, senses, agency of
action and also of inaction;
See how it all comes as MAHENDRA magic!

**28.** Without bottom or top, from the bottom to the crest
where it terminates —
What is known vividly is TURIYA consciousness;
Insert matter does not know; having understood this,
Know that what is said to remain in-between
is not knowledge.

**29.** For the man who offers his mind, flowers to
worship God
There is no other work to do;
Pick flowers of the forest; or, if not that,
By ever repeating the Maya formula Maya
will disappear.

**30.** Inert matter does not know; Knowledge has no thought
And does not articulate; knowing knowledge to be all,
Letting go, one's inner state becomes boundless;
Indeed thereafter he never suffers confined within
a body.

**31.** Without prior experience there is no inference;
This is not previously perceived with the eye;
Therefore, know that the existence of that in
which all qualities inhere
Is not known by inference.

**32.** What is known is not that in which all qualities
inhere, only the qualities;
As this, in which all qualities are said to inhere,
is not visible earth and all else do not exist;
Remember that there is only a form in knowledge
which supports.

**33.** Knowledge, to know its own nature here,
Has become earth and the other elements;
Spiralling up, back and turning round,
Like a glowing twig it is ever turning.

**34.** Mounted on the rotating wheels of a chariot which
have half moments and such for spokes,
The world rolls on;
Know this to be the beginning-less divine sport
That is ever going on in knowledge.

**35.** Like ten thousand suns coming all at once,
The modulation of discrimination arises;
The veil of transience covering knowledge is Maya;
Tearing this away, the primal Sun alone shines.

**36.** The power of knowledge is endless;
The end of all this can be marked as "Sameness"
and "the other"
Thus, in this way, there are two divisions; in this,
merging the other with sameness,
One should remain awake to that clear state of being.

**37.** The other is replete with difficulty;
And it is hard to win over without the power to
discriminate the unbroken;
Having won over the difficult,
Attain to that discrimination which is
opposed to sense interests.

**38.** What is known as many is the other,
And that which shines forth as one is sameness

Having known the state, which is going to be
spoken of, and attained release,
Remain dissolved and blended in the state of sameness.

**39.** To continue, of these forces just mentioned,
The second division, sameness, is of one quality,
While for the first, the difficult, there is no end to its
qualities
Thus, these are of two kinds.

**40.** In sameness and in the other each one's
Qualifying force always comes and becomes established;
By the fluctuating function of these two
Which comprises all, everything becomes the
object of awareness.

**41.** "This is a pot"; in that, what comes first, "this",
Is the difficult to discern; pot is its qualifying
predicate;
For intellect and such MAHENDRA magic to manifest,
This itself becomes the Karu; thus one should see.

**42.** "This is knowledge"; in that, what comes first, "this",
Is sameness; its qualifying predicate is awareness;
For intellect and all such to vanish, and for the
true path to come,
This should be meditated on.

**43.** Even those of good action are caught by nature.
And whirled round in vicious circles;
One should know that non-action does not bring
release from perverted action,
Only the non-desire for the fruit of action.

**44.** The many faiths have but one essence;
Not seeing this, in this world, like the blind men
and the elephant,
Many kinds of reasoning are used by the unenlightened
who become distressed;

Having seen this, without being disturbed, remain
steadfast.

**45.** One faith is despicable to another;
The KARU described in one is defective in
another's estimation;
In this world the secret of this is one alone;
Know that confusion prevails until it is known
to be thus.

**46.** By fighting it is impossible to win;
By fighting one another no faith is destroyed;
One who argues against another's faith, not
recognising this,
Fights in vain and perishes; this should be
understood.

**47.** To become of one faith is what everyone speaks of;
This proselytisers do not recognise;
Wise men, freed of objections to another's faith,
Know this secret in full.

**48.** The self encased in a body in his eidetic consciousness,
Understands all such as, " That is mine" and
"This is mine"
Bereft of body identity; on considering this
It is evident that everyone has truly experienced.

**49.** All beings are making effort in every way,
All the time, for the happiness of the self;
In the world, this is the one faith;
Pondering on this, without becoming subjected to sin,
be controlled.

**50.** The ground, together with water, wind, fire and sky,
The functioning ego, right knowledge and the mind —
Waves and ocean: what else is there?
All these worlds, having arisen, are changing
into knowledge.

**51.** Having existed in knowledge, an I-ness,
in beginning, emerges;
Coming as a counterpart to this is thisness;
Like two vines, these spread over the
tree of Maya
Completely concealing it.

**52.** The sky will glow as radiant sound —
On that day, all visible configurations will
become extinct in that;
Thereafter, the sound that completes the
three-petalled awareness
Becomes silent and self-luminous.

**53.** The primal energy implied in this
Is the seed from which everything here proliferates;
Having understood that, without forgetting
To Clear the mind deluded by Maya,
meditation should continue.

**54.** In sleep the wakeful state does not exist
And when one wakes up no trace of sleep remains;
Day by day, in this way, these two, having emerged
From the primal Maya woman, arise and alternate.

**55.** A long dream is this, like sleep,
this perishes everyday;
In the Same way, dream also;
The perishing intelligence does not see
What belongs to aloneness, and hence is constantly
confused.

**56.** Like waves arising in the ocean,
Bodies one by one suddenly arise, then merge again;
Alas! where is the end to this?
In the primal ocean of consciousness potent action
is said to exist.

**57.** In the waveless ocean, endless traits of Maya remain.

As potent and beginningless effects;
Water's taste and so on make a configuration
And with such embodied forms world upon world
comes to be.

**58.** Do not think in ever new terms of yesterday, today
Tomorrow or another day;
All the endless counting and measuring is due to
confusion;
One should know that there is not any difference.

**59.** Without knowledge I do not exist;
Without me there is no knowledge, light alone is;
Thus, both knowledge and knower, when contemplated,
Are of one substance, there can be no doubt.

**60.** When knowledge is spoken of as subjected to the ego
Without considering its ultimate truth,
Even if that ultimate reality is spoken of in this way,
For one who knows, knowledge does not become other.

**61.** External objects appear to be different from one another;
It is the function of the senses to posit for each
distinct dimension;
Nescience rises as sets of names, like sky and so on,
And changes into knowledge.

**62.** Do not think of the absolute truth overpowered by
the sense of "mine";
What knowledge comes from merely saying "do not"?
This will not come by mouthing a phrase;
The absolute state is attained through relentless
contemplation.

**63.** Apart from remaining in knowledge without
becoming other than it
And knowledge this knowledge here,
Struggling in frustration, one does not know;
Who sees this supreme secret of the wise man?

**64.** Dismiss your memories of each object of interest
Which cause a state of obstruction;
The vast expensive memory, which can reveal
The priceless ultimate knowledge, is not unjustified.

**65.** Nothing exists here that we have not known once;
Veiled by form, all this is not wakefully known;
Being boundless, there is no one who knows;
Who is there to know this dear wonder?
Alas! It is strange!

**66.** Food and all such always come again as a
matter of course;
That which remains free of becoming is one;
We are that knowledge itself; all others
Also remain as its forms.

**67.** One is beyond what can be counted,
The other is ordinary; other than these two there
is not any other form
Existing in waking, or in dream,
Or in some city of the Gods; this is certain.

**68.** Like snake-rope form,
The I-consciousness enters both knowledge and the
body;
Or one occasion the understanding is true,
or another untrue;
Thus one who can discern should understand.

**69.** Hearing and such as horses yoked,
Occupied by the self-image, the dexterous psychic
dynamism drives
The chariot of RATI; mounted therein, the ego
Is continuously chasing each pleasing from outside.

**70.** One RATI alone is expanding into the ego, the senses,
The mind, the body and all that is;
Where is an end to this?

Not until one knows that he is different,
none other than knowledge; remember!

**71.** No one in this world remains free from becoming,
In a state of sameness; this is said to be a beginningless play;
To him who knows this, which is unlimited,
Boundless happiness comes.

**72.** Now there is action, which is ignorance,
And again there is pure consciousness, which is knowledge;
Although these two are thus ordained by Maya to stand divided,
A non-dual vision of the Absolute brings about Turiya.

**73.** In one substance there are many,
And in many things there is one meaning; reasoning thus,
Everything becomes inseparably inclusive in knowledge;
Not all know this great secret.

**74.** Innumerable particles of dust inhere in earth,
And there is no difference in the earth that constitutes the particles;
Just as inert matter exists in consciousness consciousness finds its expression
Here in the body; therefore, when contemplated, this is one.

**75.** Nature is water, the body is form, the self is the depth;
"I am, I am" — thus a restless repetition like a series of waves;
Every inner blossom of knowledge attained is a pearl;
Indeed, whatever each finds delight in is the nectar of mortal bliss.

**76.** As countless grains of sand ceaselessly blown onto
The surface of a pond generate ripple after ripple,
By untruths successively, blown,
The inner self is transformed from within into
various forms.

**77.** The one beyond the sky, the all-pervasive energy
is wind
Knowledge is fire, senses are water, objects of interest
Are earth; thus, as five principles,
This is ever blazing; the secret of this is one.

**78.** There is no death or birth or existence;
Man, gods and all such are name and form
What exists is like the water of mirage in the desert —
It does not exist; this should be remembered.

**79.** At the time of birth there is no existence; the one
who is born
Is not in another moment; how can such a state be?
Death is also like this, and there is no birth
Everything is of the power of pure consciousness.

**80.** Like rest and motion, how can contraries such as
creation,
Existence and dissolution coexist in one place?
There is no validity for these three anywhere,
when this is considered,
Earth and such are mere words.

**81.** Prakrti divides: on one side is the agent of enjoyment;
On the other, whatever shines outside
As the here and the beyond, as an expansion of thisness,
Is the world of enjoyment.

**82.** Like fire that emerges from churning sticks,
The boundless discrimination that arises from
contemplatives
Burns as the sun that has attained the firmament

of supreme consciousness;
To this everything is fuel.

**83.** To break, to exist and to come into being is the
nature of bodies here —
One goes, another takes its place;
Remaining in the highest, the Self that
knows all these three,
The indivisible one, is free, of modifications.

**84.** As modifications of earth are known, it is said
that they exist —
This is untrue when considered; what exists is earth;
The countless entities remaining without foundation
Are all innate forms of nature existing in knowledge.

**85.** No shadow exists independent of an actual form;
As there is no original form anywhere for the
existing world,
It is neither shadow nor substance;
Everything that is seen is like a snake
painted by a master.

**86.** The body and all similar things have no being
one is another,
And become untrue for that reason; another part,
Remaining without setting from day-to-day,
Once again, as the true form, attains perfection.

**87.** Taking each kind alone, it exists,
Mutually, each excludes the other;
When this is remembered, body and all such
Are neither real nor unreal; that is indescribable.

**88.** Everything is real in itself; one who grasps the basic
truth
Will understand all this as one;
If not known introspectively,
Maya's great enmity certainly creates much confusion.

**89.** Existing in knowledge, as the being of non-being,
Countless sparks arise, causing the appearance
of the world;
So, apart from knowledge there is not another thing;
Thus one should know; this knowledge bestows the state
of oneness.

**90.** The unreal does not conceal what exists,
Such is the experience; what exists is; in this way,
At every step this is enveloped by existence;
Therefore, body and such effects are existence
through and through.

**91.** Whatever effort is made in relation to each
Object of endearment it remains ordained;
This dear value-unborn, unspent, unpredictable,
one without a second —
Remains established in happiness.

**92.** Unexpended, the law of action operates outside;
Therefore, it is eternal;
Within, endearment is inseparable;
To this, action is only an external symbol.

**93.** To one detached from the changing body,
Nothing is more dear than his self;
As the self-oriented value continuously remains
In this state, the self is eternal.

**94.** The world and the truth exist intermixed;
This state is one of great inequity;
In this, which is beyond the grasp of word and mind,
How can any right reason operate?

**95.** This extensive playful display is Maya's
Concealed energy of universal creativity;
Again and again she manifests here; her limbs
Are the ten million cosmic bodies.

**96.** The atom and the indivisible, both as being

and non-being
Shine from either side;
Thereafter, being fades away
And the experience of non-being, having no foundation,
will also cease.

**97.** The atom will disappear in the vastness of
knowledge.
Leaving no trace of its parts; on that day
indivisible will attain perfection;
Without experiencing, one does not know
this unbroken consciousness;
It is the silence filled ocean of immortal bliss.

**98.** We have not known anything here so far,
Having spoken of great happiness;
Even if intellect and such disappear,
The reality of the Self, without becoming
disintegrated, will continue as knowledge.

**99.** Knowledge and I-consciousness — both are one
To him for whom the veil is removed;
to another there is doubt;
If knowledge, having separated from "I",
can become another,
There is no one here to know knowledge.

**100.** Neither that, not this, not the meaning of
existence am I,
But existence, consciousness, joy immortal;
thus attaining clarity, emboldened,
Discarding attachment to being and non-being
One should gently, gently merge in SAT-AUM.

(Courtesy: Guru Nitya Chaitanya Yati)

COMMENTARY

1. Beyond common knowledge is *Karu*, the Supreme Being which exists inside the knower and outside him as real

knowledge. For the knowledge to be revealed to him, man should withdraw his sense unto himself and then prostrate before it in humility and invoke and learn it over and over again.

2. Conscience (which covers the mind, intelligence, consciousness and the self), the five senses which include the senses of knowledge and action, and the whole world from the human body to everything that is susceptible to knowledge, should be seen as illuminating forms of the sun of knowledge which blazes in the mental horizon, and contemplated over and over again, and the reality about knowledge which embodies in it, the soul, body, life and death. In other words, this universe is the very objectivisation of knowledge or God.

3. Objective thinking would reveal that what is seen in the universe such as the five elements, viz., the sky, fire, water, air and earth, is the transmutation of God. Transmutation means the illusion that the objects have changed though they are not like seeing snake in rope. (The creator and his creations are not different from one another. Here diversity will be seen to have evolved into unity.)

4. What is generally seen as Knowledge in the world, the object which forms the basis of that knowledge and the knowledge which accrues to the individual and associated with that object will emerge on close scrutiny, as the Original high (what is brought out here is that once the troika of knowledge, the known and the knower is destroyed, real knowledge will be attained and blended in).

5. Man residing in the world thinks while awake but not while asleep. On all those occasions his inner light which stands as witness to his mental activity blazes as the birthless and deathless eternal light. The sea of *saṁsāra* of life should be crossed over by fusing oneself in that eternal light of the spirit. (That is one should bid farewell to earthly life only after paying homage to the eternal

light.)

From here onwards Guru describes the nature of the thought process. . . .

6. Awake, sleep, eat and get physical pleasure — these are man's natural desires. In the midst of countless pleasures of this sort who will seek that truthful and temptationless Almighty God? (Who will be prepared to give up enjoying physical pleasures by allowing himself to realise the peaceful and unemotional eternal Being?)

7. Do not awake henceforth to worldly pleasures. But remain awake to the awareness that I am knowledge (*ātmā*). If felt that one is not yet deserving that awareness, one should utilise the body to serve those great sages who have absorbed the meaning of the original sound *auṁ* and conquered the cycle of birth and death. If self-realisation is found beyond reach, it would be best to serve those who have reached it and achieve that glory for oneself.

8. The five senses namely, visual, auditory, gustatory, tactile and olfactory are the gateways to physical pleasure. They are the five fruits which provide ecstasy to the physical body. Enjoying them, and entering the stinky and explosive human body and using all tricks for the satisfaction of lust, are the sense-organs namely eyes, ears, tongue, skin and nose. These are like birds vacillating in the human longing for pleasure. What cuts them down is knowledge. Guru exhorts man to acquire that knowledge and make his heart aglow.

9. The cosmic play of the Absolute is identified here as a tree which is totally comouflaged by a creeper which branches into two and enters it from both sides. The creeper symbolises the world of phenomenality and the tree it masks, the divine. A person described as doing penance at the foot of the tree is the eternal witness. Inside everyone of us, resides a spark of the all knowing witness. The one who realises this, reaches self-realisation and hence

transcends all happiness and sorrows of worldly existence and attains *mokṣa* or liberation. (There is an inner meaning, encapsulated in this stanza. That relates to the *kuṇḍalinī* lying dormant in the human body. A nerve known as *suṣumnā* runs parallel to the spinal column from the anus at the bottom to the brain at the top. Entering it from both sides are two other nerves, *jaḍa* and *piṅgalā*. At the base of *suṣumnā* lies in eight coils around the *mūlādhāra cakra* the *kuṇḍalinī* power like a snake. Guru has imagined the human body as the tree and *suṣumnā* as the creeper. Anyone who wakes the *kuṇḍalinī* transcends the cycles of birth and death and happiness and sorrow.)

**10.** "Who is that hiding in the darkness?" The person to whom this question is addressed, in order to know the questioner, asks back, "Who are you"? This sometimes happens in real life. To both the questions, the answer is "I" that is both give a single answer (since the question "who are you", is answered with a single word "I" it will be understood that the essence of the "I" in every individual is the same).

**11.** Everyone points to himself and says "I". But on close examination what is enfolded in this "I" is not many but one. At the same time what each feels as "I" is also many. Therefore it is in the form of the sum total of unity and diversity that the meaning of the real "I" or spiritual truth is to be visualised.

**12.** The skin, bones and faces and the internal urges which drag one towards misery constitute one kind of egotism or conceit which branches off into many. Just know this. But it is characteristic of this egotism to fade away. There is another egotism which is integrated and one. But perfection is to be found in the destruction of the path leading to the egotism with the propensity to diversify. One's prayer should invariably be that one may not be enslaved by the greater egotism of self pride and vain glory.

**13.** Worship with the flowers of the heart, at the Lotus Feet of

Lord Śiva whose body is smeared with the three *guṇas* (qualities) of *sattvam* (reality), *rajas* (passion) and *tamas* (darkness), and with the desires of the senses quelled, all bondage broken, worries eradicated and stark vanity suppressed merge with the splendour of the *ātmā* and become one with it.

**14.** Beyond the bounds of the three worlds, and illuminating everywhere and on the ruins of the *tripuḍis* (knowledge, knower and what is known), will be found the Great Spiritual Light. That, that light is not visible to the spiritual imposter, is a secret contained in the Upaniṣads, should be borne in mind.

**15.** Those who are fortunate to enjoy the milk of Mother knowledge, will live through ten thousand years as a single moment. Conversely those for whom knowledge is confined to ignorance will have to live through even a single moment as ten thousand years. (For the ignorant, time will be miserably tiresome. But it is bliss for one who knows. If the learned is beyond the edges of time, the ignorant toils in it.)

**16.** It is like the river flooding and inundating the vast expanse of the desert that the voice of knowledge comes through and fills one's ears and opens one's inner eye (the eye of knowledge). To be blessed with this boon, one should practise the great exercise of restraint and attain sainthood.

**17.** It is like the continuously burning and primal lamp with five petals and two decks and rotating non-stop and hung in its hook that the soul burns by shaping its own image into the physical body. As for the *ghī* (oil) in the lamp, it is the sum total of the tastes accumulated over the previous births. Its wicks represent the mental and physical exertions with the set goal of earning one's subsistence. (The five petals of the lamp represent the five senses through which we experience people and objects. When we see an object with our eyes, we have actually a dual experience, one, its physical appearance and the other, its perception. The same is the case with other sense-organs. So it has to be stated that the lamp symbolising the sense experiences has two decks. The explanation about the lamp rotating is that even though lamps ordinarily stand still, in this context, because the sense experience is a continuous phenomenon, one following the other, it is described as a rotating process.)

**18.** What we know as "I" (i.e., the soul) is not to be conceived as darkness. If it were darkness, we would be blind, unable even to repeat the word "I". So because the "I" is known, it is clear that it is not darkness. Because of that knowledge, the soul illuminates itself. This spiritual truth should be transmitted to those desirous of knowing it.

**19.** What is Truth? There are too many definitions, such as the core of everything is Truth; or what is at the apex or at the end or, this or that is Truth. Truth is the root of everything, the spiritual Reality. What has given rise to controversy is only the corpse (lifeless body). Can the wave remain apart from its oneness with water?

**20.** The universe has no root apart from the original *ātmā*. To say that there is such a root is the very travesty of reason. How can a flower garland which the idiot believes as snake, be real snake?

**21.** Fondness (love) is absolute and indivisible. The diversity about this feeling in different people is attributable to fantasy created by the fondness of different persons for diverse objects. What one should realise is that one's own fondness is indistinguishable from that of another.

**22.** Whatever is fondly held by another is the object of my own attachment also. By the same token, the object of my attachment should be held likewise by the others. If this policy is accepted, then, an act which one performs for one's own good, should be equally good for the others too.

**23.** A kind individual unhesitatingly labours day and night for other's sake. But what a greedy individual works without respite is meant exclusively for his own selfish end. Such undesirable endeavour should lead to his doom.

**24.** What we consider as different individuals such as this and that, will, on mature consideration, be found to be but multifarious aspects of the same spiritual truth which is the root of everything, in the universe. Whatever one pursues for one's own happiness should therefore be conducive to the happiness of others as well.

**25.** It should be remembered that an action which benefits one person and creates misery for another is the very antithesis of the *ātmic* (spiritual) rule. One who causes suffering to others will burn into ashes in hell.

**26.** Standing oneself as a nail which subjects all one's organs to a single condition, one feels that 'I am the body'. This feeling enwraps *ātmā*. Because of this, everyone, blinded by the indiscretion of not subjecting to *ātmā*, is led to see diversity among men.

**27.** That which knows everything by remaining in darkness is *ātmā*. So *ātmā* itself is knowledge. It is *ātmā* that fills the universe under diversified names and forms, and as conscience, senses, subject and object. What we see throughout the universe is a sort of jugglery.

**28.** The consciousness (state) to know from the bottom to the crest without differentiation between them, is called *turīya*, referred to in the *Māṇḍūkya Upaniṣad* as the fourth state after the wakeful (gross), dream (subtle) and deep sleep (causal) which are covered by what Guru calls as darkness. Non-recognition of duality is the mark of *turīya* consciousness. The corpse does not have this consciousness. It is not a state of knowledge which falls within the sphere of knowledge achieved by the thought process. This should be borne in mind.

**29.** For a person who plucks flowers from his heart and offers worship with them, there is no need for extra effort for the *turīya* consciousness to emerge. Or, by offering wild flowers in worship or if not, then by living by repeating even potential hymns, that consciousness is born.

**30.** The body which is corpse does not know anything. Nor is it capable of reason. Besides, the corpse cannot impart knowledge. If it is known that everything is condensed as a single knowledge and not diversified, it will result in the experience that *ātmā* of one's conscience permeates everthing in the universe. Then one will not suffer a state in which one is subject to the susceptibilities of the body. This is positively so.

**31.** Without explicit initial experience, knowledge through experience is unachievable. If this awareness has not been engendered through previous experience, it is not possible to identify the theory that all that are known (*dharma*) have a repository (*dharmī*). This has to be remembered.

**32.** What is known by direct experience is not *dharmī*, but *dharma*. As *dharmī* is beyond direct experience the five elements like the earth and their amalgam the universe are myths. It is not possible to experience *dharmī* directly. The premises for the knowledge of everything in the form of this Universe is *dharmī*. That this alone is the sole reality, has to be understood.

**33.** Knowledge that is *dharmī*, in order to reveal its own character and form, takes upon itself the functions of the five elements (earth, fire, air, water and the sky) and reaches a state of constant movement and whirls unceasingly into a cycle which produces the impression that the universe is real just as a gyrating fireball creates the seeming reality of a circle of fire.

**34.** The universe is in a state of constant flux. In the process the existing forms pass into the past to give place to new ones. These also are replaced in the next moment by yet more new forms. And so on goes the unending process. Thus there is interminable change. This indicates that life is a divine sport and that eternity rides on the wheels of fleeting apportionments of time such as the instant, the moment, the minute, the hour and so forth. This operation is compared to a chariot mounted on wheels which are ever whirling, touching the earth only with their infinitesimal parts at any given moment. These parts leave the earth the next moment to be replaced by other similar parts of the wheels thus continuing operation without stop.

**35.** Real light (perception) is that which is endowed with the discretionary faculty to identify knowledge in the dhārmic aspect. It emerges in the consciousness with the dazzling brilliance of a thousand suns rising simultaneously. This light is that of the primal sun which tears apart the darkness of *māyā* (illusion) that shrouds the real aspect of knowledge.

**36.** The power of knowledge is difficult to assess. This power can be seen as branching off into two namely *sama* (sameness) and *anya* (the other). By blending these two into the oneness of his own self, the seeker should remain himself in awareness of the enlightenment of knowledge so derived.

**37.** The *anya* aspect of knowledge is replete with hurdles to reach. Without the discretionary flair to imbibe the indivisibility of knowledge it would be hard to conquer it. By overcoming so resistant *anya* knowledge, one should get closer to the thereby derived detachment to worldly affiliations.

**38.** The *anya* (the other) knowledge is that which sees the being as numerous. By realising that the *sama* (sameness) is that which sees being as one, and then equipped with the comprehension of the diverse aspects of knowledge to be explained hereafter, one should merge oneself with the exact state of oneness between *sama* and *anya*, thus reach the stage from which, one feels, one is not apart.

**39.** The *sama* and *anya* aspects of knowledge have each derived one more bough, i.e., one by *sama* and one by *anya*.

**40.** *Sama* and *anya* have specific potential attached to each. These specific potentials are unlimited too in their sweep. Though beyond definition, they are known respectively as conditional or unconditional *vis-a-vis* their relation to *sama* and *anya*. In short despite their inestimable characteristics, it is through the totality of their swirls that everything is brought in the range of knowledge.

**41.** Take the sentence "This is a pot". The word 'this' which comes first points to the *anya* aspect of knowledge which one sees as many. 'This' may indicate a pot, a picture, a pen or ever so many individual things. The word 'pot' indicates a specific object. It should be seen that it is the bough specific to *anya* knowledge mentioned here that is the *karu* or primordial source from which such wonderful phenomena as *buddhi* (intellect) are seemingly experienced.

**42.** In the sentence "This is knowledge", 'This' is the *sama* aspect of knowledge, and 'knowledge' the bough specific to it. What is required to reach salvation which is beyond the sphere of intelligibility, the senses and their functioning, is to worship the *sama* knowledge with absolute surrender and devotion.

**43.** Even those who are regarded as virtuous are strangled by the whirls and swirls of Natural Forces. To secure immunity from the variegated characteristic of Nature, it is not all enough to put in effort consistent with physical infatuations however relentless and persistent the endeavour is. The only way to attain that goal is to spontaneously pursue a course of *akarma* (inaction) which means perseverent labour without consideration for reward.

**44.** The essence of all religions is one. Without imbibing this universal truth, people, like those blind men who in the belief that they had seen the elephant, had proceeded to describe it, are wandering hither and thither and reaching nowhere, raising baseless arguments to establish that their religions are greater than the others. Sensible people refrain from such meaningless scuffles.

**45.** One religion may appear unpalatable to a follower of another. The teaching of one faith may be looked at as injurious by those who believe in another. This state of mental confusion will persist until it is realised that the inner meaning of all religions is the same.

**46.** By fighting between them, it is impossible for one religion to achieve victory over another. Nor does fighting destroy a religion. Those who berate other religions should have the sense to realise that without grasping this truth, they will be treading towards their own ruin by this purposeless melee.

**47.** All advocates to religion say that the entire *homo sapiens* should become believers in a single religion. Those who indulge in arguments in the name of religion do not remember that the followers of every religion desire that theirs is the only suitable religion for mankind. Only the scholars who are not afflicted by the craze to put up arguments against other religions know the underlying secret of this in full.

**48.** The *ātmā* or the spirit that lives inside the body does not recognise the differentiation between bodies. It has an indivisibility with the *ātmā* in other bodies. Because of this oneness, one expresses one's identification with other bodies referring to them as 'that is mine', 'this is mine', etc. From this it will be evident that the *ātmā* can exist without an abode in the form of a body. Further thought would reveal that everyone is experiencing the Omnipresence of the *ātmā*.

**49.** All human beings endeavour to achieve *ānanda* or happiness. The one religion which is acceptable to one and all is to be able to attain *ānanda* which is but the exteriorisation of the *ātmā*. By realising this great truth, man should refrain from committing sins, and live in peace.

**50.** The five elements namely the earth, water, air, fire and sky together with the consciousness which awakens to awareness of the universe, right knowledge, the mind from where thought emanates, the ocean, the waves — all these and the whole universe rise into the single phenomenon of pure knowledge.

**51.** From absolute knowledge emerges at first *ahanda* or the subject, i.e., "I, the knower". Then there is the necessity for the emergence of what the knower knows. This is *idanda* or the object. Thus the original absolute knowledge is split into two like the two sides of the same coin, and then creates the continual experience in knowledge that the one knows the other. Guru conceives *māyā* as a tree which is concealed by the two creepers, the knower (subject) and known (object). These creepers grow into fruition completely hiding the *māyā* tree, and thus reveal the universe. That is to say a single truth first splits into two and then into many.

**52.** It is difficult to uncover the complete idea contained in this stanza. It can however be brought out more or less as follows:

The essential attribute of *ākāśa* (sky) is the radiant sound. When it glows into a thunderous burst of sonance, all shadows disappear in its brilliance and along with that, all the objects made visible by those shadows. Then what remains? The *tripadī* or the amalgam of sight, eye and vision which make up the totality of visual experience. The *tripadī* also disappears in the dazzle and only blindness remains. Thus what is left is neither the objects, nor the visibility, but only the brilliance, the One that shines by itself. Into that one is merged everything else as the silence of the unknown.

**53.** The primal energy that vibrates the self-illuminating knowledge is the original seed that has given birth to everything. If this is understood and retained in memory, it will destroy all thoughts generated by *māyā*. For that meditation is to be undertaken.

54. The awareness in the state of wakefulness is absent in sleep. So also sleep is free from the awareness of woken state. These two status of the consciousness are born from the primal mother *māyā*, and then disappear. She continuously brings forth this transient marvel.

55. Life is a prolonged dream. Like the dreams in sleep, this drawn out dream too will come to an end. Being preoccupied with trifling matters man is not able to realise the basic truth and is hence carried away by the dream in the belief that it is real.

56. The waves rise in the ocean endlessly one after the other and then disappear into the ocean itself. In like manner in the ocean of *saṁsāra* (birth, life and death) each body appears and disappears in an unending process. Where is this process going to end? It is the respiteless procedure going on in the Ocean of the original cause (*ātmā*) that is seen in the form of birth, life and death of individuals.

57. Like the human mind, the ocean is always active. But let us conceive the ocean as placid, with no waves. We will then find that waves are not its only attribute. For instance the sea water then tasted will be found to be salty. When this is experienced, we forget about the ocean's turbulence reflected through the waves. Similarly a pearl diver's interest in the ocean is confined to its aspect as the repository of pearl oysters. Each interest makes a world. This is created by *māyā*. In a single item like the ocean there are numerous such worlds. In the vast expanse of consciousness there are countless single items like the Ocean, each a granary as it were, of multitudinous worlds. The totality of these endless surfeit of worlds is what Guru calls *samvid*, i.e., the universe.

58. The experience, one following the other, the calculation of time in terms of yesterday, today and tomorrow — these mental activities will drag us to the conclusion that Truth

is divisible into many. Instead of directing thoughts along these lines of endless additions and subtractions it should be understood that what is experienced through them are but the result of mental confusion and that because the Truth endemic in them is but one, their essence is also one.

**59.** When knowledge is isolated, the 'I' ceases to exist. So also there is no 'I' apart from knowledge. There is only light. Hence knowledge and knower can be seen as one. There need not be any argument on this count.

**60.** Without realising that knowledge and the knower are one, knowledge is treated as an individual's own. But just as for one who knows the so-called otherness of 'that' is not separate from one, so knowledge that is treated as 'mine' does not have an existence apart from the knower.

**61.** External objects are experienced as separate from one another. This is because we feel that each sense-organ, by performing its function, perceives these objects as they appear to it. But this is due to ignorance. These objects actually merge with the countless names like the sky and earth, and are transformed into knowledge.

**62.** Blinded by ignorance, one should not say that the ultimate truth belongs to oneself. That would be wrong like saying, "the *ātmā* is mine". What is right is the statement, "I am the *ātmā*". What knowledge is gained by saying that the ultimate truth belongs to oneself? Real knowledge is not obtainable by mere utterances like that — The Supreme should be found through unrelenting meditation.

**63.** Knowledge that is *ātmā* should be realised through the stance that knowledge and 'I' are one. Instead, if the enquiry is on the premise that, that knowledge is not the 'I', it would be impossible to achieve knowledge realisation. The awareness that the knower is the 'I', and the *ātmā* that is to be known are not separate, but one, is the great secret of wise men. Who knows this?

**64.** One should dismiss from one's mind memory of all objects which hamper the mental operation towards realisation of knowledge. The priceles ultimate knowledge will be revealed by the fathomless bonanza of memories imprinted in the vast expanse of consciousness. This conclusion is reached by right reasoning.

**65.** There is nothing here that has not been known to us at one time or another. Because of the veil dropped by the heterogeniety in forms, we are denied conscious awareness of all things converging into indivisible oneness. Being unbounded, this unity which transports us to inexpressible ecstasy is normally not known to any. Who is aware of this wonderful truth? Strange indeed!

**66.** Objects which constitute knowledge and which satisfy wants of beings such as food, appear and disappear as a ceaseless operation. What remains static is the one truth namely knowledge. What could be seen as others or other things are all just luminous manifestations of the knowledge.

**67.** Apart from what cannot be known either through the visual organ or by calculation and what is ordinary and perceivable, there is nothing either in our memory or sleep or up in the heavens or anywhere. This is certain.

**68.** In dim light we see a piece of rope and suspect it to be a snake. At the same time it can be neither. Like the two forms of the rope piece, the self splits into two and settles down in knowledge (the *ātmā*) and the body. Of these one is *ārya* (righteous knowledge) and the other *anārya* (unrighteous knowledge). This reality can be unravelled by those endowed with the faculty of reasoning.

**69.** With the sense-organs like the eyes, the ears and the nose yoked to it as horses, the image of the *ātmā* seated inside as its divine occupant and conscience as its pilot, is the chariot *rati* or carnal passion. The ego enters that chariot and satisfies all the base passions outside it continuously by taking in the alluringly beauteous sights there.

**70.** It is the same carnal pleasure which blossoms into forms of ego, senses and the body as channels for the satiation of that pleasure. So long as knowledge is treated as separate from the knower, that is, the 'I', where is the end to this sordid performance? No, there can be no end to it. This is to be remembered.

**71.** In this world new objects emerge repeatedly. This process never stops and so one can stand in a static state. Change is an activity which has been going on from the beginning of time. If the ceaseless ongoing changes and the unchanging Truth which remains, are known in their entirety, then the knower experiences inestimable happiness from that knowledge.

**72.** Looked at from the one side, the action going on is ignorance appearing as real. From the other side is discerned, action which is real knowledge. This dichotomy between the worlds of ignorance and knowledge is the work of *māyā*. A mental picture of the Truth which exists beyond the dichotomy gives one the experience of *turīya*.

**73.** In one truth there are diverse forms. So also in diverse forms is the all-pervading one Truth. If this is known, all differences will disappear and merge into knowledge. This secret is not known to all because it is not an easily decipherable mystery.

**74.** The earth is constituted of countless particles of dust. But the earth has no existence apart from these particles. That is to say there can be no earth without these dust particles and there can be no dust particles without the earth. Similarly we regard the inert body and the power that gives life to it constitute what we call the 'I'. Body without life and life without body can be conjured up in our imagination only. The actuality of each apart from the other is unthinkable.

**75.** In this stanza Guru says that water in the ocean stands for nature. The bodies which are seen as various entities are the bubbles in the water. The ocean represents the *ātmā*, and the recurring consciousness 'I' am', 'I am', is compared to the never ending transitory waves. All the knowledge that is deposited in consciousness represents the pearls which lie in the ocean's depths. Hence the nectar of knowledge which everyone enjoys is nothing else but the pearls of knowledge.

**76.** Like ripples after ripples which rise on the surface of a pond consequent on ceaselessly blowing it into innumerable grains of sand, untruths prompted by *māyā* are blown into the inner self and create the impression that it has multifarious forms. Man taking this as real, feels himself embroiled, and wanders aimlessly.

**77.** The Supreme is looked upon as the sky, and the strong flowing wind as the creator of matter and forms. Fire is taken as knowledge and water, the senses. The object of the senses is seen as the earth. Thus this indivisible universe exists in these five principles. The secret of that universe and the life stirring in it are one.

**78.** Birth, life and death are non-existent. Man or Deva (the celestial being) too does not exist. All these are just names and forms, like the mirage in the desert. That they are not real may be remembered.

**79.** What is born does not have actuality. Except at the moment of birth, what is born does not exist at any other time. When seen in this light the question that arises is: how can the born have reality at any time? This is true also of death. So there is no birth and death. The birth and death which seem to exist are but the sport of pure consciousness.

**80.** How can the mutually antagonistics of creation, existence and dissolution co-exist in one place? That is impossible. When this is understood, the creations of the universe such as earth, etc., are reduced to mere words.

**81.** Nature divides itself into two. On the one side is the *ahanta* or ego which owns and consumes what is at hand. On the other side is the *idanta* or what exists here and in the beyond, the outside *ahanta*. What exists as the *idanta* is the real sphere of enjoyment.

**82.** Just as by rubbing two sticks together fire is produced, the boundless knowledge hidden in the seeker emerges by friction or pressure of the compulsions of enquiry. This knowledge blazes in the firmament of the Supreme Consciousness in whose burning fury everything is incinerated.

**83.** To die, to remain, to be born; one form giving place to another and thus continuing the process; these are innate characteristics of the body. Remaining beyond these transmutations, and knowing everything about creation, existence and dissolution, is the all-pervading *ātmā*, the indivisible and passionless.

**84.** Because we see the different forms of earth as pot, pan, etc., they are taken as real. But all these forms of sand will be found to be unreal. What is real is only the sand. What is experienced as unlimited forms as having real existence is that which is endemic in knowledge. These are but the attributes of Nature.

**85.** There cannot be a shadow without an object; what is visible as the world is not an object with any reality. Nor does it create the image of another object. Therefore it is neither shadow nor reality. Like the picture of a snake drawn by an adept artist, everything appears as visually experienced.

**86.** Every object of the world, like the body, exists apart from the others. In one body there is no other body. For this reason all bodies are transitory. On the contrary, since what exists as real in each body does not expire, it is in that reality that extinguishing bodies merge.

**87.** When each object is considered singly, it can be taken as real. But when these objects are associated with one another, it will be seen that one does not exist in the others. Looked at from this perspective, objects like the body will be found to be neither real nor unreal. This is an inexplicable phenomenon.

**88.** Each object is real by itself. One who has grasped the basic truth of existence, will see all objects as one. Unless knowledge is introspective, *māyā* will dominate the mind and plague it with confusion.

**89.** From knowledge that is Truth, emanate numerous sparks and create the impression of reality from what actually is not real, thus materialising the image of an apparently real universe. So it should be known that there is no real Truth other than knowledge. This wisdom bestows the awareness of unity (oneness).

**90.** Evanescent objects like the body will not blot out what is real. This is the experience of all. The real is what Is. On this premise every experience is permeated by the Real. Therefore the body and such objects represent the ultimate Reality in diversified forms.

**91.** For the attainment of what gives us happiness we are engaged in continuous striving. This is a changeless and unending process. Hence happiness has no beginning. It is the reality without change or dissolution and is not accessible to knowledge, and hence the one absolute Reality. It is this Reality that is being manifested in the form of experience, joyous or grievous.

**92.** Outside us the law of operation runs unexpended for securing happy ends for us. So the eternal longing for them remains struck within us for ever. For the fulfilment of this eternal longing within (i.e., for the ecstasy of the *ātmā*) the effort applied without is just an external symbol indicating its reality.

**93.** The body is ephimeral. But, for everyone there is nothing dearer than the *ātmā*. Since the love for the *ātmā* remains unchanged, the *ātmā* is eternal.

**94.** The phenomenon of the unreal world and the eternal Reality remaining intermixed is a great inequity. This endless marvel is neither verbalisable nor imaginable. To understand this, where is the place for the artifices employed for the unravelling of Truth?

**95.** The miraculous universe without beginning or end is the roadway to enjoyment. It is the all-pervading force, sometimes acting in tandem with *māyā*, and sometimes veiled by it. This force is manifested as the universe. Its limps express themselves in the multitudinous aspects of the universe.

**96.** The smallest and the largest, the reality and the unreality — these and similar opposites remain as two sides of the all-pervading force. Later, when the secret of its game-play executed through *māyā* is known, the contradiction between reality and unreality disappears on its own. The experience of existence and non-existence will cease to have its actuality in the light of this unique enlightenment.

**97.** Knowledge is vast. The atom disappears in that vastness leaving no trace of its parts. Realisation of the unique Truth will also be perfected then. This cannot be known without being experienced. It is the unbroken consciousness, the ocean of nectar materialised out of ripened silence.

**98.** Being engaged in the hunt for pleasure till now, in mind as well as through words, we have not been able to know the one object which ought to be known. Even while the intellect and other faculties and their subjects go on shifting, Knowledge of proprietorship of the *ātmā* (the I consciousness) remains as indissoluble wisdom. This should be known and made known to others. (Here 'we' refers to Guru himself.)

**99.** For one who is freed of the veil of unwisdom, knowledge and the I consciousness are identical. The others have doubt. If Knowledge is independent of the I consciousness, there will be no one here to understand and realise what knowledge is. Knowledge is a subjective experience. It does not have an independent existence of its own.

**100.** I am not this or that. Nor am I the meaning of existence or anything that is seen in this world. I am existence, consciousness and immortal joy, i.e., *sat-cit-ānanda*. This feeling should emerge in one and become the sole experience. One thus becomes the emboldened, who knows and makes others know. Thus transformed, without entertaining the indiscreet idea of any distinction between the real and the unreal, one should slowly, but steadily merge in the *praṇava* or the original sound *auṁ*.

*Ātmopadeśa Śatakam* gives the seeker answers to several questions which defy solutions in his quest for Reality. But some of the metaphysical propositions which Guru has incorporated in it, especially those relating to *māyā* and its impact on life are difficult to comprehend. Such immortal aphorisms as "Whatever one pursues for one's own happiness should be conducive to the happiness of others as well" and "the essence of all religions is one" have contributed not a little to the greatness of this poem as a timeless literary edifice. For the humanity at large strangling itself in a mad hunt for physical and transient pleasures, it presents the gateway to the spiritual world and thus the final asylum in the Reality of the Supreme where there is no differentiation between individuals, religion or caste. This work entitles Guru to the status of the modern proponent of the secular ideal.

# 4

# Sanskrit Poems

THAT Guru was proficient in composing poems of exceptional calibre in Sanskrit too with effortless ease as in Malayalam, is evidenced by his compositions in that language. Stretched to eighteen poems starting with *Vināyakāṣṭakam* and ending with *Darśanamālā*, this chain of masterly creations bears abundant testimony to his demiurgic genius. These pieces barring *Darśana-Mālā*, *Brahmavidyā-Pañcakam*, *Municaryā-Pañcakam*, *Nirvṛtti-Pañcakam*, *Āśramam*, *Dharmam*, *Elegical stanzas*, *Homamantram* and *Ślokatrayī*, have been referred to previously.

## Brahmavidyā-Pañcakam

There are five stanzas in this piece. Here is an epitome of the idea contained in them:

The preceptor reveals to the disciple that he himself (the disciple) is *Brahman*. Whatever is perceived through the senses is illusion only, created out of ignorance. He alone is the ultimate truth. That truth that is *Brahman* charges, impregnates and transfuses every grain of sand, every activity, every being and non-being, and everything that is happening and not happening in this universe. So the disciple as well as the preceptor is *Brahman*. There is and there can be nothing, apart from it.

## Municaryā-Pañcakam

This piece of five stanzas was written on the occasion of Guru's meeting with Ramana Maharshi at Thiruvilwa Malai. The poem itself was recorded by Him in Ramana Maharshi's visiting diary. Here is the gist of the idea contained in the poem:

Sree Ramana externalises the spiritual perfection reachable only by sages of the highest spiritual attainments, who abjure worldly attachments and the gratification of desires and possession, and actualise the scriptural message *tat-tvam-asi* (You are *Brahman*). The great sage fulfils himself in ultimate spiritual realisation. He is unconcerned with, and indifferent to, his personal comforts in food, drink, clothing or shelter; eating what he gets begging, sleeping where he doesn't care, and going to where his legs take him, he has attained *Brahmapāda* or the ultimate spiritual state where *jīvātmā* and *paramātmā* converge, where sages of his calibre alone reach.

## Nirvṛtti-Pañcakam

The question as to who deserves Bliss or complete happiness is answered in this five-para piece. He who forswears desire to gather information about those familiar or otherwise, abstains from imposing inhibitions on the movements and activities of others, does not show uncalled for inquisitiveness about the whereabouts of persons other than himself, desists from differentiating between persons, places and things, and treats everything known and unknown, with equanimity, deserves bliss or complete happiness.

## Āśramam

It was on the occasion of the establishment of Advaitāśramam at Aluva that Sree Narayana Guru revealed what all qualities are required by the head of hermitage. He revealed them through the five stanzas of this piece.

To be the preceptor of an Āśramam (hermitage), one must possess the qualities of generosity, equanimity, solemnity, chastity, philanthropy, kindness, honesty, courtesy, dutifulness and detachment. An organisation for good work should be formed under his leadership. Its members should be of unimpeachable character, fraternal-minded and intelligent. There should be separate schools and abodes for males and females in the *Āśramam*. It would be desirable to have an intelligent and capable person to lead the activities in each of these. Guru had propounded these ideals for the Advaitāśramam. Here will be found the nucleus of the Sree Narayana Dharma Sangh.

## Elegical Stanzas

This piece alludes to the passing away of the great spiritual contemporary of Sree Narayana Guru, Sree Chattambi Swamikal. The omniscient, detached and wise Guru Sree Chattambi Swamikal shines in the skies like full moon. Having spent his time in worldly life in a body not his own, He has left that body and entered His own *Brahma śarīra* (Spiritual Body). To be indifferent to matters of happiness or sorrow is the characteristic of great sages. Sree Narayana Guru has described Sree Chattambi Swamikal's life as one exemplifying the truth that man whose life is not his own, and who treats the body as his own, leaves it and enters what is really his. The idea that there is no sense in waiting over returning what has been borrowed and taking one's own, is brought out here.

## Homamantram

This is an invocation to the Fire God. O, the Lord of Fire, all your splendour is related to *Brahman*. Therefore You are manifestation of *Brahman*. The five senses, the mind and the intellect are your seven tongues. We are offering to you the senses and the self in the form of firewood and *ghī*. So bless us Lord.

## Dharmam

This is a homage to *dharma* or righteousness. *Dharma* is the Supreme God. It is also the greatest wealth. It always wins over everything else. Let *dharma* be hailed.

## Darśana-Mālā (Garland of Visions)

*Darśana-Mālā* can be stated to mean a garland of visions or revelations. Revelations are the visions of great spiritual thinkers expressed in words for the benefit of humanity. Here Guru has encapsulated his visions on *Advaita* (Monism) into ten gems of ten stanzas each, and created an immortal garland.

*Darśana-Mālā* is acknowledged as the most outstanding of Sree Narayana Guru's Sanskrit compositions. It reveals His mastery of the ancient language and His poetic skill, and enfolds within itself a plethora of ideas, bringing into limelight the limitless apocalyptic vistas of the layman's nightmare, the Monistic philosophy. In effect, Guru has succeeded in fulfilling His wish that a simplified version of Monism, albiet in Sankrit, should be made available. For this reason the opinion gaining ground that *Darśana-Mālā* is modern *Bhagavad Gītā*, has to be treated as carrying enough substance.

The ten gems plaited into this magnificent garland are: *Adhyāropadarśanam, Apavādadarśanam, Asatyadarśanam, Māyādarśanam, Bhānadarśanam, Karmadarśanam, Jñānadarśanam, Bhaktidarśanam, Yogadarśanam* and *Nirvāṇadarśanam*.

Now we may explain each of these *Darśanams* (Revelations).

### A. ADHYĀROPADARŚANAM (VISION BY SUPPOSITION)

**1.** In the beginning, there was
Non-existence indeed!
Dreamwise then again by mere willing
Everything existent created. He the Lord Supreme.

**2.** In the beginning, in the form of incipient memory factors
(All) this remained. Then the Lord
By his own power of false presentiment, like magician
Created all this world (of change).

**3.** This (world) before creation was
Latent within Himself,
Thereafter, like spirit from seed
From Himself, by His power, by itself
it was created.

4. The power however, as of two kinds,
Is to be known as the bright and the dark;
There is no co-existence between these two
As with light and darkness.

5. In the beginning this world
Which was in the form of mind-stuff, like a picture
Achieved with all this picturesque variety
Like an artist, the Lord.

6. Potentially what even as nature remained
Like the psychic powers of Yoga;
Like a Yogi did He, the Lord of the world, work out
His varied psychic powers thereafter.

7. When self-knowledge shrinks
Then prevails nescience fearful,
Ghost-like, taking name and form,
In most terrible fashion looms here.

8. Terrible and empty of content
Like a city infernal
Even as such a marvel
Did the Lord make the whole universe.

9. If from Sun in graded succession
This world came, such was not the case at all,
Presented as if out of slumber
At one stroke all came to be.

10. He from whom, like a fig tree as from seed,
Came out this world manifested
He is Brahma, He is Siva and Vishnu,
He is the Ultimate; everything is He indeed.

COMMENTARY

Originally this world was non-existent. Then Lord Supreme willed its creation and it came into being. This creation is not reality. It is only a fantasy. The universe emerged not in sequence, one part following the other, but in a single process. In the beginning it was a non-entity. The Lord subsequently gave it form, like a magician's jugglery. Before that as a non-entity it portended the prospect of what was coming.

Before its creation, its existence was in a state of being innate in the Lord. Then, like the spout from the seed, it was born on its own by His power. In essence creation is the objectivisation of the power inherent in the *ātmā*.

Divine power (energy) has a dual manifestation: *taijasī* (light) and *tāmasī* (darkness). They cannot exist together because of their inherent incompatibility.

The universe, before it came out into the open, existed in the Lord's imagination just as an artist's mental picture of what he is to impart into canvas. The picture takes on a beautiful form with the exquisite arrangement of colours. So also when the universe took shape through release from the Lord's mind, it was beautiful.

Like the *yogī*'s prowess, the universe was originally just nature. And like the *yogī*'s Prowess, the Lord's Omnipotence acted to transfigure nature into the universe with all its diverse manifestations. When the spiritual power is circumscribed, ignorance gains ascendency. Like a demon it appears in different aspects assuming divergent forms and shapes. The resultant terror it spreads is attributed to seeing it as real because of ignorance.

This world is a horror, not to mention that it is nothingness. Therefore the Lord made it into a demon land. As stated earlier, the universe was not created in an orderly sequence like the sun at first followed by fire, air and so on. It was born in a single action by the exercise of the Lord's will like the experience of awakening from sleep.

Like the huge banyan tree from the seed, the universe came into being. The power from which it emanated in the all-pervading *Brahman* whose might is embodied in Lords Brahmā, Viṣṇu and Śiva, the beings and everything else. Enshrined here in the opinion of some scholars is the nucleus of Guru's incontrovertible dictum

"One caste, One religion and One God for man".

B. APAVĀDADARŚANAM (VISION OF NON-SUPPOSITION)

**1.** This world which is both subtle and gross
And what has come to be from living consciousness,
If existent, then everything is existent;
If non-existent, then it exists as consciousness.

**2.** Other than the cause, the effect cannot be;
Therefore, all this is non-existent;
Of what is non-existent, how can there be any origin,
And of something unoriginated how
(can there be) re-absorption?

**3.** To that which origin and dissolution is not
That is none other than the ultimate Absolute;
(That there) is origin and reabsorption
By Maya's confusion in the self (is supposed).

**4.** Because of non-difference from cause
The effect, how could it have being?
How could there be for the same reason,
For the cause also any non-being?

**5.** By being an effect and thus non-existent
An existent cause there is, the world is
thus not indeed;
On the other hand, it is the Absolute alone
that is existent
That dull minds mistake as non-existing.

**6.** If one alone had reality
Another in it how could there be?
If existence is posited in existence, tautology (comes)
and if non-existence is so asserted
contradiction (comes).

**7.** Dividing all parts one by one
Everything then is seen there

As mind-stuff alone and as no other;
As thus banishing Maya (relativity) far away.

8. Thus it is pure mind-stuff alone that shines
There is nothing therefore beyond pure
mind-stuff at all;
What does not shine is not real either,
And what is non-real does not shine indeed.

9. High value (bliss) alone exists and shines,
Therefore not anything else at all;
Thus everything is of the stuff of the High value,
And besides this High value nothing else exists.

10. All is indeed existence — subsistence — value,
Herein there is not even a little plurality;
He who sees (this) as pluralistic.
From death to death he goes.

COMMENTARY

*Apavāda* means removing the object which shields the original object and revealing its actual form. Looked at from this aspect it will be sure that the universe shines in the Divine spirit.

This universe with macro and micro forms has evolved from the Divine power. If it is said to be real it is expressive of its grossness (*sad ṣaṇam*). If it is said to be unreal, it is expressive of the Divine consciousness (*cit ṣaṇam*). *Sad ṣaṇan* implies the underlying Divine spirit and *cit ṣaṇam* the awareness or knowledge. In either case it is clear that the universe has no identity of its own apart from God.

Cause and consequence are one. So the entire universe is unreal. How can the unreal exist or can be 'is'? What is not 'is' cannot have dissolution. The universe is the consequence and God the cause. That is the spiritual concept. The fact is that there is no reality in isolation from God.

That which has neither the beginning nor the end is *Brahman*. Nothing else deserves to be symbolic of *Brahman*. The fear the *ātmā* has beginning and end is the work of *māyā*. According to the theory of monism, *Brahman* and *ātmā* are one.

Since the consequence is not separate from the cause how can consequence have existence? By the same token how can cause non-exist? Guru here establishes the reality of the cause and the unreality of the consequence. Since the universe is the product, and unreal, it has a cause that is real. Hence the universe is illusory. But the unintelligent misunderstands it as real.

If one alone has reality, how can that state happen to another? Here Guru through an analytical approach, establishes that one alone can have reality. Where it is stated that the real is only one, it has one alone as its premise. Now supposing the real has another one as its premise, the controversial question arises as to whether that another one is real or unreal. If it is real then it leads to the defective and illogical self-dependence for the one that is real. If it is unreal it leads to the fallacy of impossibility.

When everything is dissected into its parts it will be evident that this universe is far away from *māyā* and that it is Divinely ordained and nothing else. Dissection of the cloth takes us to the threads which comprise the cloth. The threads again are reduced to cotton and the cotton further to the atom. The atom when mentally split will reveal that consciousness alone is the core of everything.

Knowledge alone will shine everywhere. Nothing else shines. Hence there is nothing else which is separate from knowledge. Everything that does not shine is unreal. *Ānanda* or ecstasy alone has reality. That therefore only shines. The others are unreal and hence cannot shine. Therefore the entire world is ecstasy and nothing else. Everything is merged into *sat-cit-ānanda*. There is nothing here which had diversity. He who sees diversity moves from death towards death.

## C. ASATYADARŚANAM (VISION OF NON-EXISTENCE)

**1.** All this (world) is of mind-stuff;
The mind, however is not anywhere;
Therefore like the blue and so on in the sky

The world is seen in the Self.

2. By nescience which is no other than the mind
All this world is a presentiment of the will;
This (nescience) by knowledge gets re-absorbed,
Then the whole world (becomes) a mere configuration.

3. Here what a coward finds through darkness
To be like a looming ghost,
That same is seen to be by the wise
Like a dream-world of a waking state.

4. This visible world results from a
willing presentiment;
Where willing is present alone
In this visible world seen; not anywhere else
As a snake too, when (alone) a rope is found.

5. Between the willl and mind
There is no difference at all;
That which is mind and called nescience and darkness
Like the magic of Indra, is a marvel.

6. Like a mirage to a wise man
The world looms in the Self,
Just as to an infant by confusion
A reflected image might real seem too.

7. The self like milk (that turns)
Does not attain to another form;
Therefore the whole (universe) as if created
By Indra's magic, exists (an eidetic) presentiment

8. Maya itself is the prime (material) cause
Of the world; what is no other
Than the Maya-maker, everything indeed
Created itself as various unreal magical effects.

9. To the mature mind this universe
Looms like a sky forest in the Self;

Even as an unreal puppet form
To a child (would seem) contrariwise.

**10.** One (alone) is real, not a second
What is unreal indeed seems as being real;
The Siva-lingam is stone itself,
Not a second made by the mason.

COMMENTARY

The universe in its entirety is the mind. But the mind exists nowhere. Hence it is like the blueness of the sky that the universe is seen in the *ātmā*. But the sky is not blue although we experience it as blue. So also the mind and its creation, viz., the universe, are nothingness. They are ascribed to their source which is *ātmā*.

Ignorance is another name for mind. This world is created by ignorance. Knowledge destroys ignorance. When knowledge is achieved the world is seen just as a picture. (The universe is the conjured up product of ignorance). It is felt visible by ignorance like the devil is felt visible by the coward. The learned regard it unreal like a dream as it appears to the dreamer when he awakes.

The universe is a supposition. Therefore where there is supposition there will be the visible universe. Nowhere else. This is like seeing rope as snake. A piece of rope found in the ground when it is dark is taken for snake. But there is no snake there. It is supposition that has created it. Similarly it is because the universe is supposed to exist that it appears as real. There is no otherness between mind and supposition (mental creation). Mind is a synonym for *tamas* (darkness). It is ignorance and is mysterious like magic.

To the enlightened this world is like mirage. A child because of its ignorance, believes its own reflection to be real. Like that the ignorant treats this world as real.

Milk changes form into curd. But *ātmā* has no such change of form. Everything appears as real as the creations of the magician. Change of form is not real. When an object really changes its form it is *pariṇāmam* or change of state. When there is no such real change for an object, but there is only the appearance of change, it is *vivartam* or apparent change of form.

The original cause of the universe is *māyā* only. Everything is created by *māyā*. Nothing exists outside this creator. Whatever appears as real is unreal. There is nothing disparate from the supreme soul, the substratum of the universe.

Monists say that the foundation of the universe lies in *māyā*. To the one who knows, it is like a forest imagined to exist in the sky. A child sees an illusory doll as real, whereas the adult has the reverse experience. The long and the short of it is that for the ignorant the world is real and to the enlightened it is unreal.

Truth is only one, indivisible, irrefutable. It is without a second. It is untruth that is felt as Truth. The *Śiva-Liṅga* (Icon of Lord Śiva) is stone itself. It is not the craftsman's another creation. But when the stone is deified it becomes worshippable. In like manner when the unreal world is conceived as the Truth, man suffers by engulfing himself in worldliness.

D. MĀYĀDARŚANAM (VISION OF NEGATION)

**1.** What is not real, that is Negation
Which by itself, as science-nescience,
Transcendence, immanence, darkness and prime potency
Of Nature, in many forms, looms.

**2.** Just as, before the origin of the pot the clay itself is
In this non-being, (so too before the origin of the
 world) as other than the world
What had no being as the Absolute itself
Such is Maya (the negative principle) of
 indeterminate possibility.

**3.** "The non-self is unreal, the Self is real",
Thus what looms is VIDYA, knowledge
As the reality of the snake (appearance)
(Superimposed) on the rope-reality is understood.

4. "The Self is unreal, the non-self is real"
Thus what looms is AVIDYA, nescience indeed
As the erroneous cognition
As between rope and snake.

5. The senses, the mind, intelligence and the five
Vital tendencies, what creates
That is the transcendent indeed even (they being)
The subtle limbs of the reasoning Self.

6. Adopting as its own these limbs, the reasoning Self
By its own negative base of error imagines,
(Itself) as if happy or suffering;
In Truth there is nothing at all.

7. The objective data of the senses which is the world
What emanates forth, that indeed
In the context of the self is the immanent
The basis of all gross presentiment of the will.

8. As the ignorance about the mother-of-pearl
The basis of the silver presentiment becomes;
So too what in the Self is the basis (of the world)
That is known as darkness (tamas).

9. Because of being that aspect (of Maya) which is a marvel
By containing in all this (universe) like tree in a seed,
Or by virtue of its importance (above others)
This here is known as the prime potent power (pradhana).

10. By its very nature, because, in a marvellous way
It diversifies, the three nature, modalities,
This (aspect of Maya) consisting of the three
Modalities is well known as Nature.

COMMENTARY

*Māyā* is illusion; that which does not exist. Whatever that is not is *māyā*. Knowledge, ignorance, this, that, darkness, excellence, Nature — *māyā* is known in such multitudinous states. It is the analytical disposition of Guru's mind that is reflected in his giving various names to *māyā*.

The pot is non-existent before it is moulded out from sand. That which is not an entity, is isolation from the oneness of *Brahman*, is *māyā*. It is a many splendoured wonder. What there is prior to the coming into being of the pot is without question, sand. So also the state prior to the coming into being of the universe is *Brahman*. It is because of the delusive characteristic of *māyā* that the impression of the world's creation is engendered.

That which occasions the idea that the *ātmā* is real and non-*ātmā* is unreal is knowledge. It is tantamount to uncovering the reality of the rope mistaken for snake due to ignorance. Conversely that which occasions the idea that the *ātmā* is unreal and non-*ātmā* is real, is ignorance (*avidyā*). When a person sees a piece of rope while it is dark, and does not see the rope as rope, but as snake only, it is due to ignorance. Similarly taking the real as unreal and the unreal as real is due to ignorance.

That which creates the micro organs of consciousness such as the senses, the mind, the intellect, the five vital airs of the body, etc., is *māyā* (the other). By 'senses' is meant the organs of action namely arms, genitals, hand, leg, and mouth and the intellectual organs namely tongue, nose, skin, eye and ear. The five vital airs of the body are *prāṇam* (life, power), *apānam* (breaking wind or downward air), *samānam* (the air that stays at the naval and performs the decaying of food), *udānam* (the air that rises from within and comes up to the throat) and *vyānam* (life breath). The microcosmic body is constituted of the five intellectual organs, the five organs of action, the five vital airs and the mind and the intellect.

The *ātmā* with its own *māyā* makes use of these organs and enjoys and suffers. These are wilful pretensions and not real. Enjoyment and suffering are *māyā* (illusory); what creates this massive universe (macrocosmic) which is experienced only by the senses, is *māyā*, 'the other'. It is because of this that the microcosmic universe is imagined to exist in the *ātmā* (The other, i.e., *para* is instrumental in the creation of the micro body, and the *ātmā*, i.e., *apara* of the marco body.)

Just as the existence of silver foisted on the pearl oyster is an experience conjured up by ignorance, so the foisting of the universe upon the *ātmā* is also the world of ignorance. That is *tamas* or darkness. (*Māyā* which occasions the imposition of what is unreal upon what is real is called *tamas*). Like the tree in the seed, everything is innate in it. Either because of that, or because it is invested with too much importance, it is accoladed pre-eminent.

The *guṇas* (attributes) are naturally divided into three, viz., *satva*, *rajo* and *tamo*. *Māyā* which encompasses these three can be turned as *prakṛti* or nature.

E. BHĀNADARŚANAM (VISION OF CONSCIOUSNESS)

**1.** Present equally within (and) without
In constant bee agitation,
Consciousness is of two kinds:
The generic and the specific.

**2.** As the concrete, the subtle, the causal and the Absolute
Basic Consciousness (is) of four kinds
So these names even, (of basic consciousness)
Are also applicable to consciousness.

**3.** Lo, here, "I am the body, this is the pot"
Depending on the concrete
What looms as consciousness
That is known as the concrete.

**4.** Here what is consciousness of the body
And the pot, that is the specific;
Likewise too, what is (the consciousness) of 'I' or 'this'
Is known as the generic.

**5.** The senses, mind, intellect, interest-items
And the five vital tendencies:
By what is made conscious, this is (known as) the subtle
Because of dependence on the subtle.

6. "I am ignorant" — such a consciousness
Is said to be the causal.
Here, that aspect which stands for 'I' is the generic,
And the specific what stands for 'am ignorant'.

7. "I am the Absolute" — Thus what consciousness attains
Is praised as the (consciousness) of the Absolute
Here the element 'I' is the generic
(And Absolute is its specific attribute.)

8. Where consciousness (exists) there the
Object of consciousness (exists); where
Consciousness exists not its object neither,
Thus both by agreement and difference certitude comes.

9. As with the eye which cannot see itself
(So) the self does not see itself;
Therefore, the Self is not indeed the object of consciousness,
That which the self sees is the object of consciousness.

10. What is the object of consciousness, that is conditioned,
What is unconditioned, that is not the object of consciousness,
What is conditioned is non-existent,
But what is unconditioned, itself the
EXISTENT IS THAT

COMMENTARY

*Bhānam* literally means light. Metaphysically it is the Supreme Soul. Its attribute is motion. It at once vibrates incessantly inside and outside. It is like an ever active beetle. It has two features, the general and the particular. *Bhānam* is an experience that it is the root cause of all activities. Its very life is motion. It stirs within and without the individual.

*Bhānam* resides in four states: *sthūlam* (material), *sūṣmam* (abstract), *kāraṇam* (causal) and *turīyam* (mental stillness). Each of these states is also referred to as *bhānam*. The name *bhānaśrayam* is also used to denote *bhānam*.

Statements such as 'I am the body', 'this is the pot', refer to material objects. So *bhānam* which depends on reference to material objects is *sthūla bhānam*. It is the illusion that material objects exist.

Reference to specific objects such as body, pot is particular *bhānam*; objects like I, this refer to general *bhānam*. Reference to the microcosmic/abstract body which is constituted of the organs of action, of intellectual process, the five vital airs, the Mind and intelligence is *sūṣma bhānam*.

The feeling that 'I am ignorant' expresses the Causal *bhānam*. Here 'I' is general and 'ignorant' is particular. In this case therefore *bhānam* has both general and particular attributes. Guru has shown that except for the *sūṣma*, the other states of *sthūlam*, *kāraṇam* and *turīyam* have both the general and particular aspects of *bhānam*.

The statement 'I am *Brahman*' represents *turīya bhānam* according to Guru. *Turīya* is the ultimate state of mental stillness — the merging of the self with *Brahman* — preceded by the three other states of *jāgrat* (awareness), *svapnam* (dream) and *suṣupti* (deep sleep) in that order. Guru has included even that state in *bhānam*.

Where there is *bhānam*, there is the invariable presence of *bhāṣyam* too. And conversely where there is no *bhānam*, there is no *bhāṣyam*. Thus the relationship can be grasped either in coordinated or differential terms. What becomes the premise or subject of *bhānam* is *bhāṣyam*. As a rule they can only be found as existing together without exception. This is the secret of *bhānam*.

Just as the eye cannot see itself, so the *ātmā* cannot see itself. Hence the *ātmā* is not illuminated by anything else. Only what *ātmā* sees is illuminated. In short *ātmā* is self-illuminating and It illuminates other objects. The *ātmā* is the knower while the other objects are the known.

What is illuminated is *adhyāsaphalam*, i.e., the result of *adhyāsam*. That which is not subject to *adhyāsam*, i.e., the action of *adhyāsam*, is not illuminated. What is subject to *adhyāsanam* is unreal. That which is not subject to *adhyāsanam* is real.

That which is subject to *bhāsana* is *adhyāstham* (attributed). That which is not *adhyāstham* (*adhyāsam*) is not subject to *bhāsana*. It will be seen that what is subject to *adhyāstham* is *asat* (unreal) and not subject to *adhyāstham* is *sat* (real). (The mental process by which what does not exist is seen as existent is *adhyāsam*. *Adhyāsam* (what is attributed) is unreal. That which is the basis of attribution is real. The *sat* is self-illuminating. The *asat* is dependent on another for its illumination. Because it is not *bhāṣya*, it can be categorically stated that the *ātmā* is *sat*.)

F. KARMADARŚANAM (VISION OF ACTION)

**1.** It is indeed the Self, tho' Self-luminous
And detached, that 'through negatively
Does action bearing many forms
Like the dream-agent in sleep.

**2.** "I think, I speak, I grasp, I hear"
In such forms whatever actions, are accomplished
By the supreme Self (which is also),
The self of pure reason and the senses.

**3.** Prior to action it is the Self (that exists);
There is nothing else at all,
Through the self by its own negative principle
By itself is accomplished (all actions),

**4.** From the Self not different from itself
There exists a certain undefinable
By that (power) all actions specificatory power,
Are falsely attributed to the actionless Self.

**5.** The Self is always detached indeed!
One performs action as if attached due to ignorance
The wise man saying, "I do nothing"
Is not interested in action.

6. The one (self) alone as fire it burns,
As wind (it) blows,
As water (it) rains,
As earth (it) supports (and), as a river (it) flows.

7. The one (self) alone remaining actionless
Moves as upward and downward vital tendencies,
Within the nervous centres,
Indeed it beats, murmurs and pulsates.

8. Here (in this visible world) as what exists, is born,
Grows, transforms, decreases and attains its end,
Is subject to six forms of becoming,
Is no other than the actionless self.

9. By means of the inner organ and the senses
Actions become self accomplished.
However, the wise man knows,
"I am the unattached, inner well founded one."

10. Because of being and object of experience
Even the 'I' is a conditioning factor
Superimposed like the mother-of-pearl gleam;
Above everything else today and tomorrow one alone is.

COMMENTARY

Even though unattached and self-illuminating the *ātmā* like the sub-consciousness during sleep, because it is on its own, assumes various forms and performs *karma* (action). It is as if the inactive *ātmā* submits to *māyā* and acts. This is like a person asleep feeling that he is performing so many activities.

The *paramātmā* which encompasses within it the Mind and the organs of action, performs such actions like thinking, saying, taking and hearing. But the *paramātmā* does not actually perform any *karma* or action. Because of the play of *māyā* it appears to perform the action. In this sense the *ātmā* is assumed to have the sense-organs capable of *karma*.

Before *karma* there is only the *ātmā*, and nothing else. Hence the *ātmā* should be conceived as doing *karma*, on its own with its own *māyā*. The *ātmā* has an inscrutable potency which is not apart from it. It is because of this potency that all *karma* is foisted on the innately inactive *ātmā*. Even though it is always inactive it pretends to be possessed by ignorance and consequently to be active, and performs *karma*. One who knows, incited by an awareness that he is not performing *karma*, maintains no affiliation with action. Only the *jñānī* (enlightened) can remain detached and do *karma*. Because the *ātmā* is inactive, the *jñānī*s thought is, even while he is immersed in action, that he is doing nothing at all.

The same *ātmā*, the one only, burns as fire, blows as wind, as cloud pouring down in rain, supports as the earth and flows as the river. The single absolute *ātmā* which exists as stagnant moves upwards through the nerves as *prāṇam*; it moves downwards as *apānam* beats, moans, groans, vibrates.

Whatever, in this world is subject to the disfigurations of existence, birth, growth, change, deterioration and destruction, is not other than the static *ātmā*. In every object in this world these six disfigurations are congenital. But they are not independent of the *ātmā*. Only they should be understood as real. They are all illusory appearances.

Through the instrumentality of the conscience and the senses, the actions take place automatically. The *jñānī* knows, that he is unattached and uninvolved. The thought of I-ness, because it is the subject of *jñāna* or knowledge, is just a feeling without substance. Hence the ego like silver in the oyster shell is enfolded in the *paramātmā*. I am for ever the *paramātmā* only, the one and only power which stands above everything else. It is eternal, without beginning or end.

## G. JÑĀNADARŚANAM (VISION BY AWARENESS OR REASON)

**1.** Awareness is one and unconditioned, indeed.
That is also the conditioned
Awareness without egoism, etc..

That is the unconditioned.

2. That which, accompanied by egoism, as if inside
And which again as qualified by thisness
Accompanied by conscious activity, such awareness,
Is to be understood conditioned:

3. That by which is experienced all things
Of the non-self such as egoism and so on
and even by which immortality is enjoyed
(As) the Witness, is Self-awareness.

4. As innumerable effects of egoism and so on
What as pertaining to the non-self
Attains to awareness, that is said to be
Awareness of the non-Self.

5. Knowing things as they really are
As when one attains to the truth of the rope
What makes for such, is true awareness
Wrong (awareness) is what is otherwise.

6. By the very presence of which everything looms
In consciousness by itself,
That awareness is indicated as empirical awareness
And also as non-transcendental awareness.

7. That function of awareness by which
The means to an end is appraised
And which arises out of associative innate disposition
That is inferential awareness.

8. On going near to an object to be ascertained
What, in the form of "this is the animal known by
such marks"
Is the functional basis for certitude,
Is (said to be) analogical awareness.

9. That awareness which is "I" and "mine"
And that other as "this" or "that" is also there;

The former as vital awareness and the latter
As sense awareness is declared.

**10.** Designated as "Aum that exists"
Attained to unity of the Absolute and the Self
Devoid of willing or other functions
That is said to be ultimate awareness.

COMMENTARY

Knowledge is one only. But it is conceived of as qualified knowledge and unqualified knowledge. Knowledge which is unattached by ego is unqualified knowledge. In reality knowledge is only one. That which is seen with attributes or qualifications is not eternal. It is in the unqualified aspect of knowledge that the character of an object is correctly known.

*Bhānam* exists within and without. That knowledge which dwells within along with the egoistic inner *bhānam*, and without along with the unegoistic outer *bhānam* is unqualified or pure knowledge.

The *ātmā* is witness to such mental states which are hostile to it, as egotism. What is experienced by that *ātmā* is *ātmajñānam* or knowledge of the self. It is by this knowledge that it is possible to experience ecstasy. Ecstasy means Salvation.

In contrast to *ātmajñānam* is *anātma jñānam*. It is knowledge about worldly experiences. That knowledge by which is known the numerous, non-Ātmic mental states such as egotism, and the consequent physical passions is called *anātma jñānam* or knowledge unconnected with the *ātmā*. In this category is included all knowledge exclusive of the *ātmā*.

What is real knowledge? In the example of the rope-snake riddle when the real fact about the rope is revealed it is real knowledge. That is to say, knowledge about objects in their factual perspective. What all is contrary to that is unreal knowledge.

That with whose presence alone everything shines on its own, is direct knowledge or *aparokṣa* knowledge. The knowledge which bestows awareness of objects is direct knowledge. It has been observed that this happens consequent on the close relationship between the senses and objects. What Guru means by *aparokṣam* (or direct) is what is experienced.

There is then *anumiti* or deductive knowledge. This is knowledge derived through deduction from two objects seen together. For instance smoke and fire. Where there is smoke there should be fire. This conclusion is reached by inference. The togetherness of smoke and fire is known to us from long experience. From this knowledge we are able to deduce that smoke accompanies fire. Here the smoke is *sādhanam* or object and fire, *sādhyam* or the conclusion arrived at, the deduction.

Related to *anumiti, jñānam* is *upamiti jñānam* or knowledge derived from similarity of objects. This can be made clear by an example. The lizard and the chameleon are similar in appearance. So a person familiar with the lizard can identify a chameleon when he happens to see one. This identification is a mental process, and the knowledge obtained is *anumiti*.

The knowledge which one gets about oneself and other external objects is *jīva jñānam*. The knowledge which is different from this is *indriya jñānam* or sensual knowledge.

The knowledge of the merger of the self/*ātmā* with the *paramātmā*, bereft of any thought, decision or indecision, is *param jñānam* or supreme knowledge. Here there is no mental activity, not even awareness of oneself.

H. BHAKTIDARŚANAM (VISION BY CONTEMPLATION)

**1.** Meditation of the Self is contemplation
Because the self consists of Bliss
A knower of the Self, meditates by the self
Upon the self for ever.

**2.** The Absolute is meditated upon
Because it consists of Bliss.

Constant meditation on the Absolute
Is thus known as contemplation.

3. It is even Bliss that all do meditate,
No one at all (meditates) suffering.
That which is meditation of Bliss,
As contemplation it is taught.

4. It is the Self alone that contemplates the Absolute;
The knower of the Self
Meditates on the Self and not on any other,
That which is meditation on the Self
Is known to be contemplation.

5. Bliss, the Self and the Absolute
Are said to be the names of this alone
In whom, there is such awareness
He, as a contemplative is well known.

6. "I am Bliss, I am the Absolute, I am the Self"
In whom in such forms,
There is always creative imagination,
As contemplative he is well known.

7. The wife does not merely adore the husband,
Nor husband merely adore the wife;
It is Self-Bliss alone (that they) adore
As lodged within every sensuous object.

8. For the wise man who sees
Thus at any place whatever
There is nothing at all other than Self-Bliss;
His contemplation verily is the highest.

9. Towards the Father of the World, to one's
Spiritual teacher, father, mother;
Towards the founders of Truth and
Towards those who walk in the same path;

10. Towards those who put down evil

And those who do good to all, what sympathy
There is, is devotion here; what here
Belonging to the Self-Supreme is the ultimate.

COMMENTARY

The mental process by which the *ātmā* is worshipped is called *bhakti*. This is because the *ātmā* is *ānanda svarūpa* or the incarnation of ecstasy. Even one who has reached enlightenment, i.e., merger with *ātmā* always performs this, albeit as an act of self-worship.

*Brahman* is the materialisation of ecstasy. It is being probed into the seeker. Such continuous search is *bhakti*.

Everyone wants *ānanda*, not misery. So everyone meditates on *ānanda* or happiness (ecstasy).

*Ātmā* is *Brahman*. Even the *ātma-jñānī* or one who has attained knowledge of *ātmā*, worships *ātmā*, nothing else. The worship of the *ātmā* is *bhakti*.

The person who entertains firm belief in the oneness of *ānanda*, *ātmā* and *Brahman* is the real *bhakta* (devotee).

A person who always imbibes within himself the belief that "I am *ānanda*, I am *Brahman*, I am *ātmā*" achieves glory as a *bhakta*.

It is not that the wife worships the husband or that the husband worships the wife. It is the *ānanda* derived from the indulgence in physical pleasure that they worship.

The person who has thus acquired knowledge of the *ātmā* sees nothing but ecstasy everywhere. His *bhakti* is more adorable than anything else.

*Bhakti* is pure Love. Love for God, Guru, Parents, one who upholds, and pursues the path of Truth, and those who fulfil others' wishes — that is *bhakti*. In short real *bhakti* is Love for, and in, the *paramātmā*.

1. YOGADARŚANAM (VISION BY MEDITATION)

**1.** That which always unites the mind

With the reasoning Self, and also gets united with it
And which is of the form of restraint
That is praised as Yoga.

2. Where the seer, the sight and the seen
Are not present there the heart
Should be joined as long as incipient memory
factors (are present);
Such is Yoga, (says) the knower of Yoga.

3. All this consisting of name-form (knowing)
As verily the Absolute, the mind ever merges
In the Absolute, what constitutes such
As Yoga is ascertained.

4. That unbroken functioning of reason
Which is the Self, like a streak of oil
Finds incessant, Joy, such as Yoga
Is by Yogis recognised.

5. To which or which other (interest) the mind goes
From that or that others into the Self
Ever restraining it, it should be joined;
In such Yoga here let it be united.

6. Uprooting those incipient memory factors of willing
The source of all human disasters, who
Together with their various willed objects
Restrains in the form of Self (saying),

7. What is seen has no existence, as such
Thus what is seen is the seer's self
He among knowers of Yoga
Is the most superior.

8. When the mind-bee drinking
Of the nectar-sweetness of Self-Bliss
Is drawn into union with Yoga-breeze
And does not flutter (Yoga takes place).

9. When meditation with gaze fixed between eyebrows,
And the tongue tip touching beyond the uvula
(take place)
Then happens that space-freedom attitude
(KHECARI MUDRA)
Of drowsiness and fatigue dispelling capacity.

10. As of wisdom and action, Yoga in this world
Is of two kinds, and within these summarily
The whole of the further elaboration of Yoga
Is comprised conclusively.

COMMENTARY

The exercise by which the mind abjures all thoughts and merges in the *Brahman* is called *yoga*. Those who are adepts in *yoga* say that *yoga* is the state of *samādhi* or oblivion in which the *tripudī* i.e., the knower, known and knowledge, disappears and the mind is blended with the *paramātmā* till the *vāsanās* or the tastes inherited from previous births last. *Yoga* involves the realisation that the universe which appears through names and forms is *Brahmam* itself and then the fusion of the mind into *Brahmam*. That is to say withdrawal of the mind from transient matter and merger with the immortal Soul.

Like an uninterrupted flow, the mind is engaged in a continuous and endless game of interaction with *Brahmam* through *yoga*. The uninterrupted flow represents the meditative process. When the *yoga* exercise is undertaken, the mind in the early stages is prone to diverse worldly matters repeatedly. This fickleness of the mind should be brought under control by constant mental exercise and thus the final merger achieved.

Temporal objectives are trouble makers. Therefore they should be destroyed along with the *vāsanās* (tastes inherited from previous births) and the mind (*ātmā*) inhibited from vacillatory urges. That is *yoga*.

What is seen has no reality. It is the act of seeing that is real. So what is seen has the form of the visual act. Whoever realises this and unites his mind is the ideal *yogī* (one who practises *yoga* to perfection).

Mind is like a beetle. The state in which it enjoys its nectar of *ānanda* is *yoga*. When the mind (*ātmā*) reaches the static, *yoga* or the fusion takes place.

That pose in *yoga* in which meditation centres under the eye-brows, the eye is brought to rest in between them and the tongue tip pulled inwards and fixed in the uvula, is called *khecarī mudrā* (*khecarī* is Durgā and *mudrā*, signet, i.e., the signet of Durgā). This pose destroys exhaustion, sleep, etc., and overcomes all hurdles to the smooth progress of the yogic exercise.

*Yoga* is of two variations —*jñānam* (knowledge) and *karmam* (action). So far as the monist is concerned knowledge alone is the means to Salvation. But Guru has given importance here to *karmam* as well. It can be stated that Guru's outlook on life is reflected in this.

J. NIRVĀṆADARŚANAM (VISION BY ABSORPTION)

1. Emancipation is of two kinds
   What is pure and what is impure
   What is without incipient memory factors,
   that is the pure;
   Likewise, what is qualified by incipient memory
   factors, is the impure.

2. As extra-pure and pure, the pure also
   Is of two kinds, likewise
   The impure also as pure impure
   And impure-impure is spoken of.

3. The extra-pure is again of three kinds;
   One is the elect, one is the more elect.
   One is the most elect, while the pure
   Exists in the (simple) knower of the Absolute.

4. The impure-pure is without passion and inertia,
   The other is with passion and inertia.

The former as in one who desires liberation.
While the latter as in those who desire psychic
powers is to be known.

5. Established in the Absolute, a knower of the Absolute,
By the fire of wisdom having burnt everything up,
Aiming at the good of the world,
Performs action according to what is considered as right.

6. He who, renouncing all action,
Always established in the Absolute,
Continues the course of bodily life, wandering
In the world, (he) is the elect knower of the Absolute.

7. He, being informed by another is able to know,
But he himself does not know;
He is the more elect, who always
Enjoys absorption in the Absolute.

8. He who by himself does not know anything
And even when made to know, (knows) not;
Such a one, always void of activity,
The most Elect is the Absolute alone (in himself).

9. Of this (world) there is certainly nothing to be
rejected or accepted
As for the self, it is self-luminous;
Having understood (thus), one should withdraw
(from all functionings);
Thereafter function does not repeat (itself).

10. The one Absolute alone there is, without a second;
Nothing else there is, no doubt herein.
Having thus understood, the well instructed one,
From duality should withdraw; (he)
does not return again.

(Translation: Nataraja Guru)

COMMENTARY

*Nirvāṇam* or salvation is of two forms, pure and impure. Of these that which is unattached to *vāsanās* is pure and that which is attached to *vāsanās*, impure. Pure *nirvāṇam* is sub-divided into very pure and simply pure. Similarly impure *nirvāṇam* is sub-divided into too impure and just impure.

Very pure *nirvāṇam* is of three kinds — *brahmavidvaran* (ordinary), *bhrahmavariyan* (purer) and *brahmavariṣṭan* (purest). All these originate from *Brahmam*.

In just impure *nirvāṇam* the two *guṇas*, *rajas* and *tamas* are absent. In the too impure *nirvāṇam* they are present. The first is found in seekers of *mokṣa* and second in seekers of power for worldly achievements.

He who has known the *Brahman* (*Brahmavit*) incinerates everything with the fire of knowledge (*jñāna*) for the welfare of the world by adopting the ordained path. He is one who has detached himself from every worldly relations. Yet he continues his activities for the good of the world. But his *karma* is devoid of temporal considerations.

He who abandons everything worldly, and who keeps his mind with thought of *Brahman*, but continues life till the body stops functioning, is *brahmavidvān* (the ideal among the *Brahma jñānīs*). Even though liberated, he continues to live as an ascetic till the duration of his body's life.

He who knows only through others and not by himself is *brahmavidyāvariyan* (the person who has reached absolute liberation). He always and for ever enjoys pure salvation. His merger with the *Brahman* is so complete that he is unaware of the external world.

He who neither knows anything by himself nor through others is *brahmavidvariṣṭan*, the perfect *yogī* who has completely merged with the *Brahman* and lost his identity to it. He is *Brahman* itself. He is knowledge. No activity emanates from within him.

There is nothing in this world which is to be accepted or dismissed. The *ātmā* is self-illuminating. Meditate on this Truth and withdraw from all actions. Then there is no occasion for the conscience to repeat activity.

*Brahman* is the only one without a second or another equal. There is no room for doubting this. Repeating this in the mind, the *jñānī* should withdraw himself from the dualistic approach. He has no rebirth then.

Guru concludes this great composition *Darśana-Mālā* with the exhortation to all that it should be everyone's goal to reach the state of salvation or the absolute merger with the *Brahman* from which there is no retraction.

# 5

# Translations

### Īśāvāsyopaniṣad

Of the ten Upaniṣads, the *Īśāvāsyopaniṣad* is regarded as the most prominent. Guru has translated it in simple and enthralling Malayalam. There are twenty-one, two-line stanzas, and one three-line stanza in the translation. The message of this Upaniṣad, conveyed through the Malayalam version is presented here, in a nut-shell.

God is Omnipotent, Omnipresent and Omniscient. No one can hide anything from Him. Therefore we should lead an ideal, unattached life without desiring for other's wealth or laying hands on it. Man should live as a paragon of virtue, doing good to others without desiring anything in return, and in absolute contentment.

There is a world around us shrouded in darkness. Living a life of avarice and desire, man is embroiled in worldly pleasures and forgets God into the bargain. He thus annihilates the *ātmā* and on death, lands in that dark world of hell.

The senses stand still unable to identify the *ātmā* dwelling so close by, in spite of being endowed with the impulse to overreach even the speed of imagination. Every action is subservient to its vibration. It is subtle and gross at the same time. It is near, yet distant. It is within and without everything.

To a person who can see the five elements in the *ātmā*, and the *ātmā* in the five elements, what is condemnable? To one who leads a selfless, humane and ideal life, the bliss therefrom is the reward. If a person who sees the oneness of everything, remains unattached to them and tries to perceive them objectively, i.e., by moving outside of himself, that will be the beginning of the end of his sorrows and longings. That is the knowledge, unblemished, pure and shining, unattached and free in the innermost recesses of the mind. That knowledge permeates the universe. It is the eternal gift of God to it.

One who worships *avidyā* or ignorance, is pushed into the depths of darkness. At the same time one who is attracted to, and looks at, *vidyā* or knowledge egoistically also lands irredeemably in the same darkness.

*Puṇḍit*s say *vidyā* and *avidyā* are different. Man's fundamental aim should be to perform *karma* through *avidyā*, and attain enlightenment (God) through *vidyā*. He who knows *vidyā* and *avidyā* together will overcome death through *avidyā*, but attain liberation through *vidyā*.

Those who worship the causal Nature go to darkness. But those who are interested in the consequential reach a darker state. What is born out of the consequential is different from what is born out of the causal. It is from *puṇḍit*s who disclose this secret to us that we understand its real meaning. Those who know both (causal and consequential), pass over death through the causal and reach the Absolute through the consequential.

The face of Truth is veiled by a golden shield. O, Lord, I yearn to uphold Truth and Righteousness. Lift that veil to enable me to see Truth.

O Sun God, You have since the birth of the universe, been performing the creation, protection and destruction of life. Remove the radiance that your rays are spraying, so that I may see your splendiferous body in all its glory. The power transfused in You is but myself. Perhaps with your magnificence withdrawn, how can I see your body? Yet it is worth seeing.

Invoke the *ātmā* by ceaseless and repeated rendering of the *praṇava mantra* '*Auṁ*.' Recapitulate the deeds of the past. O, Agni Deva (the Fire God), lead us to liberation. That is my wish. With the departure of *prāṇam* (life), this body will be reduced to ashes. But the *prāṇam* will merge in the air and reach immortality.

O, the Omniscient Lord, the witness to all our actions, save us from the sins which carry on cheating us day-in and day-out. This is our prayer.

## Thirukkural

As in Sanskrit, Guru had remarkable proficiency in Tamil too. His original creations reflect the philosophy enshrined in *Thirukkural* in all its splendour. He had translated several prominent Tamil works. But many of these translations have been lost.

*Thirukkural* is the immortal work of the great Tamil Saint Thiruvalluvar. The two thousand year-old classic is acknowledged as as authentic treatise on spiritual knowledge. *Kural* (Maxim) means the largeness of the small. The Book has three cantos, *dharma*, *artha* and *kāma*, 133 chapters and 1330 *Kural*s (ten *kural*s in each chapter). Of these Guru had translated only three *kural*s. Here is an epitome of the translated *kural*s.

### A. BHAGAVAL SWARŪP STUTHI
(IN PRAISE OF THE LORD'S REAL IMAGE)

The creator of the universe, the Almighty and the Supreme knowledge is the primordial Lord. He is Truth. He is Omnipotent. If He is not worshipped in absolute surrender at His Feet, what is the use of *vidyā* (worldly knowledge)? He who loves those who do not covet others' wealth, and cheat, will suffer no sorrow. Those who praise the greatness of God will not have to face the danger posed by darkness. He who knows the wishes of one who has conquered the senses, and moves along the path of Truth and justice, can live long. The misery of those who worship at the Lord's Feet with devotion, departs on its own. God is the sea of righteousness. No one but those who seek refuge at his Feet can cross the sea of *karma* and reach the shore of victory. The Lord has eight *siddhis* (*guṇas*) like *animā* (minuteness), *garimā* (grossness), *mahimā* (greatness), etc. The head which does not bow at the Feet of the Lord is barren of all virtues. Without worshipping at His Feet how can the *saṁsāra-sāgara* be crossed and salvation attained? On the other hand if life is dedicated at those divine Feet? Then the individual will have little hurdles in his trek across the sea of worldly life.

B. VARṢHĀ VARṆANAM
(IN PRAISE OF THE RAIN)

The basic reason why the world is not destroyed, is the rain. Rain is nectar for the world. It pours down as elixir for the world's survival. In a sense even food is provided by rain. As is known it is the ocean that generates rain. If the ocean does not give rain, the beings will be plunged in hunger. As a result there will be endless misery and suffering. The farmer cannot cultivate his land. Without rain not even a blade of grass can come up on the earth's surface. Even the ocean loses its utility if the clouds refuse to pour down. Without rain religious rites will be held up. Can life sustain without water?

C. SAṀNYĀSA MĀHĀTMYAM
(THE GLORY OF SAṀNYĀSA)

*Saṁnyāsa* (asceticism) destroys the selfishness and egotism of man. It is impossible to assess the greatness of *saṁnyāsīs*. By observing severe austerities with full grasp of the difference between attachment and liberation, one achieves immeasurable greatness. Devendra, the king of celestials, had annihilated the senses and reaped the benefits thereof. So also a person who has annihilated his senses gains Devendra's status. He who subdues the five elephants, viz., the five senses with the hook of knowledge becomes the seed that sprouts in the *mokṣa bhūmi* (the field of salvation). Great men always tide over even the most difficult of hurdles and achieve victory. But the ignorant and the lowly do not embark on hurdlesome ventures. This great world is vulnerable to the one who distinguishes between the *śabda* (sound), *sparśa* (touch), *rasa* (taste), *rūpa* (vision) and *gandha* (smell) experiences engendered by the five senses. The world is made up of *pañca-bhūta* (the five elements). The great sages have power to subjugate them and achieve anything they want. Their rage, albeit short-lived and the curses resulting therefrom, can never be stalled by anyone. Because they bestow kindness to all beings, it is the *saṁnyāsīs* who deserve to be called brāhmins.

# 6

# The Sree Narayana Gospel and Guru's View of Life

How can Sree Narayana Guru's view of life which enwraps within itself the One-World concept, be interpreted into a workable proposition? This question was put to Him by some of His prominent disciples. Guru's answer summarised here is an authentic exposition of the institutions of caste and religion, the concept of God and the virtue of righteousness. The answer is also symbolic. It is expressed in the form of a discussion. Guru establishes here how His view of life would lead to an ideal life worthy of emulation.

## Thoughts on Caste

Caste is inherited and is meant to identify man from other living beings. Brāhmaṇya (the quality of being a brāhmin), etc., does not denote man's caste. Know this as the meaning of caste, come down to us through the ages. If the union of man and woman results in the birth of the child, then that man and woman are of the same caste. If, on the other hand, they are treated as belonging to different castes, it is only an imaginary differentiation. When superficially considered, man, body, form, sound, taste, smell and touch can be taken as varied for judging caste. The constitution of an individual itself may lead to detection of his caste. But a person who is capable of conscious behaviour and has insight, never asks for a man's caste. Ignorant people allot caste to their fellow beings by the names of their profession, nationality or language. But the learned do not act likewise. Dress, language or naivity can never be the ground for deciding caste. Thus the oneness of all human beings is an indisputable conclusion. On that basis it is the duty of man to recognise this innate fratenity of humanity, and enjoy the evolving prosperity, and live in peace and amity.

### One Religion

Humanity is rooted in a single religion. The only connotation of religion as given to it by great spiritual thinkers, is opinion. The essence of religion in its entirety is embellished with beautiful enumerative worldly pronouncements. Just as the rivers emerging from various mountains, converge into the oneness of the ocean, so all religions merge in the single, eternal object. Because the great preceptors are born in different ages, there may be variations in their messages. Like the times, the lands also contribute to these variations. Still, because their faiths and goals were the same, it follows that there is one religion only. It is a fact that Christians, Muslims, Buddhists and other religionists continuously strive for the attainment of this oneness. Thus what is revealed from these endeavours is the irrefutable evidence that there is only one religion. When the essence of all religions is the same, it can be seen that there is a single religion only.

### One God

The creator of this phenomenal world is the Omnipotent, Omnipresent, Omniscient God. The articulations of great thinkers' thoughts evolve into what is called the essence. To say that this essence percolates among a diversity of Gods, is to undermine and render meaningless, what is adumbrated by essence. So it is clear that in religious parlance the ultimate God is one only.

### Dharmam (Righteousness)

*Satyam* (truth), *ahiṁsā* (non-violence), *asteyam* (non-stealing), *Avyabhicāram* (chastity) and *madyavarjanam*, (avoidance of alcoholic liquor) are the five *dharmas* or attributes of righteousness. Of these *ahiṁsā* is regarded as the greatest *dharma*. The memorable upholders of *ahiṁsā* like Buddha have merged with the Absolute. *Ahiṁsā* means non-infliction of injury to beings through thought, word or deed. All the other *dharmas* exist in *ahiṁsā* as mental attributes. Whereas in *hiṁsā* (violence), originates *adharma* (non-virtuosity). To those devoted to *dharma* as an austere observance, even wild animals do not pose any danger.

### Satyam (Truth)

Given that *satyam* is implicit in *sat*, it is the eternal *Brahman*. The world exists on *satyam* as also on its exteriorisation. Be truthful in word and deed. Never be dishonest. A person given to Truth will acquire fulfilment.

### Asteyam (Non-stealing)

Do not steal what belongs to others. Stealing leads to ruin and non-stealing to prosperity. The one paves the way for infamy and the other to high reputation. Hence non-stealing is the ideal way of life. The three modes of action (*trikaraṇa*), i.e., thought, word and deed, exemplifying truth is the path adopted by great men. People have absolute respect for them. He who steals has a heart polluted by poison. He is treated as a mad dog and driven away from society.

### Vyabhicāra (Adultery)

*Vyabhicāra* is sinful. Looking with desire at a woman other than one's own, attempting to flirt with her and even thinking of her with lust, is *vyabhicāram*. Indulgence in it may lead to loss of fame and status, wealth and knowledge and even life. For one addicted to it, daytime will be darkness. Hence such people will be denied even the pleasure to which they are legitimately entitled. No husband can bear his wife having illicit relations with another. For that reason those desiring peace either in the present life or in the life after death should abstain from this sinful act.

### Avoidance of Alcoholic Liquor

One who takes liquor digs his own grave. Liquor harms the brain incurably. So its use adversely affects the user, the society and the generations to come. That is why the Guru has said: "Liquor is poison. Do not make it, take it or give it." By the same token the use of such introxicants as the hemp (*gāñjā*) and opium should be abjured as they should be categorised as Liquor. Liquor is disastrous. Even children avoid drunkards. The sensible keep them at a distance like one afflicted by cholera. The manufacturer of liquor transudes a horrible stench. His clothes, house, even his relatives are stenchy. A liquor addict will be hated not only by his wife and children, but by God Himself. Such horrid substances should be dispensed with.

### Śuddhi Pañcakam (The Five Purities)

The basis for humanity's success lies in the observance of the five *śuddhis* or purities. Body, word, mind, senses and home are to be kept pure. That is what *Śuddhi Pañcakam* means. The ordinary people are not very interested in the five *śuddhis*. But those with knowledge pay adequate attention to it. It is essential for everyone to observe these purities. It is indispensable for the maintenance of good health. Cleanliness in body, cloth, food, air and water is necessary. The spoken word should have clarity, faultless construction, rectitude, sweetness, discretion and harmony, to have purity. Purity of mind demands sincerety, sympathy, amity, softness, consistency, modesty, faultlessness and devotion. For purity of the senses, non-utterance of unrelishable truth, non-teasing of others, and non-acclamation of the undeserving, are the pre-requisites. In regard to purity (cleanliness) of home, the interior of the house should be accessible to sunlight and air, the excretionary substances should be thrown away; and perfumery materials should be burned during morning and evening. Observance of the five *śuddhis* is beneficial to the brain, and promotes longevity.

### Guru's View of Life

Now let us examine Guru's view of life. He has gifted to society several works which lead man from the ephemeral and transient shallowness to the depths of *śānti* (peace).

It is a fact that Guru's awareness of evanescence of worldly life and of the imperishability of spiritual life was inborn in Him. He believed in God from childhood. It was by endeavouring to awaken social consciousness against superstitions, and by guiding man towards an ideal life that Guru created the atmosphere to open the doors of his view of life.

He had an aversion for worldly matters from his adolescent age. The ultimate goal of his life was self-realisation. For achieving that goal, he had held himself resolutely on to *sanātana dharma*. It helped him shape his view of life. All his works reflect his deep philosophical outlook.

It was through onerous spiritual exercises that Sree Narayana Guru had ingrained in himself the Advaita perspective. The events of His life right from childhood bear this out. He put every step forward with unfaltering self-confidence. With His recognition of *jñānam*, *bhakti*, *karma*, etc., as the means to reach His end. He was convinced that knowledge (*jñānam*) unimmersed in *bhakti* was meaningless, and that what was standing in the way of God Realisation was lust for woman and wealth. Devotional poems can sprout only a mind endowed with metaphysical intuition. With that mental disposition a spiritual bard can recognise only the philosophically astringent path. As the subtle state of *nāma* and *rūpa* (name and form) is the mind and their gross state, the world, no one can worship the nameless, formless *Brahman* except through the medium of *nāma* and *rūpa*. Therefore Guru accepted that medium for the inculcation of the Advaita precept. It was for this reason that Guru happened to compose poems in praise of Gods Vināyaka, Kr̥ṣṇa, Guha and Śiva, and Goddess (Devī). Because the Guru's Advaita is a metaphysical realisation, He had, with his eye on Advaita, synchronised spiritual pursuit with idol-worship and other religious practices. That itself is at the root of His view of life.

When Guru had set out on His mission in search of Truth through solitary penance, the following was the chain of thoughts which passed through His mind:

Let me enquire whether there is anything more Godly than

> the family. Having dedicated myself to that goal, if I find nothing of the sort, I will have to proclaim that supreme Truth before the world. If the power of God does not influence humanity, it should be possible to wean away man and his human characteristics from such vain beliefs.

Through deep contemplation on existence, Guru came to the conclusion grounded on His own experience, that the concept of God is not without reason, and that God is the only permanent Reality. He gave expression to his conclusion through His devotional poems. And that is the Guru's view of life which upholds the dignity of man.

# 7

# The Influence of Sree Narayana Literature on the Malayalam Language

KAIRALI (the Malayalam language) is immensely richer by what has come down to posterity as Sree Narayana literature embodied in sixtytwo magnificent poems.

All the poems reflect undifferentiated seriousness in the manner of presentation and in matter presented. The reincarnation they give to the Upaniṣads which constitute the core of *sanātana* culture keeps the reader in thrall. By no mean creative talent had Guru reclaimed the Vedic aphorisms, disfigured by the ravages of time.

To one undertaking a pilgrimage along the shores of the Ocean of Sree Narayana Literature, the impression that Malayalam literature had touched a turning point by its influence, is inescapable. His style is simple, His words are measured and apt and His mode of expression is replete with spiritual power. His language is figurative with the various modes of alliteration then prevalent in Malayalam poetry. He opened up the doors of the great edifice of Indian Philosophy, viz., the Advaita theory to the oriental and occidental metaphysical ideas, thus evolving a hitherto unknown methodology in Eastern spiritual thought. But many could not delve into its depths and uncover its greatness, let alone to imbibe its substance.

Into a section of the masses which believed that worldly life was a synonym for misery, He transmitted a wave of self-confidence through the introduction in Malayalam literature, of a new poetic genre which augured well for its healthy growth. He reminded the poets that more than poems about love and sex what would stand them in good stead was the acquirement and cultivation of creative flair, the products of which abounded in spiritual resplendence. Through this approach Guru was able to raise the art of poetry writing to the incorporeal plane.

It has been acknowledged that Guru who showed the way to the great Malayalam poet Kumaran Asan, had enjoined on him to keep off the love-sex theme from his poems, and that this had sparked off a revolution in the poet's creative endeavour. The upshot was that the poet threshed out a new path in Malayalam poetry with the basic thrust in the hoisting of human values, in consonance with Guru's conception. Later poets took up the cue from here. Thus the new generation of poets beginning with Kumaran Asan derived their inspiration from Guru's notion of poetry and planted the seeds of their thoughts in minds already conditioned for receiving and rearing them up. What we see today is the consummation of those seeds into a new poetic culture characteristic of the Kerala tradition, yet universal in its sweep. In short the current Malayalam poetry reflects the full impact of Guru's perspective about human beings which He had invested in His works.

Sree Narayana Guru had with his endemic pragmatism, pulled down the communal fortresses built by the priesthood, to imprison into them the oppressed and the downtrodden, and built into the human minds, an empire of love and equality. The social laws of the time also favoured the arrogation of power and privileges by the privileged classes. It was His avowed aim to expose the inequity and injustice of this order, and disintegrate it through a social reformation. And He sought to achieve this end through a social sharp medium of His masterfully evocative poems.

In the exquisitely moulded ten-stanza piece *Daiva Daśakam*, He expatiates upon a comprehensive definition of God. *Darśana-Mālā*, the epic work in Sanskrit is a compact, but indepth presentation of the *sanātana dharma* (philosophy). And His *Ātmopadeśa Śatakam*, acclaimed as the modern *Gītā*, is a masterly and succinct explication of his spiritual vision in all its deepness and amplitude. These works show that Guru's creations enjoy top rating in the visionary zone of Malayalam poetry.

Here are a few lines which glisten with some of the cosmopolitan and for that reason, emotional messages of Guru's poems:

> What each performs for the happiness of the self
> Should be conducive to the happiness of another.
> —*Ātmopadeśa Śatakam*

> You are the Existent, the Subsistent and
>   the Value-factor Supreme
> You are the Present and the Past,
> And the Future is none else but you.
> Even the spoken word, when we consider it,
>   is but You alone.
> —*Daiva Daśakam*

His poetry is a conglomerate of pieces with eight, ten and hundred stanzas, hymns, truisms and songs, all capable of imprinting increasable impresses upon the readers' minds about His poetic genius and individuality. His command of Tamil was astounding. In short Guru could handle Malayalam, Sanskrit and Tamil with equal ease and dexterity, and produce in all three, visionary works which appealed to the subtlest artistic instincts of His students. His usages, ideas and figurative syntax have been of a calibre rarely achieved even by the greatest of poets.

The works of outstanding Malayalam poets like Kumaran Asan, Vallathol Narayana Menon, Ulloor S. Paramesvara Iyer, Moolur S. Padmanabha Panicker, Pallathu Raman, K. P. Karuppan, P.K. Panicker and K. Ayyappan reflect the influence of Sree Narayana literature in no small measure. It is however in the works of Kumaran Asan, the doyen of Malayalam Poetic Renaissance, that its impact is mirrored in its crowning emotional and intellectual intensity. There was a time when Malayalam verse was ridden roughshod over by the obscene sex oriented works of the Venmony poets. The credit for having extricated it from the clutches of vulgarity and set for it a horizon of sublime love goes to Kumaran Asan. For that very reason he is acknowledged as the singer of love melodies. Because Asan had unhesitatingly trodden along the spiritual path shown him by Guru, his poems achieved a new range. As the metaphysical ideas lying inert in literature had surfaced themselves as the substance of Asan literature, Kumaran Asan emerged as a pre-eminent poet ornate with the encomium *Āsayagambhīran* (one profound in ideas).

In addition to the spiritual thread running through Asan's poems, there is a patent motive in some of them to establish a casteless society envisaged by Sree Narayana Guru, e.g., *Cāṇḍāla Bhikṣukī* (the low caste woman Buddhist) and *Duravasthā* (misfortune). It was Kumaran Asan who introduced into Malayalam literature, Guru's goal of undoing the caste-borne social set-up of Kerala and the attendant oppressive customs which perpetuated it, as an institutionalised theme. In his works designed to rewrite the upper class manoeuvred Hindu customs, and to popularise progressive ideas among the oppressed, the unquestionable pull of Guru's messages is discernible, e.g., *Duravasthā*. Taking a step further, Asan in his *Caṇḍāla Bhikṣukī* took the audacious step of voicing through Lord Buddha Himself, the irrationality and injustice of the caste system. A closer look would reveal that Asan's work *Buddha Caritam* (Biography of Lord Buddha) is a symbolic portrayal of the life of Guru Himself, besides being a slogan raiser against caste.

We may here examine how Asan's poems resplendent with human love are permeated by the spiritual effulgence of Guru's thought waves.

> Man is an impure thing even to man
> And walk on earth is regarded as sin
> By atmospheric pollution of man
> The hell itself is here, Alas! O, God!
> — *Simha Nādam* (Voice of the Lion)

> The deepest depths of darkness much
> Those formed the cruel religious laws

That chained thy children innocent
Suffer much, O Sree Guru Dev.
— *Song of Freedom*

Change you the laws yourselves, or else
the laws will change you indeed.
— *Duravasthā*

Cut asunder the chains that bind our feet
And break off these hand-cuffs and
Throw them away, O Lord

The world dawns from Love
And flourishes with Love
Love itself is the might of the world —
Love brings happiness to all
Love is life itself, Sir,
And its negative is death.
— *Caṇḍāla Bhikṣukī*

These extracts demonstrate how the poet in Asan personates to the inspiring teachings of Guru. At a time when the caste structure ruled the roost, and called the shots with unrestrained belligerence, Asan alone displayed the temerity to narrate in his poems stories featuring the low caste Hindus like Pulayas and Pariahs as their heroines. This trend can also be ascribed to the response evoked in him by Guru's power.

Asan's contemporaries, and great poets Vallathol and Ullūr, had not a little been inspired by the visionary thoughts of Sree Narayana Guru. The caste-ridden social life of the time was a curse to the downtrodden who suffered grievously by its merciless onslaughts. The intellectuals could not keep a blind eye to this. The upper castes held themselves tenaciously to their orthodoxy and resisted changes towards progress. Poetic minds were naturally perturbed. So they could not keep their pens off the revelling caste, religion and untouchability. There is no disputing the fact that Guru's poems formed the moving spirit behind this shift in contemporary Malayalam poetry.

Because Vallathol was born into the upper caste, he did not have the urge from personal experience to turn his creations to highlight the inequalities and injustices of caste, then reigning supreme in the society around him. He had the least first-hand experience of the horrors of caste. For that reason Vallathol could only float himself with abandon on the seemingly calm surface of life. For that reason too even the basic bond between man and soil was unknown to him to a large extent. As a result he had no occasion to think about life except in terms of imaginary and attractive colours.

Even though, like Asan, Vallathol could not break chains of the inequitous social inheritance, he had on occasions directed his heir upon caste, untouchability, liquor and superstitions. The most conspicuous of these expressions of wrath is the story "*Achante Chatham* (Rites for the late father), depicting the outrageous rection of an upper caste house owner, when his house is on fire and people of the lower castes are drawing water from his well in a bid to put out the fire. The house owner shouts: "You untouchables, let my house be reduced to ashes but don't touch my well and malign its purity."

Here are some of Vallathol's utterances against caste in some other poems of his:

1. O Nair! Thou art pure among pure else
   Tho' being lost the house, thou didst save the caste.
   Alas! the Tharawad or family chief
   Is flaming and becoming ash
   With angry fire of worst the Ayitham."
   — *Purest of the Pure*

2. Word Jathi or caste is risen from Hell
   The sound having two letters or syllables
   Seen in the "Yed" or book of the "Satan"
   — *The Might of Caste*

3. Thou hast welfed many "Vipras" very much,
   The appetite of Vipras and Pariahs

Are alike and equal everywhere.
The poor sick man "prayed for some Kanji"
Is it the fault greatest the sick man did?
Which caused him to be severely beaten
— *Rites for the Late Father*

4. To live and stay is dangerous for ever
Like useless thing the dross of metal iron,
All particles of Divine oblations
Are Paternal to high caste people
— *A Boat Journey*

The above lines are definite pointers to the poet's antagonistic attitude towards caste and religion. It is true that the poems of Vallathol do not portray the painful sufferings inflicted by caste upon the low-born. But however when he got the opportunity to cogitate on the existing social order, he descended from his world of imagination to have a look around. It was then that Guru's messages echoing across the Kerala atmosphere, reached his ears. He also saw how their waves had reflected upon the social consciousness. Vallathol was thus in a position to harness his unbounded poetic imagination to creating a few marvellous pieces, emphatically crying down caste.

The last (but not the least) of the poetic trio was Ulloor. In his works the influence of Sree Narayana Guru's visionary thoughts is clearly discernible. His poems have cut through the social anomalies like untouchability and oppressive customs far more deeply than did those of Vallathol. Though both were beyond the clutches of social disabilities, being members of the upper castes, Ulloor had the daring to declare that untouchability was at the root of all social grievances here, as also the target of our neighbour's scorn. Here are excerpts from some of his poems which bear out the above conclusions:

1. To wear there is no cloth
To live there is no hut
To drink there is no Kanji Neer
Doesn't say Hari with mouth opened

And hast no knowledge even to utter cry.
— *The Greatness of Chithira Thirunal Maharaja*

In this way the poet had the hardihood to proclaim that the poor are just two-legged animals. He was concerned in visualising equality among people as is evidenced by the following lines in his poem cited above:

The noble Brahmins and the poor Pariahs
Entered in temple, bowed and worshipped God
Jointly moved with fingers interfused
This scene made my eyes happy and pleasant

In a descent from his world of imagination to the world of reality, Ulloor made bold to look at the sufferings perpetrated by caste with disconcert. He expressed this feeling in no uncertain terms in a series of more than half a dozen poems. For a poet who had foredrawn in his mind's eye, the picture of what society would be like during the latter half of the twentieth century, and who had lent his ears to the transformation in society brought about by the percolation across it, of Guru's messages, could not help hearing the pulse beat of his times.

Ulloor believed that Sree Narayana Guru's vision amounted to the concept of One World and that to galvanise it into actuality was a must for the modern world. Many of his poems bear testimony to this contention. Here are quoted four lines from his poem *Vijaya Prārthanā*.

We do want only one religion of Love,
And only one caste for the mankind pure,
And we want alone one state in this world,
And one God merciful lamp for us in heart.

This stanza from his poem *Vijaya Prārthanā* (Prayer on Victory) is a restatement of Guru's well-known maxim "one caste, one religion, one God". Here are four more lines from the same poem to substantiate this surmise.

There is one way for improving mankind

And there's only one way — not other way
. . . . One caste and colour modify the world
That is all enough, enough, enough.

In one of his famous poems *Prema Saṅgītam* (The Song of Love), Ulloor has asserted that there is only one religion which sustains the universe and that is *premam* or love. The following lines confirm that this sentiment is inherent equally in the Namboodiris of Alwancherry Illam (a famous house of Namboodiris), the Pulayas, the sun and the very atom:

There dost shine the love in Alwancherry
And Ayyan Pulayan and Sun and atom"

These two lines express the boldness of ideal with which the poet's line of thinking is invested.

The influence of the Sree Narayana literature is conspicuous in many other Malayalam poets too. The foremost among them was Muloor S. Padmanabha Panicker with whose name is appended the title *sarasa kavi* (Poet Pleasing). Muloor was a memorable figure during a decisive period in the social history of Kerala. With dauntless courage and optimism he laid bare in his poems the horrors of caste, and worked for the demolition of the caste borne society in which he had been brought up, and in the process, affixed the stamp of his personality upon the life and literature of the time. He heralded the establishment of a non-communal society, envisaged by Sree Narayana Guru, and on its heels, of an ideal, welfare state in his native land. He hit at the superstitions and insane social practices which plagued human life, and plunged into the social arena with the ferocity and swiftness of a tornado through his reformatory verses. Of these the one entitled *Kavi Rāmāyaṇa*, created a sensation and was marked particularly for Guru's influence. He displayed a rare dare-devilry in ripping through the senseless superstitions and barbarous customs and practices which had played havoc on human survival, and in exposing the rank meanness and vanity of some of the upper caste poets who strove to preserve the existing order through their works. Many of his poems extended hope and inspiration to the Harijans. His assault on caste and its champions was impeccable and uncompromising.

In one of his poems Muloor declared that equality was the governing principle during the reign of an ancient king of Kerala, the mythological Mahābali. There was then no division of human beings into high and low, touchables and untouchables, nor were there the avaricious and exploitative higher-ups who treated a section of their fellow beings as animals whose rights and possessions, it was accepted as their legitimate entitlement to expropriate.

Muloor was a living example of the spark of resistance against the oppressive treatment meted out to the lower castes, which Sree Narayana Guru had lit among his followers, burgeoning into a conflagration.

Another poet who embodied Guru's messages was K.P. Karuppan. He had grown up in an environment which held out little prospect for a normal and free life. Having lived in a caste infested society paralysed by castes, sub-castes and castes within castes, Karuppan had tasted the bitterness of the atrocities of the caste system from personal experience. He had therefore perforce to live a life of confrontation with the insufferable and unwarranted categorisation of human beings. He wrote a poem *Jāti Kummi* (Announcement of caste), extolling the virtues of equality; and imbibing inspiration from it and transmitting the same to others, he laboured to redeem the underprivileged. When he discovered that in the land of Ādi Śaṅkara, the expositor of non-dualism, man could not live like a human being, he was impetuous enough to draw through his poems the picture of a social order which respected the human face. Behind this effort worked the undisputed sway of Sree Narayana Guru.

Karuppan was a revolutionary poet too. Coming as it did from such a character, *Jāti Kummi* portended far-reaching social changes. He roars therein that all poeple are children of God and hence of a single caste. He asserts that as such, to brand some of them as untouchables is to defy God Himself.

In a play captioned *Bala Kalesam*, Karuppan pursued the

theme of caste further with a passionate appeal to undo caste and treat man, whatever his class of origin, as human.

Varanappillil P.K. Panicker (1885-1925) was a prominent poet who dedicated his gifted pen to popularisation of Guru's ideals. He accepted the regeneration of the Harijans as his calling. He was one of those rare public figures whose deeds matched their words. In keeping with his avowed mission, he adopted two Pulaya boys into his household and reared and educated them. One of these T.T. Kesavan Sastri in later years donned the colours of the high office of Deputy Speaker in the Travancore State Legislative Assembly (Travancore was a former native state of India). The other named Raman earned name and fame as an outstanding Āyurvedic physician. (Incidentally Panicker's son M.K. Hemachandran distinguished himself in his career as a Cabinet Minister of the Kerala state).

It was while Panicker was in the thick of his creative effort to unfold to the masses, the substance of Guru's words that cruel death snatched him away in the prime of his life:

> All are equals by birth. Members of all the so-called communities have the right to grow and prosper. In this process lies the writ of Truth and Righteousness. Everything antithetic to it is unjust and unrighteous.

This was his declared ideal to which he held himself fast. As an insightful poet he projected his glaring individuality through his works. The exceptional figure was Sahodaran Ayyappan (1889-1968). One of the leading architects of modern Kerala, he was also a well-known social reformer who played a decisive role in shaping the social and cultural image of his generation into a refined entity. Guru's thesis that for all human beings there is only one caste, was the guiding principle of Ayyappan's multifaceted reformatory enterprise. He declared: "Caste is a superstition. It will not go of its own accord. The only way to get rid of it is to undo it". The means to that end as proclaimed by him, and in line with those proposed by Guru, were *miśra bhojana* (joint eating), intermarriages and the denouncement of the caste devil.

Ayyappan held the opinion that Buddhism was nobler than Hinduism. In his literary creations, the teachings of Lord Buddha take precedence over the enjoinments of the Hindu scriptures.

His poems abound in the influxion of new ideas in the delectability of human sentiments. His exhortations to people in a poem to organise themselves run thus:

> The powerful rule; the powerless are ruled. So you organise to achieve power.

Ayyappan says in another poem:

> God is made into man and man into God. But there is not an atom of faith in either.

In yet another piece he pays homage to Guru on the latter's demise thus:

> O, Great Guru, with the pronouncement that whatever one's religion, it is enough if man prospers, You have achieved the hitherto unaccomplished feat of denouncing and establishing religion at the same time.
>
> — *Carama Gaṇam*

The great poet Pallathu Raman (1891-1950) was another worthy name among those who wielded their pens for the propagation of Sree Narayana Guru's messages to mankind. Apart from his hostility towards caste, his interest lay centered in intensifying the predilection among people for inter-caste marriages, of which Guru was the most ardent advocate. And Raman directed his poetic endeavours towards that end. His poem *Miśra Kānthi* (Beauty through mixing) actualised those endeavours. The poem was dedicated to Guru. Guru while hailing the purity of ideal permeating it, eulogized the author as a naturally gifted poet.

The poet in Raman claimed enduring fame through the theme he adopted, which squares splendidly with the contemporary social atmosphere. He plunged himself headlong into the visionary pronouncements of Sree Narayana Guru, had traversed far into their depths with poetic creations, aimed at converting society into a casteless one as visualised by them. Raman was an accomplished writer in prose too, which also admirably served his avowed purpose. His writings, both verse and prose in concert, created tidal waves in the social revolution sparked off by Guru.

Pallathu Raman had at the very outset declared in one of his poems that he was the unrelenting warrior who had embarked on a campaign for the establishment of *dharma* by tearing through the shackles of inhuman social customs. His poem *Miśra Kānthi* had Guru Himself as the protagonist. In this respect Raman was unique and put the others in the shade. Another work, viz., *Prema-Lekhanam* (Love Letter) reverberated Guru's resounding words for all worlds and all times to pay heed to, that there was no caste in the single coloured human blood or in the salt tasting human tear.

Sree Narayana Guru's poetic marvels were essentially the outpourings of a spiritually tempered mind in the context of His first hand experiences from life. The poems besides shedding lustre to Malayalam literature, have enriched the spiritual heritage of *Bharat havarsha* on a dimension matched only by the celebrated works of Śaṅkarācārya. The ideas incorporated in them are not only profound but were well timed. The poets' attempts to simplify and popularise them, as have been briefly sketched above, were proficient, erudite and eminently fitted to accomplish the arduous task they had undertaken with a deserving sense of privilege. But for their tremendous efforts, it is doubtful if the full import of the poems with their innate intractability would have been brought home to the uninitiated. In other words, sans their emotionally inspired interpretative outputs, the value of these masterpieces would have been as good as lost upon the common folk.

In conclusion, it may be added that Guru's ideals of a casteless society have been echoed in the works of such eminent later poets as Changampuzha Krishna Pillai, G. Sankara Kurup, Viloppilly Sreedhara Menon, Bodheswaran, Vayalar Rama Varma, P. Bhaskaran, ONV Kurup, N.V. Krishna Warier, M.P. Appan, Pala Narayanan Nair, Nalankal Krishna Pillai and host of others.

# 8

# Gurus, Compatriots and Disciples

## THE GREAT GURUS OF SREE NARAYANA GURU

REFERENCE has already been made in this work to Mootha Pillai (a nephew of Chempazathi Pillai of the historic gang of Ettuveettil Pillais), the first teacher of Sree Narayana Guru. Kummam Pallil Raman Pillai Asan, the well-known Sanskrit scholar initiated, Him to the study of Sanskrit. After acquiring enough proficiency in Sanskrit, He turned to the study of *yoga* under the great master Thycaud Ayya Swamikal. It was apprenticeship under these colossuses in their respective fields that unfolded in Guru the instinctive spiritual propensities. He had acquired through past births, and mellowed them to perfection.

### Kummam Pallil Raman Pillai Asan

In those days two varieties of primary private schools were in existence: Kudippallikkudam or schools run in huts under unenthusiastic government management, and very few in number, and the teaching establishments known as charitable schools run by Christian missionaries with the cooperation of local instructors. Because of the rigorous caste discriminations of the time, the schools under government refused admission to the lower castes. But entry was permitted to them, albeit rarely, in the charitable schools. This provided them the opportunity to learn *Āyurveda* and astrology also along with Sanskrit. There were besides these two sets of primary schools, *gurukula*s modelled on Guru*kula*s of ancient India. They were a sort of residential schools where well versed teachers known as Asans imparted learning to the youngsters.

In what was called Kudippallikkudam, a rather crude learning centre, there was only one instructor. He bore the vernacular title Asan. He was however very learned and capable of teaching Sanskrit right from the alphabet to the advanced stages of study such as poem, drama and grammar. He also taught *Āyurveda* and astrology.

The Kummam Pallil family house was situated near the Puthiyidathu temple, south of Kayamkulam town. Raman Pillai was born in November 1845, the only son of rich parents. But after his father's death the young Raman Pillai and his mother were subjected to considerable molestation from paternal kins who aimed at appropriating their inherited property. The widow had to take herself and her son to a safer place. As a result the boy got little opportunity to learn Sanskrit which was his wont in keeping with the prevailing practice. He was consequently abused of being ridiculously backward in education. The insult served as a catalyst to galvanise his innate urge for learning. Under reputed masters, he learned not only Sanskrit, but also *Āyurveda* and philosophy. Equipped with this knowledge, Raman Pillai, aided by his natural adeptness for imparting scholarship, became a reputed teacher within a short-time.

At the time, the great family of Varanappillil generously offered shelter to seekers of knowledge. The head of the family was a lover of learning. Young men from far flung areas came and stayed in this family, and carried on their education with Raman Pillai Asan. Prominent among them were Sree Narayana Guru, Perunelli Krishnan Vaidyer, Velutheri Kesavan Vaidyer, Chevannoor Raman Pillai, Puthukkad Krishnan Asan, Manampoor Govindan Asan, Udayankuzhy Kochu Raman Vaidyer, amd members of the Varanappilli family such as Govinda Panicker, Kunjukrishna Panicker and Brahmavidyabhooshan P.K. Panicker.

Raman Pillai Asan had to his credit several original works and a number of translations. In a dark phase of the history of mid-

Travancore in the last century, the name of Raman Pillai shines not so much by his enlightened and enlightening erudition as by his revered standing as teacher (*guru*) of Sree Narayana Guru who brought about upheaval in the social structure of Kerala.

**Thycaud Ayya Swamikal**

Thycaud Ayya Swamikal was the *yogic guru* of both Chattambi Swamikal and Sree Narayana Guru. However our information about his life is meagre.

His original name was Subbaraya Panicker. He was the only son of his parents. However he lost both of them in his infancy. Yet he was ushered into life under the nick-name of "Ayyavu" probably because of the spiritual inclination he had imbibed from his family antecedents.

At the age of sixteen Ayyavu unexpectedly met a few ascetics well versed in *yoga*. He joined them as a disciple and wandered with them outside India. Their travels lasted several years and extended to all countries in South East Asia. During these years Ayyavu adopted full-fledged asceticism and learned *yoga* from his teachers. From any Englishman he met, he learned English too. On their return journey from abroad, they came to Tamil Nadu where Ayyavu bid goodbye to them and came to Thiruvananthapuram.

His chief ambition during this visit was to pray at the Sree Padmanabhaswamy temple. This ambition fulfilled, and as a permanent stay at Thiruvananthapuram was found not agreeable, Ayyavu returned to Tamil Nadu where he hoped to meet his teachers and continue his spiritual life. But Gurus persuaded him to matrimony. He married Kamalammal and returned to Thiruvananthapuram. After the birth of a son whom he named Lokanatha Panicker, Ayyavu turned to asceticism and remained as such for the rest of his life.

With the help of the then British Resident of Travancore Subbaraya Panicker got the post of superintendent in the Residency. This was necessary to earn his living. He retired after thirtyfour years' service. During this period also his spiritual activities continued unabated. The ruler of the state had held him in high esteem. Being domiciled in Thycaud, he came to be known as Thycaud Ayyavu, and Ayyaswami in due course. He gave prime importance to *jñānam*, *yoga* and *bhakti*, and believed in the power of meditation and the performance of religious rites for their effectuation. He opted Śivarāja *yoga* for God Realisation, and is believed to have practically demonstrated to his disciples, how all wishes could be fulfilled through this *yoga*.

Of the numerous *śiṣya*s of Ayyaswami Sree Chattambi Swamikal and Sree Narayana Guru are the most known.

## COMPATRIOTS

### Sree Chattambi Swamikal and Doctor Palpu

When one thinks of the relevance of the Sree Narayana persuasion, the two names which come to one's mind are those of Vidyadhiraja Sree Chattambi Swamikal, and the redoubtable man of action Doctor Palpu. At a time when the rigours of caste distinctions were preying upon the lowly classes in Kerala, Sree Chattambi Swamikal was the one heroic human being, who threw aside the restraints of his upper class birth, and dedicated his life for the establishment of social equality. Doctor Palpu was another remarkable lover of humanity who devoted his time and resources for the eradication of upper class tyranny. Both these noble souls expressed complete solidarity with the theme of social reformation propounded by Sree Narayana Guru, and his pronouncements and messages devised towards the attainment of that end. Further, the mutual esteem which Sree Chattambi Swamikal and Sree Narayana Guru had towards each other and their close association attracted particular social attention.

The social reformation ascribed to Sree Narayana Guru strictly speaking, was not a deliberately planned movement. It evolved itself into the social framework as a necessary operation dictated by the demand of the times. Guru was not the spokesman of a particular religion or caste. For that very reason, He was least motivated by the creation of a fresh religion. He was aware that all religions established with the noblest of motives, had by the passage of time, deteriorated to status subservient to Orthodoxy, and fell into the selfish clutches of priesthood. Hence to see the emergence of a new religion was far beyond his imagination. What was deep-rooted in his thoughts was the strong faith in a process of regeneration of humanity strictly outside religion, any religion; seeing human beings from the humanitarian aspect and giving them the respect legitimately due to them as God's creations. In the accomplishment of this great task, the activities of Sree Chattambi Swamikal and Doctor Palpu were very decisive.

**Vidyadhirraja Kunjan Pillai**
**Sree Chattambi Swamikal** (1854-1919)

The two great personalities who bore the social life and cultural thought of Modern Kerala from their dark entanglements to the brightness of enlightenment, were Sree Chattambi Swamikal and Sree Narayana Guru. They were both born in the suburbs of Thiruvananthapuram, the former at Kolloor and the latter at Chempazhanthi. By leading lives conducive to social changes, both rose to the status of world ranking preceptors.

Though Sree Kunjan Pillai was born in a family with rich traditions, poverty reigned there with chronic persistency. Hence he grew up in impoverishment right from childhood. However he managed to acquire some basic education and sprinkling of Sanskrit from a teacher nearly. After that he joined the local school (Kudippallikkudam) run by one Raman Pillai Asan of Pettah. Not long afterwards, Kunjan Pillai became the pet of the teacher who elevated him to the rank of Chattambi (Monitor). This rank name later came to be prefixed to his original name and he thus became Chattambi Swamikal. He had in his childhood, under pressure of penury, to undertake several occupations, and in the process spent some years as a document writer under his elder brother. He became a member of the organisation known as Jnanaprajagaram, established by Raman Pillai. This gave him the chance to get acquainted with Thycaud Ayyavu Swami. At that time he learned Tamil from Swaminathadesikan, and more Sanskrit from

Subbajadapati. His chief concern was the improvement of the lot of the poor. This concern engendered in him an aptitude to a spiritual way of life even from adolescence. He showed exceptional interest in philosophy, *yoga* and linguistics along with an insatiable thirst for humanitarian services.

His inherent disposition was for equal treatment of beings. At that time caste reigned society with remorseless stringency. He ignored the distinctions and took food from the houses of *avarṇa*s and people of other religions. Having cultivated such concepts as *aham brahmāsmi* (I am *Brahman*) and *tatvamsi* (that art thou), he found nothing unnatural in adopting them in practical life. This ideological resolution it was that led to the establishment of his spiritual intimacy with Sree Narayana Guru. Scholar poets, Perunelli Krishnan Vaidyer and Velutheri Kesavan Vaidyer, were the closest associates of Sree Chattambi Swamikal. Very often they met and discussed literary subjects. Frequently Chattambi Swamikal and Sree Narayana Guru sat together and chalked out schemes of social reform and made bold to adopt them in practice. Together they also came to the conclusion that only through mentally curative treatment of the social set-up, can the caste inequalities be done away with, and man converted into real human beings on terms of equality. Probably it was to acquire the spiritual perspicacity needed for fructifying this thesis that they had gone to Maruthwamalai for performing solitary penance.

Scholar and thinker, Chattambi Swamikal had certain literary works to his credit. The chief among them were *Prācīna Malayālam*, *Vedādhikāra Nirūpaṇam*, *Christu Mata Khandanam*, *Advaita Cinta Paddhathi* and *Ādi Bhāṣā*. To undo the social evils of Kerala what was more effective according to his conviction, was the dissemination of spiritual power among the masses, than the most ardent cultural and organisational endeavour.

His work *Prācīna Malayālam* is a shining star in the horizon of Kerala's historical research. It has created a thought revolution. By refuting the legend that Kerala was created, by Bhargava Raman, and presented to the brāhmins, Chattambi Swamikal was confirming his practical conclusion about the historical emergence of this land piece. "It was not gifted to anyone. It is not Bhargava Raman's property either. Before the arrival of brāhmins, the Nāyanmars inhabited this land, *cāturvarṇyam*, the theory of brāhmin overlordship can be termed '*cāturvarṇic* ribaldry', declared Swamikal.

Through his *Vedādhikāra Nirūpaṇam* the Swamikal is really blowing a rebel's trumpet across the Indian intellectual spectrum. The mad religious scheme that had placed embargos upon learning were torn to shreds by his irrefutable logic and penetrating erudition. The book advocates even reducing to ashes the Śruti-Smṛtis which deny reading and hearing of Vedic texts to *avarṇa*s.

His work *Advaita Cintā Padhathi* is an authentic treatise on Monism. The Advaidic pronouncements of Sree Chattambi Swamikal and Sree Narayana Guru are mutually amplifying. What the two achieved for society was that they were able to take to the masses Advatic concepts adumbrated in the Indian Scriptures, viz., the Vedas, *Itihāsa*s, the Purāṇas and Upaniṣads. Both has accepted all animate and inanimate objects in the universe as the creations of a single Omnipotent power.

### **Doctor P. Palpu** (1861-1950)

In the modern age it is organisations and not individuals that are significant, says Sree Narayana Guru. The one man of action who fully agreed with this opinion of Guru was Doctor Palpu. It was he who gave the name Sree Narayana Dharma Paripalana Yogam to the earlier Vavootu Sangham, which functioned at Aruvipuram during the closing years of the nineteenth century, when it spread its activities throughout Kerala as a communal (social) organisation. He laboured as the right hand man of Sree Narayana Guru in His efforts to bring about a *savarṇa-avarṇa* harmonisation in Kerala.

Doctor Palpu was an extraordinary individual. To say what he thought and to act what he said, were the outstanding characteristics of his individuality. He was a lover of mankind. He had the courage of his convictions. To see and respect everyone as equals and without reference to caste criterion was his motto.

It was the conversation he had with Svāmī Vivekānanda that led to his journey to Aruvipuram and meeting with Sree Narayana Guru. This eventually led to the emergence of Sree Narayana Dharma Paripalana Yogam. Though motivated by the loftiest of aims, the Yogam did not live up to the expectations of Guru and the Doctor. While they fondly hoped that this organisation would be capable of reforming the narrow communal foundations of Kerala's social life, with a cosmopolitan outlook generated in it by the cooption of all sections of society as its members, what really happened was that its profile displayed narrow features to mark it as an organisation pertaining to a single community. A very depressing transformation indeed. The result was that similar communal organisations guardianed and propagated by various sections of the people, came into being, thus giving rise to a muddled social set up more given to communal confusion than communal coordination. Yet with the increased tally in the organisations, the various communities bannering them only stood to gain. There was thus an impact for Guru's exhortation to get strengthened through organisation though not in the pattern envisaged.

Doctor Palpu's services to humanity are well-known. He spent the lion's share of his income to clothe the poor sleeping in streets in utter cold, and for the betterment of the lot of his suffering community. He sent at his own expense Sri. G.P. Pillai to England to make the grievances of his community, and equally disabled communities, heard in the British Parliament. This effort bore fruit abundantly.

To say that Doctor Palpu was the heart and soul of the Sree Narayana Dharma Paripalana Yogam (SNDP Yogam) would not be an exaggeration.

> Remaining behind the divine halo of Sree Narayana Guru, Doctor Palpu invested his own capabilities, mental vision, wealth and characteristic dedication, for opening up a new path for his people towards progress. Thus he led the whole of Kerala among a similar renascent path, without accepting

> even gratitude for the mighty task he had accomplished. That was Doctor Palpu.

Says P.K. Balakrishnan is his book, *Sree Narayana Yoga Phrabhavam*.

SNDP Yogam during its early existence was hard pressed for the money needed to carry on its propaganda work. It was amply provided for from the doctor's pocket. Similarly the voice of the suffering classes was heard in centres of authority through his efforts, and with the aid of his money. He led the Malayali Memorial and the Nivarthana Prakshobhanam (an agitation for withdrawal of wrongful measures), and secured representation for the oppressed in government service and the Legislative Assembly. Once in 1950, the doctor spoke to this writer thus sarcastically.

> Even if Paraśurāman's times are changed, Kerala in which worship of idols shaped like him is carried on, cannot but be a *kuriz* (Cruz) Rāma *kṣetra* (temple).

## GURU'S HOUSEHOLDER DISCIPLES

Sree Narayana Guru had besides the spiritual disciples named above, numerous householder disciples who had turned His messages and doctrines into practical adoption in society. Prominent among them were Kumaran Asan the poet, Murkoth Kumaran, C. Krishnan, Sahodaran Ayyappan, C. Kesavan and R. Sankar. It would be relevant here to examine how these accomplished and dedicated stalwarts had made use of their competence and spontaneous purposefulness and taken Swamy's ideals to the commoners' lives.

### **Paravoor Kesavan Asan** (1859-1916)

Paravoor Kesavan Asan was an outstanding scholar who evinced unreserved interest in the great utterances of Sree Narayana Guru. He was a leading Āyurvedic physician, a well-known astrologer, an outstanding journalist and acknowledged litterateur. He was a lover of the community and a staunch upholder of equality. He belonged to the earlier group of Swamy's householder disciples. As he was able to hear the pulse beat of the *avarṇa* sections of the masses, his heart began throbbing for humanity. He realised that the practical adoption of Gurudeva's messages was imperatively called for by the demands of that age.

After primary education he learned Sanskrit from Paravoor Govindan Asan, Chavara Krishna Pillai and Elanthoor Ramaswami Sastrigal. He then acquired proficiency in *Āyurveda* from Gopala Sastrigal. It was after that he entered active life.

When he witnessed the crude social practices which maligned contemporary human life and the cruelties which *avarṇa*s had to suffer from *savarṇa*s his heart was agitated with a grievous sense of insult to his self-respect. He resolved to launch a fight against these injustices. He realised that to achieve his purpose what was required was free and fearless journalistic enterprises. So to awaken the community from its age-old torpor and to open the eyes of the authorities who held the society in their grip, he founded the Kerala Bhooshanam Company and started a paper named *Sujana Nandini* in 1891. But the *savarṇa*s could not stomach this struggle for justice. Blinded by jealously and fear of losing the privileges which were hitherto monopolised by them, they let loose a vengeful violence against the valiant fighters for their rights. The resultant Nair-Ezhava riot culminated in paper *Sujana Nandini* and its press being burnt down to ashes. Asan was unhappy at this development, but he never lost his spirit in the pursuit of his fight. He now concentrated on medical profession, and started an infirmary under the name *Anandasandayini* which became a refuge to the sick, both of the hut and palace without distinction. It was at this period that Asan came into intimate contact with Sree Narayana Guru.

As indicated earlier, Asan was interested in astrology and literature, and became well-known in those disciplines. His residence was a centre of learning. The poet and musician K.C. Kesava Pillai was a prominent *śiṣya* of Asan. As a poet also Asan had several creations to his credit.

He was a Director of SNDP Yogam and was member of the State Legislative Assembly.

**Maruthoorkaniyil Kunjikkannan** (1861-1944)

Like Kesavan Asan, Maruthoorkaniyil Kunjikkannan was also one of the earlier disciples of Sree Narayana Guru. He hailed from northern Kerala. He saw Swamy at Aluva and got his blessing. He felf the need for a temple to facilitate worship for all when he came to know of Gurudeva's *pratiṣṭhās* from one end of Kerala to the other. A deputation led by him and consisting of such eminent personalities as Murkoth Kumaran and C. Krishnan called on Guru and requested Him to install an idol at Thalasserry. The famous Jagannātha Temple at Thalasserry was the result.

Kunjikkannan was born in a poor family at Kozhikode. He lost his parents at the age of seven. Having been thrown into the streets Kunjikkannan's subsequent life was a success story achieved through the process of devotion to God and the self-confidence derived therefrom.

Kunjikkannan accidentally met an Englishman who owned a medical store and struck an acquaintance with him at an early age. He worked in the medical store for twenty-seven years. The Englishman was immensely pleased with his sincerity and dedication to work. As a reward he built a medical store for Kunjikkannan at his expense. Kunjikkannan could work his way up to a fairly sound financial status through that God sent gift. Thereafter he rose to the position of a prominent citizen of Thalasserry and earned the love and affection of the ordinary people. He also got the opportunity to serve as a member of the Thalasserry Municipal Council for four terms consecutively.

He was closely connected with many of Guru's *pratiṣṭhās*. He took this as a rare privilege and blessing. He passed away at the age of eighty-three after serving Guru's mission for a long time. His body was buried under the supervision of Chaitanya Swamikal of Śivagiri.

**Mithavadi Krishnan** (1867-1938)

Mithavadi (Moderate) Krishnan was a dominant journalist and a distinguished social worker who devoted himself heart and soul to put into practical operation the social transformation enunciated by Guru. His social work bore the stamp of his personality. He was immensely popular with the masses. Even while a student, he had acquired the faculty of speaking and writing in sharp-edged and cutting verbosity. Even when he had established himself as an exemplary lawyer, his interest in journalism never abated. Though born in an opulent and influential family, he had suffered unscrupulous communal persecution. So he believed that, what was needed was to start a paper to voice social grievances and strive through its columns to root out the superstitions and irrational customs which stuck to the social plant like parasites and suck the life out of it, and reclaim and reform it into a purified organism. Without any delay he began publication of the paper *Mithavadi* and used it as an effective instrument of social reformation through his penetrative writing which exposed the social malignancies running riot at the time. *Mithavadi* has the distinction of first publishing Kumaran Asan's masterly poem *Veena Poovu* (The Fallen Flower).

*Mithavadi* was the deadly medium effectively wielded by Krishnan for restoring the rights denied to the *avarṇa*s for generations. Its guiding slogan was Guru's classic exhortation "gain freedom through acquiring knowledge". His thought was provocative, his reasoning faultless, his language inspiring and his style unmatched.

Krishnan had an insatiable desire to regenerate his community, reeling in stagnated growth inflicted upon it through centuries. This desire was set afire by Doctor Palpu's words. These words for action made him dedicate his life to the task of redressing social grievances. His thrust for action is evidenced by his share in the agitation for the removal of the 'untouchability board' that had been planted to deny freedom of movement to the Thiyas at the Thali Road in Kozhikode, and in concert with Sahodaran Ayyappan, for stopping slaughter of fowl in the Kodungalloor temple.

He did commendable work in effecting changes in the *Jenmikudiyan* (Land-Lord-Tenant) Law of Malabar to the benefit of the farmers. He himself was a landlord. The question was naturally put to him as to why he should lead an agitation detrimental to the interests of his own clan. His answer was that the majority of the tenants of Malabar who held land on payment of rent to its owner (the landlord) were Thiyas and that he did not desire to see them slaves of the landlords. This audacious reply was burst out at the face of the questioner at no less a forum than the Madras Legislative Assembly.

He had the courage to react strongly to the havoc perpetrated by caste and religion on Hindu beings. That accounted for his interest in Buddhism and prejudice against the inhuman practices indulged in by Hinduism. He did not hesitate to speak out his mind to Gurudeva himself.

Krishnan had presided over many of SNDP Yogam's anniversary meetings, at the instance of Guru. He used his intelligence and capabilities to convert Guru's messages into practical reality. He was also well-known as a free thinker.

### **C.V. Kunjiraman** (1870-1949)

C.V. Kunjiraman, the founder of the newspaper *Kerala Kaumudi*, was an ardent upholder of Sree Narayana Guru's utterances. And he tried wholeheartedly to shape the common man's mind to the idea of a new society based on the axioms contained in those utterances, through his speeches and writings. He had the temerity to proclaim that the propensity to kick more as you bow more, and to bow still more as you are kicked more, should not be permitted any more. To have organised agitation for unrestricted entry into temples to establish free worship and to drive away untouchability from their precincts, was no mean adventure in the situation obtaining in those days. At a time when monarchy with its unlimited might, wielded the administration of the native state of Travancore, C.V. Kunjiraman alone had the impetuousity to proclaim that the Ezhavas had a nobler tradition as revealed by history, than the false tradition the Namboodiris had built for themselves through fabricated legends. It was this self-assurance that had elevated C.V.'s individuality to distinction.

He had the objectivity to declare that it was the Christian missionaries who opened the doors of Kerala to world culture. While the Hindu priestly class had for their survival written up *Saṅkarasmṛti* and *Namboodiri Bhāṣyam* and commenced life under their sheltering shade, the *avarṇas* who comprised the majority of the population remained shut up in the society's dark corners. But the messages of love and the light of sympathy were passed on to those corners and the hearts of these suffering section of humanity captured by men of the calibre of C.V. Kunjiraman. Since the custodians of education were the *savarṇas*, the *avarṇas* continued to remain illiterate and hence their slaves. It was during that period that the torch-bearers of Kerala renaissance Chattambi Swamikal and Sree Narayana Guru appeared on the scene. That these two leaders of Kerala's social reformation succeeded in their venture was a positive portend to the impending social change to rescue the *avarṇas* from age-old misery. What followed through the untiring efforts of C.V. and other votaries of Guru's messages has become history.

**Mahakavi Kumaran Asan** (1873-1924)

Kumaran Asan was one of the greatest poets of modern Kerala. A poet of inborn taste and exemplary imagination, his poems chiefly dealt with such themes as love and caste. His association with Sree Narayana Guru appeared to have been preordained. It blossomed into a spiritual attachment and paved the way for the emergence of a great poet. It all started with his journey with Guru to Aruvippuram. After the *pratiṣṭhā* at Aruvippuram, Swamy sent Kumaran to Mysore with Doctor Palpu for advanced studies in Sanskrit. When the studies there were completed, Doctor Palpu decided to send him to the Sanskrit University at Calcutta for further education. Kumaran could identify himself very soon with the intellectual Renaissance which smouldered the literary firmament of Bengal during that time. That was the genesis of his victorious march into poetic world of revolutionary dimensions. Years later when Kumaran returned to Guru, he had already acquired mastery in the English language as well.

SNDP Yogam was founded in 1903. Its purpose was the regeneration of society from the shackles of superstition and irrational customs, on the lines stipulated by Sree Narayana Guru. It took over the task in right earnest. Kumaran was selected as the Yogam's convener. He straightaway plunged himself into his task and at the same time master-minded the plan of action designed to cement Guru's teachings in the public consciousness. With the motive to implement the project effectively, he opened up a new poetic genre as the medium through such works as *Veena Poovu* (the Fallen Flower), *Nalini* and *Sītā*. The ornaments he presented to Malayalam literature giving importance in them to the new tendencies which sprouted both in oriental and occidental poetry are continuing to shine even today with undiminished brilliance, acquiring fuller elegance with the passage of time. The reverberations echoing across *Duravasthā* and *Cāṇḍāla Bikṣukī* are nothing but the reflections of Gurudeva's aphorisms. The power of Asan's pen to penetrate deep into the minds of his readers was amazing and unmatched.

Asan rendered yeomen service to the cause of the community in his capacity as a member of the state Legislative Assembly. Simultaneously he travelled the length and breadth of the state and engaged himself in organisational matters of the Yogam. In the midst of this busy schedule, poems of classic proportions flowed out of his pen. During his stint as the editor of the magazine *Vivokodaya*, Asan's faculty as a fine writer of prose was also manifested.

Every line of poetry he wrote highlighted his aim to culturally uplift society and reflected the spiritual impact of Gurudeva's teachings. These lines carry the messages of eternal love, sacrifice and kindness.

### **Moorkoth Kumaran** (1874-1941)

Moorkoth Kumaran was a distinguished writer and thinker who believed that Sree Narayana Guru's messages were essential for the well-being of society and dedicated his life for their effective implementation. He accepted them as indispensable for world peace and social welfare. In his biography of Guru he had curtly declared the supreme truth. Unfortunately however many have cold shouldered that irrefutable declaration.

His stature as a litteratteur would bring out his contemporaneous relevance. An examination of the Malayalam literary output up to the latter half of the nineteenth century reveals that the writers' inner essence was reflected in the writings of Cherusserry, Ezhuthachan, Nambiar, Unnai Warrier, Poonthanam and others. The commoners' problems however were not to be handled through verse, but through prose only. This fact was established by such writers as Kesary, Chandu Menon, A.R. Raja Raja Varma and Moorkoth Kumaran consequent on their contact with English literature. With the opening up of a new genre for the development of Malayalam literature namely the narrative method in story-telling, the tempo in the flow of progressive ideas into it gathered momentum. Among the earlier promoters of narrative form in Malayalam literature, Moorkoth Kumaran occupies a conspicuous place.

In all his writings the basic essence of literature and the justification of criticism are projected. "Sweetness, joy and splendour are qualities endemic in his poems." So says Ulloor in his History of Malayalam literature. Professor Mundasserry had recorded in *Vivokodayam* that Moorkoth Kumaran who moved his pen more forcefully than the sword against injustices was the Prajāpati (Lord Brahmā) of Malayalam prose and the pioneer of Sree Narayana Movement in north Malabar. It should not be forgotten that it was on the initiative of Murkoth that a *pañcaloha* statue of Guru was installed for the first time in Kerala in the precincts of the Jagannātha temple even while Guru was alive. In this manner by popularising Gurudeva's doctrines through literary endeavour and social work, Moorkoth established his name as a genuine devotee of His.

At a time when journalism in Malayalam was in its infancy, his services to its cause were commendable. It was as occupant of the editorial chairs of such magazines and periodicals as *Kerala Sancāri*, *Gaja Kesari*, *Kerala Chinthamani* and *Atmaposhini* that his association with Kumaran Asan and work for the upgrowth of

SNDP Yogam became a realised fact. In protest against the misdeeds of Hindu priesthood he expressed solidarity with Buddhism. But Guru dissuaded him from the move and brought home to him the demand of the time to remain in Hinduism and labour for its upliftment. It was compliance with Guru's exhortation that lent imperishability to his name more than anything else.

**M. Govindan** (1874-1956)

Everyone has the right to bathe in the sea at Kanyakumari. As if to reassert that right a man was taking bath there. The then Mahārāja of Travancore was staying in the Kanyakumari palace on that occasion. An official in the service of His Highness suddenly appeared on the scene in haste and the following conversation ensued between him and the man who was having his bath in sea.

"Who are You? No one is allowed to bathe here."

"Whose order is that?"

"It is the royal command"

"I see. The Maharaja can close down every lake or tank or pond in Travancore. But what right has he in the Indian Ocean?"

So saying he continued his bath. The man who displayed such arrogance was Judge M. Govindan.

The two prominent members of the Ezhava community who in spite of their being duly qualified, on having been denied deserving posts in the Travancore Government service, had gone to Madras and Mysore, and served there in high posts were P. Velayudhan and Doctor P. Palpu. But later when the atmosphere in Travancore changed, the first man of the Ezhava community, who weathering all storms of opposition, managed to get into the service in the state and rose to the rank of Judge, was M. Govindan. When the *savarṇa* Sirkar ordained that because he was an *avarṇa* he was not eligible even for a clerical post in the Hajur Cutcherry (secretariat), he boldly entered the fray to fight out his right. As a member of the Legislative Assembly his role in getting the Ezhava Makkathaya Bill passed was memorable. He also worked as a leading figure of

SNDP Yogam and a staunch upholder of Guru's messages.

Once, Nambi Nilakanta Sarma who was a member of the Temple Entry Committee along with him had heaped insult upon the Ezhavas by calling them cāṇḍālas. He calmly retorted.

"Do you accept *Amarakośam* as an authentic work?"

"Sure" came the reply.

"If that is so, then how many brāhmin women of Kerala must have run after śūdras to give birth to the several lakhs of cāṇḍālas in Kerala?" (Cāṇḍālas are born of kṣatriyas, vaiśyas and śūdras in brāhmin women.)

Hearing this, Sarma was struck dumb with a colourless face. Sarma should have understood that Govindan was a hard nut to crack.

While engaged as a lawyer he had to argue a case. The rival lawyer commenced his argument. The case concerned a land dispute.

> My client has been maintaining the building and land under dispute nearly for the last twelve years. Therefore he has absolute right over them. So, I request the court that this right may be allowed.

Govindan replied:

> That argument cannot hold good. Just because my barber has been shaving my face for the last twelve years, can he claim ownership of my face?

This reply produced a roaring laughter in the Court. Govindan won the case.

When poet Rabīndranāth Tagore visited Travancore, the capital city was stirring with preparations for giving him a grand reception. Govindan approached his colleague Kumaran Asan and got written a poem in praise of the poet. The poem was named *Divya Kokila* (Divine Nightingale). C. Kesavan recited it in his melodious voice before the audience. Shortly afterwards when Govindan was appointed as Judge, Kumaran Asan wrote two stanzas to felicitate him. The poem was entitled *Udikkunna Nakshatram* (The Rising Star). The function to laud Govindan was held at the V.J.T. Hall. It was a grand success.

Govindan had actively taken part in functions of Śivagiri, including the Śāradā Pratiṣṭhā. After retirement from service, he took over as manager of the Sivagiri English School. It was during that period that R. Sankar was appointed Headmaster there. Govindan had prophesied then that in a short time Sankar would establish his mark as an outstanding educationalist and a prominent administrator. How true the prophesy had turned out.

**N. Kumaran** (1881-1964)

Following Kumaran Asan, the reigns of SNDP Yogam were taken over by advocate N. Kumaran. In order that his profession might not be jeopardised by the work involved, Gurudeva had shifted the organisation's headquarters to Quilon where he was practising. With the ascension of T.K. Madhavan to its Secretaryship, the Yogam's performance intensified by leaps and bounds. In one year its membership swelled form one thousand to fifty thousand. With that, all its debts were cleared and there was a substantial balance to boot. It was at that time that the Yogam's tone of appeal was converted into a voice of right.

When Kumaran jointly with T.K. Madhavan spawned their activities throughout Kerala, hope and inspiration proliferated among members of the community. As a consequence agitations and struggles for such rights as equality, temple entry, representation in Public Service, Prohibition, and *Vaikom Sathyagraha* and other movements which created social tremulations across the state, took place. The historic stir known as the *nivarthana* agitation for the establishment of rights till then denied to the *avarṇas* and non-Hindus, organised under the joint auspices of Ezhavas, Christians and Muslims, was a great success. With it, entry to revenue and Dewaswom Departments was granted to the *avarṇas*.

It was at this time that colourful anniversary celebrations of

SNDP Yogam were held in various parts of Kerala. Gurudeva's directive that all irrespective of caste or religion could join it as members helped in strengthening its sweep. Especially as member of the Law Committee, Kumaran had done memorable service to the community.

Kumaran had undiluted affection and respect for Kumaran Asan. He also had the guts to uncover and expose the conspiracies covertly hatched against Asan by the jealous. At the meeting arranged in the VJT Hall to felicitate Kumaran Asan on his receipt of Silk Robe and Bracelet from the Prince of Wales, the person who presided was Kumaran. As member of the state Assembly, he was the first to raise in it, the issue of safeguarding the interests of the labourers here. So also the speech he made in the house demanding the right to travel, through a resolution, is a memorable record.

Immediately after relinquishing the Secretaryship of the Yogam, Kumaran was appointed as Judge. Then he was elevated to the High Court. Even after retirement from service he functioned as Judge for some more time at the instance of government. As the successor to Kumaran Asan he was a success, especially when the progress of SNDP Yogam at the time is taken into reckoning (incidentally he was the son-in-law of Paravoor Kesavan Asan).

**T.K. Madhavan** (1885-1930)

T.K. Madhavan combined within himself righteous conduct and boldness of action. What brought him glory were sincerity, selflessness and sacrifice. One of the foremost householder disciples of Sree Narayana Guru, his activities were fully inspired by His messages. He was a member of the aristocratic and rich Alummood family. Yet the disabilities he had to bear in the name of caste during childhood were unendurable. The *avarṇa*s were refused the right to trek along the public pathways. He took it upon himself along with the others, the none too easy task of fighting against the injustices heaped upon the *avarṇa*s, to open the eyes of social consciousness to them and to root them out from the social arena, by the drive of the brainwave inculcated by Guru's teachings.

Due to unexpected causes, Madhavan could not complete High School education. Yet by dint of his own effort he acquired extraordinary faculty to write and speak the English language. His speech in English in the State Assembly kept everyone spell-bound. The speech centered round the grievances of the *avarṇa*s. Mahatma Gandhi's *ahiṁsā* concept and Sree Narayana Guru's spiritual vision exerted tremendous influence upon him. He had from his very youth launched an uncompromising war against social inequalities and the high-handed laws of the foreign rulers. And he could fan out his struggle to a wider field with his assumption of the editorship of the paper *Desabhimani*. When his heroic and powerful voice echoed into the social midst, and thundered against the administrative framework, the people's rejoinder to it was unconscionable.

It was at that time that he embarked on a valiant conflict for the establishment of equal rights for the *avarṇa*s and non-Hindus. In that struggle, that he achieved the active participation of the *savarṇa*s too reflect his diplomatic approach in no mean measure. He endeavoured to secure the rights of the backward classes, maintaining at the same time absolute cordiality between the various communities. His reputation rose to all India level. He asserted beyond a shadow of doubt that freedom of passage was man's birth-right. With these achievements T.K. Madhavan earned the esteem of even Mahatma Gandhi. Along with that, the right of the *avarṇa*s for admission to temples was got recognised by the authorities through the columns of the *Desabhimani*. Soon the waves of his agitation reached the State Assembly. Nair leaders like Changanacherry Parameswaran Pillai and T.K. Velu Pillai spoke out that the arguments of T.K. Madhavan should be accepted. Pursuing his efforts, he went to Tirunelveli and met Mahatma Gandhi and got signed by him a message enjoining his goal of achieving Temple entry and declared that fact at a press conference. T.K. could also succeed in getting top priority for the extermination of untouchability from the constructive programmes of the Congress.

T.K. Madhavan was a leading *bhakta* of Sree Narayana Guru, who strengthened and extended the activities of SNDP Yogam. As its Secretary, he toured throughout Kerala and admitted members into it. He had considerable love and esteem for Kumaran Asan. Yet he could not agree with Asan's moderate views. Nor could the latter endorse T.K.'s extreme canvas. But the services of T.K. to the community will ever be remembered as those of Asan. The owner of an extraordinary individuality, he gave plolitical colouring to social problems for the first time.

**K. Ayyappan** (1889-1968)

K. Ayyappan was born in a cultured family of physicians in Cherai, Kochi. He was the younger brother of Achutan Vaidyan, a devotee of Sree Narayana Guru and Sree Chattambi Swamikal. He was progressive in outlook and at the same time a rationalist in thought. When he met Guru at the Aluwa Advaitasramam, the latter entrusted him with a letter to be delivered to Kumaran Asan. It was with that letter that Ayyappan first came to Thiruvananthapuram. The assistance rendered by Asan in promoting Ayyappan's education was inestimate. Only after taking his B.A. Degree, he had returned to Cherai.

The joint eating which took place at Cherai was a decisive stage in his social life. In its name he was awarded the nick title of Pulayan Ayyappan. After sometime he could have taken up journalism as a profession. But he dedicated his life to remain in the social scene and work for the elimination of inhuman customs and superstitions there and make the attempt victorious through the ideals of Gurudeva. He had no ambition of political power. Consequently he had once thrown off his ministership in the State on other considerations.

If Gurudeva's services to social cause were accomplished through a silent revolution, Ayyappan's were rendered through writing, speech and action. *Guru* and *śiṣya* thus traversed along two paths and worked for the human progress. His paper *Sahodaran*, published his progressive thoughts in the form of touching poems. Besides, his editorials and articles in the *Sahodaran* captivated even the ordinary people. It was long before the birth of progressive literature that

Ayyappan had composed popular and appealing poems on a large scale. Those poems were given not so much importance to literature as to the popularisation of ideals.

He adored the God who blazes in our mental tabernacle and the sciences as the leading lights of modern age. The style witnessed in Ayyappan's poetic creations is the language of the ordinary man himself. His services are multifaceted. By awakening the good giving power that lies slumberous in the human mind, was he not creating a turbulent sea in the human mind and thus in a sense, administering a shock to human consciousness?

**C. Kesavan** (1891-1969)

C. Kesavan was born at a time when social justice was tearing humanity. Hence he could not help reacting to the situation and thus convert his life into a weapon of struggle against injustice. The social discriminations he had perforce to face during childhood paved the way for the vigorous struggle for equality and social justice of his later life. The teachings of Sree Narayana Guru fuelled his plan of action. He was convinced that those teachings were indispensable for peace and quietude of the world, and therefore his attention was turned towards converting them into practice. In the process he was turned towards a sponsor of the Nivarthana Agitation led by the rights denied people of Kerala for prevailing upon the authorities to release those rights from their unjust and unauthorised hold. What he did was to let loose a social and political storm.

He was born about a hundred years ago in an ordinary family at Mayyanad, near Kollam. He had had enough financial and social hurdles to his education. For sometime he occupied himself as a teacher and then as a lawyer. The administration was actually vested in a handful of *savarṇa*s in whose grip the power of the king was a mere vestige. Tax was levied on property held. So the right to vote was confined to the landholders who were chiefly *savarṇa*s. Thus the *avarṇa*s were almost divested of votes. The historic struggle against this gross injustice, launched by the Christian-

Muslim-Ezhava communities, is the Nivarthana Agitation. It swept across the state like a fierce tornado. The government legally prohibited the agitation. C. Kesavan ignored the prohibitory order and delivered his famous and masterly speech at Kozhencherry which elevated him to prime leadership status. The speech was severely critical of the administration and with that the Nivarthana Agitation crowned itself with success. The government was compelled to bow before the onrush of people's commotion. It had to concede their demands. As a result communal representation and reservation of seats and other areas of the Public Service were recognised. With the Institution of a Public Service Commission (and later P.S.C.), the *avarṇas* were given increased representation to government posts.

C. Kesavan was imprisoned because of his part in the Nivarthana venture. On his release which created a sensation all over the state, a meeting was organised by the citizens of Alleppey to honour him. For having welcomed the gathering, Sri T.M. Varghese, a top ranking leader of the State Congress, who was Deputy Speaker of the Assembly then, was dismissed from that position. C. Kesavan continued with his successful work at the Nivarthana with more work for the reclamation of the *avarṇas*. The task was facilitated by his position as Secratary to SNDP Yogam. He was also a staunch champion of Sree Narayana Guru's testimonials. He had acquired name and reputation as the Chief Minister of Kerala. His work *Jeevitha Samaram* (The Struggle of Life) constitutes a throbbing chapter in Kerala's history.

**K. Sukumaran** (1901-81)

K. Sukumaran was the son of C.V. Kunjirama, the founder of the newspaper *Kerala Kaumudi*. Through the medium of his paper he devoted his life to the promotion of communal harmony. He was an ardent adherent of Gurudeva's teachings. After graduation he entered Government Service. But soon he resigned from it as he found that it would be restrictive of his freedom, and then took over as editor of the *Kerala Kaumudi* from his father. He believed that a newspaper was the spokesman of the people, though, by living up to the ideal in running it, he never hesitated to lend his columns generously to the welfare of his own community as well as of the other backward communities. He held himself resolutely to Gurudeva's ideal "One caste, One religion and One God for man" as he believed that this would be the social concept of the future.

When the first Communist Ministry was in power in Kerala under E.M.S. Namboodiripad, the policy of financial reservation of government jobs was mooted. K. Sukumaran declared the policy as totally unconstitutional and did not dither embarking on an intense struggle for its abolition.

In a speech delivered at the Silver Jubilee of the Kulathoor Vayanasala (Library), marked by words sharper than the sword, he criticised the measure *in toto*. It was done in the presence of the Chief Minister E.M.S. who had arrived there to inaugurate the function. This added significance to the meeting. K. Sukumaran demanded the unconditional withdrawal of the measure in his very presence. Here is the relevant part of the speech:

> I wish to remind the Chief Minister in this context that the financial reservation of jobs which has assumed form and shape in the interior of the State Ministry is going to be a play with fire. Dealing with a serious matter in such light hearted manner is highly objectionable. It is my duty to resist it tooth and nail, and thwart it at all costs. This measure fraught as it is, with far-reaching consequences should be nipped in the bud. The administration in spite of its being minority led, when seen to be coming forward with financial reservation, no one is going to remain here without raising a finger against it, the minorities especially. Are these unfortunate people, because they were born in the lowest rung of society, destined to suffer? I once again remind the authorities that those who have laid their hands on reservation of jobs enjoyed and kept intact like precious organs by the minorities, should see the writings on the wall of time.

There was a period when K. Sukumaran was the President of SNDP

Yogam, and R. Sankar its Secretary. For the backward people of Kerala this period was one of great expectations. Till his death K. Sukumaran remained as unshakeable disciple of Sree Narayana Guru.

**R. Sankar** (1909-72)

R. Sankar declared with conviction that if the backward communities of Kerala thrown into the dark corners of society for historical reasons were to resuscitate, it could only be through Sree Narayana ideals. He had to tide over numerous adversities before he rose to prominence. He declared:

> The protections like Communal Reservation are temporary reliefs only. It is not right to treat a grievance as a right. What is required of young people, especially who are in possession of higher education, is that they can compete with anyone and secure jobs, any jobs. For that the required ability and strength should be achieved. Since reservation of jobs for the backward communities is not a permanent arrangement, the ideal way out is to make available all educational facilities and cultivate self dependence. That is the way to enter into any Test and be assured of grand success. But it should not be forgotten that it is not in reservation of jobs but in the sharing of power that the backward communities are to derive benefit.
>
> — *Report at the Golden Jubilee Celebrations of SNDP Yogam*

R. Sankar was born in an ordinary family at Puthoor, near Kottarakkara. Financial poverty stood in the way of his studies. Yet he tided them with great difficulties and continued his studies as a topper in all classes. R. Sankar was essentially a financial expert and proved his mettle in that expertise by his diverse cultural and political exercises. After taking his degrees, he did not enter government service. He on the other hand, reached the summit of political leadership. But he believed that the status he had earned was not greater than what he deserved. That was the corpus of his personality.

R. Sankar could boast of multiple achievements. One striking feature of his profile was his unbending pose before anybody. A practical approach to problems and sincere application in solving them accounted for his success. Because of the defiant attitude towards others, he had created numerous enemies for himself. But more than the enemies he had a horde of adoring followers. Even when he was at the apex of power he never denied what was legitimately due to the other communities though he was not at all reluctant to give his community what rightly belonged to it. He was one of those rare individuals who functioned contemporaneously in two different capacities, viz., as Sercratary of SNDP Yogam and a top leader of the Congress. This dual status benefited both the organisations. Later when Sankar held the Chief Ministership of the State, his efforts to build up the educational institutions of the Yogam had an added boost.

The S.N. Trust which left no room in it for changes in accordance with political vacillations was the child of his practical mindedness. The Ezhavas who were one deplorably backward in education had with his efforts a quantum leap to lofty heights in higher education particularly, let alone education in general. When one looks at the S.N. Colleges with their towers proudly raised high, one is impressed with reverence for the remarkable work of Sankar.

R. Sankar had made his mark upon history as the doyen of SNDP Yogam, Peerless political leader, Editor, Educational expert, member of the Indian Constituent Assembly and the Chief Minister of Kerala. Though he made his exit from life at a comparatively young age, his name will be engraved in the annals of Kerala and in the hearts of the people here in letters of gold.

## TWO REVOLUTIONARIES WHO UPHELD SREE NARAYANA MESSAGES

The two great followers of Gurudeva who had outshone the others in upholding the disciplines preached by Guru are Bodhananda Swamikal and Sahodaran Ayyappan.

## The Bodhananda March

One of that very rare creed of firebrand *saṁnyāsīs*, Bodhananda (1883-1928) believed that even where the great words of Guru could not mitigate the onslaught of caste, one would have even to resort to a bit of force to eradicate it and release society from its brutal clutches. He held himself firmly to the view that Kerala writhing in the pain inflicted by caste, can seek deliverance from it through force only, although it is in total contravention of Gurudeva's method. The scheme evolved by Bodhananda for the attainment of this goal came to be known as Bodhananda March.

He formed a Dharma Bhata Sangham for the purpose. The Swearing words of its members were:

> My caste is neither behind nor ahead of any other. I will not give my way in the name of caste. I cannot bear the untouchability practised in the name of caste. I will resist it even at the cost of my life. This is hereby sworn in affirmation.

The sworn soldiers toured places where caste was at its extreme, with directions to have recourse to violence to clip its wings. The method paid rich dividends. It paved the way for far-reaching changes in the social set up.

In the preceding century the *avarṇas* suffered untold disabilities like untouchability, restrictions on right of passage and freedom of dress. These had started disappearing with the commencement of the Bodhananda March. Travancore and Cochin had earlier vied with each other in implementing the caste anomalies. In both areas Bodhananda's new policy yielded revolutionary results. It was evident that a new social order in which caste could not play any more decisive roles as in the past, was emerging even though caste could not be driven out of peoples' minds for a long time to come.

It was after considerable travels all over India that Velayudhan met Gurudeva at Jagannātha Temple, Tellicherry. At first sight itself Velayudhan realised that he had met his Guru at last. He followed Gurudeva to Śivagiri, assumed the title of Bodhananda and started work on the expansion of Gurudeva's work. But soon tragedy struck. Bodhananda could not bear his Guru's demise. He followed suit three days after the *mahāsamādhi*.

**The Sahodara March**

K. Ayyappan had through word and deed proved that he was brother to one and all. His Sahodara March was inaugurated when on a historic occasion a joint eating ceremony was arranged in which members of all castes participated. The event created a sensation. Ayyappan spoke vociferously on the occasion expressing all his animus against caste and exposing that institution to the full nakedness of its injustice and the social calumny it had earned for itself. The swearing words of those assembled on the occasion were:

> Caste is unscientific, harmful and superfluous. Therefore I hereby undertake to affirm everything that is permissible under the law to eradicate caste.

Everyone assembled there took the oath irrespective of caste. But the next day reaction set in under the leadership of rich and influential people. The reactionaries proclaimed that what Ayyappan and his collaborators had done was a misdirected attempt to unhinge a sacred social arrangement which had been in existence for ages and that everything to undo it should be nipped in the bud. But this was only a temporary setback. Progressive ideas prevailed in the end.

Ayyappan was conferred the title Pulayan Ayyappan for his role in the event. He was also sprayed beetles and biting ants dipped in cowdung dissolved in water. Ayyappan was not deterred. He applied himself to the task with redoubled vigour. In the meantime a batch of strong adversaries cried for his blood. Ayyappan boldly told them, "Kill me if that will appease your thirst. But this march will not end until caste is buried under this soil." That speech of his lasted for an hour and instead of assault it resulted in approbation.

On another occasion Ayyappan and his followers proceeded to Kodungallur and launched struggle to end cock sacrifice and obscene songs practised in connection with annual festivals in the temple there. They were manhandled badly in connection with the event. Ayyappan resorted to the use of literature as a weapon for uprooting the caste system. In a meeting held at Cheryamangalam, Mithavadi Editor C. Krishnan, and the social reformer of Malabar, Manjeri Rama Iyer also participated. The vast assembly of people thronged there saw the form of a fearsome and horrendous monster representing caste being burnt to ashes. Its procession to the fire was marked by loud slogans "May the caste demon be incinerated" repeated incessantly. The proceedings were concluded after a fiery speech by Ayyappan and the final disappearance of the demon's figure into the flames.

# 9

# Installation of Idols (Pratiṣṭhās) and Guru's Concept of Temples

## The Historical Background

BEFORE examining the *prathiṣṭhās* of Guru it is necessary to consider what his conceptions of temples were. As a social being man has from very early times gone to temples for worship. In course of time these temples became the monopoly of the rich and influential *savarṇas*. The *avarṇas* had to take refuge with crude Gods like Madan and Maruta. This is how two varieties of Gods had evolved in Kerala. Guru reformed the Hindu religious customs and rites prevailing here and built new temples in which noble Gods were installed. The *avarṇas* were free to enter them. Here was Guru's conception about temples.

The period of Guru's *pratiṣṭhās* extented to over four decades. This period can be studied: under two phases: under the first phase the *pratiṣṭhās* were confined to idols, and under the second, they were in the form of symbols. Guru was thus breaking new ground in temple-worship. In doing so He was completely reorganising and giving new shape to it. The *praṇavākṣara pratiṣṭhā* of Murukkumpuzha and Ullala, and the mirror in the temple at Kalavancodam lead one's thoughts to the eternal regions beyond the ephemeral worldly existence. Guru had more than fifty temples in his name of which a few are mentioned here.

## Aruvippuram Śiva Prathiṣṭhā

Aruvippuram heralds the social revolution of Kerala launched by Guru. Enriched with natural beauty and decked with splendorous vales and dales, Aruvippuram had enthralled Gurudeva from His early life. In those days people of different castes used to go there, take a dip in the river and then bow to God in supplication. Hence the necessity for a place of worship there was brought home to Guru.

On the *Śivarātri* day in 1888 He did the *pratiṣṭhā* at Aruvippuram. Kumaran Asan has described the great event thus:

> Swamy imagined a rock on the eastern bank of the Neyyar river as a pedestal. Then after midnight He took a bath in the river and took the idol and stood in meditation until 3 o' clock in the morning. As He stood in that pose tears were rolling down his brilliant cheeks in profusion. The spectators poured forth the *pañcākṣara mantram* loudly in profound concentration. At 3 o' clock Swamy installed the idol on the pedestal and sprinkled water over it repeating hymns.

This was how Guru's reform of worship was inaugurated at Aruvippuram.

Here was a new concept in temple-worship. It was not only historic but momentous when the orthodox sections of society raised a hue and cry about the *pratiṣṭhā*; Swamy silenced them with a remarkable reply, "The idol of Śiva we have installed here is not that of Brāhmaṇa Śiva but of our Śiva." This reply embodies a new and hitherto unheard of approach to worship. It declared in unmistakable terms that God does not give predilections for particular castes and that worship is free and unhindered for everyone. The *pratiṣṭhā* sent shock waves to the strongholds of orthodoxy throughout the length and breadth of Bhārata.

## Chembazhanthi Gurukulam and Manakkal Temple

The Manakkal Vayalwaram house was sanctified by the birth of Sree Narayana Guru about one and a half centuries ago. The

Manakkal temple has to its credit a very long history. It was administered jointly by the Vayalwaram and Chembazhanthi families. There was an idol of Devī in the *sanctum sanctorum* of the temple. It was shrouded in superstitions. On the day next to the annual festival, Guru entered it and replaced the Devī's idol with an idol of Śiva. It was Guru's first idol breaking. It struck at the very central pivot of superstitions. Underlying the act was the motive to save society rather than His own family.

## Śivagiri and Śāradā Matom

For the propagation of His messages, Swamy selected Śivagiri as His headquarters, a most fitting choice from its location and against the background of its exquisite natural beauty.

The idol of Śāradā, the Goddess of learning was installed in the newly constructed building in 1912. It is a peculiarly modelled building, octagonal in shape. Idol of the Goddess is sculptured as in a standing pose, with foot fixed on a beautiful lotus. This idol is remarkably different from all others, being the only one of its kind in India. It was installed without the accompaniment of chanting of hymns.

## Aluva Advaitāśramam

After Śivagiri *pratiṣṭhā*, Swamy was on the lookout for a shelter for Himself. He set on a journey which took Him to Aluva. There on the bank of Periyar a plot was purchased and Advaitāśramam was built on that site. Devotees streamed into the new building. The speciality here is, apart from Guru's picture, there is no idol for worship. A Sanskrit school was opened close to Advaitāśramam just to proclaim to the world that Sanskrit was not meant for *savarṇa*s only. It was modelled more perfectly than any other school and was run most efficiently.

For Gurudeva, Advaitāśramam was a health resort too, very much to His liking.

## Talasserry Jagannātha Temple

It was Sree Narayana Guru who built a temple at Thalasserry for the Thiyas. The idol was installed in 1908. Gurudeva had apparently the Jagannātha Temple at Purī in mind when naming the new temple as Jagannātha temple. Like the Purī Temple the new temple also recognises no caste distinctions for those who go and worship there. The important ceremony there is Ilaneeratam by which tender coconut is sprinkled there as *abhiṣeka*. Even while Guru was alive a statue of his was installed on the northern side of the temple.

## Kulathur Kolathukara Temple

The Śiva Kolathukara temple at Kulathur was a long cherished dream of the natives come true. Guru broke the idol of Devī in the old temple and installed a Śiva idol. Till that time the natives went for worship outside nearby temples in which the *avarṇas* were prohibited entry. In addition to temple, Guru also provided them with educational facilities. The other landmarks at Kulathur are an oil painting of Guru preserved inside the Sree Narayana Guru Mandiram and an exemplary Library named Sree Narayana Memorial Library.

## Kunnumpara Subrāhmaṇya Temple

Sree Narayana Guru had an uncanny inspiration to spot out exceptionally beautiful places for erecting temples. Kunnumpara Subrāhmaṇya temple can boast of one such site. It is situated at Vazhamuttom near the tourist centre at Kovalam, south of Thiruvananthapuram city. The place for the temple extending to 21 acres, was donated by Pachallur Kochukutti Vaidyer. Gurudeva did the *pratiṣṭhā* work on a full moon day of 1899. Near the temple there is an artificially made spring which perpetually emits pure and crystal-clear water. The temple is in a state of constant expansion and development.

## Mannanthala Devī Temple

Mannanthala Anandavalleeswaram Temple was a major *pratiṣṭhā* by Guru after Aruvippuram. The idol was inducted in 1889. Resting in a *muṭh* built close to the temple, Swamy wrote one of His famous poems, *Mannanthala Devīstavam*. Anandavalleeswaram temple had been of immense service to the cultural and social progress of Mannanthala.

About three years back along with the centenary celebrations of the temple, its restructuralisation was conducted and a reinstallation of the idol (*punarpratiṣṭhā*) was held. The main feature of the new construction is a tall graceful and artistically rich tower (*gopuram*) with its top rising above the nearby landscape.

## Sree Narayana Mangalam, Kārttikeya Temple

The Velikkatu Sree Narayana Mangalam Kārttikeya temple is situated on the shore of the majestic and beautiful Ashtamudi lake. Kumaran Asan and Vairavan Santhi had supervised construction of the temple. The stone for the idol was brought from Aruvippuram. The *pratiṣṭhā* was done in 1898.

## The Āyiramtheṅgu Temple Pratiṣṭhā

The village, Āyiramtheṅgu lies between sea and lake. As the name suggests, it abounds in coconut trees. A temple was constructed in the heart of the village under the supervision of Varanappallil Kochukrishna Panicker. The astrologer fixed a time for the *pratiṣṭhā*. But Guru defied him and declared that the time is not what the astrologer declares but when *pratiṣṭhā* actually happens. Accordingly He did the *pratiṣṭhā* at the appropriate moment.

## Kottar Gaṇapati Temple

The Kottar Gaṇapati temple became a fact as Gurudeva gave word to a deputation of the natives that their longing for a temple would be fulfilled. Guru reached Kottar at the appointed time and fixed the idol. The temple is even today leaping towards development and further expansion.

### Peringottukara Somaśekhara Temple

The Peringottukara Somaśekhara Temple came into being in 1917. The place was donated by the Tandaserry family. A Sree Narayana Guru Mandiram had been constructed in the site earlier. Under its auspices a leading disciple of Guru named Śivalingadāsa Swamikal gave regular discourses on the works of Sree Narayana Guru with special emphasis on the spiritual insight reflecting in them. This temple has been not a little responsible for the spiritual and social advancement of Peringottukara.

### Kozhikode Śrīkaṇṭheśvara Temple

Like the Jagannātha Temple at Thalasserry, the Śrīkaṇṭheśvara Temple at Kozhikode is one of Gurudeva's most prominent creations.

The request for the creation of a temple came from a leading citizen of Kozhikode, viz., Rarichan Moopan. Very soon a beautiful structure rose on the spot selected. Guru had stated that once a temple stood on the same site and prophesied that if a temple were built on its remnants, the new temple would in due course become a *mahākṣetra* (great temple). As ordered by Guru, Chaitanya Swamikal made the *ṣaḍ dhārā pratiṣṭhā*. The Śivalingam obtained from the site was fixed in the temple tank by Guru Himself. He named the temple as Śrīkaṇṭheśvara. In addition, there are other *pratiṣṭhās* in the temple viz., Viṣṇu, Gaṇapati and Subrāhmaṇya. Quite unknown to Malabar is a Mandapan (a mound like structure) with water around it, built on the model found in Tamil Nadu. The tank around it is large and kept clean. During annual festival, the temple compound is decorated artfully and with elegance.

### The Sundreśvara Temple at Kannur

The temples at Tellicherry and Kozhikode excited the interests of the citizens of Kannur. They, under the leadership of Oyit Krishan Vakil, formed themselves into a seven-member committee and started work on temple construction. When the construction was over, Gurudeva accompanied by Chaitanya Swamikal arrived at Kannur and did the *pratiṣṭhā*. He then proceeded to Mangalapuram and conducted the *pratiṣṭhā* of Thrippatheeswara temple also.

### The Karamukku Temple

The Karamukku temple at Trichur forms a turning point in Guru's *pratiṣṭhās*. The *pratiṣṭhās* here consist of just a lamp with three tongues ever burning. In only ten cents of land the temple has over the years gathered around it a great name in that its activites have served to fill the human mind, more and more with the nectar of Guru's teachings.

### The Pratiṣṭhā at Murukkumpuzha

The *pratiṣṭhā* at Murukkumpuzha fully reflects Sree Narayana Guru's revolutionary vision. Named as Kālakaṇṭheśvaram temple, the *pratiṣṭhā* here is an inscription *auṁ* ever dazzling in brilliant light. Then as if to be sentinels to *auṁ*, the words truth, virtue, kindness and peace are engraved around it. We are worshipping these words only. Here is a lesson known loud and clear from this new mode of worship. And that is, that God lives in the mind, that God and *ātmā* are one and the same and that God can be worshipped by conceiving any form for him. Surely a very revolutionary concept.

### The Mirror Pratiṣṭhā at Kalavancodam, Shertallai

The most far-reaching and the most meaningful concept of idol-worship is enshrined in the Mirror *pratiṣṭhā* at Kalavancodam, near Shertallai. When Guru reached there He heard murmurs against idol *pratiṣṭhā*. The question was resolved by deciding to install a mirror in place of the idol, with the words *auṁ śānti* projected thereon by scrapping off from the reverse side of the mirror sufficient mercury. The *pratiṣṭhā* was done at the *brahma muhūrtam* of 14 June, 1927.

There is a belief that those who worship before the mirror will see their own faces in it. This is not correct. The mirror is not fixed in such position as to reflect the face of one looking at it.

As ordered by Guru, His teachings and messages are written

down on the temple walls in inter-mixed black and blue colours, to attract world attention.

The Kalavancodam *pratiṣṭhā* reflects Guru's deep insight and extraordinary foresight. He was actually evolving an evolutionary process in *pratiṣṭhā*. Through this process he demonstrated that worship is a psychological principle and that the effect of worship depends not on what a person worships but how he worships — in other words, his approach.

With Kalavancodam, Gurudeva withdrew from temple construction and insisted upon the construction of educational institutions. He had held *pratiṣṭhās* in seventeen important temples in addition to many smaller ones. This account could deal only with about twenty temples. The others could only have been given a feather touch. It may be hoped that more research on the subject would throw fresh light on it.

# 10

# Guru's Humour and Sarcasm

SREE Narayana Guru was endowed with a genuine gift for wit and humour. His curt replies to unwarranted questions elicited tremendous and lasting laughter. Some of those remarks have been marked by acuteness of perception and sound judgement, and have been accepted as classical wits. A few are cited here:

## The Meaninglessness of Caste

"Name?"

"Narayanan"

"Caste?"

"Has it not been known at sight?"

"No"

"If it cannot be known at sight, how can it be known when heard?"

## The Theft of the Temple's Offering Box

An event which happened at Śivagiri:

Disciple: "Swamy, yesterday the offering box in our temple was stolen."

Swamy: (Smiling) "If all the money put into that box had remained with the donors, the task would have been made difficult for the thief. When all had collected at one spot, his task became easy."

### Cārī and Brahmacārī

A youth by name Cārī came to Śivagiri, accepted Guru's discipleship and stayed there. In due course he became *brahmacārī*, and with that certain allegations also rose against him. These allegations were proved true. Guru called him to his side and said:

"Cārī does not deserve to remain *brahmacārī*. Hence Cārī may go his own way after retaining the *Brahman* here."

### If You Can Take Milk Why not Take Meat?

Gurudeva was resting in the Advaitāśramam at Aluva. A *bhakta* bowed to him and desired to clear a doubt.

Bhakta: "Swamy, we are taking goat's milk as well as cow's milk. Then why not take their meat?"

Swamy: "Doesn't matter." (After a time with a smile). "Have You got mother?"

Bhakta: "No Swamy . . . passed away."

Swamy: "Then was she buried or eaten?"

### The Golden Lance of Śāradā Matom

The *pūjā* for Śāradā *pratiṣṭhā* was held with a golden lance placed before it. After *pūjā* one day the *pujārī* clandestinely removed it. On hearing this, Swamy summoned the *pujārī* and asked him:

"Why did you take way the lance?

Pujārī: "It is our wish that nothing other than Swamy's idol should be worshipped here."

Swamy: "Then what about the Sandals?"

Pujārī: "It is kept to symbolise Swamy."

Swamy: "Then if the sandal could symbolise us, why not the lance?"

### Where is God?

Disciple: "Where does God sit? Does He know everything?"

Guru: "Yes. He is everywhere. And knows everything too. He is Supreme Being who sees without eyes, hears without ears, touches without skin, smells without nose and tastes without tongue. God is a blazing Divine Ocean. Everything that is seen in the universe is but waves of that Supreme Macrocosm."

### The Naming Ceremony

Swamy: "Why have the leading men of the place come?"

Reply: "For naming the twin children, may it please Swamy."

Swamy: "We see."

Reply: "We have come to name Kochukarunakaran."

Swamy: "Alright. That name is sufficient for them. The same name for both."

Swamy's meaning became clear to them only when they returned to their village. One of the children suddenly took ill and died. So there was need for a single name only.

### Guru had no Caste

To a question what Guru's caste was, Guru replied,

"It is a fact that we are all born in a single caste. Was not the great sage Parāśara born in a Pariah hut, and the codifier of the Vedas, Vedavyāsa in the fisherman's shelter? For that reason, were they declared as outcastes?"

"We have for long given up all thoughts of caste distinctions. Yet some particular sections are treating us as belonging to their group, and carry on propaganda accordingly. This is because we are not understood in the correct perspective. We do not belong to a particular caste or religion. This fact is hereby proclaimed for public knowledge."

### Swamy and Ayyankali

Swamy was reclining on an easy chair. It was noon time. A moustached man dressed in a long coat and *dhotī* entered through the gate and advanced towards Swamy. He came and bowed respectfully with folded hands.

Guru: "Coming from?"

Stranger: "Coming from a distance, Swamy. Ayyankali is the name. Native place is South Travancore. A worker in Sambavas Mahajana Sabha."

Guru: "Who are Sambavas?"

Ayyankali: "We are descendants of Sambhu. Lord Siva was a Sambava. We have no caste. Anyone can join our organisation (Sangh)."

Guru: "That is good, Are there non-Sambavas in the organisation?"

Ayyankali: "No, Swamy. When one joins the Sangh, one becomes Sambava."

Guru: "That is fine trick."

Ayyankali: "I am a Christian. Yet I am a member of both Sambava Mahajana Sangh and Sambava Christian Church."

Guru: "Very smart. It is such smart young men that our land requires."

### Mango During out of Season

Swamy once visited the house of Chavara Koippuzha Channar and was taking rest in the guest house. Then Swamy expressed a desire to Channar for a mango fruit. Since it was out of season for mangoes, Channar was embarrassed. Swamy Himself came to his rescue. He said: "There will be mangoes in the small mango tree standing slightly to the east. Just send someone to pluck." There were three fully ripe mangoes in the tree. The event saw the rise of Channar's family to prosperity.

## One Gold Ring and a Leper

A rich man came to Śivagiri one day and paid respects to Swamy by placing a gold ring before Him.

Swamy: "What use can we make of this ring?"

Rich man: "It is my desire to dedicate it to Swamy."

Swamy was silent. The rich man seemed to have left. Swamy had gone to the *parṇaśālā*. The rich man returned after sometime and found that the ring was gone. He saw a leper squatting there. The rich man suspected that he had stolen the ring. So he beat the poor fellow mercilessly. By that time Swamy also came back to the spot. Seeing the leper crying, Swamy said: "You gave the ring to me. Did you not? Then what is it to you whoever takes it. (To the Leper) Don't cry. By beating you he has also taken your illness upon Himself."

After a few days the leper was cured of his illness.

## The Fowl Sacrifice at Mayyazhi

Swamy was guest of Mayor Punnara Moti of Mayyazhi. One evening drumming and music were heard from the next house. Swamy asked what it was.

Mayor: "For Kuttichathan's (a crude God) pleasure, hundreds of fowls are being sacrificed, Swamy."

Swamy: "Then we should stop that cutting of fowls. We will go to the spot."

When they saw Swamy, the intoxication of those assembled there was converted into *bhakti*. The leader of the gang stood in obeisant silence.

Swamy: "Cannot this killing stop?"

Answer: "We wholeheartedly want to obey Swamy's commands. But if Kuttichathan is enraged?"

Swamy: "We shall deal with Chathan." Then looking at Chathan

Mestiri who stood nearby, Swamy asked jovially, "Will Chathan Mestiri agree?"

Everybody laughed. Chathan Mestiri too laughed. With that ended the fowl sacrifice.

### The Bhūmi (the Earth) is on Ananthan's Head

While Swamy was in Thalasserry a batch of college students approached Him. They asked:

"Is it correct that the earth stands on Ananthan's head?"

Swamy smiled: "What does your science say?"

"It is the force of gravitation between the millions of stars, sun and moon, and the planets which sustain the earth in its position."

Swamy replied: "So there is an eternal power to lead and control the world. Will it not be proper if it were accepted so. Hence why not accept also that in that eternal power rests *bhūmi*."

### The Thief and Jack Fruit

A complaint reached Swamy that a thief was stealing fruit daily from the jack tree attached to the Muttakkad temple.

Swamy: "Have you seen him after the theft started?"

Complainant: I have seen him coming and looking at the tree during day time."

Swamy: "Coming to pluck jack fruit at night entails danger of thorns and snakes. So ask him to come during day time and pluck them. How inhuman you are? From now on at least love him and tell him that."

### Judge Raman Thampi and Swamy

Raman Thampi:"I had an experience."
Swamy: "Yes?"

Raman Thampi:"When I was seated in my official chair, I

experienced loss of memory. Medicines were useless. One day Swamy's disciple T.V. Narayani Amma gave me some sacred ash. Before going to court I applied it on my forehead. My loss of memory disappeared."

Swamy: "If there is faith, it may happen."

## Guru Pūjā at Śivagiri

Cook Sankoo Bhaktan stood with hand joined for a few seconds during Guru *pūjā* (a *pūjā* in rememberance of the Preceptor) at Śivagiri before serving food to Swamy. Then Swamy said to no one in particular:

"Our picture does not know hunger. It is given food earlier. We know hunger, but will get food only late."

Hearing this, Sankoo felt unhappy.

## That is not Correct or True. We Can Never Say That.

A landlord from Nanjinad, transferred to Guru's name some property by a will. Ignoring the donor's intentions, his successors approached the court to get it nullified. A commission came to take Swamy's deposition. But Swamy refused to depose as directed by the advocate. "That is not correct nor true, we can never say that," He declared.

## The Devil Possessed Dancer

Swamy came face to face with a devil possessed dancer in a temple. He came close to Swamy, and asked:

"Do you know who I am?"

"Mere sight reveals a coarse fat fellow."

"What? Insulting? Want to see my power?"

"Yes, tooth in that mouth." Retorted Swamy. Even the man possessed could not suppress laughter.

## The Grief on Death and the Dead Body

A *bhakta* to clear a doubt asked Guru:

"Swamy, if a close relative dies, some people cry their heart out by grief."

"Crying will not bring back the dead person to life. Then why should one pour grief and cry? Will not all of us die one day? If there is birth there is also death on the other side. Why don't people think that?"

"Swamy, after death should the body be cremated or buried? Which is proper?"

"Put the body in a grinding mill and use the ground particles as manure for the coconut tree. That will be proper?"

"Oh Swamy. . . ?"

"Why will it cause pain? Only when an individual is alive can he do anything beneficial to fellow beings. If he, after death, becomes manure to plants, will that not be admirable?"

## In the Last Trial

A Christian missionary visited Sree Narayana Guru in the Gurukulasramam at Madras and asked in extreme humility:

"Swamy, some religious believers reject idol-worship. Some others approve of it. That these are natural can be accepted without reluctance. When the Muslim invaders smashed the idols of Devas and Devīs, they could do nothing to prevent the damage. Could they?"

"Is it admitted that God is Onmipresent and that Supreme power lives at least in human hearts?"

"That is admitted," said the missionary.

"While man kills man mercilessly what revenge can God perpetrate on him?"

"But in the last trial, he will be punished."

"In that case all breakers of idols will be punished in the last trial. Will they not?"

The missionary had no more question to ask.

**Man will once become God**

While Swamy was at Śivagiri some *bhakta*s approached him with a request that a temple might be arranged to be built for them with a *pratiṣṭhā*.

Swamy: "What is to be the *Pratiṣṭhā*?"

Bhaktas: Siva, Subrahmanian or Devi. Whatever Swamy is pleased to prescribe."

Swamy: "Of what use are the temples with their darkness and their bad stench?"

Bhaktas: "If temples are available, people will come for worship after purifying their bodies through bath."

Swamy: Good. The interior of the temple should be kept clean. A lamp will do in place of the *pratiṣṭhā*. Is not lamp prosperity itself?"

Bhaktas: "But with that the Bhaktas will not be satisfied. They want an idol for worship."

Swamy: "Will not pictures of Devas and Devis placed around the lamp suffice? We believe that once upon a time Vishnu, Siva and Sriraman were leaders. Siva must have become prominent by character and muscle power. Vishnu was valorous and Sriraman was saviour of Brahmins. So both were treated as Gods. Hence God worship is advisable not only inside temples, but inside one's own heart."

Guru's humour and wit are thought provoking. They reveal to us the brilliance of His heart in exposing the meaninglessness of vain arguments on profound matters and the sharpness of His intellect in touching at the exact chord to pronounce a real wit.

# 11

# The Śivagiri Pilgrimages
## Their Message

OF the messages of Sree Narayana Guru, that related to Śivagiri Thīrthadānam (pilgrimage) is the last. It was given in response to a request jointly made by Vallabhaserry Govindan Vaidyer and T.K. Kittan Writer. That was on 18 January 1928. Guru was reclining in an easy chair in the shade of a mango tree in SNDP union compound at Nagamabadam, Kottayam. Vaidyer accompanied by the Writer approached Swamy and broached the subject of Śivagiri Pilgrimage, and requested for Swamy's permission for it. Vaidyer advanced the reason that while higher caste Hindus, Christians, Muslims and others had their own pilgrim centres, those categorised as *avarṇas* (Ezhavas and several others) had nowhere to go as pilgrims. So he requested that Śivagiri might be treated as a pilgrim centre for these sections of the population.

Guru gave His consent for the project. He fixed the Pilgrimage to be once in a year and on the first of January. It was also ordained that ten days of austerity should be undertaken before the pilgrimage and that the pilgrims might wear yellow clothes. There were to be no other strict observances for the pilgrims. Enough money for the expenses should be kept at hand. The *pañcaśuddhi* of Srī Buddha, viz., purity in body, food, mind, word and deed could be desirably observed. The pilgrims could go either on foot or in conveyances.

Swamy insisted that the Pilgrimage should be least ostentatious and should involve absolute minimum expense. Yellow clothing meant only ordinary white cloth dipped in turmeric lotion.

About the goals of the scheme, Swamy explained as follows:

(1) Education (2) Purity (3) Devotion to God (4) Organisation (5) Agriculture (6) Handicraft (7) Business and (8) Training in Technology and Science. There should be a chain of speeches on these subjects by people proficient and with outstanding knowledge in them. People should listen carefully to these speeches, and put what is heard into practice. Then they and the nation along with them will march towards prosperity.

The next day itself Swamy's Pilgrimage Message was published in the daily *Desabhimani*. Thus the project received sufficient publicity. But even though it was approved in 1928, the first pilgrimage took place only in 1935 (December-January). Only five persons took part. The person who took the initiative in it was Muloor, the poet. The first batch consisted of Muloor's son P.K. Divakaran, P.V. Raghavan, K.S. Sankunni, Kesavan Muthalali and M.K. Raghavan, Ayathil.

# 12

# The Global Impact
## Nataraja Guru and Guru Nitya Chaitanya Yati

### Nataraja Guru and the English Translation of Gurudeva's Works

NATARAJA Guru (1895-1973) was the leading disciple of Sree Narayana Guru. He gave global exposure to the teachings and messages of Guru by translating into English some of His most outstanding poems. The profound and thought exciting philosophy embodied in them are brought out in all its splendour and spiritual magnitude in these translations.

Nataraja Guru had done a heroic task indeed in undertaking the translations. He did it with detachment. Underlying that detachment was unadulterated faith in God and his Guru. It was he who saw to the establishment of Narayana Gurukulas throughout the world.

During the final phase of Gurudeva's life, there was considerable hubbub at Śivagiri mainly about the properties in His name. Without joining in any of these struggles, Nataraja Guru stood by himself beside his preceptor taking in more and more spiritual knowledge from that countenance. Guru knew that Nataraja was competent to reveal spiritual secret to the *brahmacārīs*, learning in Brahmavidyalaya, and to preserve its sanctity to the world; it was probably that knowledge that prompted Gurudeva to send Nataraja to France with necessary funds for higher education. He took his D.litt. Degree from the Paris University with Triple Honours. During his stay in Europe, he came into contact with many leading personalities like Romain Roland and explained to them Guru's vision. By the time he returned, his mentor had attained *samādhi*.

Back at Śivagiri, some of the inmates there accorded an indifferent reception to him. But he turned a blind eye to this show of spite, for he had returned not to claim a chunk of Guru's wealth, but to be the successor to Guru's spiritual heritage. In keeping with his word to Guru, he took to hand preparation of a textbook for the *brahmacārīs*.

Besides Nataraja Guru, Guru Nitya Chaitanya Yati, John Spiers and P. Sankunni also played important roles in securing for Guru's ideals, worldwide popularity. The translations issued forth not only in English but in Hindi, Tamil and Sanskrit, for them to gain fast circulation. The spreading process picked up momentum through translations as well as through oral interpretations though their profoundity and endemic beauty would take a thousand years to express themselves in their full enormity.

The centre of all this spiritual eruption is Śivagiri. The place transudes spiritual resplendence which reaches out to the farthest corners of the world with Guru as the main spring of immense other-worldly ardour. Jawaharlal Nehru, the first Prime Minister of India, on his visit to Śivagiri recorded as follows about Gurudeva:

> I have great pleasure in visiting this place where a great soul lived and presented messages to the world. Places where Mahatmas stayed are converted to pilgrim centres. They become as sacred as temples. This is because their thoughts and prayers remain suspended in their atmosphere. It was here that Sree Narayana Guru lived. It was from here that the brilliance of his great message viz., One caste, One religion and One God, had percolated to the whole world. He desired to build up a society without caste. We are today more in need of Swamy's message.

After Gurudeva's *samādhi*, Nataraja Guru was invited to take part in a meeting in Punjab. More than ten thousand men and women had assembled there. Over fifty learned *saṁnyāsīs* were present to deliver speeches. Nataraja Guru was to pay toast. In his welcome speech Harikrishnadas Agarval said:

> Sree Narayana Guru is treated in south India with as much esteem as we treat Guru Nanak in the north. Nataraja Guru is the most prominent of His disciples. He has been going round the world to unite humanity into a single brotherhood bound by love without caste or creed. Pilgrims in yellow coloured clothes thronging into Sivagiri, the place of Guru's Samadhi, during the Christmas season are multplying by the year. I had also been to Sivagiri last year to pay homage to the great Guru. I was able to see how Nataraja Guru could realise there the concept of one world encompassing the entire humanity as a whole without difference of caste, religion, race or language. I welcome him and along with Yati and Paul Guvert, heartily to this vast assembly.

Nataraja Guru's speech was as follows:

> In the morning session I listened to the great speeches of three illustrious men. I felt my heart yearning. When I saw that, subtle thoughts were being discussed with thread bare precision before that acutely listening vast human concourse, I recalled to my mind the history of *guru-śiṣya* (preceptor-disciple) relationship, in this Divine Land still surviving as a heritage.
>
> When the dress, language, ideas and ideals of human beings are wanting in uniformity, the route to peace will be shut down. In the light of a homogeneous science we should be able to synchronise life's values and ideals. We may boast of our National Freedom. But its consequences have reached only to society's surface and not even near the suffering and the needy. For that very reason ideological

> freedom is even now far away from us. Only truth can lead people along the right path and realise the effects of freedom. In the name of that truth my humble obeisance to you all.

The most authentic work on life and teachings of Sree Narayana Guru, viz., *The Word of the Guru* has been written by Nataraja Guru. It is the great Preceptor's voice that is echoing all along in this treatise. The first part of the book titled, *The Way of the Guru*, is contained in nine chapters which deals with the path designed by Guru. The second part *The Word of the Guru* is, in its eleven chapters, concerned comprehensively with Swamy's Monistic Philosophy, internationally relevant Theories and His conception of *guru-śiṣya* relationship. In the third part is included the English translations of some of the important works of Swamy, under the following titles: *The Critique of Caste, Parental Gratitude, Kindness to Life, Song of the Kundalini Snake, Thought and Inertia, Scriptures of Mercy*, and *The Science of the Absolute*.

Having come to know of Sree Narayana Guru from *The Word of the Guru*, Romain Roland has in his life of Śrī Rāmakṛṣṇa, the following words to say about Him:

> Glasenapp does not say anything regarding new religious manifestations in south India which are not negligible. Such for example is the great Guru, Sree Narayana, whose beneficient spiritual activity has been exercising its influence, during the past forty years in the State of Travancore on nearly two millions of his followers. His teaching, permeated with the philosophy of Sankara, shows evidence of a striking difference of temperament compared with the mysticism of Bengal, of which the effusions of Love, (Bhakti) inspire in him a certain mistrust. He was, one might say, a Jnani of action, a grand religious intellectual, who had a keen living sense of the people and of social necessities. He has contributed greatly to the elevation of the oppressed classes in south India, and his

> work has been associated at certain times with that of Gandhi.
>
> — Romain Roland
> *The Life of Ramakrishna* 1930

Several of Guru's works have been translated into English recently. His Sanskrit poems have been translated into Malayalam, English, and Hindi. The reputed work *Ātmopadeśa-śatakam* has been translated into English by Guru Nitya Chaitanya Yati. Similarly P. Sankunni's translation of *Daiva Daśakam* into English has also been published. Swamy Dharmathirther's *The Prophet of Peace* and *Sree Narayana Guru, The National Builder*, have also come out in English. More biographies of Guru in Malayalam have appeared of late.

## Guru's Global Reputation and Guru Nitya Chaitanya Yati

Sree Narayana Guru was well known in Kerala and parts of Tamil Nadu during His lifetime. But his reputation did not reach the other parts of India with such rapidity. This was because of the language barrier.

Even while Guru was alive, Nataraja Guru had taken steps to establish Narayana Gurukulas in different parts of the world. Their headquarters was fixed as the Gurukula at Varkala. Along with that, their supervision was entrusted to Guru Nitya Chaitanya Yati. As a result Gurukulas are being built throughout the world with simultaneous endeavour to develop them to flourishing status.

He is Jayachandra Panicker, son of Pandalam Raghava Panicker and related to the poet Muloor S. Padmanabha Panicker. With this literary and cultural legacy, Jayachandra Panicker, who found the sublimation of his spiritual propensity to become an accomplished fact, was very much facilitated. He had further received the spiritual tutelege of Nataraja Guru with whom he lived as disciple as well as colleague for quarter of a century. As if in continuation of this training, he, in due course, became the spokesman as well as the operator of the word of Guru.

Sree Narayana Guru had never expressed himself against any religion. Peaceful co-existence of religions was His creed; He had absolute faith in the core of every religion namely morality, rites and practices, and its awareness of its goal. He insisted upon the study of every religion with an open mind. Even if one had little faith in religion, it would suffice if one had faith in pure human love based on ideal and truth. It was by his premise on this conception that Nataraja Guru took up the establishment of *gurukulas* world-wide on the ancient Indian *gurukula* model, evolving a blueprint designed to put the Gurudeva vision into practice in all zones of life. That was laid down, as the *modus operandi* of the *gurukulas*. While giving directions as to how that could be accomplished successfully, its Gurus — Nataraja Guru and Nitya Chaitanya Yati — lived as its ideal exemplifications. Though Nataraja Guru is no more, Yati is carrying on his work relentlessly for more than fifty years now.

Yati had a short split with Nataraja Guru in the meantime. But they were reconciled not long afterwards. He took over work on the *gurukulas*. The latter part of his life has been dedicated to define Sree Narayana vision in the light of the realities of the present and the possibilities of the future. The insight for the new venture was received from Nataraja Guru.

Both Nataraja Guru and Yati are writers of spiritual works. But Guru was not a speaker. Yati on the other hand is a litterateur and speaker. He has listeners all over the world. His capacity for talk and writing has endeared him to many families in foreign lands. But he never stays for long at any place. He travels throughout the world, to places including Singapore, Australia, Japan, Fiji, France, England and so on.

The East West University of Brahmavidya of which Yati is the chairman, is the expanded version of *brahmavidyālaya*. There are centres at Varkala and Patna for the faculties functioning in various centres of the world to assemble. The real power behind the centre of Nataraja Guru's *samādhi* having become the East West centre of *brahmavidyā*, is Guru Nitya Chaitanya Yati.

## The Nataraja Gurukulas Reflecting Gurudeva's Spirit

As a result of Nataraja Guru's perseverent efforts, *gurukulas* sprung up at several centres both in India and abroad. To hear Advaita from Guru's face and to assimilate it through reflection and meditation — the *gurukulas* were to provide facilities for this process. Knowledge was imparted in ancient India in the *gurukulas*. Such names as Adinarayanan, Padamasambhavan, Vasishtan, Parasaran, Vyasan, Sukran and Sankaracharier are associated with the *gurukula* system.

Nataraja Guru's work was taken over and continued with unabated zeal by Nitya Chaitanya Yati. A magazine under the name *Gurukula* is published from Varkala. The theories on, and interpretations of Gurudeva's visions were brought to the world by Nataraja Guru, Yati, John Spiers and Dharamathirdhar.

The first *gurukula* was founded at Kunoor in 1923. A second one arose in Kaggalipuram near Bangalore. The spiritual magazine '*Values*' was published from there under the supervision of John Spiers. Eight km away from Kaggali is Somanhalli where a *gurukulam* was established in 1950. In Kerala *gurukulams* were built in Wyanad. The headquarters of the Arts and Science section of Brahmavidya Mandiram is at Vaithiri. The first *gurukula* outside India came into existence in Singapore. In Belgium Nataraja Guru established a *gurukulam* in 1950. Today *gurukulams* are found all over the world.

The Brahmavidya Mandiram as conceived by Sree Narayana Guru at Śivagiri was inaugurated in 1970. The one at Narayana Giri in Varkala followed suit in 1974. On the same day another Brahmavidya Mandiram came up in Washington, USA.

## The Transfusion of Sree Narayana's Messages and the Media

Although Gurudeva's messages disseminated to different parts of India through the various Indian languages, it is through Malayalam that they have been given a fair deal in publicity. The prominent newspapers *Kerala Kaumudi, Malayala Manorama* and *Mathru Bhoomi* are giving the eminence due to them. There are besides innumerable magazines issuing forth from various parts of Kerala such as *Sivagiri* Magazine (from Śivagiri), *Gurukulam* (from Narayana Gurukulam), *Gurudevan* (from Aluva), *Gurusabdam* (from Trichur), *Gurusannidhi* (from Kannur), *Prasanna Keralam* (from Kottayam) and *Kerala Kausthubham* from Nilgiris. This apart, the spiritual Magazines of India codify the universal theories of Guru and publish them as souvenirs and other yearly publications come out in countries outside India such as Singapore, Sri Lanka, Persia, France, Germany, England, America and Australia.

Detailed commentaries on Guru's teachings are available in various languages. But a majority of them are found in Malayalam. Those by Nataraja Guru, Guru Nitya Chaitanaya Yati, Balarama Panicker, Balakrishnan Nair, M.A. Sastrigal and Narayana Prasad are outstanding. *Sree Narayana Vijayam*, a massive work published simultaneously in Malayalam and Sanskrit by Balarama Panicker, is the pick of the lot. Similar works have been written by Kilimanoor Kesavan (*Gurukarṇāmṛtam*) and Raman Tholoor (*Sree Narayana Smrithi*). Further there have been published innumerable poems, studies, souvenirs and songs.

There is a large number of artistic and literary organisations devoted to spreading Guru's words. Sree Narayana Samskarika Samithi, Sree Narayana Academy, Sree Narayana Samskarika Sangh, Sree Narayana Research Centre, Gurudeva Kalavedi, Sree Narayana Study Circle, Sree Narayana Guru Pracharana Sabha, Sree Narayana Cultural Movement, Sree Narayana Women's Samajam and many more are doing tremendous work in India and abroad. The Sree Narayana Study Centre under the University of Kerala is an institution of government.

# 13

# Guru in Smṛtis

THE failure to record and preserve the frequent conversations of Guru and the mode of His approach to problems has resulted in great loss to posterity. To compensate for that loss at least marginally, is to collect from those who have directly heard from the Master's lips and who are alive today, His pieces of conversations and gems of teachings to humanity.

As Doctor N.A. Karim has rightly stated:

> Sree Narayana Guru was a many faceted personality. With marvellous spiritual accomplishments, He was the greatest social revolutionary this country has seen. He was scholar, poet, visionary, physician and social revolutionary all combined into one. Above all he was an unequalled lover of mankind. An indefinable spiritual power surrounds that life. It is therefore impossible to confine his life and personality within the narrow confines of biography. As such if His greatness can be expressed at least in part, and at least in vital aspects, that would be an achievement.

Kunju Swamy, a disciple of Sree Ramana Maharshi, has the following account of the meeting between Sree Narayana Guru and the Maharshi:

> Once when Sree Narayana Guru visited Kancheepuram Asram with disciples, I was present there. In accordance with my wish, it was Govindananda Guru who prevailed upon Gurudeva to agree to meet the Maharshi at

Arunachalam. In the ordinary course great souls Tagore and Mahatma Gandhi had visited Guru at Sivagiri itself. On the other hand, behind Guru's decision to go to the Maharshi's place for the visit, underlies the presence of intuition of relationship in previous lives. I have also belief in previous lives' relationships.

I had informed Sree Ramana of Guru's visit. Swamy arrived at the right time with Sishyas. He sat in the chair specially kept in the shade of the mango tree. Food was ready by then. Ramana Maharshi came out of the Asram and came to the tree shade and saw Swamy. Then He invited His guest for meals. They sat near each other and took food.

After the meals, Sree Ramana prepared to go to the mountain top. Swamy went to the tree shade to take rest. He then asked for a piece of paper and pencil. I brought them and stood aside. Swamy then wrote the poem 'Nirvriti Panchakam.' Within a short time the Maharshi came back. Swamy dedicated the poem to Him. He read it and was satisfied. When the Maharshi departed for His Mut, Swamy expressed to his disciples the following opinion about Sree Ramana Maharshi:

The Maharshi is a King serpent. He has enough spiritual prowess to give salvation to a person with one glance. Today He remains unknown to the world like the lamp inside a pot. No one is attempting to make good use of His spiritual wealth.

Prof. N. Krishna Pillai recollects:

From Form I to Form III, I had studied in the Sivagiri English School. The then Head Master was R. Sanker, a handsome young graduate. Swamy visited the school frequently with fruits and distributed them to us. When Swamy attained Samadhi, the teachers took us to Sivagiri Mut. We could see only that face. The body was draped in ochre robes.

Professor Krishna Pillai remembers one more thing. It is a real life story told by his classmate Sadanandan:

> One of Gurudeva's cooks, though an Ezhava was sent away without Swamy's knowledge, on the ground that he was of poor ancestry. Swamy pretended not to have known it. A few days later, on His return from a journey, Swamy brought with Him a boy to be engaged as cook. He belonged to the Pariah community. This was Swamy's sharp, but silent answer to His disciples who saw caste within caste in defiance of their master's stance above and beyond caste distinctions. By virtue of His exceptional self restraint, His mental power acquired through concentration and His unmatched capacity for observation, Swamy stands above ordinary people like a Mahameru (huge mountain).

Prof. Krishna Pillai also recounts the story of an asthma patient who was cured by small doses of petrol.

Muloor S. Padmanabha Panicker records:

> I remember the first time I saw Guru. He came to our house as our guest. I was only twelve years old then. He asked me to recite the first stanza of Nishadham. I recited and He was pleased. Next I saw Swamy at Kollam where the second anniversary of SNDP Yogam was being celebrated. He enquired about our family affairs. My father had passed away in the meantime. I saw Him a third time at Chengannur where I had been travelling with T.K. Madhavan and A.K. Govinda Das. At a meeting attended by Swamy I spoke. He was satisfied. That night, on the way to Sridhar Asram, when a Bhakta named Kunjusankaran shouted at a Pulaya to get out of the path, Swamy asked, "What, is there untouchability at night too?" The next day Swamy arranged free worship in the temple there for all the untouchables in the locality.

The Pichanad Kurups of Poovathoor were being persecuted by the Nairs of mid-Travancore. Swamy freed them and

> treated them like Ezhas and others.
>
> Poet Ulloor S. Parameswara Iyer visited Swamy at Sivagiri during his official tour to Varkala as Diwan Peishkar. They talked for sometime. Ulloor left Sivagiri after taking lunch from there.

Bhargavan Vaidyer was a great devotee of Swamy. He recollects how Swamy had arranged the marriage of the business magnate K.C. Karunakaran to his German bride in His presence at Sivagiri.

Vaidyer also recounts the story of a mad man. His people took him to Swamy. Suddenly the mad man shouting "My Swamy" bit at Swamy's face. Swamy's followers frightened at the event, closed in on him to retaliate. Swamy checked them. He said, "Doesn't matter. He did it out of love. Only his expression of love was like this. That was because of his madness." The lunatic stayed at Sivagiri for some days, and his madness was gone.

Kuttippuzha Krishna Pillai states how Swamy emphatically deprecated the brāhmaṇa theory that śūdras had no right to learn the Vedas. Kuttippuzha had the occasion to take part in a joint eating feast arranged by Swamy in which members of all communities except brāhmins were present. He sat near Swamy. When the feast was about to be over, Swamy asked him. "Is every thing gone?" Sensing that the question implied whether all untouchability had gone, he replied. "Everything has gone Swamy." Kuttippuzha concludes, "In the presence of Gurudeva I saw the real human being on that occasion which was my first joint eating session." He confesses that he had been converted into a relationalist and a Monist because of his heart to heart relationship with Swamy.

Pazhampally Achuthan considers the time of his first meeting with Swamy as one of the greatest moments of his life. While resting in a disciple's house at Prakkulam, Karunagappally, Swamy heard of Sree Chattambi Swamikal stricken with illness at Panmana. Swamy with His troupe proceeded to Panmana. He entered the room in which the sick saint lay. Both sat in the same cot, hands locked in affection, and talked for some time. They were two brilliant stars of Kerala's social horizon, who fought together to wipe out the social inequalities in this land, branded as a lunatic asylum because of the havoc caused by the chronic caste system.

Once Swamy visited Dr. E.K. Madhavan's house at North Purur. A new house was under construction. But the construction had to be stopped as at a corner of the old house there was a small room used by the household for prayer. There was objection from some members in dismantling this room. Hence the construction was held up. The matter came before Swamy. Swamy didn't respond then. Next morning before departure He asked that the idol and the sword kept inside the prayer room be brought and laid on His boat. In midriver He threw the idol into the water and gave the sword later to a blacksmith for making kitchen knives. Thus Gurudeva accomplished another idol breakage and removed the hurdle to the construction of the building.

Sadanamata T.V. Narayani Amma has the following memories to relate.

> I have heard that Sree Narayana Guru, Perunelli Krishnan Vaidyer and Velutheri Kesavan Vaidyer were my father's co-students at Varanapally. I was introduced to Swamy by Mundakkal Kesavan Asan.
>
> In those years, girls, especially Ezhava girls, coming to Thiruvananthapuram for higher college studies, had no place to stay. When my husband's sister Devayani got admission to the college, her accommodation became a problem. The two of us went to Sivagiri and placed the problem before Gurudeva. Gurudeva directed that a building be secured on rent and the girls accommodated in it. He also appointed me as the *Sadanamata*. Thus the SNV *Sadanam* was born in Thiruvananthapuram and later such *Sadanams* were established in most of the cities and towns in the state.

R. Kunjukrishnan from Mannanthala reminisces thus:

> Swamy, Doctor Panicker (Superintendent, Mental Hospital, Oolenpara) and myself were on our way to Kawdiar when Swamy directed that the car be taken to Sankummukham (Beach). At Sankummukham Swamy got out of the car and walked towards the Mandapam. Inside it a Sanyasi was meditating in Padmasana pose. As Swamy reached near him he awoke from meditation and prostrated at His feet. He said that, that day he attained realisation as he had seen his Guru after long search. He referred to his presentiment earlier in the day that Swamy would come to him later that day itself. Swamy blessed him and invited him to visit Sivagiri during Navaratri and then left.

Gurudeva's car driver Janardhanan has this event to narrate:

> Once when Gurudeva was at the Nagambadam temple, a women came and placed five rupees at His feet. Gurudeva asked his helper to return the money to the woman. But the woman refused to accept it and started crying her heart out, stating that she got only so much on pledging her locket. Then Swamy Himself took the money from the helper and gave it to her. He also blessed her with imminent prosperity. I have known that she had become wealthy shortly afterwards. I was Swamy's driver for about four years. During this period what astounded me was that when Swamy started on a journey He never mentioned His destination, but the car went straight and stopped at His intended destination, and that when the petrol had been used up, it was before a petrol bunk that the car went and stopped.

Former M.L.A., T.K. Narayani Amma remembers with gratitude:

> It was because of Swamy's blessing that I was born as daughter to my parents. I believe that Gurudeva's kindness alone is behind my triumphs in life. It was He who gave me my name and approved of my marriage. My husband Nanu Pillai, Engineer was also a staunch Gurudeva devotee.

Here is an account of his experience by Gurudeva's *bhakta* K.S. Palpu:

> The Kettukalyanam which Swamy had stopped at Karimkulam was that of the girl whom I married later. With that ended the atrocious Kettukalyanam, in Kerala. My marriage was held in Swamy's presence. I had the fortune to take the wedding garland from His hands. While working as Headmaster of the SNV High School, Nedunganda, I used to go to Sivagiri with my wife and see Guru and accept his famous hospitality. Once he cured my wife of chronic stomach pain with a simple medicine — an Ayurvedic mixture consisting of Brahmi juice and milk. Once when Swamy was resting in the Arumanoor temple a drunkard came and stood in front of Him and created considerable nuisance. Swamy asked for a bucket of water being drawn from the nearby well and a glassful given to him. He drank the water with relish and declared it to be excellent arrack. Swamy asked to give him the whole bucket. It is said that he never drank liquor again.

Vaidikacharya Kottayam Gopalan Thanthri describes Gurudeva's daily routine while he was an inmate at Śivagiri. He would get up at 3 a.m. regularly. After the morning ablutions, etc., He would take breakfast. Then He attended to sick persons, coming to Him. He abjured travel in carts drawn by bullocks; but He travelled in rickshaws pulled by men. I was present during the Kalvancodam *pratiṣṭhā*. It was there that He declared, "No more temples hereafter, but only educational institutions."

Manakkodam Kesavan Vaidyer spoke thus:

> The place was Thanneerumukkam. Swamy was resting in the house 'Kalathra.' Besides me, there were other non-spiritual disciples too. In the special room in which Swamy slept I was given permission to enter. The others were left outside. I was surprised as no one was given entry in Swamy's room. In the early hours of the morning Swamy got up, went out and came back soon with a sleepy

> consciousness. I saw an inexplicable shining flame of light enfolding the whole room. On close look I saw that the light emanated from Gurudeva's face. Within a few seconds a deep breath from Him and a contraction of the flame was seen in Him. After the Yoga exercise, as Swamy walked along the verandah, I leaned myself on one side of the door and looked at that face. The face had the radiance of blood-red colour. After a stroll in the verandah, He returned to the room. I found the face calm and normal as before.

Dr. G.O. Pal, the well-known dental surgeon staying on the opposite side of Government Secretariat at Thiruvananthapuram, has numerous experiences to narrate about his connection with Swamy. He keeps with him a tooth of the sage which he treasures with considerable pride. He also corroborates Gurudeva's car driver Janardhanan's statement that Swamy never mentioned his destination when the journey was begun, but that the car would stop at the place He had in mind.

Dr. G.O. Pal had taken a photograph of Guru stealthily. He preserves the photograph even today. He claims that this photograph is different from any other he has seen and that it is like Swamy's actual appearance.

N.R. Krishnan, Ex. M.L.A. of Shertallai had been taking only topioca flour as food because of stomach ache. Swamy persuaded him to take a regular meal in His company. The stomach ache was cured with that meal.

Pandalam Raghava Panicker describes how Guru rejected the request of the people of Karakkad (near Chengannur) to conduct *pratiṣṭhā* in a new temple built by them and asked them to build a school. Thus came into being the Padmanabhodayam High School in memory of the poet Muloor.

Agamananda Swamikal had an experience while he was working as Headmaster of the English Middle School at Chengannur. Swamy went to the school and spoke to the students for more than an hour. This was very unusual with Him as He never made speeches, and was known as a person of few words.

Vallabhaserry Govindan Vaidyer was a deeply dedicated devotee of Gurudeva. He even gave up his profession to work for SNDP Yogam and the propagation of Guru's messages. This resulted in tightening of his financial position. Guru realised this and allowed him to pursue his profession instead of organisational work. He prospered well and soon, with Guru's blessings.

It was early night. Swamy accompanied by Mundakkal Kesavan Asan went to the house of Paramu Pillai. As soon as they were at the gate, a fierce dog barked and pounced on them. Kesavan Asan tried to beat off the brute with his umbrella. Swamy checked him and said that the dog would understand that they were not thieves or robbers. The dog immediately stopped barking.

The well-known writer Moorkoth Kunjappa narrates the episode of how Sree Narayana Guru had saved a young brāhmin woman from the attack of *brahmarākṣas* (the spirit of a brāhmin who met with violent or gruesome death). Guru was resting in the house of a prominent citizen of Thalasserry. Many people had assembled there for obtaining the sage's blessing. Then a Tamil brāhmin woman came with her young daughter. The woman bowed to Swamy with palms joined. The young woman remained still. The strange expression on her face indicated that everything was not allright with her. To Swamy's query the woman said her daughter was possessed by *brahmarākṣas*. She also explained what *brahmarākṣas* was. Swamy enquired whether she had faith in Him. She answered in the affirmative and touched His feet. Swamy then looked at the young woman's face unwinkingly for a few seconds. Now the girl lowered her head, and saluted Swamy with hands joined. Swamy's face blazed red. He assured the girl that everything was gone. Then He smiled and the fearful redness on that face was transformed into a tranquil but shining expression. He advised some Āyurvedic treatment for the girl and then dismissed the mother and daughter.

The former Superintendent of Government Presses K. Swaminathan narrates the story of three of his friends M.R. Konni Masthiri, M.P. Moothedath and Arumughom Mudaliar who had acquired wealth and status with Swamy's blessings. Their stories are almost similar.

Konni belonged to Thrisoor. He wished to be a Railway contractor. But he was financially ill-equipped. He believed that if he saw Sree Narayana Guru and obtained His blessings, his ambition would be realised. So he presented himself before Guru at Aluva, and placed a few silver coins before Him and represented his grievance through a silence. Swamy who knew his grievance gave him a silver coin and blessed him with direction to take up Railway contract. In a short time he grew rich and prosperous.

Moothedath was doing a clerk's job under Konni. He also belonged to Thrisoor and entertained the same desire as his employer to become a Railway contractor. Financial stress stood in his way too. So he approched Sree Narayana Guru and placed a few silver coins at His feet. Guru knew his hardship and gave him three coins from those presented by him, and asked him to take up Railway contract. Swamy blessed him with the words, "Be sincere in your work. You will prosper." Moothedath in later life rose to be a leading and immensely rich Railway contractor. He kept those three coins in his *pūjā* room and prayed before them everyday till his death. Moothedath gave expression to his devotion and gratitude to Gurudeva in the form of the imposing *Samādhi Mandiram* for the sage at Śivagiri.

Arumughom was a low paid Railway employee at Kollam. Unable to keep his body and soul together within a pitiably low pay, he thought of taking refuge with Gurudeva for redressal of his disability. So he went to Śivagiri and like the other two, placed a few silver coins at His feet. He did not answer to Guru's questions. "Right, you are interested in type foundings? Are you not?", asked Guru. He answered in the affirmative. Guru gave him a silver coin and blessed him. Arumughom resigned his job and went to Madras. There he started a type founding business on a small scale at first. It grew by leaps and bounds within a short period and rose to be the largest type foundry in Asia. Arumughom Mudaliar became famous, but death snatched him away. He was succeeded by his son

Subramanian who also was deeply devoted to Gurudeva.

Bharathi Amma, wife of the Magistrate, Kottappuram Madhavan has recounted some events asssociated with Sree Narayana Guru. The first of these is the story of how her uncle Kochappy Vaidyer had cured a young woman belonging to a rich Nair family, of insanity at the command of Guru. Bharathi Amma herself was a victim of disabling stomach pain during her school days. Gurudeva cured her by giving her a plantain fruit to eat. Her mother had been taken to Gurudeva with suspected madness. Swamy cured her with the words: "Lakshmi has no madness. Madness is for those who say she has." Since then she gave birth to six children including Bharathi Amma.

Here is an episode about Guru narrated by the ninetyseven-years-old Vattavilakom Velayudhan of Kowdiar who was acquainted with Him closely. It was during Guru's visit to a house in Kawdiar. A *saṁnyāsī* expressed desire to see Him. He agreed to meet the *saṁnyāsī*. They sat together and talked till late night. Then Guru retired to the next room for sleep. At dawn the *saṁnyāsī* was found gone without even taking leave. Later it was discovered that some money which was in Guru's possession was missing. Suspicion naturally fell on the *saṁnyāsī*. After about an hour the Police presented the *saṁnyāsī* before Guru as the culprit. Guru appeared on the scene and declared, "O, the *saṁnyāsī* was in need of money. I gave the sum to him. Please release him." Here Guru showed deep love of humanity. Only a person with a great and magnanimous heart can show such profound and ideal love to a person who, by a heinous act, had covered himself with hate from everyone around.

Retired Controller of Stationery K. Sadanandan recounts an event of his childhood, told him by his parents. He was a six-month-old infant when he contracted diarrhoea. Treatment by experts only aggravated the condition to chronic state. The child appeared to be losing his grip on life. The alarmed parents took him to Sree Narayana Guru. Guru gave him a small piece of sugar candy, and asked the parents to treat him with pomegranate juice two or three times. It was not the season for pomegranate fruit. After considerable search a dry fruit only could be obtained . The semblance of juice was extracted from it with the aid of water and given to the child. Two doses and the child was cured completely.

G. Janaki, retired Additional Law Secretary, describes the story of her parents thus:

> My parents didn't have the fortune to see a child of theirs even after ten years of married life. People around began to look at my mother with contempt and call her barren woman. My parents were turned into a miserable lot. They went to Gurudeva and represented their misery to Him. He looked at my mother who was crying in great agony. He was holding a neem tree twig consisting of five leaves. He handed it to my mother and asked her to eat the leaves. Because of the bitter taste she could not eat all the five leaves. She spit out one. Before long she became pregnant. Of the children she gave birth to only four survived. This is attributed to her failure to eat all the five neem leaves.

Swamy Dharmanandaji remembers some details about Guru's dress and nature.

> Ordinarily Guru does not wear ochre robes. He wears only colourless and borderless white clothes. He will have a thin white cloth piece to cover His body. He does not grow his hair, or beard. He will tonsure his head often. He has not accepted symbols of Sanyasa like rosaries, the Yoga stick (Dandu) or water jug (Kamandalu). Swamy does not pray. Nor does He prostrate before idols. He never reads books or newspapers. Yet He knows everything that happens in the world.

Matam Parameswaran Namboodiri had just one meeting with Gurudeva. He was introduced to Him by Kuttippuzha. Gurudeva ascertained from the Namboodiri that he was studying Sanskrit at another *illam* (Namboodiri house). Then Gurudeva asked for the details of his lessons, and advised him not to give up because of the difficulties he would face with Sanskrit grammar. Parameswaran

Namboodiri was astounded by Gurudeva's amazing knowledge of Sanskrit grammar and scholarship in Sanskrit. He was convinced that he was standing before an extraordinary personage. But he regrets that unfortunately for him he was not destined to meet that personage once again.

# 14

# The Organisations

### Sree Narayana Dharma Paripalana Yogam (SNDP Yogam) and Sree Narayana Guru

WHEN one thinks about Sree Narayana Guru who advised to enlighten with *vidyā* (education) and acquire strength through organisation, one would be convinced of how Guru's daring prophesy as the Founder-President of the first social organisation of Kerala namely Sree Narayana Dharma Paripalana Yogam, had reflected on society.

For the Yogam founded about ninety years ago, spiritual power was provided by Guru, and material power by Dr. Palpu. Under instructions from Gurudeva, Dr. Palpu and Kumaran Asan convened a meeting of prominent Ezhava leaders from various parts of Kerala at Thiruvananthapuram. The meeting was held at Kamalalayam Bunglow and presided over by Guru. It was this meeting that transformed the Varoothu Sangham of Aruvippuram into SNDP Yogam. It was registered on all Kerala basis and started with permanent members. That opened the flood gates of victory for the *avarṇa* sections of the population.

The Yogam commenced its work at a time when the ordinary people were lacking in social consciousness, and the circumstances for the emergence of political plenitude were at low sky. The Nivarthana agitation, embarked under the joint auspices of Ezhavas, Muslims and Christians for equal rights with higher castes for government jobs, was a success. The role of the Ezhavas in the struggle for Responsible Government in Travancore was decisive. Success loomed large with these turmoils among the ordinary people.

As a result of the relentless work of SNDP Yogam, the basic rights of the ordinary people in the social, economic and educational spheres were on the verge of being established one by one. Within fifteen years of the Yogam's establishment, the superstitions which had run their banal roots into the social reformation process, the economic reconstruction endeavour and the orthodox thinking showed conspicuous vibrations towards change. This paved the way for a social renaissance.

Sahodaran Ayyappan describes the goal of Yogam's activities thus:

> The Yogam is not an organisation for establishing caste. It is on the other hand an organisation for destroying caste. There are two types of people who want to destroy caste. One type believes that caste is uncalled for and harmful. The other believes that because of the social disabilities generated by caste, it should be done away with. In Kerala the one power capable of eradicating caste is the Yogam. The panacea for it is, joint eating and inter caste marriage.

Guru held the Presidency of the Yogam for about a quarter of a century during which period He kept close liaison with the organisation by presiding over its annual gatherings and rendering His advice about reformatory programmes to be adopted. He had declared:

> No community will acquire prosperity and power except through organisation. It was by keeping this idea in view that we had established the Yogam, quarter of a century ago itself. The name Ezhavan does not denote a caste or religion. Hence members can be enrolled in the Yogam without regard for the differences in caste. Therefore we bless that numerous people may embrace Yogam.

The last message of Guru to the Yogam is memorable. He had said:

> We feel happy to note that you are seriously thinking of community reshuffling and religious reformation. But to bring together members of a particular caste and create a community should not be the aim of the organisation. Even religious reform should not be a hurdle. Our communal institution should be one which admits every human being into its ranks. Religion should allow freedom of belief. It should be acceptable to the cultured sections of society and should lead the people along the right path. The Sanathana religion "One caste, One religion and One God for man" is such a religion. To unite together all those who belong to this Sanathana Dharmam is to add a jewel to the organisation. To those who believe that without religious conversion inequalities and difficulties cannot be dispensed with, accepting this Sanathana Dharmam will tantamount to their religious conversion and declaration of independence.

## The Sree Narayana Trust and Sree Narayana Colleges

Under the Sree Narayana Trust fourteen colleges are functioning with distinction from Thiruvananthapuram to Kannur. Most of these institutions owe their proud existence to R. Sankar, the matchless political and educational activist Chief Minister of Kerala. That college education which had been the monopoly of the few, had to be made available to the children of ordinary people, struck him as the sole aim of higher education and that he set himself heart and soul to achieving that goal, was but the greatest blessing of the backward classes of Kerala. At the dawn of Indian Independence the Dewan of Travancore, Sir C.P. Ramaswami Iyer invited Mannath Padmanabhan and R. Sankar, and gave permission to start one college each. Mannath Padmanabhan started the Mahatma Gandhi college at Kesavadasapuram in the name of the Nair Service Society. R. Sankar started the Sree Narayana College at Kollam under SNDP Yogam. This was in 1948. Then in 1951 the Sree Narayana Women's College was opened at Kollam itself. The S.N. College at Kannur was established in 1960. In 1964 when R. Sankar was the Chief Minister of Kerala, the T.K.M. College at Nangyarkulangara, and the S.N. Colleges at Chembazhanthi, Shertalai and Varkala were started along with the Colleges sanctioned for the Christians, Nairs, and Muslims. S.N. Colleges at Punalur (1965), Nattika (1967), Chelannur (1968) and Alathur followed. The list was completed by the colleges at Chathannur, Chengannur and Shoranur (all three in 1981). The College at Shoranur was named M.P. Moothedath Memorial College. In addition, a Training College was opened at Nedunganda near Varkala in 1958. During the last academic year there were 34961 students, 1852 teachers and 730 other hands in all the S.N. Colleges taken together.

To facilitate the administration of the S.N. Colleges the Sree Narayana Trust was formed in 1952. R. Sankar took over as the first Secretary. The Trust performed its task efficiently and effectively under Sankar's able stewardship. But Sankar's untimely demise was a shocking blow to the Trust.

P.S. Karthikeyan succeeded Sankar. But that was only a stop gap arrangement. The next Secretary was M.K. Raghavan. He carried matters to a level of efficiency expected of Sankar. Yet the Trust had been found to betray a want of interest in encouraging the education of children of the poor members (of the Yogam) and to appoint sufficiently qualified candidates to deserving posts under the Trust. Complaints are not rare that in the colleges built with money collected from members of the community, their children are not given their fair share of admissions; and this is an expression of utter irreverence to Gurudeva.

That in almost all institutions (save the Polytechniques at Kottiyam, the I.T.I., at Koorkancherry and the I.T.I., (run under the responsibility of C.R. Kesavan Vaidyer) run by the Trust, corruption is rampant, is a fact the new office-bearers should take into their urgent and serious reckoning. It is essential in this context to remind those related that it is the duty of the Yogam to save its youngling, the Trust, from the depravity alleged to it. Incidentally some of the educational institutions run directly by the Yogam have the same story to tell though the deformity does not deteriorate to alarming dimensions for the simple reason that the salary of the teachers is disbursed directly by the government.

A redeeming feature about the Trust is the hospitals (Sankar Memorial Hospital, Kollam, Sankar Memorial Hospital, Punalur, Dr. Palpu Memorial Sree Narayana Hospital, Ayoor, etc.) run by it. They are very well conducted. So also the six Hostels under the Trust are functioning without blemish.

### The Five Stalwarts Who Piloted the Yogam after its Golden Jubilee

The Golden Jubilee of SNDP Yogam celebrated under the expert leadership of Sankar stands out as a feather in his brilliant cap. These celebrations had served to gravitate the members of the community towards Gurudeva's famous message to organise and acquire power. The celebrations have proved beyond a shadow of doubt that it is not only shameful but also dangerous so far as the *avarṇas* are concerned, to be porters' rests to carry members of the higher castes to political leadership. The Jubilee has pointed a finger at those who, in spite of realising the danger involved in such an attitude, have betrayed the interests of the community in return for cheap rewards. That they are questioning their very noble traditions, these people do not realise. The dauntless men who reached the upper rungs of leadership viz., V.K. Velayudhan, K.R. Narayanan, C.R. Kesavan Vaidyer, P.S. Velayudhan, M.K. Raghavan and K.K. Viswanathan, had striven hard to drive home to such people these stark truths in the tradition of R. Sankar.

#### V.K. VELAYUDHAN

The success of the Nivarthana Agitation in Travancore owed not a little to the prodigious services of SNDP Yogam leader V.K. Velayudhan. C. Kesavan, a top political leader and former Chief Minister of Kerala, had said: "If Velayudhan's leadership had not been available for the Yogam, it is impossible for me to declare what the result of the Nivarthana Agitation would have been."

When C. Kesavan was arrested at the orders of Sir C.P. Ramaswami Iyer, it was on V.K.Velayudhan's shoulders that the mantle of leadership of the Yogam fell. He vindicated himself in that capacity by continuing the struggle for basic rights of the underprivileged with uncompromising zeal. However towards the fading years of his life he accepted the Chairmanship of the State Public Service Commission, bidding goodbye to his blemishless public life. This action of his is by and large, looked upon with disapproval as it had a blackening effect on all the praiseworthy job he had done in his early days.

## C.R. KESAVAN VAIDYER

C.R. Kesavan Vaidyer rose into a prominent industrialist by dint of hard work, and the discreet exercise of his exceptional intelligence. He had started with practically a blank slate. Wealth has only reinforced the nobility endemic in his nature. He spends a sizeable chunk of his wealth for beneficiary causes. He is devoted to Sree Narayana Guru, heart and soul, and works without rest for the espousal of His cause of social revolution. Today he is a happy and contented man, blessed as he is, to see more than a thousand full moons.

Having been drawn towards Guru's teachings from early life, he was actively involved in the programmes of the Yogam and with Gurudeva's blessing, went on with work connected with the regeneration of the community. After initial business setbacks he started the manufacture of *Chandrika* medicinal soap. Soon it made its presence felt in the commercial world and with it Vaidyer's prosperity took on wings. His activities were extended to other fields as well. As a good Āyurvedic Physician, he was editor of magazines like *Ayurveda Ratnam* and *Dhanwanthari*. In the co-operative zone also he was an active worker. Politically his sympathies lay with the Congress and that led to his close connection with R. Sankar and K. Ayyappan. He affixed his individual stamp on the educational and cultural spheres too. Under the Chandrika Educational Trust, Vaidyer established two high Schools at Irinjalakuda, his headquarters. He is a voracious reader and has written several books. He took over Kumaran Asan's magazine Vivakodayam, and carried on its publication for two years. He also started the Vivakodayam Publications, a publishing house. He was President of SNDP Yogam for a term. He continues his activities on all the fields without break despite his age.

K.R. NARAYANAN

K.R. Narayanan is well-known as a great social worker, a leading fighter in the Nivarthana agitation, an exceptional Parliamentarian, a very capable Secretary of SNDP Yogam and a top ranking Congress leader. He made his mark in all the fields he had placed hands on. He worked shoulder to shoulder with T.K. Madhavan in the *Vaikom Satyagraha*. He was a genuine devotee of Gurudeva.

Hailing from Thalayolaparambu, Vaikom, Narayanan gained admission to the government school after prolonged agitation as *avarṇas* were denied that privilege those days. Even there he suffered discrimination. He was not permitted to sit on the bench during the first year. He endured similar disabilities in all the government schools he had studied.

K.R. entered public life with the determination to fight off every attempt of the *savarṇas* to appropriate the basic rights of the *avarṇas*. He established a branch of the *Poura Samathwa Vada Sangha* (organisation for fighting for equality) at Thalayolaparambu. He was an active participant in the founding of the Temple Entry League. He directed his efforts towards strengthening and accelerating the activities of SNDP Yogam. His speeches in the Legislative Assembly were awe-inspiring and awakened the layman to an awareness of his rights.

As Secretary of the Yogam, his services will be remembered for ever. He played a conspicuous part in establishing the Dewaswom Board College at Thalayolaparambu. He is held high as a writer of scholarly articles, orator and leader of backward classes.

P.S. VELAYUDHAN

Professor P.S. Velayudhan opened a fresh chapter in the history of

SNDP Yogam by breaking new ground in its style of functioning. As General Secretary of the Yogam he revived Kumaran Asan's magazine *Vivakodayam* under a new name *Yoganadam*. Along with that he established a printing press at Kollam. This facilitated the printing of all matters connected with the Yogam's work. P.S. Velayudhan's outstanding achievement was the release of the Yogam from the clutches of self-motivated vested interests. He reformed the Election process of the Yogam in such manner as to be free from interference in its affairs by profit seekers. This naturally made him a target of opposition from wealthy circles. But he stood four square against all opposition and fortified the Yogam from disruption. When all other communities began creating political parties, the Professor did not hesitate to form the Socialist Republican Party (SRP) to fight for, and achieve the rights of the backward classes through political activity. But unfortunately those who secured seats of power through the Yogam misused their positions in a manner detrimental to the interests of the Yogam, and to its very good name itself. This placed the S.R.P. in a precarious situation and its final and complete alienation from the Yogam. As the oldest social organisation of Kerala, it was during Professor Velayudhan's tenure that a complete history of the Yogam was compiled and published. The book published in connection with the Platinum Jubilee of the Yogam, is a glaring exemplification of his knowledge of history. The procession organised by him at Thiruvananthapuram, demanding the preservation of the constitutionally allowed reservation of jobs for the backward classes, was perhaps the mightiest the city had seen.

## K.K. VISWANATHAN

K.K. Viswanathan was an outstanding spokesman of the messages of Sree Narayana Guru. He had established his own individual impress upon the history of Kerala. He was a former President of SNDP Yogam and of the Sree Narayana Trust.

He entered public life in association with K. Ayyappan. He was concerned with the protection of the interests of the Harijans and backward classes. He served as Head of Government, Legislator and K.P.C.C. President with distinction. As Governor of Gujarat (1973-78), the native state of Mahatma Gandhi, his work for the eradication of untouchability outstripped all his other reforms. Where two Harijans lost their lives at the hands of the upper castes the Governor himself went in person to console the aggrieved. He effected several reforms to subserve the rights of Harijans, including raising of the reservation rate for the Harijans, and the formation of the Harijan Development Corporation.

As Head of the Government, his most notable achievement was the propagations of the Sree Narayana teachings in Gujarat and the formation of the Sree Narayana Cultural Mission, an organisation intended to start the spread of Narayana messages and doctrines throughout India. The Secretariat march and *dharṇā* he had led against the argument of economic reservation advanced by interested parties including the government, for upsetting implementation of the Mandal Commission Report, will remain in public memory unfaded for a long time.

## 15

# Sree Narayana Dharma Sangham and Gurudeva Vision

OF the institutions created by Sree Narayana Guru for promoting the ideals enunciated by Him, the prime of place goes to Dharma Sangham. Gurudeva had in mind the spiritual and cultural regeneration of the people when constituting it. Brahmavidyalayam or Centre for the teaching of Religion was its nucleus. Gurudeva had bequeathed all his property to this institution. He appointed Swami Bodhananda as His successor. With that, SNDP Yogam or other organisations ceased to have any claim over those properties. The Will was written in 1926 and registered at Trichur in 1928.

At the time He wrote the Will, India had not entered the democratic age yet. Asceticism in India operates almost on the hermitage system. According to precedent the current head of the hermitage nominates his successor. As in everything he did, Gurudeva brought to bear on the system he established, His divine outlook and the stamp of his inherent sagacity. Along with the adoption of the hermitage system, he also accepted the democratic method in administrating it. His will remains unquestioned testimony to His democratic credentials.

On the same day as the will was registered, a special meeting of *saṁnyāsīs* was held under the presidency of Swami Bodhananda. Under directions from Guru, Swami Sathyavratha spoke on the subject of *dharma*. Hearing that speech Gurudeva expressed a desire to bring his conception about Brahmavidya Mandiram to fruition. He said: "Select young men disposed to spirituality as *saṁnyāsīs* and send them to work for the good of humanity. Not only here, but throughout the world the gentle breeze of Dharma Sangham's message should blow." These words of Gurudeva had been realised through the Dharma Sangham.

Guru emphasised that for worldly happiness, *yoga*, and for spiritual happiness, Dharma Sangham are necessary. But unfortunately after His *samādhi* some selfish people dragged the Sangham into unnecessary civil litigation which prolonged for several years before a settlement was reached. From then on the Dharma Sangham became Sree Narayana Dharma Sangham Trust.

### Gurudeva's Will

> This Will Deed is executed with the intention of passing title to the charitable institutions like temples, ascetic asylums, educational institutions, industrial concerns which are owned by us and which are in our possession and enjoyment, and also to all the movable and immovable properties attached to them after our passing away, to our chief disciple Bodhanandan, inmate of Sivagiri Mut, who was consecrated as our successor on the 27th of September this year at Sivagiri Mut, the headquarters of all our charitable endowments. The free enjoyment and possession of all these institutions and the properties connected with them will be vested in us until the end of our life and this deed will come into force only after our demise. We have the full power to make amendments to this deed. After our passing away, Bodhanandan shall take possession of all the above said charitable institutions and properties and shall administer them and after the end of Bodhanandan's life the right of succession shall be to a Sanyasin who will be selected by the majority of the Sanyasins from among the chain of our disciples and this right shall pass on through the succeeding chain of our disciples. No hindrance shall be caused to the pious objectives or the permanent existence of the said institutions by the administration of

the Sanyasins hereby engaged and if any disorder is foreseen, then the group of disciples shall have full right to exercise control properly.

Narayana Guru

The Will was registered in the presence of Guru and was signed by eleven *saṁnyāsīs* of the Dharma Sangham.

The idea of Brahmavidyalaya had taken shape at Guru's instance through a resolution adopted in the concluding session of the conference of religions held in the Advaitāśramam at Aluva in 1924. Swamy Sathyavrathan had read it at the meeting in the form of proclamation. It was Guru's idea that the Brahmavidya Mandiram should be an educational institution where all religions, visions and theoretical phenomena are taught. He had fixed its assets at rupees five lakhs. But it took considerable time for His idea to take concrete shape.

Before detailed thought on Brahmavidya Mandiram is bestowed it is necessary to examine at some length the Indian spiritual visions and their nucleus, viz., the thesis of Sree Narayana Guru. Visions are in reality philosophy itself. Even though the search for Truth is followed through diverse paths, the end is the same. What emerges from that search in the form of realities associated with life evolve themselves as visions. When a wonder world of words emanates in the process the visions materialise in six meaningful forms. It is then that their architects Ganthaman, Kanada, Kapila, Patanjali, Jemini and Vyasa come to our attention. The ultimate aim of all visions is the unearthing of proper solutions for life's problems. They point to passages through which to get rid of the hard issues which beset worldly life. Hence it can be categorically stated that Gurudeva's visions are meant for the welfare and progress of mankind.

What was Gurudeva's vision? A vision is a consolidated thesis which materialises from the spiritual fusion of life's ends and means. Those who have effected that fusion are *jñānīs*. Sree Narayana Guru was such a *jñānī*. He was a great saint who had realised His visions through the mode of quest for them adopted in

India from ancient times. His works *Darśānamālā* and *Ātmopadeśa-śatakam* are glowing testimonials to His success.

There is a school of thought which holds that Sree Narayana Guru's Monistic Vision differs from that of Śaṅkarācārya. But during the thousand and odd years which have elapsed since the Ācārya's time, his theory must have undergone unavoidable changes. Hence it would be appropriate to assert that, ideologically Gurudeva was in agreement with the Ācārya, though He differed from His precursor in the methods prescribed. In this respect Guru showed His preference for the methods divergent from those of the Ācārya, advocated by *ācāryas* Madhva and Rāmānuja, the progenitors of Viśiṣṭādvaita.

According to Śaṅkara, Knowledge is the *ātmā*. But for Viśiṣṭādvaitists knowledge only qualifies the *ātmā*. The atom equated *ātmā* is not subject to expansion or contraction. Only knowledge is susceptible to those metamorphoses. But Gurudeva defines knowledge as *Karu* thus:

> Beyond Common Knowledge is KARU, the supreme Being which exists inside the Knower and outside him as real knowledge.

According to Him God created the universe as a sport, and thus enhanced knowledge by giving transfiguration to ignorance, and body and sense-organs to consciousness in conformity with tastes inherited from previous births. The Advaita theory says that simultaneous with the evanescence of individual entity, for the liberated, that entity transmutes itself as the finer aspect of *Brahman*. In the light of that theory Guru can be discerned as a full-fledged *advaitī* (Monist).

Our philosophy respects human values. That tendency is clearly traceable in both Vaiṣṇavism and Śaivism. While one set gives importance to the synonyms of Viṣṇu, the other holds on tenaciously to those of Śiva. Guru's preference is for Śiva. The essence of Śiva and Ātmā are one. Lord Śiva is the original cause of creation, preservation and annihilation, and exists untransfigured as the God who is the cause of all transfiguratives.

Spiritual Knowledge is pure knowledge. Knowledge bestows happiness. He who knows is never unhappy. These who are unhappy are the knowledgeless. The holder of knowledge does not only not make others unhappy, but also transmits the joy of consolation to the sorrow-stricken. The root of Gurudeva's vision in this respect is the word in the Upaniṣads that the preceptors impart solace to those seekers approaching them for knowledge by passing on to them the nectar of enlightenment unreservedly, and to the heart's content of the seekers.

Buddha, Jesus Christ, Muhammed the Prophet and Guru Nanak were divine souls who stood for kindness, love, fraternity and truth respectively. Sree Narayana Guru stands as the noble compendium of all these virtues. What He did was to accept as His spiritual weapon the visionary concept of pulling down the ideational fortresses built of Smṛtis (scriptures memorialised) by the this Śrutis (scriptures transmitted through word of mouth) which are the very sources of Smṛtis.

God leads and controls the universe. Even though man is the most prominent of His creations, he neglects the Quest of God by preoccupying himself with his flesh and blood and worldly achievements. Thus the duty invested in him passes into oblivion. As a result, he falls exhausted without being able to reach God at the fag end of his earthly existence. This spiritual ineptitude is acquired and life itself is rendered meaningless, to the detriment of the inherent spiritual powers lying dormant in him. To awaken him to his Godly prowess and lead him on to the right path towards realisation of that prowess, was the mission of Sree Narayana Guru's incarnation.

Man who is surmounted by an overwhelming consciousness of the physical basis of his existence does not run inwards to his *ātmā*. But the body is short-lived whereas the *ātmā* is eternal. In *Ātmopadeśa Śatakam* Guru has drawn an analogy between the indestructible *ātmā* and the similarly indestructible sunlight which reflects on a pot and which survives the pot's breakage.

Of the *darśana*s (visions) which have enriched ancient India's culture with unsurpassed spiritual enormousness, those of Sāṁkhya, Yoga, Dvaita, Advaita, Śaiva, Vaiṣṇava, Cārvāka, Sree Narayana *etc.*, are the most outstanding. Among these, the Sree Narayana *darśana* rose as a star in the emerging firmament of Nationalism shining in ubiquitous radiance.

While assessing Guru's inestimable place in the Dārśanic expanse, His commentaries on the Vedas, Upaniṣads and *Brahmasūtra* should be taken into one's reckoning to have correct evaluation.

The Upaniṣads which are recognised as the fountain spring of the Advaita theory, have their origin in the five thousand and odd year old Vedas. The Vedas are four in number namely *Ṛgveda*, *Yajur-veda*, *Sāmaveda* and *Atharvaveda*. Taken together they have 1180 divisions with each division having three sub-divisions named *Mantram*, *Brāhmaṇam* and Upaniṣad. Of the Upaniṣads, 108 are known. Ten of these however, viz., *Īśa*, *Kena*, *Kaṭha*, *Praśna*, *Muṇḍaka*, *Māṇḍūkya*, *Taittirīya*, *Aitareya*, *Chāndogya* and *Bṛhadāraṇyaka* are accepted as the most exceptional ones. These ten Upaniṣads are clubbed together to be titled the Book of knowledge.

Sāṁkhya, Yoga, Nyāya, Vaiśeṣika, Pūrva-Mīmaṁsā and Uttara-Mīmāṁsā are known as *Ṣaḍ Darśanas* (six visions). Of these Vedānta Darśana is accredited to Uttara-Mīmāṁsā; while some ascribe its authorship to Bādarāyaṇa, others assign that honour to Vyāsa. There is also a view that both are the same.

*Brahmasūtram* is a great work which codifies the Upaniṣad sayings comprehensively. Śrī Śaṅkara has annotated the *Brahmasūtram* and the *Gītā* monistically on the premise of their being enriched with the rationality inherent in the Śrutis (i.e., what has come down through spoken word). Nevertheless in expanding the horizon of Monistic vision, the services of the exalted visionaries Śrī Rāmakṛṣṇa, Śrī Ramana, Sri Chattami Swamikal and Sree Narayana Guru are incalculable. "The Advaita Theory which originated with the Buddha, blossomed through Śrī Śaṅkara and popularised through Sree Narayana Guru, has tremendous relevance in the modern age." Prof. Balarama Panicker.

Now we may examine the conditions upon which Sree Narayana Dharma Sangham is designed to function:

1. To disseminate Guru's messages and thoughts on *dharma* as "One caste, One religion and One God for man". To sustain in perpetuity the saintly personages who are members of the Sangham in the mission to love humanity on lines envisaged by Guru and to fulfil the aims of the Sangham.
2. To take hold of and administer the movable and immovable properties bequeathed by Guru through His Will, with particular motivation to achieve their relentless growth and enlargement. To protect the *muṭh*s, temples, places of worship and educational institutions and the assets attached to them.
3. To protect and preserve the house of Guru's birth and the place of His final rest.
4. To establish schools of religion to train young men gifted with aptitude, sense of responsibility and disposition for service, and to enrol them as members of the Sangham if found deserving of initiation into *saṁnyāsa* on termination of the training.
5. To endeavour for the eradication of caste and religious fanaticism, and to popularise Guru's dictates. To promote universal brotherhood and love of God. To establish spiritual *sabhā*s (units) with their headquarters at Śivagiri.
6. To arrange translation of Guru's works into other languages. To foster the emergence of research works on Swamy's life and compositions. To bring forth along with contemporary publications, works and interpretative commentaries on them in conformity with the Sangham's goal.
7. To open and operate centres of worship, *gurukula*s, hospitals, educational institutions and charitable establishments.

8. To take over or amalgamate the temples of *muṭhs* established by Guru.
9. To collect funds from the public, the government, the Devaswom Board and other institutions, and make use of them in undertakings meant for public good.
10. To do everything necessary to bring into operation the declared aims of the Sangham.

Of the 25 *saṁnyāsī* members of the Sangham at the start, only 9 are to be members of the Board. Their term of service is five years.

Guru's intention was to give popular recognition to His vision through organised effort. He had envisaged that a separate group of *saṁnyāsīs* who were life-long *brahmacārīs* was essential, and that it should exist permanently and unhindered after He was gone. For this scheme He had accepted Buddha and the organisational set up for the spread of Buddhism as the model. Guru had accepted Lord Buddha's slogan "*Buddham, Sangham, Dharmam*" as the guiding dogma for the formation of the Dharma Sangham. In the year of constitution of the Sangham itself Guru attained *samādhi* (eternal rest). But its uninterrupted functioning is guided by Guru's spiritual inspiration.

A period of 42 years had to elapse since the creation of Sree Narayana Dharma Sangham before Guru's idea of a Brahmavidyalayam had come true. In the year 1970 Sankarananda Swamikal performed its inauguration. When, on the 28th of February 1971, the Head of the *muṭh* opened the inaugural class of Brahma-vidyalayam, the light of *dharma* fell on the minds of all devotees of Guru. Among the first batch of students were Gopinathan and Manoharan, Purushothaman, Sugathan, Sudhakaran, Somanathan and Sasidharan.

Guru's conception that like the mendicants of Lord Buddha, there should come into existence a Dharma Sangham engaged in spreading the message of *dharma* across the length and breadth of the land with Śivagiri as its centre of work, has taken shape at last. The Secretary of the Trust Pavithrananda Swamikal and his colleague Sooshmananda Swamikal are the driving spirits behind the Sangham today.

The following is the syllabus accepted for the scheme of teaching in Brahmavidyalaya:

1. The spiritual beauty of the works of Sree Narayana Guru.
2. The teaching of Vedānta covering the Upaniṣads, *Brahma Sūtram*, *Bhagavad Gītā*, and *Ṣaḍ Darśanas*.
3. Knowledge of the languages, Sanskrit, Malayalam and English.
4. Knowledge of world religions.
5. Enough common knowledge to facilitate the study of modern science.
6. Study of the Scriptures.

The institution bases its functioning on Guru's visions. It aims at creating a chain of *saṁnyāsīs* constituted of young men motivated by inherent urge to lead a life of dedication and to mould into being a generation of world citizens who are imbibed with a deep sense of human values in absolute disregard of caste or creed. A course of seven years completed with commendable brilliance is rewarded with the Degree of "BrahmaVidyacharya". However those who are not predisposed to *saṁnyāsa* are permitted to lead worldly lives, though as propagators of *dharma* and as champions of humanitarian enterprises.

The students of Brahmavidya Mandiram should be of impeccable character. They should be innately committed to *ahiṁsā*, truth, humility, *brahmacarya* and unreserved surrender to God. They should be the inmates of Śivagiri and should acquiesce in unquestioningly to the rules of the *muṭh*. The expenses of the students are fully borne by the Dharma Sangham Trust. In terms of current prices the total assets of the Trust can be fixed at around rupees twenty-five crores.

The important institutions under the administrative control of the Śivagiri Dharma Sangham are the following:

Sivagiri Mutt, Sree Narayana Gurukulams at Chempazhanthi and Aruvippuram, Aluva Advaitasramam, Kunnumpuram Temple, Ramaswami Mut, Kollam, Advaitasramam, Kurichi, Kottayam, Sree Narayana Asramam, Peringotukara, Trichur, Sree Narayana Seva Mandiram, Kurichikkara, Trichur, Dharmagiri Subrahmonia Temple, Thirthala, Narasiṁhasramam, Eroor, Thirupramkundram, Madura, Sree Narayana Sevasramam, Kancheepuram, and Sree Narayana Mandiram, Thirunarayana Road, Madras. Recently the Kerala Government has sanctioned half an acre of land at Kanakakkunnu, Thiruvananthapuram for accommodating the proposed Sree Narayana World Cultural Centre. The then President of India Sri. R. Venkataraman inaugurated this research centre.

In addition to the institutions listed above, there are numerous schools, hospitals, and various other institutions functioning under the protective wings of the Trust. Further, there are a few more institutions and properties owned by Guru which have not come under the possession of the Trust.

# 16

# Memorials

### The Samadhi Mandiram of Sree Narayana Guru and M.P. Moothedath

THE Project for creating a suitable memorial for Sree Narayana Guru never became a reality even after twenty-five years of Guru's *samādhi*. This led to unhappiness among His followers. Several persons had come forward with offers of assistance for building a tower-like memorial at the top of the Śivagiri Hill. But nothing substantial had resulted. It was then that M.P. Moothedath, a leading *bhakta* of Guru, appeared and took over construction of the Samadhi Mandiram to perpetuate the memory of the great social revolutionary of Kerala.

While this writer and his class-mates were standing on the top of the Śivagiri Hill enjoying the picturesque surroundings extending up to the horizon on all sides, during an excursion from the college, a middle-aged person, good looking and modest in appearance, approached and introduced himself. He belonged to Shornur. He said his name was Govindan and he was the Manager of M.P. Moothedath. His master had entrusted him with the task of construction of the tower. In a few minutes Moothedath himself appeared on the scene and talked to us. He narrated the story of his early life, his association with Gurudeva and rise to prosperity with His blessings. Though his original name was Paran, he took Railway contracts under the name M.P. Moothedath by which name he was known.

When the Samadhi Mandiram was complete, the idea that Gurudeva's full size statue should be installed on the spot of the original *samādhi* gained among the Dharma Sangham members including Moothedath. For Moothedath the desire was to get the statue sculpted in marble by an expert in the art in Madras, at his own expense. It was decided thus. While work was in full swing, a team visited Madras to monitor its progress. The team was not satisfied. R. Sankar's story that Gurudeva appeared to the sculptor in a dream and directed him to make the statue in the form he saw in the dream, comes to mind in this context. Anyway the statue was carved out to the satisfaction of one and all and brought to Śivagiri with all ostentation and fanfare via Coimbatore, Palakad, Shornnur, Thrisoor, Cochi, Kottayam, Kollam and Thiruvananthapuram. Receptions in grand scale were accorded to the statue in these places. It was then installed at the Samadhi Mandiram the construction of which had been complete by then. The inauguration of the Samadhi Mandiram was witnessed by one of the largest crowds Śivagiri had seen. The function was attended by the elite from every field of public life, political, social, religious and so on. The celebrations ended with an exhibition lasting two weeks. M.P. Moothedath was awarded the stamp of honour namely Sree Narayana Bhakttothamsam (unequalled in devotion to Sree Narayana Guru), in recognition of his services.

In this connection the services of Govindan, manager of Moothedath, is equally worthy of reckoning as those of his master. But he was too humble to claim credit for what he had done. He said that everything was done by Gurudeva Himself with the money provided by Moothedath. But it is a shameful truth and an indication of the community's ingratitude that the name of Moothedath who turned the Memorial into a reality does not appear anywhere in the Monument. But great hearts do not do anything for reward.

### Sree Narayana Shashtyabdapoorthi Memorial

The Sree Narayana Shashtyabdapoorthi Memorial building was inaugurated at Kaithamukku, Thiruvananthapuram on the 26th of January 1992. It belongs to SNDP Yogam. The inaugural function was attended by the elite and ordinary people from all walks of life. The six-storeyed structure is the pride of all Sree Narayana *bhaktas*, and the consummation of their long cherished wish.

The original Shashtyabdapoorthi Memorial had been inaugurated at the same spot more than seventysix years ago by the then Dewan of Travancore, Krishnan Nair, in the presence of an enlightened audience. The spade work for the construction of the new structure was done during the tenure of Professor P.S. Velayudhan as President of the Yogam, in 1979. About sixty lakhs of Rupees were collected during a period of ten years and the work was completed. The first floor of the building is used for the Yogam's purposes. The remaining floors are rented out.

Men like R. Sankar and T.K. Divakaran had rendered unforgettable service for the construction of the Memorial. The names of numerous others also stand out worthy of remembrance. By their tremendous efforts the Monument stands with its head held high as the proud symbol of their victory in the long drawn out struggle of the *avarṇas* for rights, lasting more than a hundred years.

# Landmarks in the life of Sree Narayana Guru

1855 Birth Vayalwaram House, Chempazhanthi, Trivandrum.

1861 Basic Education: Under Chempazhanthi Pillai.

1871 Higher Education: Kummappally Raman Pillai Asan-Varanappally.

1884 Yogic Practices: Under Ayyasami along with Sri Chattampi Swamikal.

1882-87 Sanyasa, Tapas, Travels.

1888 Sivaprathishta at Aruvippuram.

1893 Conditioning of temple affairs.

1895 Guru's journey to Bangalore accompanied by Kumaran Asan.

1898 The Aruvippuram Temple meeting: Vavoottu Sangham.

1903 The establishment of S.N.D.P. Yogam.

1904 Guru exempted from appearing in Court.

1904 The first anniversary of the S.N.D.P. Yogam.

1904 Meeting in Sivagiri, Varkala-Defiance of Anaacharas.

1908 Installation of Jagannatha Idol at Thalasserry.

1910 The Sreekanteswara Temple at Kozhikode.

1911 The Sundareswara Temple at Kannur.

1912 Stoppage of 'Kettukalyanam' at Karumkulam.

1912 Installation of Goddess Sarada at Sivagiri.

1915 Establishment of the Advaitasramam at Aluva.

1916 The Guru in Mezhuveli.

1916 Installation of the Idol of Jnaneswara in the temple at Anchuthengu.

1916 Establishment of Sanskrit School at Advaitasramam.

1916 The Shashtipoorthy (60 years) of Gurudeva.

| | |
|---|---|
| 1918 | Installation of the Idol in the temple at Koorkancherry. |
| 1920 | Journey to Ceylon (Sri Lanka). |
| 1921 | Installation of the Idol in the Temple at Karamukku. |
| 1922 | The Prathishta at Murukkumpuzha Temple. |
| 1922 | Tagore in Sivagiri. |
| 1924 | The premature death of Kumaran Asan. |
| 1924 | The all religious congregation at Aluva. |
| 1924 | The Vaikom Sathyagraha. |
| 1924 | The Guru in Sivagiri. |
| 1925 | Mahatma Gandhi in Sivagiri. |
| 1926 | Establishment of the Dharma Sangham. |
| 1927 | The Mirror Prathishta at Kalavamkodam. |
| 1928 | The Dharma Sangham registered. |
| 1928 | The Samadhi. |

# Bibliography

## Books in Malayalam


*Antharastra Gurudeva Varshakhosham*, Thiruvanthapuram, 1977.

*Aruvippuram* (Darsanika Novel) by Vijayalayam Jayakumar, Thiruvananthapuram, 1984.

*Atmopadesa Satakam Prabandhhangaliloode*, Thiruvananthapuram, 1980.

*Atmopadesasatakam* by Swamy Satchithananda, Valappad, 1966.

*Atmopadesasatakam Sanyasaramam* by Swamy Vimalananda, Gujarat, 1981.

*Brahmananda Swamigal, Rishi Vamsadeepam* by Narayanan Palamattam, Thrisoor, 1961.

*Brahmasree Narayana Guru* by M.K. Sekharan, Kannur, 1934.

*Brahmasree Sree Narayana Guru Devan* (Vanchippattu) by V.K. Ananthan, Kannur, 1940.

*Brahmasri Sree Narayana Guruvante Jeeva Charitra Samgraham*, by Kumaran Asan, Thonnakkal, 1979.

*Chempazhanthiyile Karmayogi* by G. Venu, Clappana, Kollam, 1962.

*Christu Matha Chhethanam* by Chattambi Swamigal, Kottayam, 1982.

*Darsanamala* by Koppunni Master, Kollam, 1980.

*Ente Gurudevan* (Kavitha) by P.K. Kochu, Kollam, 1949.

*Ente Narayanan* by M.K. Vasu, Thiruvananthapuram, 1929.

*Guru Charanangalil Vicharapanam* by C.R. Kesavan Vaidyer, Irinjalakuda, 1977.

*Guru Samadhi Stothram* by Chaithanya Swamigal, Kozhikode, 1942.

*Guru Sannidhiyil* (Kavitha) by K.V. Dev, Kollam, 1969.

*Guru Swamy Charitham* (Oonjalpattu) by A.B. Narayanan Vaidyan,

Thrisoor, 1962.

*Guru Swamy Thrippadamgalude Jeeva Charitra Samgraham* by T.K. Narayanan, Kollam, 1922.

*Guru: Kshetra Sankalpam.*

*Gurudarsanam* by K. Madhavan Artist, Varkala, 1981.

*Gurudeva Charamam* (Padyam) by Nalpadi Krishnan, Thrisoor.

*Gurudeva Charitham Mahakavyam* by Kayamkulam Murali, 1972.

*Gurudeva Jeevacharitram* by M.K. Sekharan, Kottayam, 1917.

*Gurudeva Keerthanangal* by Valadi, Kesava Kurup Chempazhanthi, 1963.

*Gurudeva Krithikal, Savyakhyanam 10 Volyangal* by G. Balakrishnan Nair, 1978.

*Gurudeva Mahasamadhi* by K.V. Ramoti, Thalaserry, 1929.

*Gurudeva Poojathantravum Dhyanangalum* by C. Velu Vaidyan, Kollam, 1962.

*Gurudeva Samranakal* by Sivaprasad Sadhu Kollam, 1931.

*Gurudeva Smaranakal* by R. Gangadharan, Thiruvananthapuram, 1982.

*Gurudevante Ascharyangal* by Gopalan Thanthri, 1983.

*Gurudevante Thiruvachanangal* by Dharmatheerdhar Swamy Thiruvananthapuram, 1984.

*Gurudevante Thiruvachanangal* by Dharmatheerdhar Swamy, Kollam, 1953.

*Gurudevasmaranakal* (Jeeva Charitram) by Sathyanandan, 1947.

*Gurupadakeerthanam* by K.C. Appan, Thiruvananthapuram, 1961.

*Guruvarual, Guruvum Sishyanum* by Nitya Chaithanya Yati, Thiruvananthapuram, 1967.

*Guruvarul (The Word of the Guru)* by Nataraja Guru, tr. by Nitya Chaithanya Yati, Varkala, 1967.

*Irulil Ninnu: Guru Jeevacharitham* by V. Sankaran, Thrisoor, 1934.

*Jagad Guru Sree Narayana Paramahamsan* by M.K. Krishnan, 1955.

*Jnanavum Karmavum* by Trisoor Kuttippuzha Krishna Pillai.

*Keralathinte Samskarika Charithram* by P.K. Gopalakrishnan, Thiruvananthapuram, 1974.

*Kuttikalude Sree Narayana Guru* by C.N. Kamakshykkutty Amma, 1994.

*Mahasamadhi Prabandham* by M.K. Kumaraswamy Sanyasi, 1934.

*Mangala Bharathi* — Mangalananda Swamy — Mathrubhoomi, Thiruvananthapuram, 1969.

*Mangalamala* (Kavitha) by Bhaskaran Vaidyer, Mullaserry, 1980.

*Mathamethyalum Manushyan Nannayal Mathi* by Sukumara Sastri, Thiruvananthapuram, 1958.

*Mayatha Ormmagal* by N.R. Krishnan, Thrissur, 1969.

*Misrakaanthi* by Pallathu Raman, Kochi, 1924.

*Nammude Guru Devan* by S.V. Kadavil, Kadavil, 1970.

*Narayana Guru—Anthology* by P.K. Balakrishnan, Palluruthy, 1984.

*Narayana Guruswamy* by M.K. Sanu, Irinjalakuda, 1978.

*Narayanasmarana* (Kavitha) by Sankaran Adiyodi, Thalaserry, 1992.

*Navayuga Loka Guru* by M.K. Kumaraswamy Sanyasi, 1962.

*Om Maha Sandesam* by Sree Narayantheerdhar, Sivagiri, 1965.

*Phalithangal*, 1-9 Bhagangal, Thalaserry, 1977.

*Poorvakala Smarnakal* by Gopalan Thanthri, Kottayam, 1963.

*Prakasam Konduvarunna Sree Narayana Guru* by John Spiers, Kollam, 1950.

*Prardhana Pushpangal*, Thalaserry, 1974.

*Samadhi Gana Navakam* by Sahodaran Ayyappan, Thalaserry, 1963.

*Sarada Stavara Malika* (Padyam) by Kulathoor Jeothy, Thiruvananthapuram, 1961.

*Satsanga Muhoortham*: *Kochi SNDP Sovenirer* by Pallathu Raman, Kochi, 1946.

Several translations of *Daivadasakam* Published by K. Neelakantan, Madras, 1965.

*Sivagiri* by Santhakumari Amma, Balakrishnan Nair, Sivagiri, 1980-88.

*Sivagiri Theerdhadana Geethangal* by Sangeethswamy Sugunanandanda, Kottayam, 1973.

*Sivagiri Theerdhadanam* (Padyam) by P.O. Kunjan Panicker, 1977.

*Sivagiri Theerdhadanam* by T.K. Kittan, Kottayam, 1930.

*Sivagiri Theerdhayatra* by Mulor S. Padmanabha Paniker, Kollam, 1928.

*Sivalingadasa Swamigal* by K.R. Bhaskaran, Irinjalakuda, 1978.

*Sivasatakam* by T. Bhaskaran, Thiruvananthapuram, 1981.

*Smaranakal* by Kuttikrishna Marar, 1978.

*SNDP Yoga Charitram* by P.S. Velayudhan, Kollam, 1978.

*Sree Chathaya Thirunal* by M.K. Kumaraswamy Sanyasi, 1930.

*Sree Narayana Academy Sovinier (Convener)* by Dr. Vijayalayam Jayakumar (editor) Thiruvananthapuram, 1984.

*Sree Narayana Charitham* (Gadha) by Kotukoikkal Velayudhan, Kollam, 1972.

*Sree Narayana Charitham* (Kilippattu) by P.K. Kesavan, Ernakulam, 1942.

*Sree Narayana Chinthakal* by C.R. Kesavan Vaidyer, Irinjalakuda, 1972.

*Sree Narayana Geetham* by Kayamkulam Murali, Kayamkulam, 1976.

*Sree Narayana Geetham* by P. Vasudevan, Thiruvananthapuram, 1977.

*Sree Narayana Guru — Navodhanathinte Pravachakan* by P. Parameswaran, Kozhikode, 1971.

*Sree Narayana Guru* (Bale) by Ambikadas, Thiruvananthapuram, 1961.

*Sree Narayana Guru* (Bale), (Sthuthikal) by Mohan, Thiruvananthapuram, 1978.

*Sree Narayana Guru* (Darsanika Novel) by M. Viswambharan, Kottayam, 1980.

*Sree Narayana Guru* (Jeevacharithram) by Kottukoikkal Velayudhan.

*Sree Narayana Guru* (Jeevacharithram) by Kunjappa, Moorkoth, 1977.

*Sree Narayana Guru* (Laghu Charitham) by G. Kamalamma, 1981.

*Sree Narayana Guru* (Oattanthullal) by Meeran Krishnan Pillai Ernakulam, 1967.

*Sree Narayana Guru Ashtothara Namavali* by S.N. Chaithanya, Kottayam, 1969.

*Sree Narayana Guru* by K. Ramachandran, 1981.

*Sree Narayana Guru Charitham* (Jeeva) by Kumaran, Kottayi, 1924.

*Sree Narayana Guru Charitham* by Krishnakumar, Kollam,1959.

*Sree Narayana Guru Charitham* by T. Achuthan, Kannur, 1916.

*Sree Narayana Guru Chinthamony Stothram* by Ramananda Swamy, Thalaserry, 1931.

*Sree Narayana Guru Deva Krithikal* by G. Balakrishnan Nair.

*Sree Narayana Guru Devan* (Atma Geethanjali) by Dharmananthaji Swamy, Thiruvananthapuram, 1967.

*Sree Narayana Guru Devan* (Bale) by K. Dharmadas, Thiruvananthapuram, 1967.

*Sree Narayana Guru Devan* by K. Balarama Panicker Thiruvananthapuram, 1968.

*Sree Narayana Guru Devan Stuthi* by K.R. Ramankutty Sastri, Kottayam, 1975.

*Sree Narayana Guru Devante Padyam* by M.K. Karunakaran, 1943.

*Sree Narayana Guru Namavali* by Guruprasa Swamigal, 1947.

*Sree Narayana Guru Prabandhhangaliloode*, Varkala, 1969.

*Sree Narayana Guru Smaranakal* by Pazhampilly Achuthan, Thonnakkal, 1960.

*Sree Narayana Guru Swami* by A. Sankaran, Thakazhy, Alappuzha, 1957.

*Sree Narayana Guru Swamigal* (Gadyam) by C.V. Gopalan, 1934.

*Sree Narayana Guru Swamigal* by K.R. Bhaskaran, Puthukad, 1975.

*Sree Narayana Guru Swamigal* by Sankaran Karipai, Cherai, 1956.

*Sree Narayana Guru Swamy Smaranakal* by Choikuttan Master, Kottayam, 1943.

*Sree Narayana Guru Vijayam* (Thullal) Gopalakurup, 1972.

*Sree Narayana Guru, Oru Samagrapatanam* by Vijayalayam Jayakumar, 1994.

*Sree Narayana Guru, Thiruvachanangal* by M.K. Kumaraswamy Sanyasi, 1947.

*Sree Narayana Gurudeva Keerthanam* by Moolur S. Padmanaba Paniker, Thalaserry, 1930.

*Sree Narayana Gurudeva Krithikal — Sree Narayana Guru* (Bale), Thiruvananthapuram, 1969.

*Sree Narayana Gurudeva Smaranakal* by G. Gangadharan, 1983.

*Sree Narayana Gurudevan* (Bale) State Institute of Education, Thiruvananthapuram, 1968.

*Sree Narayana Gurudevan* (Ganakavyam) by V.V. Sukumaran, Kuzihimbam, Thrisoor, 1949.

*Sree Narayana Gurudevan* (Ganakayam) by Satchithananda Swamigal.

*Sree Narayana Gurudevan* (Jeeva Charitram) by Vadyil Sadasivan, Thiruvananthapuram, 1983.

*Sree Narayana Gurudevan* by Krishnananda Swamigal, 1948.

*Sree Narayana Gurudevan* by P.K. Kesavan, Ernakulam, 1984.

*Sree Narayana Gurudevan* by Vasudevan Nair, Thiruvananthapuram, 1966.

*Sree Narayana Gurudevarude Phalithangal* by M.A. Vidwan Sukumaran, Thalaserry, 1968.

*Sree Narayana Guruswamikalude Jeeva Charitram*, by Moorkoth Kumaran, Thalaserry, 1930.

*Sree Narayana Guruswamy* (Jeeva Charithram) by K. Damodaran, 1929.

*Sree Narayana Guruswamy Charitham* by M.C. Kunjan, Kottappuram, 1931.

*Sree Narayana Guruswamy Mahatmyam* by N.K. Kunjan Pillai, Kottappuram, 1931.

*Sree Narayana Guruvinte Darsanam* by M. Prabha, 1980.

*Sree Narayana Guruvinte Jeevacharithram* by Nalapadi Krishnan Thalaserry.

*Sree Narayana Guruvinte Sahityavum Darsanavum: Oru Patanam* by A. Padmanabha Kurup, Kozhikode, 1987.

*Sree Narayana Guruvinte Sampoornakritikal* by Sivagiri, 1974.

*Sree Narayana Guruvum Kumaran Asanum* by C.R.K. Vaidyer, 1993.

*Sree Narayana Guruvum Sishyanmarum* by Kotukoikkal Velayudhan, Kollam, 1971.

*Sree Narayana Hamsa Charitham* by G. Nanoo, Vazhavila, Thiruvananthapuram, 1987.

*Sree Narayana Jayanthi* (Khandakavyam) by V.V. Sukumaran, Kuzhimbam, Thrisoor, 1949.

*Sree Narayana Jayanthi* by C.V. Gopalan, 1935.

*Sree Narayana Jeeva Charitram* by Kotukoikkal Velayudhan, Kollam, 1974.

*Sree Narayana Karnamritham* by Kesavan, Kilimanoor, 1981.

*Sree Narayana Kavanahastham* by Sukumar Azhikode, Ernakulam, 1954.

*Sree Narayana Kavyatheerdham* (Prabhashanam) by Sukumaran Pottackad, Ernakulam, 1966.

*Sree Narayana Keerthanam* by Chellappan, Kaithavana, 1962.

*Sree Narayana Marggam* (*The Way of the Guru*) by Nataraja Guru, tr.

by Muthukulam Parvathy Amma, Kollam, 1950.

*Sree Narayana Matham* by B. Kalyani Amma, 1928.

*Sree Narayana Matham* by C. Parameswara Menon, Kozhikode, 1951.

*Sree Narayana Namasankeerthanam* by V.R. Nanoo, Kayamkulam, 1946.

*Sree Narayana Paramahamsa Charitham* by K.V. Kunjan, 1931.

*Sree Narayana Paramahamsa Devan* by S.V. Kadavil, Kadavil, 1929.

*Sree Narayana Paramahamsan* by K.K. Panicker, Alappuzha, 1960.

*Sree Narayana Paramahamsan* by Ramananda Swamy, Thalaserry, 1932.

*Sree Narayana Prabhodhanam* by C. Sudhamony, Thrisoor, 1977.

*Sree Narayana Sankeerthanam*, 1936.

*Sree Narayana Sidhaantangal* by K. Balarama Panicker, Kollam, 1953.

*Sree Narayana Sidhanthangal* by Swamy Brahmananda Thiruvananthapuram, 1959.

*Sree Narayana Stothra Mala* by Maunanandan Swamy, Varanapally, 1948.

*Sree Narayana Stuthikal* by Moolur S. Padmanabha Panicker, Thalaserry, 1928.

*Sree Narayana Sudarsanam* by Unniparan Vaidyer, Karimbram, 1924.

*Sree Narayana Vijayam* (Mahakavyam), Thiruvananthapuram, 1972.

*Sree Narayana Vilasom* (Kummi) by Ramakrishanan Santhi, Kannur, 1932.

*Sree Narayanadarsa Manjari* by B. Karunakaran, Kollam, 1981.

*Sree Narayanakeerthanam* by K.C. Appan, Thiruvananthapuram, 1961.

*Sree Narayanante Dharma Sasanangal* by Kotukoikkal Velayudhan, Ochira, 1977.

*Sree Narayanante Ekalokam* by Abu. O., Kozhikode, 1948.

*Sree Narayanante Sandesam* by A.K. Pavithran, Thalaserry, 1956.

*Sree Narayanante Swadheenatha Malayalathil* by Prasobham, Thiruvananthapuram, 1982.

*Sree Narayanodantham Jnanakummi* by Pandalam Raghva Panicker, Kollam, 1929.

*Sree Smrithi* by M.A. Peethambaran, Irinjalakuda, 1984.

*Swamy Thirunal* by M.K. Theyyunni, Kottayam, 1949.

*Thatwachinthakkoru Mukhavura* by S. Sukumaran Nair, Kottayam, 1980.

*The Sivagiri I Saw* by Ambikadas, Thiruvananthapuram, 1961.

*Vedantha Parichayam, Nooru Dhayagal* by A.B. Narayanan Vaidyan, Varkala, 1985.

*Vilapa Gana Manjari* by K.R. Krishnan, Kollam.

*Viswa Vandya Guru Sree Narayanan* by M.K. Kumaraswamy Sanyasi, 1962.

*Viswadeepam* by K. Dharmadas, Mayyanad, 1969.